Interdisciplinary Studies in Human Rights

Volume 17

Human rights are one of the normative cornerstones of contemporary international law and global governance. Due to the complexities of actual or potential violations of human rights and in light of current crises, new and interdisciplinary research is urgently needed. The series Interdisciplinary Studies in Human Rights recognizes the growing importance and necessity of interdisciplinary research in human rights. The series consists of monographs and collected volumes addressing human rights research from different disciplinary and interdisciplinary perspectives, including but not limited to philosophy, law, political science, education, and medical ethics. Its goal is to explore new and contested questions such as the extraterritorial application of human rights and their relevance for non-state actors, as well as the philosophical and theoretical foundations of human rights. The series also addresses policy questions of current interest including the human rights of migrants and refugees, LGBTI rights, and bioethics, as well as business and human rights.

The series editors are Members of the Centre for Human Rights Erlangen-Nürnberg (CHREN), an interdisciplinary research center at Friedrich-Alexander-University Erlangen-Nürnberg. The Advisory Board brings together human rights scholars from a wide range of academic disciplines and regional backgrounds. The series welcomes suggestions for publications of academic research falling into the series subject matter.

Otgontuya Davaanyam

Conceptualising the Corporate Human Rights and Environmental Responsibilities

A Bottom-Up Analysis through OECD Case Law

Springer

Otgontuya Davaanyam
University of Erlangen-Nuremberg, CHREN
Nuremberg, Bayern, Germany

ISSN 2509-2960 ISSN 2509-2979 (electronic)
Interdisciplinary Studies in Human Rights
ISBN 978-3-032-21429-4 ISBN 978-3-032-21430-0 (eBook)
https://doi.org/10.1007/978-3-032-21430-0

This work was supported by Deutsche Forschungsgemeinschaft (462211419).

This Springer imprint is published by the registered company Springer Nature Switzerland AG
The registered company address is: Gewerbestrasse 11, 6330 Cham, Switzerland

Acknowledgment

Proverbs 31:8-9

"Speak up for those who cannot speak for themselves, for the rights of all who are destitute. Speak up and judge fairly; defend the rights of the poor and needy." (Bible, NIV)

Transitioning from a career in business law to a focus on human rights was a meaningful turning point in my professional journey. This shift has enabled me to apply my legal expertise to supporting individuals and communities facing structural disadvantage, and to contribute to efforts aimed at fairness, accountability, and respect for human dignity. I value the opportunity to work in a field that closely reflects my personal commitments and long-standing belief in justice.

Leaving my home in Ulaanbaatar, Mongolia and moving to Nuremberg, Germany, to begin this doctorate was both an exhilarating and daunting journey. It was not merely about adapting to a new academic challenge, but also learning to navigate an entirely different culture, language, and way of life. The beginning was far from easy—there were moments of self-doubt, homesickness, and the overwhelming reality of a PhD. But reflecting on it now, I can say with absolute certainty that it was one of the best decisions I have ever made. This journey has been as rewarding as it has been challenging, and I am profoundly grateful to those who supported me and made it all worthwhile.

First and foremost, I extend my heartfelt gratitude to God for His strength, wisdom, and unwavering guidance throughout this process. Without His help and grace, I would not have had the courage or perseverance to see this journey through to its conclusion.

My deepest gratitude goes to my supervisor, Markus Krajewski, whose trust and belief in my abilities gave me the confidence to undertake and successfully complete this challenging project. Thank you for selecting me for this programme and for having faith in my potential, even when the task seemed insurmountable. Your expertise, thoughtful guidance, and continuous encouragement have been instrumental in shaping not only this project but also my growth as a researcher and as an individual. Your patient mentorship and insightful feedback have been invaluable. I am particularly grateful for your leadership and direction throughout the OECD case law project—this work would not have been possible without your support and guidance.

I would like to extend my deepest gratitude to my two student assistants, Marie-Louise and Luise. Without your dedication and hard work, I could not have achieved so many of the project's key outcomes, including the OECD case law database and the edited volume. Your meticulous efforts in analysing and coding the OECD case law, combined with your invaluable support in reviewing and editing my papers, were instrumental in bringing this work to fruition. Thank you for your unwavering commitment, collaborative spirit, and for making this journey both productive and fulfilling.

To my family, thank you for being my rock. To my son, my endless source of joy and inspiration: your boundless enthusiasm, curiosity, and ability to lift my spirits even on the darkest days have been my greatest motivation. You are the reason I persevered, and I hope this work demonstrates to you the power of resilience and determination.

To my partner: You are the true reason this book was completed. Thank you for consistently reminding me that I needed to sit down and write, even on the days when I would rather have done anything else. Your love, encouragement, and (occasionally firm) nudges made all the difference. You believed in me when I doubted myself, and your unwavering support has been my anchor throughout this process.

To my colleagues at the chair, thank you for your collaboration, kindness, and steadfast support. Working alongside you reminded me daily how much I could learn from others and how much more we could accomplish together. You have shown me that German people can be not only highly professional but also incredibly kind, warm, and willing to help. Your humour, advice, and encouragement brightened this journey, and I feel truly fortunate to have shared this experience with you.

I am also deeply grateful to my wonderful colleagues from the International Doctorate Programme on Business and Human Rights (IDP-BHR). You made the most difficult days so much easier. It was comforting—and at times, a relief—to know that others were experiencing the same highs and lows of PhD life. Sharing our struggles, successes, and even moments of laughter reminded me that I was never truly alone on this journey. Thank you for being more than colleagues—you became friends and companions on this wild adventure.

In addition, I would like to extend my heartfelt thanks to all the OECD NCP enthusiasts—academic scholars and practitioners—who contributed to the successful completion of this research project. I am deeply grateful to the scholars who participated in our workshop and shared their knowledge in our edited volume, as well as to the different NCP staff who attended my interviews, the OECD RBC headquarters, OECD Watch, and others who joined our webinars. Your willingness to engage with my project, listen, and provide valuable feedback has been truly invaluable. Your kindness and generosity in dedicating your time to support my research have not gone unnoticed, and I am incredibly thankful for your insights and encouragement.

Lastly, this work is dedicated to all those striving for justice and accountability in the field of business and human rights. May this book contribute, in some small way, to advancing the principles and practices that guide us towards a fairer and more sustainable world.

Competing Interests The author has no competing interests to declare that are relevant to the content of this manuscript.

Contents

List of Abbreviations

ALS	Australian Laboratory Services
BHR	Business and Human Rights
BTC Pipeline	Batu-Tbilisi-Ceyhan Pipeline
BWI	Building and Wood Workers' International
CGMs	Corporate Grievance Mechanisms
CHRB	Corporate Human Rights Benchmark
CSDDD	Corporate Sustainability Due Diligence Directive
CSR	Corporate Social Responsibility
ECHR	European Court for Human Rights
ESG	Environmental, Social, and Governance
EU	European Union
FDI	Foreign Direct Investment
FFI	Fibres & Fabrics International
FIs	Financial Institutions
FPIC	Free, Prior, and Informed Consent
GBVH	Gender-based Violence and Harassment
GRI	Global Reporting Initiative
HHRDD	Heightened Human Rights Due Diligence
HRC	Human Rights Council
HRDD	Human Rights Due Diligence
HREDD	Human Rights and Environmental Due Diligence
HRIA	Human Rights Impact Assessment
IACmHR	Inter-American Court of Human Rights
ICCPR	International Covenant on Civil and Political Rights
ICESCR	International Covenant on Economic, Social and Cultural Rights
ICJ	International Court of Justice
IFC	International Finance Corporation
ILC	International Law Commission
ILO	International Labour Organisation

IUF	International Union of Food, Agricultural, Hotel, Restaurant, Catering, Tobacco and Allied Workers' Associations
JKPL	Jeans Knit Pvt. Ltd
LBI	Legally Binding Instrument
LkSG	Lieferkettensorgfaltspflichtengesetz (German Supply Chain Act)
LPHR	Lawyers for Palestinian Human Rights
mHRDD	Mandatory Human Rights Due Diligence
MNE	Multinational Enterprise
MSE	Meaningful Stakeholder Engagement
NAPs	National Action Plans
NCP	National Contact Point
NGAM	Natixis Global Asset Management
NGOs	Non-Governmental Organisations
NHRI	National Human Rights Institute
NPOs	Non-Profit Organisations
OECD Guidelines	OECD Guidelines for MNEs on Responsible Business Conduct
OECD	Organisation for Economic Co-operation and Development
OHCHR	Office of the United Nations High Commissioner for Human Rights
OPT	Occupied Palestinian Territory
PACTA	Paris Agreement Capital Transition Assessment of European Financial Markets and Institutions
PvM	Perfetti Van Melle
QHSE	Quality, Health, Safety, and Environment
RAID	Rights and Accountability in Development
RBC	Responsible Business Conduct
RDS	Royal Dutch Shell
RSPO	Roundtable on Sustainable Palm Oil
SCA	Systematic Content Analysis
SDGs	Sustainable Development Goals
SOEs	State-Owned Enterprises
SPDC	Shell Petroleum Development Company of Nigeria Limited
SRSG	Special Representative of the Secretary General
TCFD	Task force on Climate-related Financial Disclosure
TEPN	TotalEnergies E&P Norge AS
UDHR	Universal Declaration of Human Rights
UN	United Nations
UNDHRD	UN Declaration on Human Rights Defenders
UNDP	United Nations Development Programme

UNGA	United Nations General Assembly
UNGPs	United Nations Guiding Principles on Business and Human Rights
VOG	Victoria Oil and Gas PLC
WBA	World Benchmarking Alliance
WGBHR	Working Group on Business and Human Rights (UN)
WPRBC	Working Party on Responsible Business Conduct (OECD)

List of Figures

Chapter 1
Introduction

1.1 Background and Context

In light of growing global concerns about corporate adverse impacts on human rights and the environment, a turning point came in 2005 when the United Nations (UN) appointed a Special Representative on Business and Human Rights (BHR). This appointment sparked a groundbreaking initiative, ultimately leading to the creation of two landmark frameworks: the 'Protect, Respect, and Remedy' Framework, endorsed by the UN Human Rights Council (HRC) in 2008, and the UN Guiding Principles on Business and Human Rights (UNGPs), adopted in 2011.[1] These frameworks have since become essential cornerstones in shaping corporate responsibility and accountability on a global scale.

The UNGPs, forged through extensive collaboration among governments, businesses, civil society, and other key stakeholders, represent an 'authoritative normative framework' and serve as a comprehensive 'blueprint' for both states and enterprises to uphold human rights.[2] The UNGPs provide a unified language and set of expectations that facilitate meaningful dialogue between states and private entities, particularly businesses, regarding the imperative to respect and protect human rights in the context of commercial activities.[3]

---

[1] 'UN OHCHR, Guiding Principles on Business and Human Rights: Implementing the United Nations "Protect, Respect and Remedy" Framework (2011) UN Doc A/HRC/17/31'; 'UN Human Rights Council 'Promotion And Protection of All Human Rights, Civil, Political, Economic, Social and Cultural Rights, Including the Right To Development "Protect, Respect and Remedy: A Framework for Business and Human Rights: Report of the Special Representative of the Secretary-General on the Issue of Human Rights and Transnational Corporations and Other Business Enterprises, John Ruggie" 7 April 2008 A/HRC/8/5.

[2] Choudhury (2023), p. 1.

[3] Ibid.

O. Davaanyam, *Conceptualising the Corporate Human Rights and Environmental Responsibilities*, Interdisciplinary Studies in Human Rights 17,
https://doi.org/10.1007/978-3-032-21430-0_1

At their core, the UNGPs are designed to prevent and mitigate the adverse impacts on human rights that can arise from business operations. They clearly delineate the responsibilities of both states and corporations, establishing a polycentric system involving multiple actors, including businesses, governments, and civil society.[4] This collaborative approach ensures that when human rights abuses occur within the realm of business, there are effective and accessible remedies available.[5] Over time, the UNGPs have evolved into the global benchmark for responsible business conduct, influencing the development of policies and practices that ensure business operations are conducted with a deep respect for human rights.[6]

The UNGPs establish a 'global standard of expected conduct' for multinational enterprises (MNEs), outlining their human rights due diligence (HRDD) responsibilities to avoid causing, contributing to, or directly linked to human rights violations anywhere in the world. At the core of these principles is the fundamental concept of 'do no harm', which embodies the corporate responsibility to respect human rights by preventing any infringement. This responsibility is put into practice through concrete measures, including a written commitment to uphold human rights and the thorough implementation of HRDD processes.[7]

HRDD demands that corporations conduct thorough risk assessments and implement robust management strategies to proactively identify, prevent, and mitigate potential and actual human rights and environmental risks in their operations.[8] The concept of HRDD, as introduced by the UNGPs, has been further reinforced in the global regulatory landscape. The Organisation for Economic Cooperation and Development (OECD) integrated this principle into its Guidelines for Multinational Enterprises on Responsible Business Conduct (OECD Guidelines) as risk-based due diligence, complemented by the introduction of a dedicated human rights chapter in its 2011 revision.[9] Compared to the UNGPs, the OECD Guidelines hold more binding authority over member states, as the Declaration on International Investment and Multinational Enterprises mandates these states to actively promote the OECD Guidelines within their jurisdiction.[10]

In the 14 years since the establishment of the UNGPs and the incorporation of risk-based due diligence in the Human Rights Chapter of the OECD Guidelines, significant advancements have been made in business practices concerning corporate human rights responsibilities. Various multi-stakeholder initiatives have emerged, both sector-specific and regionally focused, reflecting a growing global

---

[4] Prenkert and Scott (2014), pp. 467–468.

[5] UN OHCHR, Guiding Principles on Business and Human Rights: Implementing the United Nations "Protect, Respect and Remedy" Framework (2011) A/HRC/17/31.

[6] Wolfsteller and Li (2022), p. 5 https://link.springer.com/10.1007/s12142-022-00656-2 (accessed 11 January 2026).

[7] McCorquodale and Blanco-Vizarreta (2023), p. 126.

[8] Chiussi Curzi (2020), p. 245.

[9] Organisation for Economic Cooperation and Development (OECD) (2023); OECD Guidelines for Multinational Enterprises (2011).

[10] 'OECD (2023).

consensus on corporate accountability for human rights.[11] This is further evidenced by the adoption of the Corporate Sustainability Due Diligence Directive (CSDDD), which affirms a broader regional agreement on holding companies accountable for their impacts on both human rights and the environment.[12]

Moreover, as states increasingly recognise their crucial role in shielding individuals from corporate abuses, many are adopting the National Action Plans (NAPs) on BHR.[13] These plans outline strategic approaches to fulfilling their duty to protect, through both legislative and policy measures. Additionally, UN, including the Working Group on the issue of human rights and transnational corporations and other business enterprises, also referred as Working Group on Business and Human Rights (WGBHR) international organisations, and states are issuing sector-specific guidance for MNEs and enhancing judicial and non-judicial mechanisms to improve access to remedies for victims of corporate misconduct.[14] Despite these advancements, addressing corporate responsibility remains a formidable challenge, particularly in regions where the rule of law is weak, and governments are heavily reliant on foreign investment. The complex interplay of structural issues and pervasive poverty further complicates the ability to assess whether corporations are truly upholding their fundamental responsibility to respect human rights as outlined by the UNGPs and other international standards.[15]

---

[11] For example, 'UN 'The Principles for Responsible Investment, https://www.unpri.org (accessed 1 March 2024)'; 'UNICEF, UN Global Compact and Save the Children 'Children's Rights and Business Principles (CRBP) https://www.unicef.org/media/96136/file/Childrens-Rights-Business-Principles-2012.pdf (accessed 15 January 2026).'; 'Equator Principles: A Financial Industry Benchmark for Determining, Assessing and Managing Environmental and Social Risks in Projects, July 2020'.

[12] Directive (EU) 2024/1760 of the European Parliament and of the Council of 13 June 2024 on Corporate Sustainability Due Diligence and Amending Directive (EU) 2019/1937 and Regulation (EU) 2023/2859 (5 July 2024).

[13] For example, according to the National Action Plans (NAPs) development website managed by the Danish Institute for Human Rights, 19 countries are currently implementing NAP on Business and Human Rights, while 14 countries are in the process of developing such plans. See 'Global National Action Plans on Business and Human Rights,' available at [https://globalnaps.org/country/] (accessed 31 January 2026).

[14] For example, the Working Group on the issue of human rights and transnational corporations and other business enterprises (WGBHR) recently issued a report on investors, environmental, social, and governance (ESG) approaches, and human rights. See UN Human Rights Council, 'Investors, Environmental, Social, and Governance Approaches and Human Rights: Report of the Working Group on the Issue of Human Rights and Transnational Corporations and Other Business Enterprises,' 2 May 2024, A/HRC/56/55.

[15] Although there are many cases, a recent case filed in the French Court against TotalEnergies for environmental damage and human rights abuses caused by the Tilenga and EACOP projects in Uganda and Tanzania can be one clear example. Business and Human Rights Resource Centre (BHRRC), 'TotalEnergies lawsuit' (regarding reparations for damages caused by Tilenga and EACOP projects in Uganda and Tanzania), 27 June 2023 https://www.business-humanrights.org/en/latest-news/totalenergies-lawsuit-re-reparations-of-damages-caused-by-tilenga-et-eacop-projects-in-uganda-and-tanzania/ (accessed 31 January 2026).

The global supply chain, characterised by its vast and intricate network spanning various sectors, continues to witness severe and persistent human rights abuses. These violations are not confined to large MNEs but also impact small and medium enterprises (SMEs), along with a broad spectrum of stakeholders including international and national banks, export credit agencies, state-owned enterprises, suppliers, and informal business entities.[16] Abuses such as child labour, forced labour, gender-based violence in the workplace, forced land grabs, and violations against marginalised groups—including Indigenous Peoples, minorities, children, women, and migrant workers—are often perpetrated in remote, unregulated, and difficult-to-monitor areas within the global supply chain.[17]

The entangled relationship between powerful MNEs, which profit from these exploitative practices, and the ongoing human rights violations further complicates the landscape. There remains considerable ambiguity regarding the theoretical and legal connections between MNEs and these harms, as well as the practical steps they must take to fulfil their obligations under the international business and human rights framework. One pressing issue is that the guidance provided by the UNGPs remains somewhat ambiguous and challenging to implement in real-world contexts.[18] The shortcomings in the practical application of HRDD, as highlighted by the Corporate Human Rights Benchmark (CHRB), emphasise this challenge.[19] There is a critical need for corporate practices to reflect on how companies are practically fulfilling their human rights and environmental responsibilities, addressing the obstacles they encounter, and identifying actionable steps that can be implemented across different sectors, countries, and risk situations.

A promising avenue for addressing these critical issues lies within the specific instances handled by the National Contact Points (NCPs) of OECD member countries, which are tasked with ensuring MNEs adherence to the OECD Guidelines.[20] Member states are not only required to promote these guidelines among MNEs headquartered in their territories and those operating abroad, including in developing nations, but they are also obligated to receive and process complaints from individuals, civil society organisations, and other legitimate stakeholders concerning non-compliance with the OECD Guidelines by MNEs.[21] Upon receiving a

[16] Halifax Initiative 'Export Credit Agencies and Human Rights' Failure to Protect 2015 https://halifaxinitiative.org/sites/default/files/Failure%20to%20Protect_0.pdf (accessed 31 January 2026).

[17] Ford and Nolan (2020), p. 27 https://www.tandfonline.com/doi/full/10.1080/1323238X.2020.1761633 (accessed 31 January 2026).

[18] See Sect. 1.2.1.

[19] In 2023, CHRB report show that while 61 percent of the 112 global top companies have human rights due diligence in place, only 27 percent of them engage with rightsholders during the process. World Benchmarking Alliance, '2023 Corporate Human Rights Benchmark,' 20 November 2023.

[20] Organisation for Economic Cooperation and Development (OECD) "OECD Guidelines for Multinational Enterprises on Responsible Business Conduct" OECD Publication 2023, Part 2: Procedural Guidance.

[21] Ibid.

complaint, NCPs are mandated to provide a 'good office,' which typically include mediation, conciliation, and, in rare cases, arbitration between the parties involved.[22]

Since their inception in 2000s, NCPs have played a pivotal role in ensuring the implementation of the OECD Guidelines, particularly in examining the involvement of businesses in contributing to, causing, or being linked with harms worldwide, with a significant focus on developing countries. Over the past 24 years, more than 650 cases have been submitted to over 40 NCPs, with over 500 of these cases scrutinised to address pressing human rights and environmental concerns.[23] Notably, more than 400 cases have been resolved through the NCPs' case handling mechanism, offering invaluable insights into how MNEs should meet their responsibilities to respect human rights and engage in responsible business practices at both the operational and group management levels.

These cases not only exemplify the ways in which MNEs can fulfil their specific responsibilities but also shed light on the unique human rights and environmental responsibilities borne by different corporate actors within various business relationships, sectors, and country contexts. Scholars emphasise the crucial role of NCPs in offering authoritative interpretations of corporate-specific responsibilities across diverse business and situational contexts.[24] These interpretations often extend beyond the general provisions of the UNGPs, providing a more nuanced and comprehensive framework for understanding and addressing corporate accountability on a global scale. While previous research has focused on individual instances handled by NCPs, which interpret certain corporate responsibilities, there has been no exhaustive analysis of the totality of specific instances—approximately 400 cases (exactly 394)—that cover corporate human rights and environmental responsibilities. Such an analysis could yield profound insights into what these cases reveal about specific corporate responsibilities in various contexts, such as climate change, environmental degradation, global supply chains, conflict-affected areas, and the roles of different actors, including investors, state-owned entities, and non-profits engaged in commercial activities.

Additionally, it is crucial to investigate how HRDD responsibilities are being carried out by different corporate actors within varied business relationships. A comprehensive understanding of both the NCPs' interpretations of corporate human rights and environmental responsibilities, including the effectiveness of the HRDD and the effectiveness of their case handling mechanisms is essential for discerning the actions that have enabled NCPs to successfully resolve cases and bring about tangible change and effective remedies.

This research aims to conduct a thorough analysis of total 394 specific instances managed by 32 NCPs over a 24-year period from 2000 to 2024. These instances will

---

[22] Ibid.

[23] See OECD 'Database of specific instances' https://mneguidelines.oecd.org/database/ (accessed 31 January 2026).

[24] Bağlayan (2018), p. 371 https://www.tandfonline.com/doi/full/10.1080/18918131.2018.1547533 (accessed 31 January 2026); Buhmann (2018), p. 390 https://www.tandfonline.com/doi/full/10.1080/18918131.2018.1547526 (accessed 31 January 2026).

be meticulously examined through the method of systematic content analysis to explore the diverse responsibilities of businesses concerning human rights, disclosure practices, general policies that include risk-based due diligence, environmental impact assessments, and labour standards as articulated in the OECD Guidelines. By systematically analysing all relevant cases through various different codes and conducting a more in-depth examination where necessary, it aims to shed light on how MNEs have navigated and addressed key challenges and established expectations in corporate responsibilities during the specified timeframe. To achieve this, it will focus on the theoretical and normative aspects of NCPs by examining their interpretations of corporate human rights responsibilities.

Building on the systematically coded data and the inductive and grounded theory–based analysis, the book is structured around three main parts. These parts emerged from the categorisation of codes developed during the research process, reflecting the core analytical dimensions identified through the data which will be explained in the Sect. 1.2. The first part will examine the fundamental corporate human rights and environmental responsibilities within the context of the UNGPs, including key actions such as conducting HRDD, establishing human rights policies, ensuring transparency, and meaningfully engaging with various stakeholders. The second part will delve into the specific responsibilities of different corporate actors, exploring the unique responsibilities associated with different business relationships and operations, such as the responsibilities of financial institutions, investors, parent companies or global group-wide entities, state-owned enterprises, and non-profit organisations engaged in commercial activities. The third part will address corporate responsibilities in specific contexts, including environmental and climate change impacts, sustainable development goals, and obligations towards marginalised groups such as workers, children, women, minorities, and indigenous peoples. This section will also include a brief analysis of the shared and collective responsibilities of companies regarding specific human rights impacts. The conclusion will synthesise the key insights from this section and offer recommendations for policymakers, scholars, and other stakeholders on the future development of these issues.

1.2 Research Framework: Research Question and Research Context

The central focus of this book is to explore and conceptualise corporate human rights and environmental responsibilities through an in-depth analysis of OECD case law, utilising a bottom-up approach. This research is anchored by a primary research question that seeks to elucidate how corporate human rights and environmental responsibilities are interpreted and enforced within the frameworks of the UNGPs and the OECD Guidelines, particularly in complex and challenging situations. This inquiry is set against the backdrop of a broader research context that encompasses the dynamic and evolving landscape of international human rights law, the critical role of MNEs in upholding these rights, and the effectiveness of existing accountability mechanisms. An essential component of this analysis is the concept of HRDD, which plays a vital role in ensuring that companies proactively identify, prevent, mitigate and address adverse human rights impacts associated with their operations.

The book is structured around three key underlying assumptions each of which contributes to a comprehensive understanding of the intricate interplay between corporate actions, human rights responsibilities, environmental stewardship, and accountability. By integrating the concept of HRDD, this research not only examines how corporations address human rights risks but also evaluates the effectiveness of due diligence processes in aligning with international standards and guidelines.

The research questions associated with the main research include:

1. How can OECD case law provide deeper insights into the processes of human rights due diligence, enabling a more comprehensive evaluation of the effectiveness of HRDD practices?
2. How do interpretations of corporate human rights and environmental responsibilities vary across different sectors and corporate actors as reflected in OECD case law?

These questions, alongside the primary research question, guide the analysis and provide a structured approach to examining the multifaceted nature of corporate responsibility in the context of international human rights and environmental standards. By investigating the implementation of HRDD, this research aims to highlight the proactive measures companies can take to align with global expectations, reduce risks, and enhance accountability within the complex framework of business operations.

1.2.1 Underlying Assumption 1: Justifying Corporate Human Rights Responsibility within the Scope of the UN Guiding Principles on Business and Human Rights

The first underlying assumption of this research addresses the necessity of clarifying corporate human rights responsibilities within the framework established by the UNGPs. The UNGPs, while providing a global standard for preventing and addressing the risk of adverse human rights impacts linked to business activity, leave room for interpretation regarding the extent and nature of corporate responsibility.[25] Corporate human rights due diligence, as outlined in the UNGPs, is rooted in both

[25] Wettstein (2013), pp. 243–268.

business management practices and international law.[26] Ruggie's approach of 'principled pragmatism' resulted in a hybrid concept of due diligence, blending legal and non-legal elements.[27] This has led to some critiques, suggesting that the UNGPs lack clarity in defining the legal implications of this process, particularly in distinguishing it from voluntary corporate actions aimed at assessing risks related to their business activities.[28] This complexity further complicates the understanding of corporate involvement in harm and adverse impacts as defined by the UNGPs—specifically in terms of 'caused,' 'contributed,' and 'directly linked'.[29] Although the UNGPs provide commentary on each of these terms, the previous efforts to clarify the involvement of financial institutions in such harms have highlighted the difficulty in clearly distinguishing between them.[30]

Tara Van Ho has also argued that the explanations regarding 'directly linked' and 'contributed' remain unclear, advocating for more detailed elaboration to better define corporate responsibility to the harm.[31] Confusion regarding how corporations are associated with harm often results in a lack of accountability, particularly when it comes to the actions required once a business identifies its involvement in causing harm.[32] When a business either causes or contributes to harm, it is obligated to cease the harmful activity, prevent its recurrence, and, where necessary, provide remediation. However, if a business is directly linked to the harm, it is expected to use its leverage to mitigate the impact. The concept of leverage, however, remains unclear within the UNGPs.[33] Although the Interpretative Guide and various organisations have attempted to clarify what specific actions leverage entails, the practical application of this concept remains elusive for many companies, making it challenging to effectively execute this critical responsibility.[34]

Furthermore, the scope of corporate human rights and environmental responsibilities remains ambiguous. The 'responsibility to respect' is often interpreted as a more passive responsibility, primarily focused on avoiding harm rather than taking active measures. HRDD, as outlined in the UNGPs and OECD Guidelines, adopts a

---

[26] Martin-Ortega (2014), p. 44. http://journals.sagepub.com/doi/10.1177/016934411403200104 (accessed 31 January 2026).

[27] Bilchitz (2009) http://www.ssrn.com/abstract=1394367 (accessed 31 January 2026).

[28] Bonnitcha and McCorquodale (2019), pp. 899, 900 http://academic.oup.com/ejil/article/28/3/899/4616670 (accessed 31 January 2026); Chetail (2014), p. 124 https://brill.com/view/book/edcoll/9789004262393/B9789004262393_006.xml (accessed 31 January 2026).

[29] 'United Nations, Guiding Principles on Business and Human Rights: Implementing the United Nations "Protect, Respect and Remedy" Framework (2011) A/HRC/17/31, Principle 13.

[30] OHCHR response to request from BankTrack for advice regarding the application of the UN Guiding Principles on Business and Human Rights in the context of the banking sector OHCHR 13 June 2017 https://www.banktrack.org/download/letter_from_ohchr_to_banktrack_on_application_of_the_un_guiding_principles_in_the_banking_sector/banktrack_response_final.pdf (accessed 31 January 2026).

[31] Van Ho (2021), p. 625.

[32] Fasterling (2023), p. 115.

[33] Mares (2018), p. 26.

[34] Wood (2012), pp. 63–98.

risk-based management approach, serving as a standard of conduct intended to mitigate risks to stakeholders. However, this approach can create a false sense of security, leading to the mistaken belief that merely managing risks is sufficient to address the needs of those impacted.[35] Critics contend that the 'do no harm' principle is not enough; corporations should bear a more proactive responsibility to 'do good' and actively promote positive outcomes, rather than just minimising negative impacts.[36]

Also, when it comes to assessing risks and adverse impacts, the UNGPs provide a broad definition, stating that this includes the infringement of all internationally recognised human rights. Many scholars commonly equate adverse human rights impacts with direct violations or abuses of rights. However, David Birchall presents a more expansive view, arguing that the concept of impact extends beyond mere legal and regulatory breaches.[37] For instance, he suggests that business activities, such as financial decisions that restrict individuals' access to housing, can constitute adverse human rights impacts even if these actions do not technically violate the law.[38] Birchall's perspective challenges the traditional understanding of human rights impacts, emphasising that corporate responsibility should encompass broader considerations, including the indirect consequences of business practices on people's well-being and access to essential resources.

Beyond the legal and other implications of these critical concepts, their practical implementation is even more complex, especially given the lack of clarity in their normative content. Numerous cases reveal that some corporate actors still struggle to understand their responsibilities for certain harms, such as financial institutions' contributions to adverse human rights impacts and climate change, or technology companies' linkages to conflict-affected areas.[39] This research contends that a more precise definition of corporate human rights responsibilities is essential for ensuring that businesses are held accountable for their impacts. It supports this argument by highlighting the limitations of current interpretations and examining the consequences these ambiguities have for both corporations and the communities they affect. Without clear and enforceable standards, businesses may continue to evade accountability, perpetuating harm and undermining efforts to protect human rights and the environment. Therefore, refining these definitions is not just a legal necessity but also a moral imperative to foster genuine corporate responsibility and sustainable development.

---

[35] Taylor (2020), pp. 88–107.

[36] Bilchitz (2013), pp. 107–137; Wettstein (2012), p. 739 https://www.cambridge.org/core/product/identifier/S1052150X00005261/type/journal_article (accessed 31 January 2026).

[37] Birchall (2019), p. 120 https://www.ssrn.com/abstract=3425733 (accessed 31 January 2026).

[38] Ibid, 121.

[39] Macchi and Bernaz (2021), pp. 1–21; BHRRC 'Switched off: Tech company opacity & Israel's war on Gaza' Briefing 18 April 2024 https://www.business-humanrights.org/en/from-us/briefings/tech-sector-opt-analysis-2024/#_findings (accessed 31 January 2026).

1.2.2 *Underlying Assumption 2: Recognising the Significance of Analysing Corporate Human Rights Responsibility within the OECD Guidelines on Multinational Enterprises*

The second underlying assumption emphasises the critical role of analysing corporate human rights responsibilities within the framework of the OECD Guidelines. The OECD Guidelines complement the UNGPs by offering specific recommendations to MNEs on conducting their operations in a socially responsible manner, with a particular focus on human rights and environment. The OECD Guidelines, addressed to corporations operating in or from 51 adhering countries, set forth principles and standards related to sustainable development, governance, disclosure, human rights, labour relations, environmental protection, anti-corruption efforts, consumer interests, and taxation.[40]

While the UNGPs provide a broad framework, the OECD Guidelines exert a comparatively stronger influence on states and, indirectly, on corporations due to their quasi-binding nature. Although the Guidelines employ non-mandatory language, such as ‘should,’ and prefer terms like ‘adverse human rights impacts’ over ‘violations,’ which might blur their legal standing, they nonetheless hold significant weight.[41] This is particularly true given the OECD Guidelines’ legally binding effect on member states, which in turn exerts pressure on companies to comply. The establishment of NCPs to monitor and enforce adherence to the Guidelines further strengthens their impact, making them a more robust tool for states compared to the UNGPs.[42] From the perspective of state responsibility, the OECD Guidelines represent more than just a political commitment; they embody a pledge to uphold responsible business conduct in line with internationally recognised standards of good practice.[43] For some EU countries with strong responsible business conduct policies embedded in their governmental frameworks, the implementation and promotion of the OECD Guidelines are robust.[44] In terms of scope and regulation, the OECD Guidelines provide a broader and more detailed framework compared to the UNGPs. They encompass various sector-specific recommendations developed after the initial guidelines, offering clearer guidance on the specific actions MNEs should take

[40] OECD, OECD Guidelines for Multinational Enterprises.

[41] Curzi (2020), p. 24.

[42] McCorquodale (2024), p. 195.

[43] Krajewski and Davaanyam (2023). https://novabhre.novalaw.unl.pt/guardians-of-rights-the-role-of-government-in-promoting-responsible-business-conduct-under-the-updated-oecd-guidelines-for-multinational-enterprises/ (accessed 31 January 2026).

[44] For instance, the Dutch government has a separate responsible business conduct policy that complements and supports the implementation of the OECD Guidelines. Government of Netherlands ‘Responsible Business Conduct Policy (2020) https://www.government.nl/topics/responsible-business-conduct-rbc/documents/policy-notes/2020/10/16/from-giving-information-to-imposing-obligations (accessed 31 January 2026).

based on their sector or activities.[45] This makes the OECD Guidelines arguably more comprehensive, particularly in addressing corporate responsibility related to managing diverse human rights risks.

Moreover, the corporate responsibility outlined in the OECD Guidelines, specifically under Chapter 2: General Policies, Section 1, goes beyond the principles established by the UNGPs. While the UNGPs emphasise respecting human rights and avoiding harm, the OECD Guidelines extend this responsibility to include contributing to economic, environmental, and social progress with the goal of achieving sustainable development.[46] The commentary on the OECD Guidelines further elaborates on this, underscoring that corporate activities must align with and support sustainable development objectives.[47] Certain cases under the NCP mechanism provide further analysis of this enhanced responsibility, highlighting the importance of corporate efforts not just to avoid harm, but to actively contribute to the sustainable development of stakeholders.[48] This reflects a more proactive and positive corporate responsibility, emphasising the role of businesses in fostering sustainable progress.

Furthermore, scholars argue that the OECD Guidelines offer a more comprehensive approach to addressing environmental impacts compared to the UNGPs, outlining specific responsibilities for MNEs in mitigating their adverse environmental effects.[49] The most recent updates to the OECD Guidelines further pointed out this point, as they now incorporate climate change impacts—an area notably absent from the UNGPs.[50] This also demonstrates the OECD Guidelines' agility in evolving to meet emerging global challenges.

Although the OECD Guidelines are more comprehensive and specific compared to the UNGPs, they remain a non-binding instrument. This non-binding nature can significantly undermine their effectiveness, particularly in instances where companies choose to disregard the Guidelines. The limitations of the OECD Guidelines become starkly evident in certain NCP cases, where companies have blatantly ignored the Guidelines and refused to participate in mediation processes, even when faced with substantial evidence and credible complaints from victims. In these situations, NCPs often find themselves powerless, with no means to enforce compliance or impose penalties. Consequently, they may be forced to close cases without any

---

[45] OECD (2016) https://www.oecd-ilibrary.org/governance/oecd-due-diligence-guidance-for-responsible-supply-chains-of-minerals-from-conflict-affected-and-high-risk-areas_9789264252479-en (accessed 14 September 2024); OECD (2018) https://www.oecd-ilibrary.org/finance-and-investment/oecd-due-diligence-guidance-for-responsible-business-conduct_15f5f4b3-en (accessed 31 January 2026).

[46] OECD, OECD Guidelines for Multinational Enterprises, Chapter 2: General Policies, Section 1.

[47] Ibid, Commentary to the Chapter 2: General Policies, Section A.1.

[48] Ibid, See Chap. 3 of this book, Sect. 3.6.

[49] McCorquodale (2024), p. 70.

[50] OECD 'Working Party on Responsible Business Conduct Summary of input received during the public consultation on the targeted update of the OECD Guidelines for Multinational Enterprises' V/RBC/RD (2023) Unclassified Organisation for Economic Co-operation and Development (21 March 2023) DAF/INV/RBC/RD (2023): 1.

resolution, leaving the victims without justice and the offending companies free of consequences.[51] This highlights a critical weakness in the current framework, where the lack of binding authority can lead to significant gaps in accountability and undermine the overall objectives of responsible business conduct.

Nevertheless, in situations where states possess a strong mandate, some NCPs have effectively leveraged the Guidelines as a powerful tool, leading to substantive outcomes. While external factors play a crucial role in these successes, these cases illustrate that the OECD Guidelines can indeed be impactful when applied appropriately.[52] Also, the OECD Guidelines' comprehensive approach to corporate responsibility, particularly in addressing human rights and environmental risks, continues to be referenced across international, regional, and domestic instruments. This includes recent mandatory human rights due diligence (mHRDD) laws such as the CSDDD, the Swiss Ordinance on Due Diligence and Transparency in relation to Minerals and Metals from Conflict-Affected Areas and Child Labour (DDTrO), and the Norwegian Transparency Act, among others.[53]

This research project situates the OECD Guidelines as a crucial instrument in advancing corporate accountability, especially in the realms of human rights and environmental sustainability. It highlights the unique and evolving features of the Guidelines that make them particularly relevant for an in-depth analysis of corporate responsibility. By exploring the intersection of the OECD Guidelines with the broader international human rights framework, this discussion lays a comprehensive foundation for understanding how the OECD's approach can influence and reshape global business practices.

1.2.3 Underlying Assumption 3: Exploring Corporate Human Rights Responsibility Through Specific Cases Handled by the OECD National Contact Points

In the third underlying assumption of this research, the focus transitions to the practical application of corporate human rights and environmental responsibilities, with a particular emphasis on cases overseen by the OECD NCPs. These NCPs play a pivotal role in implementing the OECD Guidelines, acting as essential forums for mediation and resolution when MNEs and other companies are accused of

[51] For example, NCP Canada, Individuals against Barrick Gold, Final Statement, 17 May 2024.

[52] For example, NCP Netherlands, Former employees vs. Bralima, Heineken, Final Statement, 18 August 2017.

[53] Directive (EU) 2024/1760 of the European Parliament and of the Council of 13 June 2024 on Corporate Sustainability Due Diligence and Amending Directive (EU) 2019/1937 and Regulation (EU) 2023/2859 (5 July 2024); The Swiss Federal Council 'Ordinance on Due Diligence and Transparency in relation to Minerals and Metals from Conflict-Affected Areas and Child Labour (DDTrO) of 3 December 2021; The Government of Norway 'Act relating to enterprises' transparency and work on fundamental human rights and decent working conditions (Transparency Act).

breaching these guidelines.[54] Through their case-handling processes, NCPs investigate and assess the extent of corporate involvement in alleged human rights and environmental adverse impacts, scrutinising the responsibilities that corporations should have upheld under the Guidelines and other international frameworks, such as the UNGPs.[55] Where necessary, NCPs also provide tailored recommendations to companies on the actions they should take to address and mitigate these impacts.[56] By analysing the assessments, recommendations, determinations, and dialogues between parties captured in some initial and final statements of specific instances, it offers a comprehensive exploration of how corporate responsibilities concerning human rights and environment are interpreted, implemented, and enforced in practice. This examination not only sheds light on the practical implications of these responsibilities but also highlights the role of NCPs in guiding and holding corporations accountable to international standards. Through these case studies, it delves into the real-world challenges and successes of applying corporate human rights and environmental obligations, offering a nuanced understanding of how these principles are operationalised in diverse contexts.

Since the early 2000s, the OECD case database has documented over 650 cases across 36 NCPs globally.[57] The research narrows its focus to 394 predominantly resolved cases, deliberately excluding those that deal exclusively with issues such as taxation, science and technology, competition, and anti-bribery measures. Through the analysis of these selected cases, it offers valuable insights into the normative dimension of the NCP framework, focusing specifically on how NCPs interpret and establish expectations for companies in alignment with the OECD Guidelines and the UNGPs framework. The analysis concentrates on the substantive, normative aspects of corporate human rights and environmental responsibilities, while deliberately excluding the procedural and remedial challenges of NCP case handling, as the research had already grown considerably in scope. These procedural and remedy-related dimensions of the OECD case law project will be developed separately in a forthcoming academic paper.

Building on the insights of scholars, this analysis highlights several key advantages of undertaking a comprehensive examination of case law. Firstly, since NCP statements are based on evaluations of specific corporate behaviours within varied contexts and situations, they provide invaluable guidance to a wide range of corporate actors on the nuanced requirements of due diligence responsibilities.[58] Secondly, such analysis can assist MNEs and other companies whether directly involved in

[54] Christine Kaufmann 'OECD MNE Guidelines Quo Vadis? Making responsible business conduct work for better lives' in *'OECD Guidelines for Multinational Enterprises: A Glass Half Full'.* (Liber Amicorum for Dr. Roel Nieuwenkamp, Chair of the OECD Working Party on Responsible Business Conduct 2013-2018) https://www.zora.uzh.ch/id/eprint/160967 (accessed 31 January 2026), 29–37.

[55] Ibid, 31.

[56] Ibid.

[57] OECD Database of specific instances.

[58] Bağlayan (2018), p. 371; Buhmann (2018), p. 390.

cases or not—in aligning their human rights and environmental due diligence practices more closely with the expectations set out in the OECD Guidelines and, by extension, the UNGPs.[59] Thirdly, as stated, these statements enhance the collective knowledge base of NCPs by offering practical examples and detailed guidance on human rights due diligence, thereby facilitating the development of a more coherent and unified body of jurisprudence across different NCPs.[60]

Although the state-based nature of NCPs implies that they operate independently within diverse organisational frameworks, this diversity can also be viewed as an asset.[61] It allows for a more tailored and context-sensitive promotion of the Guidelines, thereby improving their application among companies operating in the numerous countries that adhere to them. Finally, NCP statements provide critical insights for scholars and stakeholders committed to RBC, offering real-life examples and guidance that can be used to either advise corporations or hold them accountable for their actions. This real-world applicability of NCP statements enhances their value, making them a vital resource for understanding and advancing responsible business practices globally.[62]

Overall, building on the significant impacts of the OECD case law analysis, this research aims to comprehensively cover the full spectrum of NCP analysis and recommendations that focus on corporate human rights and environmental responsibilities. The first part of the book delves into corporate human rights and environmental responsibilities as interpreted through OECD case law. This section lays the groundwork by examining these responsibilities within the framework of the 'Protect, Respect and Remedy' using OECD case law as a critical lens. The analysis centres on HRDD responsibilities under the UNGPs, contrasting international human rights standards with actual corporate practices, and underscoring the necessity of robust human rights policies. Subsequent chapters of the first part provide an in-depth exploration of specific issues such as environmental degradation, climate change, and corporate responsibilities in conflict-affected and high-risk areas, offering a nuanced understanding of how these responsibilities are operationalised through case law examples.

1.3 Methodology: Mixing the Traditional Legal Analysis with Systematic Content Analysis

This research adopts a multifaceted methodology, blending traditional legal research method including doctrinal and black-letter law analysis, and systematic content analysis to yield in-depth qualitative insights. By integrating traditional legal

[59] Ibid.

[60] Ibid, Buhmann, 391.

[61] Ibid, 392.

[62] Ibid.

analysis with specific case studies, alongside systematic content analysis facilitated through MAXQDA, the study offers a robust and comprehensive evaluation of corporate human rights and environmental responsibilities within the NCP framework. This interdisciplinary approach ensures a nuanced understanding of the complexities involved.

1.3.1 Understanding the Conceptual and Authoritative Value of OECD Case Law Through Traditional Legal Analysis

Traditional legal analysis, comprising doctrinal legal method and the black letter law approach, forms the central methodological foundation of this research project. The doctrinal method systematically examines legal principles, precedents, and interpretations, considering judicial reasoning and academic commentary.[63] In contrast, the black letter approach focuses on established legal rules found in statutes, case law, and regulations, without engaging with broader socio-political contexts.[64] Grounded in traditional legal scholarship, these methods provide a structured framework for understanding the conceptual and authoritative significance of OECD case law through a detailed examination of NCP statements.[65] They involve analysing legal principles and doctrines to interpret how laws and guidelines are applied in the NCP reasoning and determinations.[66] In this research, traditional legal analysis serves several key functions: clarifying the legal framework, interpreting the normative content of human rights and environmental responsibilities, and examining how NCPs articulate expectations of corporate conduct in alignment with the OECD Guidelines and the UNGPs.

However, it also recognises that applying doctrinal legal analysis to OECD NCP cases presents methodological particularities. Unlike judicial bodies that render binding decisions, NCPs are sui generis, quasi-judicial mechanisms whose determinations are non-binding and grounded in soft law. Consequently, the doctrinal approach is adapted to account for the interpretive and persuasive—rather than coercive—authority of NCP statements. The analysis therefore focuses not on the enforcement of legal norms but on how NCPs interpret, internalise, and operationalise the normative expectations embedded in the OECD Guidelines.

This reflective adaptation highlights the added value of doctrinal analysis in a non-binding, governance-oriented context.[67] It allows for a systematic understanding of how normative principles evolve and gain authority through interpretive

---

[63] Hutchinson (2018), p. 13.

[64] Legalgetaway 'Understanding Black Letter Law: The Basics' https://legalgetaway.com/blog/what-is-black-letter-law/ (accessed 31 January 2026).

[65] Egan (2017), pp. 1–17 https://www.ssrn.com/abstract=3082194 (accessed 31 January 2026).

[66] Ibid, 13–14.

[67] Ngwoke et al. (2023), pp. 8–9.

practices rather than judicial enforcement.[68] By examining both past and current NCP decisions alongside academic literature, it identifies emerging patterns, trends, and divergences in the interpretation of corporate human rights and environmental responsibilities. This comprehensive legal understanding is essential for evaluating the normative influence of NCPs in shaping corporate accountability frameworks, even in the absence of binding outcomes.

1.3.1.1 Application of the Traditional Legal Analysis in OECD Case Law: Key Implications

The application of traditional legal analysis in this research plays a pivotal role in interpreting how OECD NCPs establish, apply, and evolve normative standards of corporate human rights and environmental responsibility. Through a systematic doctrinal examination of OECD case law, the research clarifies the legal and policy standards articulated in NCP statements and explores how these standards are embedded within the broader framework of the OECD Guidelines and the UNGPs. The analysis focuses on how NCPs interpret and operationalise expectations for multinational enterprises, particularly in relation to HRDD and corporate accountability.

The black-letter approach provides a solid basis for identifying ambiguities and inconsistencies in the application of global standards. By engaging closely with case-specific reasoning, it critically evaluates how NCPs apply these normative principles across different contexts and legal cultures. Rather than assessing compliance through the lens of binding enforcement, the study examines how normative authority is constructed through interpretation, dialogue, and consensus within the non-binding, quasi-judicial setting of the NCP system. This adaptation acknowledges the sui generis nature of the NCP mechanism, which functions as a soft-law forum for persuasion and standard-setting rather than adjudication.

Ultimately, the research leverages the strengths of traditional legal analysis to deepen the discourse on corporate human rights and environmental responsibilities. It demonstrates how doctrinal interpretation, even within a soft-law system, provides valuable insights into the normative foundations and evolving authority of corporate accountability frameworks. Through close reading of case law and relevant literature, it distils the legal and conceptual significance of OECD case law, clarifying how HRDD and related normative standards are interpreted and advanced within the OECD NCP system.

[68] In this context, the UNGPs serve as a formal source for guiding corporate human rights responsibilities.

1.3.2 Enhancing the Traditional Legal Analysis with Systematic Content Analysis Using MAXQDA

While the traditional legal analysis forms the core of this research project, its limitations—particularly its inability to systematically handle large volumes of data—necessitate a broader approach. To address this, the research integrates systematic content analysis (SCA) and socio-legal methodologies, thereby strengthening the overall research rigor. While the doctrinal approach provides a solid legal foundation, it lacks the tools to efficiently process and interpret large datasets. Unlike traditional legal methodologies that often focus on idiosyncratic leading cases, SCA emphasises the relevance of applicable case laws that the researcher deems significant for the study.[69] By comprehensively analysing approximately 400 cases, this interdisciplinary approach offers both empirical insights and practical perspectives that the doctrinal method alone may overlook. As a result, it ensures a comprehensive understanding of the OECD NCP mechanism, blending theoretical analysis with real-world applications and insights.

1.3.2.1 Processes of Systematic Content Analysis

This legal-empirical methodology generally consists of three key stages: first, developing a database of representative legal texts—such as court judgments or rulings by administrative agencies—selected using rigorous criteria; second, systematically documenting the quantitative and/or qualitative characteristics of these cases according to a predefined set of guidelines (referred to as 'coding'), either manually or through automated processes; and third, a reflective stage where the researcher groups the cases into common themes and draws conclusions about their significance and interpretation.[70]

The SCA is conducted through MAXQDA, specialised software for qualitative data analysis.[71] MAXQDA enables the creation of a structured coding framework, allowing for the systematic categorisation of text segments ('codes' or 'coded segments') derived from OECD NCP case statements.[72] This tool is highly effective for exploring diverse sources and comparing different cases and groups.[73] The first step involved importing all completed final statements, along with selected initial statements of NCP cases from 2000 to 2024, in PDF format into MAXQDA. These cases were then organised by NCP countries within the software's 'document system' (see Fig. 1.1).

[69] Brook (2022), p. 190.

[70] Ibid, 193.

[71] Salehijam (2018), pp. 34–42; Gizzi (2018) https://www.maxqda.com/blogpost/maxqda-and-the-four-stages-of-research (accessed 31 January 2026).

[72] Ibid.

[73] Maene (2023), pp. 109–178.

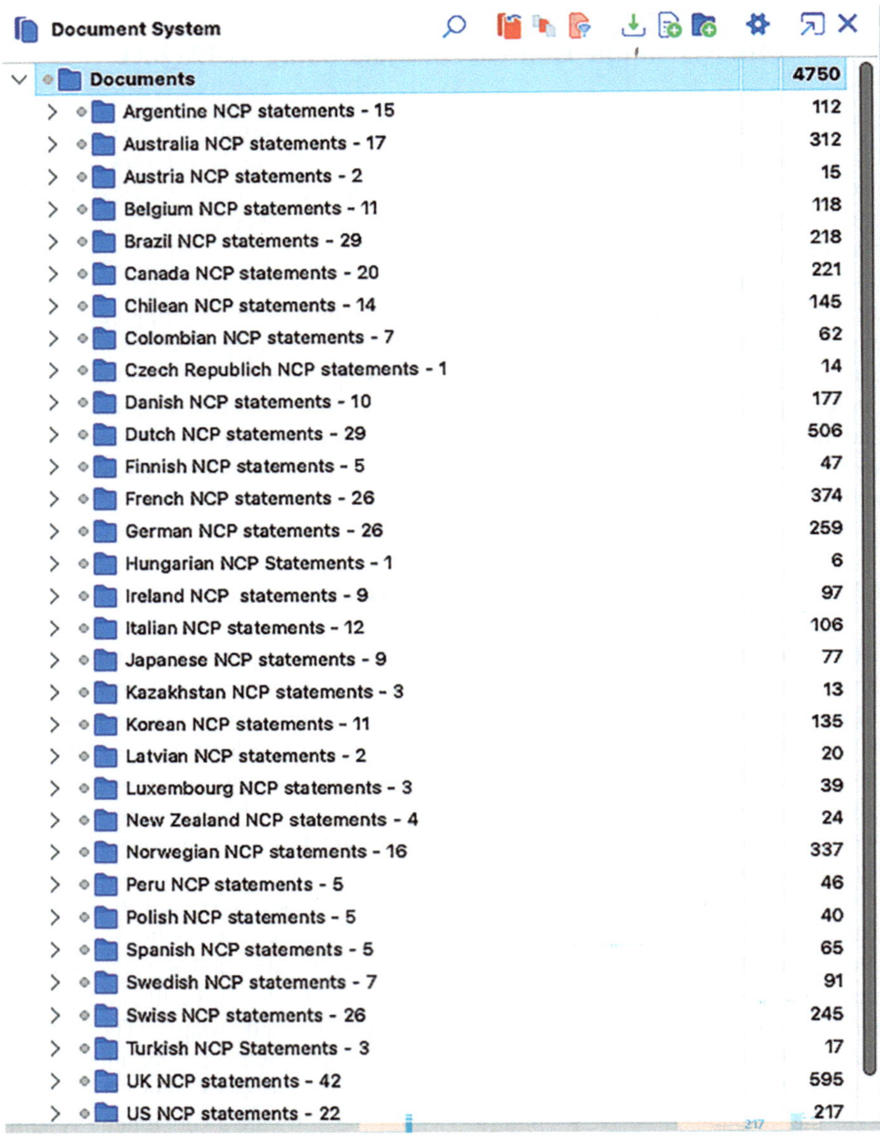

Fig. 1.1 394 NCP cases in document system of MAXQDA

Some of the initial statements contain relevant text that can be used for substantive and procedural analysis in this research, which is why they were included. The image below shows the number of NCP documents on the left, while on the right, the corresponding analysed sections are displayed as numbers of coded segments.

The research aims to conduct a systematic analysis of all relevant cases handled by functioning NCPs—defined as those that have received at least one case to resolve—addressing human rights and environmental issues. To achieve this, a comprehensive set of cases spanning from 2000 to 2024 was collected from multiple sources, including the official OECD case database, the OECD Watch database, and individual NCP websites. The analysis focuses primarily on final statements, as these represent fully resolved cases by the NCPs. However, as mentioned earlier, some initial statements provide valuable insights into how NCPs interpret corporate responsibility. Therefore, a few initial statements were also included in this research.

1.3.2.2 Development of Parent and Sub-Codes

Once all cases—primarily final statements, with occasional initial statements from the NCPs—were uploaded, the software facilitated the systematic coding of individual sentences or paragraphs within these documents. These codes were organised into a 'code-system' for further analysis. Throughout the research, the codes evolved to address key questions about how NCPs interpret corporate human rights and environmental responsibilities and how they provide effective remedies. This coding process was inspired by the grounded theory, which employs a bottom-up (inductive) approach, allowing the data itself to shape the primary analysis, rather than relying solely on predefined hypotheses.[74] This means that the initial codes were not predetermined but instead emerged inductively through close reading and iterative analysis of the NCPs' final statements.

During the analysis phase, relevant sentences and paragraphs from the NCP statements were highlighted to assess the NCPs' interpretation, explanation, and elaboration of corporate human rights and environmental responsibilities. This process also focused on their role in mediating and resolving complaints to provide effective remedies for victims. The systematic coding aimed to comprehensively evaluate the effectiveness of NCPs in addressing human rights, environmental, and labour rights issues, both procedurally and substantively.

From the initial review through the completion of 394 cases, a comprehensive and detailed coding system was developed to analyse corporate human rights responsibilities within OECD case law. This process identified a total of 15 parent codes, which were deemed crucial for evaluating corporate human rights and environmental responsibilities, as well as the effectiveness of the OECD NCP mechanism (see Fig. 1.2: Parent Codes of OECD case law Analysis in MAXQDA). These parent codes addressed diverse and significant areas, such as corporate involvement in harm, the application of risk-based due diligence, stakeholder engagement processes, and the extent of state involvement. Together, these elements provided a structured framework for a thorough and substantive exploration of corporate responsibilities and their alignment with the OECD Guidelines.

[74] Saldaña (2013), pp. 51–52.

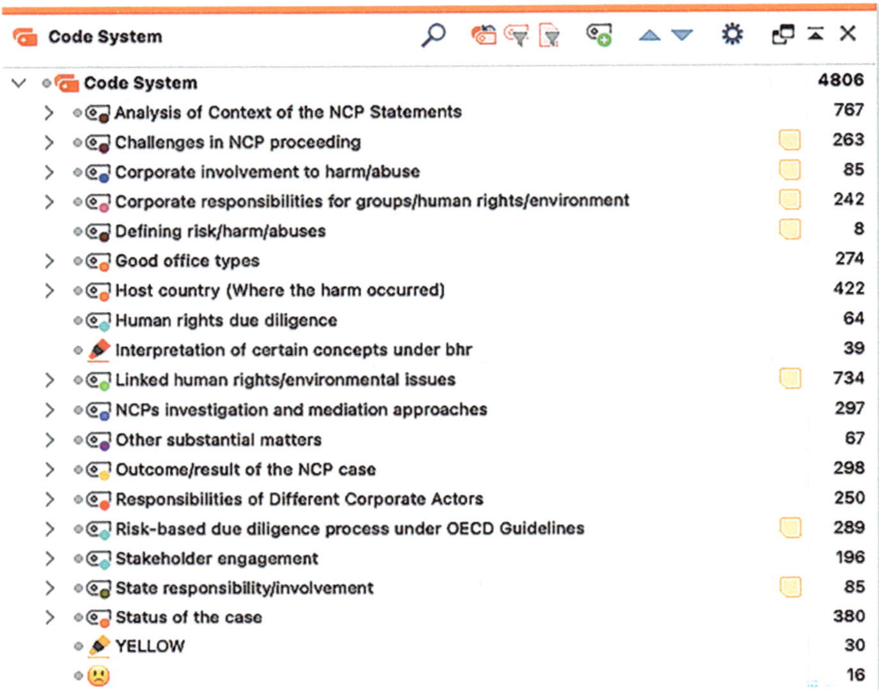

Fig. 1.2 Total parent codes of the OECD Case Law Project

In addition to the general codes, five specific parent codes were dedicated exclusively to assessing the effectiveness of the OECD NCP mechanism. These codes focused on identifying challenges in NCP proceedings, analysing different mediation approaches, evaluating final outcomes, and providing a contextual analysis of NCP statements. While these codes were part of the OECD case law project, this research project focuses solely on the substantive analysis of corporate human rights responsibility. It does not address the procedural aspects of NCPs' grievance mechanisms—such as investigations and mediation approaches—which will be examined in a separate academic article.

This multi-layered coding system was instrumental in uncovering common challenges, trends, and patterns within the NCP framework. By doing so, it provided valuable insights into the practical functioning of the OECD NCP mechanism, highlighting its strengths, limitations, and broader implications for corporate human rights and environmental responsibilities.

1.4 Explanation of Research Material Source and Structure

1.4.1 Material Source: Focus on OECD Specific Cases from 2000 to 2024

The primary source material for this research consists of OECD-specific cases from 2000 to 2024, including final statements issued by 32 functioning NCPs worldwide. These cases address various corporate human rights and environmental responsibilities, excluding those related to Chapters 7, 8, 9, 10, and 11 of the OECD Guidelines. However, cases that cover both one of these chapters and issues related to human rights, labour rights, general policies, or the environment are included.

In addition to English-language final statements, this research incorporates statements published in other languages, such as Spanish, Dutch, and French. For non-English statements, DeepL translation tools and native language translators contracted for the project were utilised to ensure accurate and reliable translations. This approach allows for a comprehensive analysis of the full range of NCP decisions, enriching the study by including perspectives from different jurisdictions and languages, thereby broadening the scope of the research.

Ultimately, it is important to note that the coding and categorisation processes developed through the OECD Case Law Project—including 15 parent codes and their respective subcodes—were consolidated into a publicly accessible online database comprising 394 cases.[75] This database enables researchers and practitioners to explore and utilise the coded data for further analysis.

1.4.2 Book Structure: Description of the Main Three Chapters

The analysis is structured into three parts, derived from a subset of the ten parent codes developed for the substantive assessment of corporate human rights responsibility (see Fig. 1.3). The eventual codings were informed by the frequency and salience of issues that repeatedly emerged across the case law—such as corporate HRDD responsibilities, differentiated obligations of various corporate actors, and responsibilities towards environmental protection or climate change. Based on these recurrent themes, it delineates three major analytical parts that collectively capture the core dimensions of corporate accountability within the OECD case law.

---

[75] OECD case law database: www.oecdcaselaw.com/statements (last accessed 10 July 2025). All coding, data structuring, and categorisation were carried out with the support of two student assistants and a web developer within the OECD Case Law Project team.

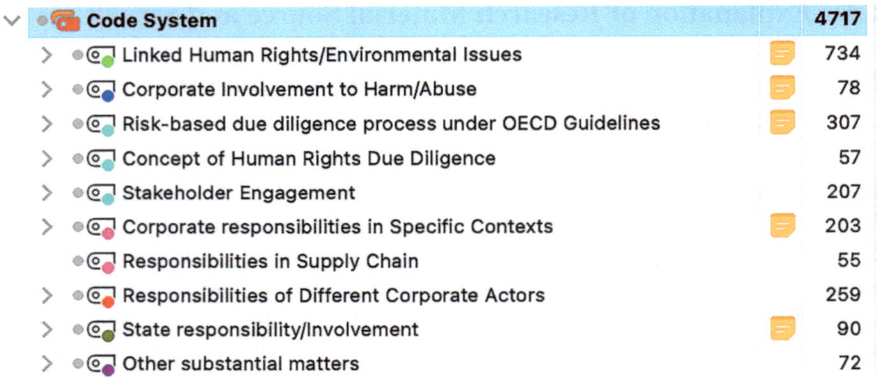

Fig. 1.3 Total parent codes: Exploring Substantive Analysis of Corporate Human Rights and Environmental Responsibilities

1.4.2.1 Chapter 1: Substantive Analysis of Corporate Human Rights and Environmental Responsibilities

The first part of the book provides a foundational examination of corporate human rights and environmental responsibilities, focusing on their substantive legal and policy dimensions. It analyses the normative content of the UNGPs and OECD Guidelines, exploring their role in shaping corporate human rights due diligence obligations. The section further explores the legal frameworks that operationalise these responsibilities, outlining how corporations are expected to implement each step of HRDD. This includes establishing a human rights policy, identifying and assessing adverse impacts, integrating findings into decision-making processes, and ensuring the establishment of effective grievance mechanisms to remedy actual harm.

A critical component of this analysis is the examination of how the UNGPs and the OECD Guidelines influence corporate conduct within the OECD NCP mechanism, which serves as an implementation and accountability framework. By systematically reviewing NCP cases, the section assesses how corporate due diligence responsibilities are interpreted and implemented in practice. Special attention is given to the evolving expectations placed on businesses by the OECD NCPs to prevent and mitigate adverse human rights and environmental impacts through due diligence mechanisms.

1.4.2.2 Chapter 2: Contextual Analysis—Key Issues in Corporate Responsibility Cases

The second chapter of this book shifts from a broad normative analysis to an in-depth, case-specific examination of corporate human rights and environmental responsibilities. Rather than discussing corporate responsibility in abstract terms, this section focuses on how businesses navigate legal and ethical challenges within different thematic and sectoral contexts. Drawing on OECD NCP case law, it explores real-world instances where corporate actors have been held accountable for human rights and environmental impacts. This analysis is guided by a coding framework that systematically categorises key themes emerging from NCP complaints and decisions, providing a structured approach to evaluating corporate accountability trends.

One of the central issues examined in this section is corporate responsibility towards vulnerable groups, including workers, women, Indigenous peoples, and ethnic minorities. Many NCP cases have raised concerns about how businesses engage with these communities and the extent to which they fulfil their due diligence obligations to prevent harm. The analysis explores how NCPs have interpreted corporate responsibilities in these contexts, highlighting trends in decision-making and enforcement.

The book also examines corporate human rights responsibilities in conflict-affected areas, where businesses often operate in high-risk environments with heightened due diligence expectations. The analysis explores whether corporations are expected to adopt more stringent HRDD measures in such contexts and how these responsibilities have been framed in OECD NCP cases. Given the complexity of operating in conflict zones, this section investigates whether companies have been held accountable for complicity in human rights abuses and whether NCPs have provided clear guidance on corporate responsibilities in these situations.

Climate change and environmental impacts represent another key area of corporate responsibility. This section analyses how businesses are held accountable for greenhouse gas emissions, deforestation, pollution, and resource exploitation. By examining OECD NCP decisions, the analysis assesses how corporate due diligence obligations intersect with environmental sustainability goals. It also explores how companies have responded to allegations of environmental harm and whether NCPs have effectively addressed corporate contributions to climate change.

Another emerging area of focus is corporate responsibility in advancing the Sustainable Development Goals (SDGs). Businesses are increasingly expected to align their operations with global sustainability objectives, and this section explores how OECD NCP cases have linked corporate conduct to the broader SDG agenda. The analysis investigates whether companies are actively integrating human rights and environmental considerations into their business strategies and how NCPs have interpreted corporate contributions to sustainable development.

Finally, this section explores the concept of shared responsibility in addressing global human rights challenges. Given the complex and interdependent nature of global supply chains, there is growing debate over whether corporations should collaborate to mitigate systemic human rights risks. This section examines OECD NCP cases that address collective corporate responsibility, assessing whether businesses are expected to work together in tackling shared human rights and environmental challenges.

By systematically coding and analysing NCP case law and complaints, this section identifies patterns in corporate accountability across different industries and sectors. It also evaluates the effectiveness of NCP processes in ensuring remedial measures are implemented, shedding light on the practical application of human rights due diligence obligations. This structured approach allows for a nuanced understanding of how corporate responsibility is evolving in response to regulatory frameworks, stakeholder expectations, and emerging human rights challenges.

1.4.2.3 Chapter 3: Different Actors and Their Specific Responsibilities

The third and final part of the book moves from a general analysis of corporate responsibilities to a more focused examination of specific corporate actors and their distinct obligations in implementing HRDD. Corporate responsibility is not uniform across all business entities; rather, different types of actors have varying degrees of influence, oversight, and accountability depending on their roles within corporate structures and global value chains. This section explores how different corporate entities engage with HRDD, highlighting key challenges and responsibilities through the lens of OECD NCP cases. A coding analysis is applied to systematically identify patterns and trends in corporate accountability across different sectors.

One of the central categories examined in this section is parent companies, particularly within transnational corporate structures. These entities play a critical role in shaping HRDD practices across their subsidiaries and supply chains. The analysis considers how parent companies influence corporate policies, the extent of their legal and ethical obligations, and the ways in which they can be held accountable for human rights violations committed within their business networks. OECD NCP cases provide insight into evolving expectations regarding parent company liability, particularly in industries where supply chain risks are high.

Another key group analysed in this section is financial institutions, including banks, investors, and lenders. These actors have significant leverage over the companies they finance, and their due diligence obligations are crucial in preventing human rights abuses linked to investment activities. It examines how financial institutions assess and mitigate human rights risks in high-risk sectors, as well as how OECD NCPs have interpreted their responsibilities in past cases. The findings highlight the role of financial actors in shaping corporate behaviour and the challenges in ensuring meaningful HRDD in investment decisions.

The role of state-owned enterprises (SOEs) is also explored, as these entities operate at the intersection of corporate and state responsibilities. Unlike private corporations, SOEs are both business entities and public institutions, meaning they are subject to corporate responsibility norms as well as state-imposed governance frameworks. This section examines how SOEs have approached HRDD obligations, particularly in cases where their business activities intersect with public policy objectives or state interests. OECD NCP cases provide important insights into how SOEs balance economic interests with human rights responsibilities and the extent to which they are held accountable for their actions.

In addition to traditional corporate actors, this section also considers the responsibilities of non-profit organisations and international bodies, such as FIFA, the International Olympic Committee (IOC), and the World Wide Fund for Nature

(WWF). Although these entities are not conventional businesses, their global influence and operational activities raise important questions about their responsibility to conduct HRDD. The analysis explores how these organisations apply—or fail to apply—the UNGPs and OECD Guidelines in their decision-making processes, using case studies to illustrate key challenges.

Finally, the section addresses the role of states in regulating corporate responsibility. While businesses are expected to conduct due diligence independently, states also have a duty to establish regulatory frameworks that enforce corporate human rights obligations. This analysis evaluates how different OECD countries have incorporated HRDD requirements into national law and assesses the effectiveness of state intervention in ensuring compliance. It also considers how state regulation has influenced corporate behaviour in practice, drawing on OECD NCP cases to illustrate the varying degrees of state involvement in corporate accountability.

By structuring the analysis around these different actors, this section provides a comprehensive examination of how HRDD obligations are distributed across the corporate landscape. Through a combination of normative analysis and case-based insights, the research seeks to highlight the distinct challenges and responsibilities faced by different corporate actors, offering a nuanced perspective on the evolving expectations surrounding corporate human rights and environmental due diligence.

References

Documents

Directive (EU) 2024/1760 of the European Parliament and of the Council of 13 June 2024 on Corporate Sustainability Due Diligence and Amending Directive (EU) 2019/1937 and Regulation (EU) 2023/2859 (5 July 2024).

The Government of Norway 'Act relating to enterprises' transparency and work on fundamental human rights and decent working conditions (Transparency Act).

The Swiss Federal Council. '*Ordinance on Due Diligence and Transparency in relation to Minerals and Metals from Conflict-Affected Areas*' (DDTrO) of 3 December 2021.

Documents

Global National Action Plans on Business and Human Rights. https://globalnaps.org/country/. Accessed 31 Jan 2026

Government of Netherlands 'Responsible Business Conduct Policy (2020). https://www.government.nl/topics/responsible-business-conduct-rbc/documents/policy-notes/2020/10/16/from-giving-information-to-imposing-obligations. Accessed 31 Jan 2026

OECD (2011) OECD Guidelines for Multinational Enterprises. OECD Publication

OECD (2016) OECD Due Diligence Guidance for Responsible Supply Chains of Minerals from Conflict-Affected and High-Risk Areas: Third Edition. OECD. https://www.oecd-ilibrary.org/governance/oecd-due-diligence-guidance-for-responsible-supply-chains-of-minerals-from-conflict-affected-and-high-risk-areas_9789264252479-en. Accessed 31 Jan 2026

OECD (2018) OECD Due Diligence Guidance for Responsible Business Conduct. OECD. https://www.oecd-ilibrary.org/finance-and-investment/oecd-due-diligence-guidance-for-responsible-business-conduct_15f5f4b3-en. Accessed 31 Jan 2026

OECD (2023) 'Working Party on Responsible Business Conduct Summary of input received during the public consultation on the targeted update of the OECD Guidelines for Multinational Enterprises' V/RBC/RD (2023) Unclassified Organisation for Economic Co-operation and Development (21 March 2023) DAF/INV/RBC/RD (2023), 1

OHCHR response to request from BankTrack for advice regarding the application of the UN Guiding Principles on Business and Human Rights in the context of the banking sector OHCHR 13 June 2017. https://www.banktrack.org/download/letter_from_ohchr_to_banktrack_on_application_of_the_un_guiding_principles_in_the_banking_sector/banktrack_response_final.pdf. Accessed 31 Jan 2026

Organisation for Economic Cooperation and Development (OECD) (2023) OECD Guidelines for Multinational Enterprises on Responsible Business Conduct. OECD Publication

UN Human Rights Council 'Promotion and Protection of All Human Rights, Civil, Political, Economic, Social and Cultural Rights, Including the Right to Development "Protect, Respect and Remedy: A Framework for Business and Human Rights: Report of the Special Representative of the Secretary-General on the Issue of Human Rights and Transnational Corporations and Other Business Enterprises, John Ruggie" 7 April 2008 A/HRC/8/5.

UNICEF, United Nations Global Compact and Save the Children 'Children's Rights and Business Principles (CRBP) https://www.unicef.org/media/96136/file/Childrens-Rights-Business-Principles-2012.pdf. Accessed 31 Jan 2026

United Nations (2011a) Guiding principles on business and human rights: implementing the united nations 'protect, respect and remedy' framework. United Nations, New York and Geneva

United Nations (2011b). Guiding Principles on Business and Human Rights: Implementing the United Nations 'Protect, Respect and Remedy' Framework. UN Doc A/HRC/17/31

United Nations (2024) Human Rights Council, 'Investors, Environmental, Social, and Governance Approaches and Human Rights: Report of the Working Group on the Issue of Human Rights and Transnational Corporations and Other Business Enterprises,' 2 May 2024, A/HRC/56/55

United Nations. The Principles for Responsible Investment https://www.unpri.org. Accessed 31 Jan 2026

Bibliography

Bağlayan B (2018) Searching for human rights norms for corporate conduct in domestic jurisprudence: a bottom-up approach to international law. Nordic J Human Rights 36:371–389. https://www.tandfonline.com/doi/full/10.1080/18918131.2018.1547533. Accessed 31 Jan 2026

BHRRC (2023) TotalEnergies lawsuit (regarding reparations for damages caused by Tilenga and EACOP projects in Uganda and Tanzania), 27 June 2023 https://www.business-humanrights.org/en/latest-news/totalenergies-lawsuit-re-reparations-of-damages-caused-by-tilenga-et-eacop-projects-in-uganda-and-tanzania/. Accessed 31 Jan 2026

Bilchitz D (2009) The Ruggie framework: an adequate rubric for corporate human rights obligations? SSRN Electr J:1–87. http://www.ssrn.com/abstract=1394367. Accessed 31 Jan 2026

Bilchitz D (2013) A Chasm between "Is" and "Ought?" a critique of the normative foundations of the SRSG's framework and the guiding principles. In: Deva S, Bilchitz D (eds) Human rights obligations of business, 1st edn. Cambridge University Press, pp 107–137

Birchall D (2019) Any act, any harm, to anyone: the transformative potential of "Human Rights Impacts" under the UN guiding principles on business and human rights. SSRN Electr J:120–147. https://www.ssrn.com/abstract=3425733. Accessed 31 Jan 2026

Bonnitcha, Jonathan and McCorquodale, Robert. 'The concept of "Due Diligence" in the UN guiding principles on business and human rights' Eur J Int Law 28 (2019): 899-919. http://academic.oup.com/ejil/article/28/3/899/4616670. Accessed 31 Jan 2026

Brook O (2022) Politics of coding: on systematic content analysis of legal text. In: Bartl M, Lawrence JC (eds) The politics of European legal research: behind the method. Edward Elgar Publishing, pp 109–123

Buhmann K (2018) Analysing OECD national contact point statements for guidance on human rights due diligence: method, findings and outlook. Nordic J Human Rights 36(4):390–410

Business and Human Rights Resource Centre (BHRRC) 'Switched off: Tech company opacity & Israel's war on Gaza' Briefing 18 April 2024. https://www.business-humanrights.org/en/from-us/briefings/tech-sector-opt-analysis-2024/#_findings. Accessed 31 Jan 2026

Chetail V (2014) The legal personality of multinational corporations, state responsibility and due diligence: the way forward. In: Alland D et al (eds) Unité et diversité du droit international/Unity and Diversity of International Law. Brill | Nijhoff, pp 105–130. https://brill.com/view/book/edcoll/9789004262393/B9789004262393_006.xml. Accessed 31 Jan 2026

Choudhury B (2023) The UN guiding principles on business and human rights and principles for responsible contracts: an introduction. In: Choudhury B (ed) The UN guiding principles on business and human rights: a commentary. Elgar Commentaries, pp 1–10

Curzi LC (2020) General principles for business and human rights in international law. Brill Nijhoff

Egan S (2017) The doctrinal approach in international human rights scholarship. SSRN Electr J:1–17. https://www.ssrn.com/abstract=3082194. Accessed 31 Jan 2026

Equator Principles: A Financial Industry Benchmark for Determining, Assessing and Managing Environmental and Social Risks in Projects, July 2020

Fasterling B (2023) Guiding principles 19: action upon human rights impact assessments. In: Choudhury B (ed) The UN guiding principles on business and human rights: a commentary. Elgar Commentaries, pp 115–136

Ford J, Nolan J (2020) Regulating transparency on human rights and modern slavery in corporate supply chains: the discrepancy between human rights due diligence and the social audit. Aust J Human Rights 26:27–45. https://www.tandfonline.com/doi/full/10.1080/1323238X.2020.1761633. Accessed 31 Jan 2026

Gizzi MC (2018) MAXQDA and the Four Stages of Research – an Analysis Methodology Guide (1 August 2018) MAXQDA. https://www.maxqda.com/blogpost/maxqda-and-the-four-stages-of-research. Accessed 31 Jan 2026

Halifax Initiative 'Export Credit Agencies and Human Rights' Failure to Protect 2015. https://halifaxinitiative.org/sites/default/files/Failure%20to%20Protect_0.pdf. Accessed 31 Jan 2026

Hutchinson T (2018) Doctrinal research: researching the jury. In: Watkins D, Burton M (eds) Research methods in law, 2nd edn. Routledge, pp 8–39

Kaufmann Christine, 'OECD MNE Guidelines Quo Vadis? Making responsible business conduct work for better lives' In: OECD Guidelines for Multinational Enterprises: A Glass Half Full. Liber Amicorum for Dr. Roel Nieuwenkamp, Chair of the OECD Working Party on Responsible Business Conduct 2013-2018), 29-37 https://www.zora.uzh.ch/id/eprint/160967. Accessed 31 Jan 2026

Krajewski M, Davaanyam O (2023) Guardians of rights? The role of government in promoting responsible business conduct under the updated OECD guidelines for multinational enterprises. Nova Centre on Business, Human Rights and the Environment Blog, 30th November 2023. https://novabhre.novalaw.unl.pt/guardians-of-rights-the-role-of-government-in-promoting-responsible-business-conduct-under-the-updated-oecd-guidelines-for-multinational-enterprises/. Accessed 31 Jan 2026

Legalgetaway 'Understanding Black Letter Law: The Basics'. https://legalgetaway.com/blog/what-is-black-letter-law/. Accessed 31 January 2026
Macchi C, Bernaz N (2021) Business, human rights and climate due diligence: understanding the responsibility of banks. Sustainability 13(15):1–21
Maene C (2023) NVivo: an introduction to textual qualitative data analysis with software. In: Stevens PAJ (ed) Qualitative data analysis: key approaches. SAGE Publishing, pp 109–178
Mares R (2018) Human rights due diligence and the root causes of harm in business operation: a textual and contextual analysis of the guiding principles on business and human rights. Northeast Univ Law Rev 10(1):1–71
Martin-Ortega O (2014) Human rights due diligence for corporations: from voluntary standards to hard law at last? Neth Quart Human Rights 32:44–74. http://journals.sagepub.com/doi/10.1177/016934411403200104. Accessed 31 Jan 2026
McCorquodale R, Blanco-Vizarreta C (2023) Guiding principle 17: human rights due diligence. In: Choudhury B (ed) The UN guiding principles on business and human rights: a commentary. Elgar Commentaries, pp 123–136
McCorquodale R (2024) Business and human rights: element of international law. Oxford University Press
Ngwoke RA, Mbano IP, Helynn O (2023) A critical appraisal of doctrinal and non-doctrinal legal research methodologies in contemporary times. Int J Civil Law Leg Res 3(1):8–17
Prenkert JD, Scott J (2014) Schackelford 'Business, Human Rights and the Promise of Polycentricity'. Vanderbilt J Transnatl Law 47(2):467–468
Saldaña J (2013) The coding manual for qualitative researchers, 2nd edn. SAGE Publications, pp 51–52
Salehijam M (2018) The value of systematic content analysis in legal research. Tilburg Law Rev 23(1):34–42. https://doi.org/10.5334/tilr.5. Accessed 31 Jan 2026
Taylor M (2020) Human rights due diligence in theory and practice. In: Deva S, Birchall D (eds) Research handbook on human rights and business. Edward Elgar Publishing, pp 88–107
Van Ho T (2021) Defining the relationships: "Cause, Contribute, and Directly Linked to" in the UN guiding principles on business and human rights'. Human Rights Quart 43(4): 625–658. https://muse.jhu.edu/article/837782 Accessed 31 Jan 2026
Wettstein F (2013) Making noise about silent complicity: the moral inconsistency of the protect, respect and remedy framework. In: Deva S, Bilchitz D (eds) Human rights obligations of business. Cambridge University Press, pp 243–268
Wettstein F (2012) CSR and the debate on business and human rights: bridging the great divide. Bus Ethics Quart 22(4):739–770. https://www.cambridge.org/core/product/identifier/S1052150X00005261/type/journal_article. Accessed 31 Jan 2026
Wolfsteller R, Li Y (2022) Business and human rights regulation after the UN guiding principles: accountability, governance effectiveness. Human Rights Rev 23:1–17. https://link.springer.com/10.1007/s12142-022-00656-2. Accessed 31 Jan 2026
Wood S (2012) The case for leverage-based corporate human rights responsibility. Bus Ethics Quart 22(1):63–98
World Benchmarking Alliance (2023) 2023 Corporate Human Rights Benchmark. 20 November 2023

Websites

OECD. 'Database of specific instances' https://mneguidelines.oecd.org/database/. Accessed 31 Jan 2026
OECD case law database: www.oecdcaselaw.com/statements. Accessed 31 Jan 2026

Chapter 2
Analysing Corporate Human Rights Responsibilities Through the Lens of the UN Guiding Principles and OECD Case Law

2.1 Introduction

This chapter examines corporate human rights responsibilities through the lens of the UNGPs, using OECD case law as a practical foundation for analysis. The UNGPs set a global standard for preventing and addressing human rights abuses in business operations, while the OECD Guidelines provide more detailed, sector-specific guidance tailored to the various industries and activities in which MNEs operate. The primary objective of this chapter is to critically assess how the corporate human rights and environmental due diligence responsibilities outlined in the UNGPs are applied in practice through the OECD NCP system. As highlighted in the previous chapter, the core responsibility of corporations regarding human rights and the environment is centred on HRDD.

By analysing cases from different NCPs, this chapter explores how corporate human rights responsibilities have been interpreted, enforced, and contested. Special emphasis is placed on the alignment between the UNGPs and OECD case law, with a particular focus on how the HRDD framework outlined in the UNGPs and the OECD Guidelines, as a 'risk-based due diligence concept', has been adopted and expanded by different NCPs (see Fig. 2.1). It explores how companies have responded to these responsibilities, how NCPs assess their actions, and how businesses can better align their practices with the UNGPs and OECD Guidelines after the case proceeding.

O. Davaanyam, *Conceptualising the Corporate Human Rights and Environmental Responsibilities*, Interdisciplinary Studies in Human Rights 17,
https://doi.org/10.1007/978-3-032-21430-0_2

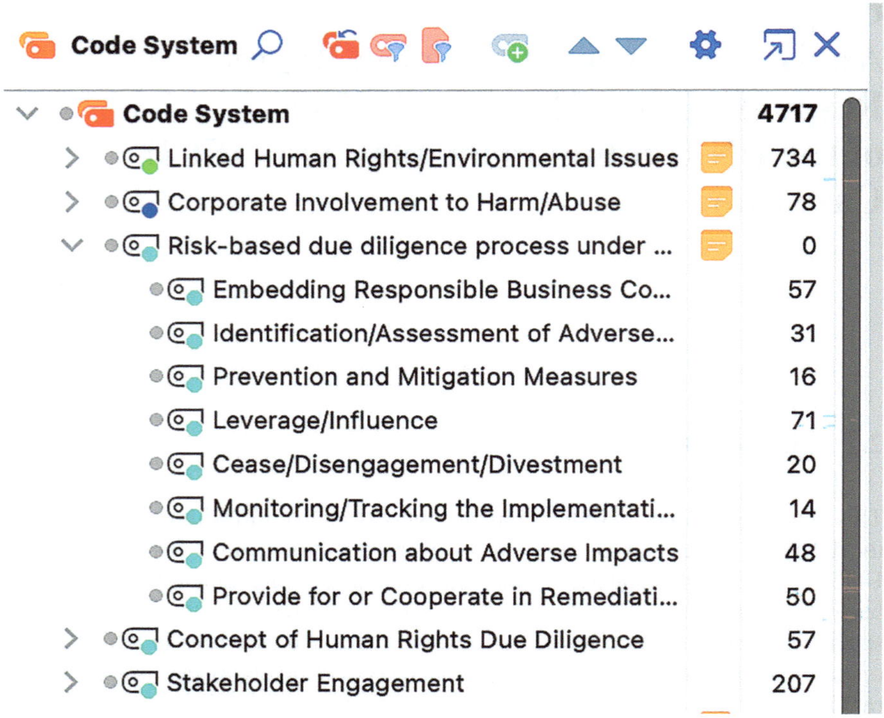

Fig. 2.1 Sub-codes of the Parent code: Risk-based due diligence process under the OECD Guidelines

2.2 Establishing a Corporate Human Rights Policy Framework

2.2.1 The Critical Role of Comprehensive Human Rights Policies: Aligning Corporate Conduct with the UNGPs and OECD Guidelines

Adopting a human rights policy is a crucial part of a corporation's HRDD responsibilities. Alex Newton wrote that, 'In many instances, in the process of developing their human rights policy, companies have uncovered various issues that were previously overlooked. On the other hand, without a human rights policy, a company seeking to respect human rights is fumbling along in the darkness without a torch'.[1] Principle 16 of the UNGPs asserts that companies must establish a human rights policy endorsed by senior management, informed by both internal and external

[1] Newton (2019), p. 93.

expertise.[2] This policy should outline the company's human rights expectations for personnel, business partners, and other entities directly linked to its operations, products, or services. It must be publicly accessible, communicated internally and externally to all relevant stakeholders, and integrated into operational policies and procedures to ensure its implementation across the enterprise.[3]

John Ruggie, the architect of the UNGPs, emphasised that developing a human rights policy and conducting HRDD are essential because they demonstrate what companies know about human rights and how they communicate these expectations globally.[4] The UNGPs commentary highlights the importance of transparent internal and external communication of the human rights policy and stresses the need for policy coherence throughout the business to align operations with human rights commitments.

The OECD Guidelines provide more specific guidance on the adoption of human rights policies, particularly in Chapter 2: General Policies, A.7 and A.8. These sections emphasise the importance of developing and applying effective self-regulatory practices and management systems that foster a relationship of confidence and mutual trust between enterprises and the societies in which they operate. This is a crucial directive, as it highlights how corporate human rights policies can play a vital role in building trust among stakeholders and rightsholders, ensuring that society understands the company's commitment to human rights and environmental standards.[5] Moreover, the Guidelines addresses the importance of promoting awareness and compliance among workers employed by MNEs. This is to be achieved through the appropriate dissemination of company policies, including training programs designed to ensure that workers are fully informed about the company's human rights expectations.[6] In this way, the Guidelines not only call for the adoption of human rights policies but also stress the importance of internal communication and training to ensure these policies are integrated into daily operations and upheld at all levels of the organisation.

While the adoption of corporate human rights policies has not traditionally been a central focus in academic literature—where much of the discussion has revolved around the operational impacts of HRDD processes—CSOs and multistakeholder initiatives, such as the UN Global Compact, Shift, and others have consistently highlighted the significance of these policies.[7] They emphasise that a well-formulated human rights policy is not merely a corporate formality, but a critical

[2] UN Guiding Principles on Business and Human Rights, Principle 16.

[3] Wettstein (2022), pp. 145–146.

[4] John F. Sherman III 'Are there risks knowing and showing? BSR Human Rights Working Group 22 October 2012, Shift https://shiftproject.org/wp-content/uploads/2012/10/Sherman_risksknowingshowing2012.pdf (accessed 31 January 2026).

[5] UN Guiding Principles on Business and Human Rights, Commentary to the Principle 16; Neglia (2023), p. 119.

[6] Ibid.

[7] Global Business Initiative (GBI) Making Policy Commitment https://gbihr.org/business-practice-portal/making-a-policy-commitment (accessed 31 January 2026).

instrument for demonstrating a company's commitment to human rights.[8] It serves as a clear and public declaration of responsibility, helping to communicate this to a wide array of external stakeholders, including CSOs, local communities, affected rights holders, and investors. Furthermore, initiatives such as the Corporate Human Rights Benchmark (CHRB) actively assess how companies are implementing HRDD, paying particular attention to the establishment and operationalisation of human rights policies.[9] These assessments rely on publicly disclosed human rights policy, reports, and other documentation produced by global companies, underscoring the vital role of transparency and accountability in corporate human rights efforts.[10]

Recent mHRDD legislation, such as France's Devoir de Vigilance (Duty of Vigilance), Germany's Lieferkettensorgfaltspflichtengesetz (LkSG) and the CSDDD, signals a significant shift from voluntary frameworks to legally binding obligations for corporations.[11] These regulations require businesses to not only adopt human rights policies but also define specific content and processes that these policies must incorporate. For instance, France legislation demand big French companies to adopt and publish the 'Vigilance Plan' assessing the risks of human rights and environmental abuses in their supply chain.[12] The LkSG, Section 6(2) mandates that companies issue a policy statement on human rights strategy, which must be adopted by senior management.[13] This policy should establish clear procedures for meeting legal obligations, prioritise key human rights and environmental risks, and define the company's expectations for upholding human rights across its supply chain.[14] Unlike the broader scope of the French Duty of Vigilance Law, the LkSG adopts a more selective approach, focusing specifically on human rights and environmental risks explicitly outlined in its annex.[15]

Similarly, the CSDDD specifies in Article 7 that companies must integrate due diligence into all relevant policies and risk management systems, develop a due diligence policy in consultation with employees, and ensure the policy addresses long-term approaches to due diligence, codes of conduct, and procedures for implementing

---

[8] Ibid.

[9] Corporate Human Rights Benchmark, https://www.worldbenchmarkingalliance.org/corporate-human-rights-benchmark/ (accessed 31 January 2026).

[10] Ibid.

[11] Law 2017-399 of March 27, 2017 on the duty of vigilance of parent companies and contracting companies, Respect International 'French Corporate Duty of Vigilance Law (English Translation)' https://respect.international/french-corporate-duty-of-vigilance-law-english-translation/ (accessed 31 January 2026); The Act on Corporate Due Diligence Obligations in Supply Chains (Lieferkettensorgfaltspflichtengesetz, LkSG) 22 July 2021 https://www.csr-in-deutschland.de/EN/Business-Human-Rights/Supply-Chain-Act/supply-chain-act.html (accessed 31 January 2026).

[12] Ibid, Duty of Vigilance Law, Article 1.

[13] The Act on Corporate Due Diligence Obligations in Supply Chains (Lieferkettensorgfaltspflichtengesetz, LkSG) 22 July 2021, Section 6(2).

[14] Ibid.

[15] The Act on Corporate Due Diligence Obligations in Supply Chains (Lieferkettensorgfaltspflichtengesetz, LkSG) 22 July 2021, Annex.

and verifying compliance.[16] Furthermore, these policies must be reviewed and updated regularly to address changing risks and impacts.[17] While the CSDDD references a broad spectrum of key international human rights instruments, it conspicuously omits several crucial agreements.[18] These include the UN Declaration on the Rights of Indigenous Peoples (UNDRIP), the International Convention on the Protection of the Rights of All Migrant Workers and Members of Their Families (ICMW), the UN Declaration on Human Rights Defenders (UNDRHD), the Convention on the Elimination of All Forms of Discrimination Against Women (CEDAW), and International Humanitarian Law (IHL).[19] The absence of these key frameworks creates a significant divergence between the CSDDD and established international business and human rights standards, such as those embodied in the UNGPs and the OECD Guidelines. These omissions undermine the directive's ability to enforce a holistic and robust corporate human rights policy.[20]

By selectively excluding these critical agreements, the CSDDD fails to account for the full spectrum of human rights concerns that companies should address, particularly those impacting vulnerable groups. The absence of explicit references to Indigenous peoples' rights, migrant workers' protections, gender equality, and human rights defenders dilutes the mandatory obligations that the CSDDD seeks to impose. This selective approach weakens the directive's potential to create comprehensive corporate human rights policies that are in line with international standards, leaving significant gaps in addressing pressing human rights issues.

Considering the analysis above, while the increasing adoption of mHRDD legislations for MNEs is a positive step, driven by emerging regulations such as the CSDDD and LkSG, this progress is undermined by the selective approach that lawmakers are taking. This is the deviation from the UNGPs' core principles risks diluting the effectiveness of corporate human rights efforts. While the UNGPs and OECD Guidelines recognised the vital importance of establishing human rights policies, they left it largely up to states and businesses to determine which rights to be recognised. Moreover, the selective application of human rights standards could

---

[16] Corporate Sustainability Due Diligence Directive, Article 7.

[17] Ibid.

[18] Nele Meyer and Christopher Patz '*Dividing the Indivisible: Human Rights under the EU Corporate Sustainability Due Diligence Directive*' *VerfassungBlog,* 1 June 2024 https://verfassungsblog.de/dividing-the-indivisible-human-rights-under-the-eu-corporate-sustainability-due-diligence-directive/, DOI: https://doi.org/10.59704/a61ef927af06b44f> (accessed 31 January 2026).

[19] UN General Assembly, United Nations Declaration on the Rights of Indigenous Peoples: resolution / adopted by the General Assembly, A/RES/61/295, 2 October 2007; UN General Assembly, UN Declaration on Human Rights Defenders, A/RES/53/144, 8 March 1999; UN General Assembly, International Convention on the Protection of the Rights of All Migrant Workers and Members of their Families, A/RES/45/158, 18 December 1990, UN "Convention on the Elimination of All Forms of Discrimination against Women." 1988 Treaty Series 1249: 13.

[20] Meyer and Patz (2024).

have unintended consequences.[21] MNEs, now mandated to adopt policies, may find themselves navigating complex and inconsistent human rights expectations across different jurisdictions, leading to fragmented and inconsistent practices. This not only creates confusion but also risks undermining the universality of human rights by forcing companies to prioritise certain rights over others based on legal requirements, rather than a holistic approach aligned with international standards. Furthermore, by failing to mandate the consideration of all internationally recognised human rights, these regulations narrow the lens through which businesses must operate. This selective approach risks fostering a 'compliance culture', where companies focus on meeting the minimum legal requirements rather than genuinely engaging with the full scope of human rights issues.[22]

Beyond the scope and necessity of establishing a corporate human rights policy, it is essential to consider the real-world impacts these policies can have. Research from management scholars indicates that companies operating in high-risk sectors—such as oil and gas—are more likely to prevent, mitigate, and address severe human rights risks when they implement robust, comprehensive, and well-developed human rights policies.[23] This suggests that both policy commitment and operational preparedness are necessary for firms to reduce human rights abuses effectively.[24] The hypothesis put forward by these scholars argued that strong human rights policies, when combined with a company's readiness to act on them, reinforce each other to mitigate 'means-ends decoupling'—the gap between what a company claims to do in terms of human rights and the actual impact of its practices.[25]

From a legal perspective, establishing a human rights policy can serve as a key indicator of a company's duty of care. As Nadia Bernaz noted in her article, companies can be held accountable for their human rights policy statements because such policies demonstrate that they are aware of the risks and potential impacts associated with their activities.[26] This awareness imposes a responsibility to take adequate measures to prevent or address harm. This concept was notably affirmed in the landmark UK Supreme Court case against Vedanta, where the court held that Vedanta, a UK-based parent company, could be liable for the actions of its

[21] Mares (2024) Https://Verfassungsblog.De/Csddd-The-Unintended-Consequences-Of-Mandatory-Due-Diligence/ (accessed 31 January 2026).

[22] CCC, ECCHR (2022) https://www.ecchr.eu/fileadmin/Publikationen/PublicEye_Report_Respecting-Rights_1-22.pdf#page=2.26 (accessed 31 January 2026), Sherman III 'Beyond CSR: The Story of the UN Guiding Principles on Business and Human Rights' *Corporate Responsibility Initiative, Harvard Kennedy School Working Paper* March 2020 https://www.hks.harvard.edu/sites/default/files/centers/mrcbg/files/CRI_AWP_71.pdf#page=11.17 (accessed 31 January 2026).

[23] Olsen et al. (2022), pp. 1512–1557.

[24] Ibid.

[25] Ibid.

[26] Bernaz (2013), pp. 493–511, https://doi.org/10.1007/s10551-012-1531-z 10 April 2019 UKSC/2017/0185 https://www.supremecourt.uk/cases/uksc-2017-0185#judgment-details (accessed 31 January 2026).

subsidiary operating in Zambia.[27] The case highlighted that Vedanta's public human rights policy and sustainability commitments signalled an acknowledgment of risks in its operations, thereby reinforcing the company's duty of care toward those affected by its activities.[28] This ruling set a significant precedent, demonstrating that corporate human rights policies are not just aspirational statements, but can create legal obligations.[29] When companies recognise human rights risks through such policies, they may face heightened scrutiny and accountability, particularly when they fail to act in accordance with their stated commitments. This shift stresses the importance of companies adopting comprehensive and actionable human rights policies, not only to mitigate risks but also to fulfil their legal and ethical responsibilities in a global business environment.

In terms of implementation of corporate policies on human rights and environmental risks, it has sparked significant debate, particularly considering lessons learned from the Duty of Vigilance Law. While this legislation prompted many companies to consider these risks in their business activities and supply chains, significant challenges remain. As Neglia pointed out, there are critical flaws, such as the lack of precision and detail in company plans, which make it difficult for stakeholders to measure their effectiveness. Additionally, the absence of clear communication about these plans, combined with weak implementation, creates a substantial risk that regulatory efforts may become overly focused on reporting requirements rather than addressing the fundamental disconnect between corporate policies and real-world behaviours.

Neglia further emphasised that despite the widespread adoption of policies following the UNGPs, companies with even the most detailed policy frameworks, such as Adidas and H&M, continue to be linked to severe human rights risks.[30] He argued that the adoption of policies should be viewed as an obligation of result, meaning that companies must focus on respecting human rights through tangible actions, rather than simply fulfilling an obligation of means—adopting and reporting policies without ensuring their actual implementation.[31] In conclusion, true progress in corporate human rights responsibility requires a shift in focus from mere policy adoption and reporting to meaningful, result-driven actions that bridge the gap between corporate commitments and actual impact on the ground.

---

[27] UK Supreme Court, Vedanta Resources PLC and another (Appellants) v Lungowe and others (Respondents).

[28] Hogan Lovells 'The Implications of the UK Supreme Court's Decision in Vedanta for the Management of Human Rights Risk in Overseas Operations and Supply Chains' 30 May 2019 https://blogs.law.ox.ac.uk/business-law-blog/blog/2019/05/implications-uk-supreme-courts-decision-vedanta-management-human (accessed 31 January 2026).

[29] Ibid.

[30] Neglia (2023), pp. 121–122.

[31] Ibid, 121.

2.2.2 *Insights from OECD Case Law: Best Practices for Implementing Effective Corporate Human Rights Policies*

From 2000 to 2024, OECD NCP case law has examined around 44 cases (57 coded segments) focused on corporate human rights policies, with an emphasis on their scope and implementation. These cases provide essential guidance on how companies should develop and adopt these policies, not just in terms of their content—ensuring comprehensive coverage of all internationally recognised human rights—but also how they are communicated internally and externally. The NCP case law pointed out that human rights policies cannot be mere formalities. Instead, they must serve as actionable frameworks, fully integrated into the company's operations and communicated transparently to stakeholders. These insights are critical benchmarks for businesses seeking to align with international standards and ensure meaningful engagement with human rights concerns.

One of the primary contributions of OECD NCP cases has been their detailed examination of whether corporate policies truly address all internationally recognised human rights. A consistent issue that arises is the omission of protections for vulnerable groups, particularly Indigenous Peoples' rights and the principle of Free, Prior, and Informed Consent (FPIC). This oversight is especially troubling, as these rights are crucial to ensuring that Indigenous communities are respected and involved in decisions that impact their land rights and livelihoods. For instance, in the case against PanAust before the Australian NCP, as well as cases against Norconsult at the Norwegian NCP and WWF and Credit Suisse at the Swiss NCP, the NCPs emphasised the critical need to incorporate Indigenous Peoples' rights and FPIC into corporate human rights policies.[32] In the PanAust case, the Australian NCP further stressed that financial compensation alone does not satisfy the obligation of consent, underscoring the necessity of fully aligning corporate policies with international human rights standards, particularly regarding vulnerable groups.[33] Furthermore, many OECD NCP cases have exposed broader failures by companies to address the rights of other vulnerable groups, such as gender-based harassment and women's rights. In cases involving APG Asset Management at the Dutch and US NCPs, the importance of incorporating gender-based harassment and violence in human rights policies—not only in the fast-food sector but also within investor

[32] NCP Australia, Project Sepik and Jubilee Australia Research Centre on behalf of Sepik River communities v. PanAust Limited, Final Statement, 3 October 2023; NCP Norway, Association for International Water Studies (FIVAS) v. Norconsult AS, Final Statement, 23 June 2015; NCP Switzerland Survival international v. WWF, Final Statement, 21 November 2017; NCP Switzerland, Society for Threatened People v. Credit Suisse, Final Statement, 16 October 2019.

[33] NCP Australia, Project Sepik and Jubilee Australia Research Centre on behalf of Sepik River communities v. PanAust Limited, Final Statement, 3 October 2023, para 111.

due diligence systems—was emphasised.[34] Similarly, the case against JCB at the UK NCP highlighted the importance for companies operating in high-risk or conflict-affected areas to adopt human rights policies that go beyond mere compliance with laws like the UK Modern Slavery Act and demonstrate a proactive commitment to protecting human rights.[35]

As noted earlier in the previous section, and similar to some mHRDD initiatives, corporations also tend to selectively recognise certain international human rights—whether intentionally or unintentionally—while excluding others. Consequently, their human rights policies often lack the necessary depth and comprehensive coverage of internationally recognised rights, particularly those protecting vulnerable groups. By identifying these shortcomings, OECD NCP case law plays a crucial role in pushing companies to align more fully with global human rights standards.

However, having a written human rights policy is insufficient. In previous section, scholars emphasised that the true value of such policies lies in their effective implementation and in the company's preparedness to act on them. Wettstein highlighted the challenge companies face in embedding these policies into their corporate culture and operations.[36] This aligns with the UNGPs, which emphasise that successful integration of human rights policies requires not only embedding them into operations and management systems but also ensuring clear and consistent internal and external communication.

Several OECD NCP cases illustrate the critical importance of moving beyond written commitments to tangible action. In the case against Mallee, the Australian NCP noted that having a human rights policy is foundational for embedding respect for human rights throughout a company's operations.[37] Similarly, in the case against Walmart before the Chilean NCP, the NCP recommended reinforcing internal communication through training programs focused on supplier relationships, incorporating the Trade and Commercial Guidelines Agreement (TCGA) to promote understanding and compliance.[38] Cases before the Belgian NCP involving Etex Group and the Czech NCP involving a textile company further emphasised that executive management must be well-informed about human rights policies to make

---

[34] NCP Netherlands, 4 Trade Unions International Union of Food, Agriculture, Hotel, Restaurant, Catering, Tobacco, and Allied Workers Associations (IUF), European Federation of Food, Agriculture and Tourism (EFFAT), Service Employees International Union (SEIU), Unión General de Trabalhadores (UGT) (IUF, EFFAT-IUF, SEIU, UGT) v. APG Asset Management, Final Statement 3 February 2022; NCP United States International Union of Food, Agriculture, Hotel, Restaurant, Catering, Tobacco, and Allied Workers Associations(IUF), European Federation of Food, Agriculture and Tourism (EFFAT), Service Employees International Union (SEIU), Unión General de Trabalhadores (UGT) against McDonald' s Corporation, Final Statement, 14 March 2022.

[35] NCP United Kingdom, Lawyers for Palestinian Human Rights against JCB, Final Statement, 12 November 2021, 5.

[36] Wettstein (2022), p. 146.

[37] NCP Australia, Publish What You Pay Australia against Mallee Resources Limited, Final Statement, 2 August 2023, para 75–76.

[38] NCP Chile, Arpal SpA v. Walmart, Final Statement, 20 May 2021, 16.

effective decisions.[39] The NCPs stressed that such policies should be regularly updated—ideally on an annual basis—due to the evolving nature of human rights risks.[40] Moreover, the Danish NCP in the case against Bestseller highlighted that these policies should be adapted to the local contexts where companies operate to capture potential and actual risks more effectively.[41]

Furthermore, in the case against Moeller, the Danish NCP stressed the importance of internal communication, recommending mandatory human rights policy training for employees, particularly those managing operations.[42] Moreover, the French NCP in the case against Teleperformance emphasised the need for global companies with multiple branches to have coherent, comprehensive policies addressing critical human rights issues.[43] The NCP criticised Teleperformance for failing to address health risks to workers during the Covid-19 pandemic, stressing the importance of a unified group-wide policy to manage health risks in such a large organization.[44] The collective insight from these cases is clear: corporate human rights policies must not only be implemented but regularly reviewed, communicated, trained and adapted to the unique risks faced by the business. As emphasised by the NCPs, policies must be publicly available to all relevant stakeholders, aligning with the recommendations of the UNGPs. Ultimately, companies that fail to move beyond compliance and adopt proactive human rights policies risk falling short of their legal and ethical obligations, leaving vulnerable groups unprotected.

2.3 Undertaking Human Rights Due Diligence: Risk Identification and Assessment

2.3.1 Unpacking Risk Assessment: The Importance and Practical Steps for Corporations Under the UNGPs and OECD Framework

The UNGPs, particularly Principle 18, set out the corporate responsibility to conduct human rights risk assessments. This principle emphasises that businesses must identify and assess any actual or potential adverse human rights impacts that they may be involved in, either through their own activities or via business relationships.

[39] NCP Belgium, Building and Wood Workers' International (BWI) v. Etex Group, Final Statement, 17 October 2017, 4; NCP Czech Republic, A Czech Interest Group v. A Czech Company in Textile Industry, Final Statement, 20 May 2022, 9.

[40] Ibid.

[41] NCP Denmark, Christian Juhl v. Bestseller AS, Final Statement, 30 September 2022, 9–10.

[42] NCP Denmark, Former Employees of the Joint Venture Douala International Terminal S.A. in Cameroun v. A.P. Moeller—Maersk A/S, Final Statement, 06 May 2024, 18.

[43] NCP France, UNI v. Teleperformance, Final Statement, 05 July 2021, 14.

[44] Ibid.

To ensure a thorough risk assessment, the process should: (a) draw upon internal and/or independent external human rights expertise, and (b) involve meaningful consultation with potentially affected groups and other relevant stakeholders, proportionate to the size of the enterprise and the nature and context of its operations.[45] Similarly, the OECD Guidelines, under General Policies A.11, reinforce the significance of conducting risk-based due diligence.[46] Companies are encouraged to integrate this process into their enterprise risk management systems to identify, prevent, and mitigate actual and potential adverse impacts, as detailed in paragraphs 12 and 13 of the Guidelines.[47]

The scope and depth of HRDD must be carefully adapted to the specific circumstances of each situation, recognising that different contexts demand tailored approaches. Both the UNGPs and the OECD Guidelines emphasise that the requirements for HRDD can vary based on factors such as the size of the business, the severity of human rights impacts, and the nature and context of its operations. Principle 17 of the UNGPs notes that for businesses with large and complex supply chains, it may be challenging to address all potential risks comprehensively.[48] In such cases, companies should prioritise the most salient human rights risks. McCorquodale and Cristina Blanco-Vizarreta further argued that the more robust and engaged HRDD becomes, particularly with the direct involvement of rights holders, the greater the likelihood that businesses will be able to effectively identify, prioritise, and address the most severe human rights and environmental risks.[49]

In practice, however, conducting robust and effective human rights risk assessments is challenging, especially in the context of complex global supply chains.[50] Many human rights violations, such as child labour, forced labour, different types of modern slavery, and abuses against women or migrant workers, are hidden deep within the supply chain, often beyond Tier 1 and Tier 2 suppliers.[51] As a result, most companies are still unable to identify risks beyond their direct suppliers. For the downstream supply chain, businesses also struggle to understand how to conduct effective risk assessments within their distribution channels.[52] This highlights a significant gap between the expectations set by the UNGPs and the realities faced by businesses. Nora Götzmann has criticised the UNGPs for setting the expectation that businesses should assess their human rights impacts without specifying how

---

[45] UN Guiding Principles on Business and Human Rights, Principle 18; Bright and da Graça Pires (2023), p. 138.

[46] OECD Guidelines for Multinational Enterprises, General Policies A.11.

[47] Ibid, paras 12 and 13.

[48] UN Guiding Principles on Business and Human Rights, Principle 17.

[49] McCorquodale and Blanco-Vizarreta (2023), p. 130.

[50] Natour and Pluess (2013) Https://Www.Bsr.Org/En/Blog/How-To-Conduct-An-Effective-Human-Rights-Impact-Assessment (accessed 31 January 2026).

[51] Ripley (2020) Https://Www.Ilo.Org/Sites/Default/Files/2024-05/Wcms_759213.Pdf#Page=3.05 (accessed 31 January 2026).

[52] Schilling-Vacaflor (2021), pp. 1–15, Https://Www.Mdpi.Com/2071-1050/13/17/9666 (Accessed 31 January 2026).

this should be done or what essential features are necessary to ensure that these assessments align with international human rights standards.[53] She argued that more guidance is needed to ensure such assessments contribute meaningfully to enhancing corporate accountability in preventing and addressing adverse human rights impacts on workers and communities.

With increasing societal pressure on MNEs, a diverse array of tools has emerged to support human rights risk assessment. The evolving practice of Human Rights Impact Assessment (HRIA) in the BHR field highlights a wide spectrum of methodologies and approaches. Some scholars argue that an overreliance on external audits by certain companies has become a significant impediment to addressing severe human rights issues effectively, as these audits often lack depth and fail to identify root causes within business operations.[54] This dependence on superficial assessment suggests a reluctance to engage in genuine, transformative practices that can lead to meaningful change. Conversely, other researchers have identified instances, albeit limited, where companies demonstrate a willingness to undertake more comprehensive, in-depth analyses to genuinely address the pressing human rights risks tied to their operations.[55] This divergence in approach and capability draws attention to the necessity of aligning risk assessment practices with the unique nature of business activities and the specific context in which they are conducted. Companies must move beyond the 'tick-box' mentality associated with external audits and commit to customized, context-specific assessments that truly reflect the intricacies of their impact.

Since the enactment of the mHRDD legislation, the responsibility of risk assessment has increasingly become a mandatory legal requirement for companies. This concept of risk assessment has been further integrated into binding legislation, such as the LkSG, the CSDDD, and Modern Slavery Acts in countries like the UK, Australia, and Canada.[56] These laws build on the foundations laid by the UNGPs and OECD Guidelines, transforming the identification, prevention, and mitigation of human rights risks from a voluntary standard into a legal obligation for businesses. The CSDDD, inspired by the risk-based due diligence outlined in the OECD Guidelines, defines the requirements for companies in conducting risk assessments to identify and evaluate both human rights and environmental risks.[57] It is important to note that, while the UNGPs do not extensively address environmental risks, the OECD Guidelines and the CSDDD both incorporate environmental risk assessment alongside human rights considerations.[58] This integration represents a step forward

---

[53] Götzmann (2017), pp. 87–108.

[54] Ford and Nolan (2020), pp. 20–29 https://ssrn.com/abstract=3612492 (accessed 31 January 2026).

[55] Smit et al. (2020), pp. 945–793.

[56] Corporate Sustainability Due Diligence Directive, The Act on Corporate Due Diligence Obligations in Supply Chains (Lieferkettensorgfaltspflichtengesetz, LkSG) 22 July 2021; Modern Slavery Act UK 2015 c 30; Modern Slavery Act Australia 2018 No. 153; Fighting Against Forced Labour and Child Labour in Supply Chains Act (S.C. 2023, c. 9) 11 May 2023.

[57] Corporate Sustainability Due Diligence Directive, Recital 6 and Article 5.

[58] OECD Guidelines for Multinational Enterprises, Chapter VI: Environment. 6.1.

in recognising the interconnectedness of human rights and environmental impacts and ensuring a holistic approach to risk assessment.

Without a clear concept and understanding, companies are likely to fail in conducting effective human rights risk assessments, which undermines their responsibility to respect human rights. Current cases involving Amfori and SEDEX—two of the most widely used tools for multinational companies to identify and assess human rights risks—serve as a striking example that common practices are not adequately addressing these issues.[59] It is evident that a one-size-fits-all approach is insufficient when it comes to human rights risk assessments, as each company's context, including its supply chain and operational environment, is unique. Newton has pointed out that in order to identify and assess risks effectively, companies must first understand how the process will be shaped by their specific business model.[60] Factors such as subcontracting from high-risk areas and navigating complex supply chains complicate monitoring efforts. As supply chains extend and business relationships grow more intricate, monitoring and management become increasingly difficult, exacerbating the risk of human rights violations.[61] Furthermore, the nature and location of work—including the use of cheap labour and the presence of vulnerable workers—are critical considerations. Women, children, migrants, minorities, and workers with disabilities are especially susceptible to exploitation, and ignoring these vulnerabilities contributes to an ineffective and superficial assessment of risks.[62]

Considering these issues, Götzmann argued that effective HRIA must meet five key criteria.[63] First, companies must apply international human rights standards as benchmarks, ensuring that impact identification, analysis, mitigation, and remedy are grounded in universally recognised norms. Second, they need to consider the full scope of impacts, including both actual and potential adverse impacts that are caused, contributed to, or linked through business relationships. Third, adopting a human rights-based process is essential—this means emphasising participation, inclusion, equality, non-discrimination, accountability, and transparency. Fourth, companies must ensure accountability by identifying rights-holders and duty-bearers, assigning responsibilities, allocating sufficient resources for impact management, and focusing on access to remedy, including transparent public reporting. Lastly, they must address impacts based on their severity, making sure all identified human rights risks are effectively mitigated.

Götzmann further emphasised that companies must apply a human rights-based approach to their risk assessments, which includes three crucial principles: inclusion and participation, non-discrimination and equality, and transparency and

[59] Human Rights Watch 'Bangladesh: Social Audits Shortchange Workers: Shahidul Islam's Killing Underscores Heightened Risks for Independent Unions' 14 September 2023 https://www.hrw.org/news/2023/09/14/bangladesh-social-audits-shortchange-workers (accessed 31 January 2026).

[60] Newton (2019), p. 101.

[61] Ibid, 102.

[62] Ibid.

[63] Götzmann (2017), pp. 86–87.

accountability.[64] This argument underlines the inadequacy of current practices and the need for a more comprehensive framework that acknowledges the rights and vulnerabilities of affected communities. Additionally, she highlighted that a further area for attention is the potential connection between company-conducted HRIAs and methodologies developed for community-based HRIAs. By drawing on the proposed criteria and focusing on rights-holders, there is an opportunity for these methodologies to inform and learn from one another. Addressing the power dynamics embedded in project contexts is essential for fostering a more authentic and impactful risk assessment process. Götzmann's perspective urges companies to go beyond surface-level procedural compliance, advocating for deeper, structural changes that place human rights at the forefront.

Supporting this argument, Blair Kanis stated that a more effective approach to addressing adverse human rights impacts through HRIA lies in the identification of rightsholders and their associated risks.[65] This critical process ensures that the necessary actions to prevent, mitigate, or remedy human rights violations are not only defined but also actionable. A well-executed HRIA pinpoints specific at-risk groups and identifies the precise impacts they are likely to face. These findings enable enterprises to continually adapt their strategies as projects evolve, ensuring that human rights obligations are met with precision and responsiveness to changing conditions on the ground.[66]

The HRIA must be seamlessly integrated into an ongoing risk-monitoring framework, allowing for timely updates as new rightsholders or new risks emerge. For instance, certain communities may not initially be recognised as affected, but as circumstances shift, they may become vulnerable, necessitating modifications to the company's remediation strategies. This adaptability is crucial. The structured HRIA rating system, as recommended by Kanis, provides a roadmap for mapping out specific human rights impacts across different regions, ensuring targeted and effective monitoring.[67] By incorporating such commitments into project contracts with clearly defined, measurable obligations, both companies and governments can create a mutual understanding of expectations. This not only safeguards the rights of vulnerable groups—such as the right to housing or clean air—but also ensures that human rights commitments are upheld in practice, making them concrete, enforceable, and resilient against evolving risks.

Putting this into practice, Irit Tamir and Sarah Zoen's development article offers a comparative analysis of PepsiCo and Coca-Cola's human rights impact assessments in Brazil. Focusing on the Sirinhaém estuary islands and the Usina Trapiche sugar mill, the article emphasizes the critical role of stakeholder and community engagement during the HRDD risk identification and assessment process,

[64] Götzmann (2017), p. 89.

[65] Kanis (2015), pp. 413–441.

[66] Ibid, 430.

[67] Ibid.

illustrating how meaningful participation can shape more just and effective outcomes.[68] The authors highlighted the significance of the inclusion and participation of local communities in the identification and assessment processes, as well as ensuring transparency and accountability.[69] One of the key limitations of company-led assessments today is the lack of effective community engagement. Companies often struggle to connect with local communities—they may not know who to engage with, how to establish contact, or how to build the trust necessary to fully understand the impacts of their operations. This affirms the importance of genuine community involvement in human rights assessments, not merely as a procedural step but as a fundamental aspect of responsible business conduct.

In conclusion, while the UNGPs and OECD Guidelines have laid the groundwork for corporate human rights risk assessments, there remain significant gaps between expectations and actual practices. The complexity of global supply chains, the challenges of engaging affected communities, and the lack of a standardized approach have hindered the effectiveness of human rights due diligence. Moving forward, companies must adopt a more comprehensive, rights-based approach that includes meaningful community participation, transparency, and accountability. Only through genuine commitment and structural shifts can businesses effectively mitigate human rights risks and contribute to responsible, sustainable operations.

2.3.2 Key Lessons from OECD Case Law: Best Practices in Conducting Human Rights Due Diligence

Within the cases addressed through the OECD NCP mechanism, there are 20 instances in which NCPs specifically focused on evaluating companies' risk identification and assessment approaches, analysing their alignment with OECD Guidelines and other international standards. Examining OECD case law reveals that NCPs' analysis and recommendations for corporate risk identification and assessment align closely with the approach advocated by Götzmann, which emphasised genuine commitment from companies to understanding and mitigating human rights risks.

Firstly, there are several cases in which NCPs criticised companies for their lack of commitment in assessing and identifying risks. A prominent example is the case against ANZ Bank regarding allegations of its involvement in providing a loan to a project that resulted in the forced eviction of more than 600 local community members.[70] ANZ defended its actions by asserting that its business practices were in line with OECD Guidelines and claimed they neither knew nor had the opportunity to

[68] Tamir and Zoen (2017), pp. 371–377.

[69] Ibid.

[70] NCP Australia, Equitable Cambodia and Inclusive Development International v. ANZ Group, Final Statement, 27 June 2018.

know about the risks at the time of providing the loan.[71] However, the NCP's findings pointed out significant discrepancies in ANZ's statements. The NCP wrote that: 'There is some doubt in this case around the extent to which ANZ's actual business practices aligned with its stated approach to human rights (and therefore the purpose of the OECD Guidelines).[72] As the notifiers have pointed out, there was publicly available information at the time (in 2010) that suggested the existence of risks associated with ANZ's former client and its project—including the well-publicised dispute between the project and the affected community around the time that ANZ commenced financing the sugar refinery and factory.'[73] The NCP emphasised that there was sufficient information available in the public domain that should have prompted ANZ to recognise and address the potential human rights risks associated with the project. For instance, protests from local villagers and involvement of civil society representatives highlighted the contentious nature of the project early in 2010.[74] Thus, NCP criticised ANZ for failing to align its internal policies and procedures with its actual business practices, questioning how ANZ could continue financing the project in 2011 given the ongoing public disputes.[75] This case highlights the importance of companies moving beyond mere claims of adherence to standards, demonstrating instead an active and informed approach to risk assessment.

Another example case reviewed by the UK NCP involved British American Tobacco (BAT).[76] While the NCP acknowledged that BAT had financially supported an impact assessment focused on the living and working conditions of migrant workers involved in tobacco harvesting in North Carolina, USA, it raised concerns about the extent of BAT's involvement beyond merely funding the assessment.[77] The NCP questioned whether BAT actively engaged in the assessment process or simply limited its role to providing financial support. The UK NCP emphasised that for any information-gathering and research process of this kind to be effective, it must result in a commensurate response that ensures compliance with standards. Financial contributions alone are insufficient if not followed by tangible actions to address the identified issues. Specifically, the NCP recommended that BAT actively participate in procedures to address the problems highlighted during interviews with workers.[78] These procedures should be time-bound and subject to quality inspections by an independent third party to ensure they are appropriate and effective. This case highlights that effective human rights due diligence requires more

---

[71] Ibid.

[72] NCP Australia, Equitable Cambodia and Inclusive Development International v. ANZ Group, Final Statement, 27 June 2018.

[73] Ibid.

[74] Ibid.

[75] Ibid.

[76] NCP United Kingdom, IUF and FLOC v. BAT, Final Statement, 6 May 2022.

[77] Ibid, para 59–60.

[78] Ibid.

than funding the third-party assessments—it demands active involvement from the company in addressing and mitigating risks. BAT's approach was criticised for falling short of the genuine commitment needed to align its practices with international standards. The NCP's recommendations highlight the importance of active participation of the company in the risk identification and assessment processes.

To better delineate the scope of risk assessment, several cases handled by the OECD NCP mechanism offer valuable insights. These cases emphasised the significance of integrating stakeholder perspectives into the processes of risk identification and assessment—a central component of HRIA, as highlighted by various scholars in the previous section. For example, in the case against Imperial Metals brought before the Canadian NCP, the NCP recommended that Imperial Metals include the interests of the Tahltan Nation—a tribal council representing the governments of two Tahltan band governments in British Columbia—within their due diligence assessments.[79] This marks the necessity of considering Indigenous communities' views when assessing the risks of corporate projects that impact their lands and livelihoods. Similarly, in a case involving Dredging International, the Belgian NCP directed the company to consult with a local NGO in India to identify risks at an early stage of the project.[80] This also highlights the importance of engaging CSOs that have on-the-ground insights into potential social and environmental harms, thereby improving the effectiveness of risk mitigation strategies. In the case against Moeller, the Danish NCP evaluated the company's impact assessment process, with particular attention to whether stakeholders had been properly consulted.[81] These cases collectively illustrate that stakeholder engagement is not merely a procedural formality but a critical element in creating a comprehensive human rights approach-based risk assessment. Companies are increasingly being called upon to integrate these diverse perspectives to ensure that their business practices are both responsible and responsive to the needs of affected communities.

In the case against Vedanta brought before the UK NCP, the NCP's final statement highlighted critical shortcomings in the company's approach to HRDD.[82] The UK NCP found that Vedanta failed to implement a human rights policy and risk assessment specifically addressing the needs and rights of local communities, including Indigenous communities.[83] Moreover, the UK NCP observed that the company failed to engage meaningfully with affected stakeholders during its operations, despite substantive evidence indicating that such communities were present near its project area. Vedanta neither undertook any action to consult these communities nor established a human rights policy or mechanism to identify, assess, and address the risks arising from its business activities and their potential human rights

[79] NCP Canada, SEACC v. Imperial Metals Corporation, Final Statement, 08 May 2020.

[80] NCP Belgium, Greenpeace India v. Dredging International, Final Statement, 11 March 2011, 2.

[81] NCP Denmark, Former Employees of the Joint Venture Douala International Terminal S.A. in Cameroun v. A.P. Moeller—Maersk A/S, Final Statement, 06 May 2024, 27–28.

[82] NCP United Kingdom, Survival International v. Vedanta Resources PLC, Final Statement, 25 September 2009, paras 64–65.

[83] Ibid.

impacts. Consequently, the UK NCP concluded that Vedanta had breached its responsibility to conduct risk-based due diligence as required under the OECD Guidelines. This case clearly illustrates how the UK NCP's finding of non-compliance highlights the fundamental importance of integrating stakeholder perspectives into the risk assessment process. As previously addressed in the earlier section, it demonstrates that neglecting engagement with local and Indigenous communities not only undermines effective due diligence but also constitutes a failure to uphold RBC.

Furthermore, specific activities recommended by the NCPs align with the standards reflected in the CSDDD, which includes broad mapping and in-depth analysis, incorporating rigorous methods tailored to company activities, sector-specific, and country-specific risk contexts. For example, in the case involving Bestseller, the Danish NCP provided specific guidance on what companies should do to effectively identify and assess human rights risks.[84] This includes: (1) conducting a broad mapping exercise and (2) researching and analysing relevant information regarding sector-specific, country-specific, and product-specific risk factors. Furthermore, the Danish NCP emphasised that such mapping should enable the company to prioritise the most significant risk areas that require further assessment.[85] The guidance also highlighted the importance of considering the local legal and governance framework, as well as the socio-economic and political context.[86] Additionally, information from international organisations, civil society groups, NHRIs, government agencies, trade unions, and industry bodies may be relevant to include in the mapping process.[87]

Furthermore, the Danish NCP recognised Bestseller's approach to risk assessment as a best practice. This recognition was due not only to Bestseller's consistent reassessment of risks whenever there were changes in the risk landscape but also to their proactive and multifaceted approach.[88] Rather than relying solely on one-time assessments or third-party audits, Bestseller conducted its own in-depth evaluations, directly engaged with different stakeholders to gather diverse perspectives, and documented these processes. The Danish NCP recognised Bestseller's commitment to ongoing risk assessment, emphasising that this continuous effort reflects a deeper understanding of the dynamic nature of human rights risks.[89] By integrating stakeholder input and going beyond external audits, Bestseller demonstrated a genuine engagement with the complexities of their operating environment. The approach outlined by the Bestseller could exemplify a comprehensive framework for risk identification that transcends superficial assessment. It demands that companies immerse themselves in understanding the intricacies of their operational con-

[84] NCP Denmark, Christian Juhl v. Bestseller A/S, Final Statement, 30 September 2022, 6–7.

[85] Ibid, 6.

[86] Ibid, 7.

[87] Ibid.

[88] Ibid.

[89] Ibid, 7–8.

texts and incorporate diverse insights to develop a holistic view of potential risks. Such practices are increasingly in line with the evolving standards for corporate accountability, underscoring that effective risk management is not a one-time procedural formality but rather a robust, context-specific, and ongoing commitment to addressing and mitigating human rights impacts effectively.

In addition to emphasising risk assessments, NCPs have successfully used mediation to convince companies to conduct comprehensive risk assessments to identify and address actual adverse impacts linked to their operations. Notable examples include the cases involving Michelin Group before the French NCP, APG Asset Management before the Dutch NCP, and FIFA before the Swiss NCP.[90] In these instances, the NCPs facilitated agreements where the companies committed to conducting thorough risk assessments. In the French NCP case, Michelin Group agreed to undertake a comprehensive environmental and social impact assessment, with the NCP rigorously following up to ensure that the company not only completed the assessment but also took concrete actions to address the identified impacts.[91] Similarly, in the cases concerning APG Asset Management before the Dutch NCP and FIFA before the Swiss NCP, both companies agreed to strengthen their risk assessment processes by focusing on specific human rights issues and cooperating more closely with the complainant parties. In the APG case, this involved addressing gender-based violence and harassment in the fast-food sector and recognising APG's responsibility as an investor.[92] In the FIFA case, the company committed—through dialogue with the Building and Wood Workers' International (BWI) union—to address labour rights risks affecting migrant workers on construction sites in Qatar.[93] These examples demonstrated how NCPs, through facilitated mediation and systematic follow-up, can play a crucial role in pushing companies beyond superficial compliance and towards meaningful change.

2.4 Developing Prevention and Mitigation Strategies

2.4.1 Mitigation and Prevention in the Human Rights Due Diligence Process: A Comprehensive Review Under the UNGPs and OECD Guidelines

After conducting a HRIA, businesses must design and implement strategies to prevent and mitigate both actual and potential human rights risks. Principle 19 of the UNGPs requires companies to integrate these findings into their operations and

---

[90] NCP France, Sherpa et al. v. Michelin Group, Follow-Up Statement, 29 February 2016, 5–6.

[91] Ibid.

[92] NCP Netherlands, 4 Trade Unions v. APG Asset Management, Follow Up Statement, 21 December 2023, 2.

[93] NCP Switzerland, BWI v. FIFA, Final Statement, 2 May 2017, 5–6.

ensure that identified risks are addressed.[94] Similarly, the OECD Guidelines, particularly Chapter 2: General Policies, Sections 11–13, emphasised that businesses must prevent or mitigate adverse impacts, even when they are not directly responsible but are connected through business relationships.[95]

The core aim of HRDD is to ensure that companies do not cause, contribute to, or directly linked to human rights adverse impacts. Ruggie, the principal architect behind the UNGPs, described HRDD as a proactive, comprehensive process that identifies both actual and potential risks throughout the entire business lifecycle, with a primary focus on prevention and mitigation.[96] What distinguishes the UNGPs' approach is its focus on the responsibility that arises from a business's activities and relationships.[97] However, as Mark B. Taylor noted, the distinctions between causing, contributing to, or being linked to harm often blur in practice.[98] These categories exist on a continuum of responsibility, further complicated by the dynamic nature of modern business operations, supply chains, and technological advances.[99]

Furthermore, even if a company has not directly caused harm, it still holds a responsibility to exercise leverage over entities connected to human rights abuses. Leverage refers to the company's ability to influence the practices of an entity responsible for harm.[100] The UNGPs require businesses to take action based on several factors, including their level of influence, the severity of the harm, and the nature of the relationship.[101] However, the concept of leverage is especially challenging in practice, particularly for corporate actors such as investors and financial institutions, who are often only directly linked to harm.[102] When companies are connected through their business relationships, their primary responsibility is to use leverage to influence the behaviour of the directly responsible entity. Despite its importance, leverage has not been fully developed within the UNGPs framework, especially in relation to mitigation.[103] This creates practical challenges in assessing how companies have exercised leverage as part of their HRDD obligations. In practice, it can be difficult to evaluate whether companies have adequately fulfilled this responsibility, as leverage is often difficult to measure and may vary depending on the business relationship and context.[104] This ambiguity further complicates the broader challenges businesses face in understanding and implementing their human

[94] UN Guiding Principles on Business and Human Rights, Principle 19.

[95] OECD Guidelines for Multinational Enterprises, Chapter 2: General Policies, Sections 11–13.

[96] Ruggie and Sherman, III (2017), p. 923.

[97] Ibid.

[98] Taylor (2020), pp. 88–107.

[99] Ibid, 97.

[100] UN Guiding Principles on Business and Human Rights, Commentary to the Principle 19.

[101] Ibid.

[102] Wörsdörfer (2015), pp. 193–218.

[103] Ibid, Wood (2012), pp. 65–66.

[104] Ibid.

rights responsibilities, especially when their involvement in harm is indirect.[105] Therefore, clearer guidance and standards on how companies should exercise leverage and be held accountable are crucial in the evolving landscape of corporate human rights obligations.

In addition to the confusion surrounding corporate involvement in harm, the legal clarity of mitigation and prevention responsibilities remains ambiguous. McCorquodale and Jonathan Bonnitcha highlighted that the distinction between the terms 'avoid' and 'seek to prevent' in the UNGPs is not clearly defined.[106] The UNGPs do not further specify the relevant standards of conduct, making it challenging to determine the appropriate standards applicable to each aspect of corporate responsibility. Adding to this critique, Radu Mares argued that the concept of mitigation under the UNGPs—focused on reducing harm—implicitly tolerates some level of residual harm.[107] From a human rights perspective, this raises concerns about the types of adverse impacts that are acceptable and where the threshold lies.[108] Mares questioned whether mitigation adds value beyond what prevention and remediation already provide, or if it introduces redundancy or ambiguity into the framework.[109] He also argued that the relationship between mitigation, prevention, and remediation needs more precise conceptualisation and clearer textual and contextual interpretations of the UNGPs.[110]

However, Björn Fasterling contended that the absence of precise definitions for certain terms should not impede the implementation of prevention and mitigation measures.[111] He further explained that the purpose of the UNGPs is not to function as strict legal regulations but to provide guidance, encouraging companies to take more appropriate actions based on their involvement in causing or contributing to harm. The UNGPs aim to foster a proactive approach, where businesses assess and address risks effectively, even in the absence of detailed legal prescriptions.

In addition to these conceptual challenges, businesses often face difficulties in determining the best ways to prevent and mitigate human rights risks in practice. McCorquodale suggested that for mitigation strategies to be successful, businesses must allocate responsibility for managing human rights risks to appropriate departments or levels within the organisation.[112] They must also allocate adequate resources and establish robust oversight mechanisms to ensure effective responses to identified risks.[113] Wettstein emphasised that integrating HRDD into a company's operations requires embedding human rights commitments into everyday business

---

105 Ibid, 67–68.

106 Bonnitcha and McCorquodale (2017), pp. 899–919.

107 Mares (2018), pp. 1–71.

108 Ibid, 8–17.

109 Ibid.

110 Ibid.

111 Fasterling (2017), pp. 225–247.

112 McCorquodale, *Business and Human Rights*, 154–156.

113 Ibid.

practices rather than treating them as symbolic gestures.[114] For human rights policies to be truly effective, they must shape decision-making at all levels of the organisation. Only by doing so can a company meet its human rights obligations and promote responsible, rights-respecting practices.[115]

Corporate responsibility for preventing and mitigating human rights and environmental impacts has increasingly shifted from voluntary commitments to enforceable legal frameworks. A key development is the CSDDD, which imposes binding obligations on businesses to manage risks throughout their operations and supply chains.[116] Articles 10 and 11 of the CSDDD outline a comprehensive framework for addressing different types of risks.[117] Article 10 focuses on prevention, requiring businesses to implement strategies to avoid potential human rights and environmental harms.[118] The extent of a company's responsibility is based on whether it caused, jointly caused, or is linked to the harm. Companies are required to take preventive measures, secure contractual assurances from partners, and, when necessary, offer financial or other forms of support to avoid and prevent the potential risks. The CSDDD encourages a collaborative approach, particularly fostering partnerships with SMEs to help them meet due diligence and contractual requirements.[119]

Article 11 provides guidance on how businesses should respond to identified adverse impacts, requiring corrective action plans with clear timelines and measurable indicators.[120] The directive stresses that terminating business relationships should be a last resort, particularly for companies operating in the Global South. Instead, companies are urged to focus on corrective actions that address the root causes of harm.[121] This guide provides a comprehensive interpretation for businesses on the use of termination or temporary suspension of business relationships as a mitigation measure, based on Principle 19 of the UNGPs. According to the commentary on Principle 19, when a business enterprise causes or may cause an adverse human rights impact, it is obliged to take all necessary steps to cease or prevent the harm.[122] However, the concept of 'ceasing adverse impacts' has been subject to debate and remains inadequately defined, as highlighted by various scholars. For example, past cases, such as companies withdrawing from Myanmar or the DRC due to escalating conflict, have demonstrated the lack of clarity around responsible exits and the failure to properly mitigate adverse impacts on local workers and

[114] Wettstein (2022), pp. 148–149.

[115] Ibid.

[116] Corporate Sustainability Due Diligence Directive.

[117] Ibid, Articles 10 and 11.

[118] Ibid, Article 10.

[119] Ibid, Recitals 56 and 57.

[120] Ibid, Article 11.

[121] Ibid, Recitals 69–71.

[122] UN Guiding Principles on Business and Human Rights, Principle 19.

communities.[123] In response to these challenges, the CSDDD offers clearer guidance to companies, helping them navigate decisions about when to terminate or suspend operations in alignment with the principle of ceasing adverse impacts, ensuring that responsible exit strategies are in place.[124] By implementing concrete actions, such as preventive and corrective action plans, collaboration with suppliers, and assistance to SMEs, the CSDDD addresses many of the questions scholars have raised about corporate prevention and mitigation responsibilities.[125] However, it remains to be seen how effectively companies will bring these demands into real-world contexts. Moreover, as will be discussed in the next section, the OECD case law provides further insights into how companies can discharge their mitigation and prevention responsibilities.

2.4.2 Case-Based Best Practices: How OECD Case Law Shapes Corporate Strategies for Human Rights Prevention and Mitigation

Analysing the prevention and mitigation measures implemented by companies, as assessed and recommended by NCPs through various cases, presents significant challenges. This complexity arises from the need to address a range of interconnected issues. These include the nature of corporate involvement—whether a company is causing, contributing to, or directly linked to adverse impacts—as well as mitigation strategies for indirect impacts, such as the use of leverage. A key area of focus has been on termination, disengagement, and divestment, which are viewed as forms of ceasing adverse impacts and are considered critical mitigation measures in certain cases. As a result of the OECD case law analysis, four key categories were identified (See Fig. 2.2). These include: (1) corporate involvement, which encompasses the degrees of causing, contributing to, or being directly linked to adverse impacts; (2) prevention and mitigation measures taken by companies; (3) the use of leverage to influence business partners and improve outcomes; and (4) disengagement, which includes termination and divestment as responses to address and cease adverse impacts.

[123] The International Peace Information and Service (IPIS) insights on Due Diligence in Mineral Sourcing Regulating responsible sourcing of 3TG minerals: Comparative analysis of Section 1502 of the US Dodd-Frank Act and the EU Conflict Minerals Regulation, lessons learned and risks for implementation, Antwerp, 20 December 2019; Stoop et al. (2018) https://journals.plos.org/plosone/article?id=10.1371/journal.pone.0201783 (accessed 31 January 2026).

[124] Corporate Sustainability Due Diligence Directive, Article 10.6

[125] Ibid, Recital 69 and Article 10.5.

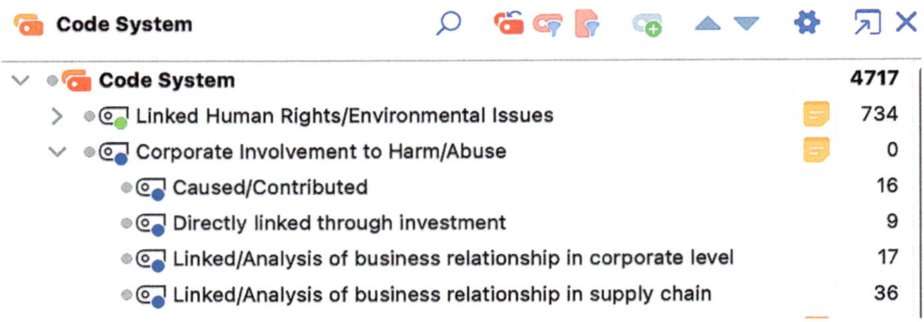

Fig. 2.2 Sub-codes of Parent code: Corporate involvement to the alleged harms

2.4.2.1 Corporate Involvement in the Harm

2.4.2.1.1 OECD Case Law Analysis on Causation and Contribution to the Harm

This book explores how NCPs assess and determine corporate involvement in adverse impacts, whether by causing, contributing to, or being directly linked to them. Given the non-judicial and voluntary nature of NCP mechanisms, they often rely on dialogue with companies rather than making definitive rulings. In many instances, if a company does not acknowledge its role in the alleged harm, the NCP cannot conclusively determine its responsibility. However, in some cases, NCPs have independently assessed whether a company caused, contributed to, or was directly linked to the harm. While only 10 out of 394 cases addressed the causation and contribution of companies to the harm, these instances, though relatively rare, are highly significant and merit thorough analysis. Some of these cases provide valuable insights into how NCPs evaluate corporate involvement, considering various factors outlined in the UNGPs and OECD Guidelines, such as business relationships, the degree of direct or indirect control by parent companies, and other relevant factors.

For example, the French and Norwegian NCPs faced significant challenges in cases involving Natixis Global Asset Management (NGAM) and TotalEnergies E&P Norge AS (TEPN) related to the crane accident at Samsung's Martin Linge Project.[126] In the Norwegian NCP case, the project, led by Samsung, included various companies such as TEPN, Equinor ASA, and Technip Energies N.V. The Norwegian NCP had to carefully assess how these companies were involved in the harm by analysing their business relationships.[127] After consulting with the

[126] NCP Norway, Samsung Heavy Industries Martin Linge Project Crane Accident Workers Support Team and Korean Transnational Corporations Watch v. Totalenergies E&P Norge As, Equinor Asa, Technip Energies N.V., Final Statement, 22 February 2023; NCP France, Unite Here v. Natixis/NGAM, Final Statement, 5 December 2017.

[127] Ibid.

companies and reviewing project documents, the Norwegian NCP concluded that TEPN and other companies did not cause or contribute to the alleged harm. While it was clear that Samsung, as the main executor of the project, was responsible for the direct causation, the NCP undertook a thorough analysis to determine whether TEPN had contributed to the harm by facilitating or enabling Samsung's actions or omissions. In addition to the project documents detailing the specific roles of each company, the NCP examined how TEPN conducted its due diligence to ensure a safe working environment.

During the mediation process, TEPN outlined the steps it had taken, including regular check-ups and reviewing reports prepared by Samsung.[128] While questions arose regarding how effectively TEPN and other companies used their leverage over Samsung to ensure safety in workplace, the Norwegian NCP ultimately concluded that, based on the available evidence, TEPN and the other companies did not cause or contribute to the harm.[129] However, they were still linked to the harm through their business relationships with Samsung. As a result, the Norwegian NCP encouraged TEPN and the other companies to use their leverage to push Samsung to provide remediation to the victims of the crane accident. Although discussions about possible remediation through the linked companies took place during the mediation, the issue was not adequately resolved. This case highlights the limitations of leverage in ensuring corporate accountability, particularly when companies are only linked to harms through business relationship.

The case against Natixis and its asset management subsidiary, NGAM, highlights a complex situation involving allegations of labour rights violations, specifically the infringement of workers' collective bargaining rights at a hotel property owned by AEW Capital Management, a client of NGAM's U.S. subsidiary, AEW Capital Management.[130] The French NCP faced the intricate task of determining the level of responsibility for each entity involved, analysing whether they caused, contributed to, or were directly linked to the adverse impact.[131] The NCP's analysis first addressed the primary responsibility, identifying the hotel operator as the direct employer of the workers and therefore likely the party directly responsible for the labour violations.[132] This responsibility involved remedying the harm, ceasing the violation, and taking preventive measures to avoid future issues. The hotel operator's role as the employer placed it in a position of direct causation, a critical element in the chain of responsibility.

Regarding contribution, the NCP investigated the role of investment funds and their holding company, which were said to exercise control over the hotel operator. These entities may have contributed to the adverse impact either through direct decisions or by failing to act when they had the authority to do so. In particular, if

[128] Ibid, TEPN, 16.

[129] Ibid, 17–18.

[130] Ibid, NGAM, 1–2.

[131] Ibid, 5–7.

[132] Ibid, 6.

AEW Capital Management played a role in identifying financial and operational partners during the hotel acquisition process or provided advice that influenced operational decisions beyond financial matters, it could be seen as having contributed to the violations. In this case, the NCP highlighted that both AEW and the investment funds had a responsibility to use their leverage to prevent and stop the harm, including actions such as urging the hotel operator to engage with the complainants or facilitating meaningful stakeholder engagement.

The NCP also explored the concept of 'direct link' under the OECD Guidelines, analysing the relationships between various entities in the investment chain. It concluded that entities like URS, a pension fund with equity interests, as well as AEW, NGAM, and Natixis, were directly linked to the adverse impacts due to their business relationships.[133] Although Natixis and NGAM contested this characterisation, the NCP referred to the OECD guidelines for institutional investors, which state that ownership ties, even at certain percentage levels, can create a direct link between a parent company and its subsidiary's activities. As such, the NCP clarified that NGAM were directly linked to the labour violations, even if they did not directly cause or contribute to them. However, the NCP also reiterated that being directly linked does not shift responsibility from the entity causing the harm (the hotel operator) to the company linked through business relationships. As a result, the hotel operator remained accountable for the violations, while URS, AEW, NGAM, and Natixis were expected to leverage their influence to prevent and mitigate further harm.[134] In particular, NGAM and Natixis were urged to ensure that AEW performed thorough due diligence in this case and in its broader operations. Consequently, the mediation concluded successfully, as Natixis and NGAM effectively used their influence on their U.S. subsidiary, AEW Capital Management, to integrate the OECD Guidelines for institutional investors into AEW's management contract for the Westin Long Beach Hotel.[135] Consequently, AEW adhered to the OECD Guidelines during the hotel's sale, leading the new operator, HighGate Hotels, to engage in immediate social dialogue with workers and support the unionisation process, which was successfully formalised in September 2017.[136]

From examining the cases involving TNEP and NGAM, the analysis of roles and responsibilities highlighted the complexity of corporate accountability within business relationships, particularly the nuanced distinction between being directly linked to harm and contributing to it. The significance of this distinction lies in whether a company that is directly linked to the harm knew, or should have known, about the violations occurring within its supply chain or business operations. When a company is aware of ongoing harm yet chooses to remain passive, it demonstrates complicity by enabling the direct perpetrator to continue its harmful actions. This inaction can be perceived not only as a failure to prevent further harm but as an

[133] Ibid, 6–7.

[134] Ibid, 7.

[135] Ibid, 7–9.

[136] Ibid.

implicit endorsement of the violations. In such cases, the company's failure to intervene, despite its capacity and responsibility to do so, places it in a morally and legally precarious position, further entrenching the harms it could have mitigated.

Aside from these two cases, most of remaining cases did not deeply explore corporate involvement. Although cases such as the case against Bonsucro in the UK NCP, or the case against Gramercy Funds Management in US NCP, and the one against BHP in Australian NCP determining whether the companies caused, contributed to, or were directly linked to harm, they often lacked thorough examination and explanation.[137] Moreover, there are no clear cases where companies explicitly acknowledged their involvement in violations. However, in the Australian NCP case against Mercer concerning the alleged breach of individuals' privacy, there was a tentative acknowledgment from the company regarding its role in the privacy violation.[138]

This highlights that NCPs are not judicial bodies and lack the authority to impose legally binding decisions. As such, they may avoid assigning blame directly to encourage companies to participate in voluntary mediation. Instead of employing a confrontational approach, NCPs often focus on fostering dialogue and cooperation to achieve resolution. However, in some cases—such as those involving Natixis and TNEP—the thorough analysis provided by NCPs like the French and Norwegian ones, combined with clear advocacy and detailed explanations of corporate involvement, played a significant role in resolving the cases successfully. Even in cases like the Samsung crane accident, where there was no visibly successful outcome, the process itself facilitated meaningful discussions between the companies directly linked to the harm, showcasing the value of such actions.

2.4.2.1.2 OECD Case Law Analysis of Corporate Involvement As Directly Linked to Harm

The OECD case law analysis of corporate involvement as directly linked to alleged harms can be divided into three main categories. First, corporations may be directly linked through their investments. Second, they may be connected via internal business relationships, such as between a parent company and its subsidiary. Third, they may be linked through supply chain relationships, including contracts and partnerships with other businesses.

[137] NCP United Kingdom. IDI, EC and LICADHO v. Bonsucro Ltd., Final Statement, 11 January 2022; NCP United States André Amisi Rushingwa, Delvaux Bwisibo Mukunda, and Raymond Minani Muganira, v. Gramercy Funds Management LLC, Final Statement, 29 August 2023; NCP Australia, GLAN v. BHP Group Ltd. and other enterprises, Final Statement, 31 July 2023.

[138] NCP Australia, Australian Women Without Borders v. Mercer PR for its conduct in relation to activity in Nauru, Final Statement, 9 July 2019, para 19.

Directly Linked Through Investment

Under the UNGPs and the OECD Guidelines, investors are expected to consider not only business, operational, and financial risks but also human rights and environmental risks when making investment decisions. This broader approach ensures that investments align with responsible business conduct, addressing potential negative impacts on people and the environment alongside financial returns.

In cases involving investors, such as those against Danish financial institutions, ING, Atradius Dutch State Business (ADSB), and Credit Suisse, the NCPs concluded that these investors were directly linked to adverse impacts through their financial products, including loans and other forms of investment.[139] When investors are found to be directly linked to the harm through their investments, NCPs may assess their mitigation responsibility accordingly.

For example, in the case involving Danish financial institutions, the Danish NCP determined that the respondent's role in the project was to provide a financial guarantee for the Danish Pension Fund, which financed a loan to a Russian bank.[140] This bank, in turn, provided a loan to a company operating a mine in Armenia.[141] The Danish NCP concluded that the respondent (the Danish financial institution) was directly linked to the project through its operations and, according to the OECD Guidelines, fulfilled responsibility to identify and mitigate adverse impacts through the value chain. In the case of ADSB, the Dutch NCP also found that ADSB was 'directly linked' to potential adverse impacts caused by a business relationship with Van Oord, a company involved in dredging activities. The NCP referred to OECD Guidelines, paragraphs 11 and 12 of the Chapter 2, section A, affirming that ADSB had a responsibility to leverage its influence over the business relationship to prevent or mitigate adverse impacts.[142]

In situations where a company is directly linked to adverse impacts through its business relationships, the OECD Guidelines make clear that this linkage does not absolve the company of responsibility. Instead, it requires the company to conduct risk-based due diligence to identify, prevent, and mitigate potential harms. Where actual harm has already occurred, the company is expected to use its leverage to influence the entity causing or contributing to the impact, including by negotiating corrective measures, ensuring remediation is provided, and pressing for accountability. In the case concerning Anglo American before the UK NCP, the NCP

[139] NCP Netherlands, Milieudefensie/Friends of the Earth Netherlands, WALHI/Friends of the Earth Indonesia and SDI/Friends of the Earth Liberia v. ING, Final Statement, 7 April 2022; NCP Netherlands Both ENDS, Associação Fórum Suape Espaço Socioambiental, Conectas Direitos Humanos and Colônia de Pescadores do Município do Cabo de Santo Agostinho v. Atradius Dutch State Business, Final Statement, November 2016; NCP Switzerland, Society for Threatened People v. Credit Suisse, Final Statement, 16 October 2019.

[140] NCP Denmark, Two NGOs v. a Danish Financial Institutions, Final Statement, 19 June 2018.

[141] Ibid, 2.

[142] NCP Netherlands Both ENDS, Associação Fórum Suape Espaço Socioambiental, Conectas Direitos Humanos and Colônia de Pescadores do Município do Cabo de Santo Agostinho v. Atradius Dutch State Business, Final Statement, November 2016, 7.

emphasised that although Anglo American did not manage the daily operations of the Cerrejón mine, it nevertheless retained a responsibility to exercise its leverage to address the adverse impacts caused by the operating company. This illustrates how responsibility under the OECD Guidelines extends beyond direct causation and includes the duty to act where a company is linked to harm through its business relationships.[143]

Moreover, the case against ING, brought forward by Friends of the Earth, raised a critical question: at what point does a financial institution's direct link to harm evolve into contributing to that harm? The complainants argued that despite ING's knowledge of potential harm, the bank failed to conduct sufficient due diligence or exercise adequate leverage.[144] The NCP acknowledged the complexity of assessing when a bank's relationship with a client shifts from a 'direct link' to a 'contribution' to human rights violations. According to the OECD Guidelines, this shift can occur when a bank becomes aware of an ongoing human rights issue linked to its operations, products, or services and fails to take reasonable steps to address it.[145] Such steps might include raising the issue with the client's leadership, persuading other banks to join in pressuring the client, or making further financing conditional on corrective action.

Directly Linked Through Business Relationships within Corporate Structures

In 15 out of 394 cases, NCPs investigated how companies were directly linked to alleged harms through their business relationships within corporate structures. In most of these cases, NCPs presumed a direct link due to the corporate relationships between a parent company and its subsidiary operating in the host country. For instance, in the case against Bonsucro concerning its subsidiary MPGT, the UK NCP immediately recognised the direct link.[146]

Parent companies frequently argue they are not liable for harms caused by their subsidiaries, contending they do not exercise direct control over their subsidiaries' day-to-day operations. However, NCPs have successfully challenged this argument in several instances, concluding that parent companies are still responsible due to their business relationships, regardless of operational oversight. For example, in the case against ENRC, the UK NCP determined that from December 2012, ENRC wholly owned Camrose and Comide—companies directly responsible for the harm.[147] Consequently, ENRC was considered to have direct control over their

---

[143] NCP United Kingdom, Global Legal Action Network (GLAN) v. Anglo American, Initial Statement, 10 January 2022 (Pending).

[144] NCP Netherlands, Milieudefensie/Friends of the Earth Netherlands, WALHI/Friends of the Earth Indonesia and SDI/Friends of the Earth Liberia v. ING, Final Statement, 7 April 2022.

[145] Ibid, 5.

[146] NCP United Kingdom, IDI, EC and LICADHO v. Bonsucro Ltd., Final Statement, 11 January 2022.

[147] NCP United Kingdom, Rights and Accountability in Development (RAID) v. ENRC, Final Statement, February 2016.

actions. While ENRC did not fully own Africo/Swanmines, it acquired a controlling interest in Africo and held board positions, providing it with significant leverage over decision-making and daily operations.[148] The NCP's analysis primarily relied on ownership percentage, suggesting that significant ownership can establish a direct link, even without detailed evidence of operational control.

Another notable case is the Belgium NCP's investigation of ES-KO International, where the NCP analysed the nature of corporate branches.[149] The NCP concluded that, although branches may operate with some managerial autonomy, they lack separate legal personality and function in the name and on behalf of the parent company. Despite this, the case was dismissed due to jurisdictional constraints—the parent company was based in the DRC while the subsidiary was located in Belgium.[150] This restricted the Belgian NCP's ability to hold the subsidiary accountable under the OECD Guidelines for the actions of the parent company in the DRC.

The case against Perenco, handled by the French NCP, further illustrated parent company responsibility.[151] Initially, Perenco France denied liability, claiming the local company in Tunisia was independently managed and not subject to the parent company's decision-making. However, the French NCP's investigation revealed evidence that Perenco France was actively involved in its subsidiary's activities.[152] Publicly available data showed that several Perenco Group managers were French Foreign Trade Advisers (CCEFs), a role involving the promotion of France's international business interests. Perenco also participated in the Franco-Tunisian Economic Forum in 2019, and the group's Commercial Development Director was involved in discussions on energy transition challenges.[153] Additionally, employee testimonies and job descriptions indicated that Perenco France had advisory or decision-making responsibilities toward its subsidiaries, including PTCL in Tunisia.[154] Based on this evidence, the French NCP concluded that there was a business relationship between Perenco France and its subsidiary in Tunisia, which warranted further examination of Perenco France's due diligence obligations concerning the subsidiary's activities. This case is significant in highlighting the French NCP's ability to establish the responsibility and link of parent companies. However, given that Perenco was aware of the allegations and failed to conduct adequate due diligence, the company could have potentially been considered as having contributed to the harms, rather than merely being directly linked.

---

[148] Ibid, para 47–49.

[149] NCP Belgium, Adimed-Kilu Group v. ES-KO International, Final Statement, 2 July 2018.

[150] Ibid, 6–7.

[151] NCP France, Avocats Sans Frontières (ASF) and I WATCH v. Perenco, Initial Statement, 4 December 2019.

[152] Ibid, 2–3.

[153] Ibid.

[154] Ibid, 6.

A similar situation arose in the case involving Glencore, where allegations surfaced regarding the company's subsidiary in Chad.[155] Glencore initially claimed that responsibility for the alleged harms rested solely with its subsidiary, PetroChad Mangara (PCM), and that it was not directly liable. However, the UK NCP, after reviewing various documents, determined that Glencore was indeed directly linked to the harms.[156] The NCP found that Glencore UK in London provided technical planning, financial services, and broader corporate support to PCM, establishing a direct link between the parent company and the subsidiary's operations.[157]

These cases highlight a key principle: regardless of jurisdictional or organisational complexity, parent companies can and should be held accountable for harms linked to the activities of their subsidiaries, given their managerial oversight and control within the corporate structure. Under the UNGPs and the OECD Guidelines, business relationships of this kind trigger a responsibility to prevent and mitigate adverse impacts. This obligation is rooted in the concept of leverage, requiring parent companies to use their influence to address or avert harm rather than distancing themselves from it. The specifics of parent companies' responsibilities, including their duties related to mitigation and prevention, will be discussed in greater detail in Sect. 4.2 of this book under 'Managerial Responsibilities of Parent Companies towards Subsidiaries'.

Directly Linked Through Business Relationships in Supply Chains

In OECD case analyses, direct business links within supply chains are more frequently identified than those stemming from broader corporate ties, such as investments. NCPs often prioritise these direct links when adverse impacts arise from a company's operations, products, or services through its business relationships in the supply chain, in line with the OECD Guidelines. According to the commentary on the UNGPs, when companies are directly linked to abuses within their supply chains, they are required to conduct HRDD and take appropriate action to prevent and mitigate potential and actual risks. OECD cases demonstrate how NCPs critically examine both contractual and non-contractual business relationships on a case-by-case basis to determine a company's human rights and environmental responsibilities within its supply chain.

In most cases concerning direct links within supply chains, the Canadian NCP's case against Endeavour Mining offers deeper insights.[158] The NCP referred to commentary paragraph 15 of the Chapter 2—General Policies of the OECD Guidelines, which clearly obliges companies to conduct due diligence aimed at preventing or mitigating adverse impacts directly linked to their operations, products, or services

[155] NCP United Kingdom, AJTZP, RAID and PILC v. Glencore UK Ltd., Initial Statement, 22 January 2021.

[156] Ibid, 11–12.

[157] Ibid.

[158] NCP Canada, The Secretary General of the Labour Union Federation nationale des Mines et de l'Energie (FENAME) v. Endeavour Mining, Final Statement, 24 October 2017.

through business relationships, including subcontractors or labour brokers.[159] This responsibility applied to Endeavour in relation to its contractor, ALS (the mining laboratory operator), and labour brokers like SAER Emploi.[160] The NCP emphasised that Endeavour's due diligence is not a one-time investigation but should be a continuous, proactive process.[161] This requires the establishment of systematic procedures to identify human rights and environmental risks and to address such risks within the operations of contractual partners.

Similarly, in the case against Mylan, handled by the Dutch NCP, the NCP emphasised that Dutch companies conducting business abroad must comply with the OECD Guidelines, which provide the normative framework for responsible business conduct.[162] The Dutch NCP reaffirmed that companies must address adverse impacts, even if they did not directly contribute to them, so long as these impacts are linked to their operations, products, or services through a business relationship.[163] The Mylan case is particularly significant, as it is one of the few examples that sheds light on human rights risks arising in the downstream supply chain, specifically at the level of end users of the company's products.

Both cases pointed out that companies are responsible for addressing risks throughout their supply chains, even those stemming from third-party relationships. Companies can implement due diligence measures for subcontractors by leveraging their influence to embed RBC expectations into contracts or by supporting capacity-building programs. For example, the Canadian NCP recommended that Endeavour Mining implement such measures to align with the OECD Guidelines.[164] Similarly, the Dutch NCP's recommendation to Mylan reiterated that companies are obligated to address adverse impacts, even when they are not the direct contributor but are linked through a business relationship.[165]

Further critical analyses of companies' responsibilities for adverse impacts directly linked to their operations through business relationships in supply chain can be found in UK NCP cases involving G4S and JCB.[166] In the case against JCB, Lawyers for Palestinian Human Rights (LPHR) alleged that JCB violated the OECD Guidelines by allowing their construction machinery to be used in the demolition of Palestinian property and settlement-related construction.[167] The UK NCP clarified company responsibilities in complex cases where a company has not directly

---

[159] OECD Guidelines for Multinational Enterprises, Chapter 2, commentary para 15.

[160] Ibid.

[161] Ibid.

[162] NCP Netherlands, Bart Stapert attorney v. Mylan, Final Statement, 11 April 2016.

[163] Ibid, 5.

[164] NCP Canada, The Secretary General of the Labour Union Federation nationale des Mines et de l'Energie (FENAME) v. Endeavour Mining, Final Statement, 24 October 2017.

[165] NCP Netherlands, Bart Stapert attorney v. Mylan, Final Statement, 11 April 2016, 5.

[166] NCP United Kingdom, Lawyers for Palestinian Human Rights (LPHR) v. JCB, Final Statement, 12 November 2021; NCP United Kingdom, LPHR v. G4S, Final Statement, March 2015.

[167] NCP United Kingdom, Lawyers for Palestinian Human Rights (LPHR) v. JCB, Final Statement, 12 November 2021, 12.

contributed to adverse human rights impacts, yet those impacts are directly linked to its operations, products, or services through a business relationship.[168] The paragraph 13 of the Chapter 2 of the OECD Guidelines stressed that this provision does not shift responsibility to the company with a business relationship; instead, it mandates that companies use their leverage to influence the responsible entity to prevent or mitigate the harm.[169] JCB's argument that its relationship with Comasco, its distributor, was arm's length was rejected.[170] The NCP concluded that JCB had a clear contractual business relationship with Comasco, which falls within the OECD Guidelines' definition of a business relationship. Consequently, JCB was required to use its leverage over Comasco to address any adverse human rights impacts.

Similarly, in the case against G4S, the UK NCP emphasised the company's responsibility to address human rights impacts arising from its business relationships.[171] The complaint, raised by again LPHR, linked G4S to facilities and operations of Israeli state agencies accused of breaching international human rights and humanitarian law.[172] Although G4S was not directly responsible for the violations, the UK NCP concluded that G4S had an obligation to use its leverage to mitigate or prevent these adverse impacts, as stipulated by the OECD Guidelines.[173] The UK NCP's decisions in both the G4S and JCB cases underlined that companies must leverage their influence to ensure that business partners or entities within their supply chains uphold human rights standards. The OECD Guidelines require companies to engage proactively with their business partners to prevent or mitigate harm, even if their connection to such partners through services or products is limited in scope.

The crucial of existence of the business relationship also addressed in the case against Adidas in German NCP. The case against Adidas brought before the German NCP provides a crucial example of how business relationship analysis can be instrumental in addressing the responsibilities of MNEs.[174] The analysis of Adidas' relationships with its subcontractors in Indonesia, particularly concerning labour rights violations, reinforced the need for companies to assess their entire supply chain critically, not just their direct business partners. Adidas was linked to the subcontractor's adverse labour practices, including wage disputes and union-busting activities, even though it argued that its influence was limited by its small share of orders.[175] This argument was rejected, as the NCP emphasised that under the OECD Guidelines, Adidas had a responsibility to use its leverage within its business

[168] Ibid, 12.

[169] OECD Guidelines for Multinational Enterprises, Chapter 2, para 13.

[170] Ibid, 13.

[171] NCP United Kingdom, LPHR v. G4S, Final Statement, March 2015.

[172] Ibid, 9–10.

[173] Ibid, 11–12.

[174] NCP Germany, SÜDWIND Institut, Sedane Labour Resource Centre (Lembaga Informasi Perburuhan Sedane, (LIPS"), Bogor (West Java, Indonesia), Clean Clothes Campaign v. Adidas, Final Statement, 14 March 2018.

[175] Ibid, 5.

relationships to prevent and mitigate human rights violations.[176] The case illustrated that the responsibilities of MNEs extend beyond direct contractual obligations. Adidas' business relationship with its subcontractor created a direct link to adverse human rights impacts, such as wage violations and the suppression of union activities. The German NCP highlighted that Adidas, despite representing a small portion of the subcontractor's production, was still expected to exercise due diligence in addressing these impacts.

By exercising leverage over business partners in the Global South, MNEs indirectly influence and elevate the RBC standards of smaller and local companies. A prime example is the case involving PWT Group before the Danish NCP, where the NCP emphasised that companies must uphold the OECD Guidelines by ensuring their suppliers comply with health and safety standards.[177] The NCP stressed that this responsibility extends to all relevant human rights and labour rights risks, including working conditions and the structural safety of supplier facilities.[178] This case affirms the critical importance of labour rights-related risks that MNEs must prevent, identify, and address within their supply chain relationships to effectively meet their obligations. Beyond labour rights, other cases have shown that companies are also expected to address broader human rights issues, such as environmental and community impacts.

2.4.2.2 Prevention and Mitigation Measures Implemented by Companies

Most cases addressing preventive and mitigation measures focus on corporate involvement directly linked to adverse impacts, with NCPs primarily recommending that companies leverage their influence and conduct due diligence within their operations and supply chains. However, these recommendations—particularly those relating to leveraging influence and ceasing harm through engagement or divestment—are significant enough to warrant separate analysis. This section shifts focus to other preventive and mitigation measures beyond leverage and disengagement, which are relatively rare. Out of 394 cases, only 13 explicitly addressed preventive measures and among these, only few provide clear guidance. These cases offer unique examples of NCPs recommending or companies taking specific actions, which deserve closer examination.

One such example is the case against Bestseller, which was previously discussed in this book.[179] In this instance, the Danish NCP recognised that Bestseller had implemented preventive and mitigation measures effectively. The NCP recommended that, in accordance with the OECD Guidelines, when a company identifies

---

176 Ibid, 5–6.

177 NCP Denmark, Clean Clothes Campaign and Active Consumers v. PWT Group, Final Statement, 17 October 2016.

178 Ibid, 5.

179 NCP Denmark, Christian Juhl v. Bestseller AS, Final Statement, 30 September 2022.

risks of contributing to adverse impacts, it must use its influence to address the business relationship and mitigate those risks.[180] Factors such as the volume of goods purchased, the company's size relative to its supplier, and the availability of alternative suppliers play a key role in determining the company's ability to influence its partners. Additionally, the NCP emphasised that collaboration is a key component of effective mitigation measures. Companies can collaborate within their industry or across sectors, as well as with relevant stakeholders throughout the due diligence process, to enhance their leverage and mitigate risks more comprehensively.[181]

Similarly, in the case involving a Danish financial institute, the Danish NCP highlighted the importance of preventive measures related to environmental and social risks.[182] The case involved the development of an Environmental & Social Action Plan (ESAP), which detailed the actions, responsibilities, and timelines for both the construction and operational phases of a project.[183] The ESAP, developed by a third-party consultant, ensured that qualified experts were involved in overseeing the project and that access to information and reporting were upheld. When the financial institute became aware of issues regarding the company's compliance with IFC standards, it used its leverage to influence the management and owners by referring to the ESAP. This case demonstrated how financial institutions can engage in mitigation efforts to address environmental and social risks through their own due diligence actions, even in complex projects.

In addition, the case of Industri Energi against DNO ASA before the Norwegian NCP provided a good example of preventive measures that extend beyond leverage and disengagement.[184] The NCP issued specific recommendations for DNO on how to better align its operations with the OECD Guidelines, particularly in high-risk areas.[185] These recommendations included conducting risk-based due diligence, establishing comprehensive emergency planning procedures, and promoting meaningful cooperation between trade union representatives and management during crises or situations where regular dialogue might be challenging. Additionally, the NCP advised DNO to make its guidelines and procedures readily accessible to employees and stakeholders through internal communication channels and the company's website. These recommendations illustrate proactive mitigation and prevention strategies, demonstrating how companies should take diverse, concrete steps to address risks in advance, tailored to the specific nature of those risks.

Similarly, in a case related to a Samsung accident, the Norwegian NCP evaluated the preventive measures taken by TEPN and deemed them effective in mitigating

---

[180] Ibid, 9.

[181] Ibid.

[182] NCP Denmark, Two NGOs v. Danish Financial Instittute, Final Statement, 19 June 2018.

[183] Ibid, 4–5.

[184] NCP Norway, Industri Energi v. DNO ASA, Final Statement, 9 April 2018.

[185] Ibid, 12.

potential risks.[186] The NCP did not find that TEPN caused or contributed to the adverse impact but considered whether TEPN could have anticipated the risk of the crane collision and whether its actions helped reduce the likelihood of adverse impacts.[187] The NCP emphasised the importance of embedding RBC into business relationships by setting pre-qualification or bidding criteria, as highlighted in the OECD Due Diligence Guidance.[188] TEPN followed this guidance by conducting a thorough pre-qualification process, identifying potential risks with Samsung's health, safety, and environmental (HSE) performance. To address these risks, TEPN deployed an on-site HSE team, participated in meetings and safety walks with Samsung, and consistently used its leverage throughout the construction phase to improve HSE practices.[189] In its assessment, the NCP noted that TEPN effectively implemented well-engaged preventive and mitigation measures to minimise future risks. These cases above illustrate the broader range of preventive and mitigation measures NCPs can recommend when a company is directly linked, extending beyond traditional approaches centred on leverage and disengagement.

2.4.2.3 Leveraging Influence on Business Partners and Enhance Outcomes

Leverage is a fundamental concept in the framework of corporate responsibilities for preventing and mitigating human rights risks. In situations where MNEs have neither caused nor contributed to harm but are directly linked to it through business relationships, leverage becomes particularly critical. Despite its recognised importance, leverage has not been clearly defined or interpreted in a way that enables scholars, policymakers, or companies to fully understand its scope and application. Furthermore, questions remain about whether leverage constitutes a legal responsibility from a jurisprudential standpoint.

Both the OECD Due Diligence Guidance and the Shift Project have explored leverage extensively, demonstrating how it can be applied across a variety of contractual and non-contractual business relationships.[190] These frameworks urge different actors—MNEs, suppliers, and investors—to effectively engage in leveraging

[186] NCP Norway, Samsung Heavy Industries Martin Linge Project Crane Accident Workers Support Team and Korean Transnational Corporations Watch v. Totalenergies E&P Norge As, Equinor Asa, Technip Energies N.V., Final Statement, 22 February 2023.

[187] Ibid, 16.

[188] OECD 'OECD Due Diligence Guidance for Responsible Business Conduct' 2018, 60 https://www.oecd.org/en/publications/oecd-due-diligence-guidance-for-responsible-business-conduct_15f5f4b3-en.html (accessed 31 January 2026).

[189] NCP Norway, Samsung Heavy Industries Martin Linge Project Crane Accident Workers Support Team And Korean Transnational Corporations Watch v. Totalenergies E&P Norge As, Equinor Asa, Technip Energies N.V., Final Statement, 22 February 2023.

[190] OECD 'OECD Due Diligence Guidance for Responsible Business Conduct' 2018, 60 https://www.oecd.org/en/publications/oecd-due-diligence-guidance-for-responsible-business-conduct_15f5f4b3-en.html (accessed 31 January 2026); Shift 'Using Leverage in Business Relationships to Reduce Human Rights Risks' November 2013 https://shiftproject.org/wp-content/uploads/2013/11/Shift_leverageUNGPs_2013.pdf (accessed 31 January 2026).

their influence to promote responsible practices within their spheres. The Shift Project has further conceptualised leverage as a core component of corporate responsibility in mitigating human rights risks, outlining how companies can use leverage to influence suppliers, joint venture partners, customers, and even governments through both direct and collaborative means.[191] The primary goal is for companies to use their leverage to prevent or mitigate adverse human rights impacts. Ultimately, the exercise of leverage is about changing the behaviour of key actors involved in human rights risks, with a focus on practical and innovative strategies that businesses can adopt to meet their responsibilities in respecting human rights.

In addition, Wood argued that leverage should be seen as a legal concept of responsibility, particularly in the context of human rights.[192] He asserted that even when a company is not directly responsible for harm, its ability to influence the actions of others creates both a moral and potentially a legal obligation to act.[193] This responsibility is activated when there is a significant connection between the company and the rights violation, when the company has the capacity to influence the outcome, when the costs of intervention are reasonable, and when the rights violations are serious.[194] Wood further critiqued the traditional focus on 'impact-based' responsibility, which emphasises direct contributions to harm, and advocates for a recognition of 'leverage-based' responsibility.[195] This perspective encourages companies to use their influence to prevent or mitigate human rights abuses through their business relationships. Such an understanding challenges and expands existing frameworks, including the UNGPs and the OECD Guidelines, by emphasising the moral imperative for companies to intervene when they have the power to make a meaningful difference.

Moreover, OECD case law provided significant insights into how leverage should be interpreted as a critical aspect of corporate human rights responsibility. Approximately 40 of 394 cases, NCPs have analysed or recommended that companies exercise leverage in their direct business relationships. In some cases, complainants have argued that companies failed to comply with the OECD Guidelines because they did not use their leverage, and in certain instances, NCPs agreed and recommended that companies take action. These cases span various corporate actors, illustrating direct links to harm through different business relationships, including those between parent companies and subsidiaries, investors and investees, buyers and suppliers, and producers and purchasers. Further specific analysis of leverage, such as the responsibility of investors and parent companies to exercise the leverage, will be discussed later in this book, particularly in Chaps. 3 and 4.

[191] Ibid Shift, Using Leverage in Business Relationships to Reduce Human Rights Risks, 6.

[192] Wood (2012), pp. 82–83.

[193] Ibid.

[194] Ibid.

[195] Ibid, 82–85.

These sections will offer a more comprehensive understanding of leverage as a responsibility across all corporate actors.

In most cases, NCPs have assessed how effectively companies exercised their leverage and emphasised the importance of using their influence to ensure that business partners engage in responsible business practices. However, a closer examination reveals that leverage is not the vague concept it may appear to be under the UNGPs. OECD case law highlighted a structured approach: first, companies must identify and understand their potential influence and the degree of that influence (assessing their power to influence and determine the degree of influence); second, they must act on that influence by exercising leverage; and finally, if their leverage proves insufficient, they are expected to collaborate with others to increase their collective influence and enhance their ability to bring about responsible business conduct.

Some OECD cases have demonstrated the critical role of leverage in promoting responsible business practices, particularly in highlighting instances where companies failed to adequately influence their business partners. For instance, cases involving Mallee in the Australian NCP, Socfin and Socapalm in the Belgian NCP, Minera Candelaria and a mining MNE in the Chilean NCP, and Bresser in the Dutch NCP emphasised how these companies missed opportunities to use their leverage effectively, resulting in non-compliance with OECD Guidelines.[196] In these cases, the NCPs recommended that the companies should have exercised their influence to encourage their business partners to conduct RBC in their operations.

Conversely, other cases such as Moeller in the Danish NCP, Shell in the Dutch NCP, the APG Assessment, and the Finnish NCP case against Pöyry PLC provided more detailed examples of how leverage was, or could have been, effectively applied. These cases offer clearer insights into the specific actions companies can take to influence their partners. For instance, in the case involving Pöyry Energy AG, a leading company in the industry, Pöyry and its Swiss subsidiary provided consulting services for the Xayaburi hydropower project on the Mekong River in Lao PDR.[197] 13 NGOs, including Friends of the Earth, filed complaints against Pöyry, alleging that the company violated the OECD Guidelines by failing to adequately address the human rights and environmental risks associated with the project, particularly regarding fish migration.[198] The Finnish NCP concluded that Pöyry had an opportunity to influence the progress of the Xayaburi project.[199] Despite working under a limited commission that restricted its ability to engage with stakeholders, the company was still responsible for addressing uncertainties related to the environmental and human rights impacts of the project.[200] Pöyry's report to its client

---

196 NCP Australia, Publish What You Pay Australia v. Mallee Resources Limited, Final Statement, 2 August 2023.

197 NCP Finland, the Siemenpuu Foundation, Friends of the Earth Finland, and 13 other NGOs v. Pöyry Plc and the Xayaburi hydropower project, Final Statement, 10 June 2013.

198 Ibid, 2–3.

199 Ibid, 12.

200 Ibid.

could have more clearly highlighted these concerns, especially uncertainties around the interpretation of the Mekong Agreement.

Despite its limitations, NCP analysed that Pöyry made several detailed recommendations to enhance the project's environmental impact, such as conducting new environmental studies, constructing fish passages, and modifying technical designs to improve sediment and nutrient flow.[201] Although there was scientific disagreement about the adequacy of these recommendations, Pöyry's efforts to mitigate environmental risks demonstrated the importance of leverage in promoting RBC, even in complex situations. The Finnish NCP recommended that greater attention be given to risk assessment and the inclusion of stakeholder perspectives through open dialogue in future large-scale projects, especially those with significant environmental risks that impact multiple countries and are governed by international treaties.[202] The NCP also advised that projects similar to Xayaburi should not proceed until thorough environmental studies are conducted. This case illustrated that the company should have understood and identified its degree of leverage from the outset and exercised it fully to comply with the OECD Guidelines.

Leverage is a complex concept, as demonstrated in the case against Moeller—Maersk in the Danish NCP. In this case, 337 former employees of the joint venture Douala International Terminal S.A. (DIT) filed a complaint against Moeller.[203] The complaint alleged that Moeller failed to observe the OECD Guidelines during its engagement with DIT, particularly in relation to harsh working conditions and the withholding of workers' administrative documents after the concession agreement for the Douala-Bonaberi port in Cameroon ended.[204] In response to this, Moeller responded that Moeller held a 44% share in DIT, alongside its joint venture partner Bolloré, which also held 44%, with the remaining 12% split between the Port Authority of Douala and private shareholders.[205] This structure meant that Moeller did not have full control over DIT, sharing decision-making power with Bolloré and other stakeholders.[206] Nevertheless, the Danish NCP examined the degree of leverage Moeller possessed and how it was used.[207] It found that while Moeller had a substantial degree of leverage—having appointed the General Director of DIT and several board members—its influence may have been limited by the presence of the Port Authority of Douala and the fixed-term nature of the 15-year concession agreement.[208] The Port Authority's administrative role in the port, combined with its ties

[201] Ibid, 12.

[202] Ibid, 12–13.

[203] NCP Denmark, Former Employees of the Joint Venture Douala International Terminal S.A. in Cameroun v. A.P. Moeller – Maersk A/S, Final Statement, 06 May 2024.

[204] Ibid, 8–9.

[205] Ibid, 11.

[206] Ibid, 19.

[207] Ibid.

[208] Ibid.

to the Cameroonian government, could have complicated efforts to address systemic issues.

Despite these challenges, the NCP concluded that Moeller still held significant leverage through its ownership percentage and management positions in DIT.[209] The NCP expected Moeller to have used this leverage to promote responsible business conduct, even in the face of external constraints. Furthermore, Danish NCP recommended that Moeller consider how to address the use of leverage within its joint venture framework.[210] Moeller was encouraged to implement practices to analyse its degree of leverage in various operations and business relationships when engaging in new activities and to develop strategies to use that leverage to promote responsible business practices.[211] If Moeller finds it lacks sufficient leverage, it should consider ways to build additional leverage through senior management outreach, commercial incentives, government engagement, or industry collaborations. Danish NCP also recommended that Moeller track its use of leverage by, for example, saving minutes from board meetings.

The analysis and recommendations by various NCPs regarding leverage—determining, exercising, tracking its effectiveness, and increasing it—have been consistently applied across multiple cases. In the Dutch NCP case against Shell, where Shell was alleged to have breached several OECD Guidelines chapters, including those on human rights, environmental protection, labour rights, and anti-bribery measures in its Nigerian subsidiary, the Shell Petroleum Development Company of Nigeria Limited (SPDC), the NCP addressed Shell's responsibilities as a Netherlands-based parent company.[212] The NCP recommended that if Shell had exercised its leverage to the fullest extent without achieving the desired behavioural change in the SPDC joint venture, it should explore ways to build additional leverage with its SPDC JV partners.[213] This could be done through senior management outreach, commercial incentives, or by collaborating with other actors in the industry to exert collective leverage. The NCP highlighted that cooperative approaches within the industry could strengthen leverage in accordance with the OECD Due Diligence Guidance.[214]

In some cases, companies have claimed an absence of meaningful leverage, especially where state participation constrains their capacity to influence business conduct. This line of argumentation was evident in the case concerning the KPO Consortium.[215] The consortium was accused of failing to comply with the OECD Guidelines while operating the Karachaganak oil and gas condensate field in

[209] Ibid, 19–20.

[210] Ibid.

[211] Ibid, 19–21.

[212] NCP Denmark, Aminigboko Community v. the Shell Petroleum Development Company of Nigeria Limited and Shell Headquarters, Final Statement, 10 February 2023.

[213] Ibid, 8–9.

[214] OECD Due Diligence Guidance, Section 3.2.d.

[215] NCP United Kingdom, Crude Accountability v. KPO Consortium, Final Statement, 25 September 2019.

Kazakhstan, where many Kazakh families were forcibly relocated.[216] KPO argued that it had no influence or control over the resettlement process, which was managed by Kazakh authorities. However, the UK NCP held a different view. The UK NCP stated that KPO had, at a minimum, an obligation to engage with both the affected households and the authorities, regardless of whether the resettlement of the households were conducted by the state authorities.[217] NCP stated that KPO had been conducting a new review of the Sanitary Protection Zone from 2011, and during this process, it had opportunities to communicate with the households and raise their concerns with the authorities. In relation to the authorities, the UK NCP referred to the IFC standard, which emphasises that businesses should engage with authorities to ensure that resettlement meets the appropriate standards.[218] While KPO's involvement may not have necessarily changed the authorities' approach, there was no indication that the authorities had restricted or prohibited KPO's involvement. If resources were a factor in the delays, KPO was in a strong position to offer assistance, as evidenced by its ability to fund the Tungush relocation and its ongoing funding of the current relocation efforts.

The UK NCP further noted that even if a business believes it cannot change the outcome or behaviour of a partner, it still has a responsibility to explore what actions it can take. The obligation is to seek to prevent or mitigate adverse impacts. In KPO's case, the information provided did not suggest that the company made any formal or informal appraisal to support its claim that it was not appropriate to intervene. This case demonstrates that, regardless of how limited a company's influence may be, it must always seek ways to exercise leverage and explore all possible avenues to mitigate or prevent adverse impacts.

A compelling example of this principle was demonstrated by the US NCP in its handling of the case involving Coca-Cola Amatil's alleged misconduct at its Indonesian subsidiary, in violation of the OECD Guidelines.[219] In response to Coca-Cola's claim that it lacked direct control over the management of its Indonesian operations, the US NCP emphasised that the company was still responsible for using its leverage to prevent or mitigate adverse impacts, citing the OECD Guidelines (Commentary on General Policies, paragraphs 19–20).[220] The US NCP highlighted that leverage is a complex issue, with the extent of a company's influence in supplier relationships varying based on specific factors unique to each situation.[221] Companies may not fully recognise the extent of their leverage until they attempt to exercise it. Nonetheless, the OECD Guidelines are explicit that a lack of leverage is not a valid excuse for inaction. While the Guidelines acknowledge the practical limitations

---

[216] Ibid, 3.

[217] Ibid.

[218] Ibid, 11–12.

[219] NCP United States, the International Union of Food, Agriculture, Hotel, Restaurant, Catering, Tobacco, and Allied Workers Associations' v. Coca Cola Amatil, Final Statement, 25 May 2018.

[220] Ibid, 2–3.

[221] Ibid, 8.

businesses face in influencing supplier behaviour—such as product characteristics, the number of suppliers, or the complexity of supply chains—they stress that companies can still exert influence.[222] The US NCP suggested that businesses can achieve this through mechanisms such as contractual agreements, voting trusts, or by participating in industry-wide collaborative initiatives to enhance their leverage.[223]

In conclusion, leverage plays a crucial role in the corporate human rights responsibility framework, particularly in cases where MNEs are directly linked to adverse impacts through their business relationships. The cases analysed across various NCPs highlight that even when companies lack direct control over their business partners, they still bear the responsibility to exercise leverage to its fullest extent, track, and enhance their leverage to promote responsible business practices. Whether through contractual agreements, collaborative industry efforts, or senior management outreach, companies must explore all available avenues to prevent or mitigate human rights and environmental risks. The OECD Guidelines and related case law emphasised that inaction, due to perceived limitations in leverage, is not acceptable. Instead, companies are expected to continuously assess their influence and take meaningful steps to drive positive change, even in complex or constrained situations.

2.4.2.4 Stopping the Harm: Key Steps in Disengagement and Divestment

In situations where mitigation and prevention efforts are either impracticable or ineffective and leverage proves insufficient, the last resort under both the UNGPs and the OECD Guidelines is to terminate the business relationship. However, as Fasterling has argued, the UNGPs caution against a 'cut and run' approach, where companies simply sever relationships to avoid negative impacts in their supply chains.[224] Instead, if the negative impacts are severe and other strategies have failed, companies must carefully consider whether terminating the relationship is the most responsible course of action.[225] As mentioned earlier in this chapter, the termination of business relationships—whether referred to as withdrawal, divestment or exit, especially in conflict-affected areas—must be done in a responsible manner to avoid further human rights violations affecting, for example, local employees. Several cases have addressed the need for companies to end their business relationships in a way that is consistent with the UNGPs and the OECD Guidelines and ensures that the process is managed responsibly and prudently to avoid exacerbating negative impacts. For example, in the cases involving Mallee in the Australian NCP, Bestseller in the Danish NCP and Unilever in the Dutch NCP, the NCPs discussed how companies should end or terminate their relationships in a responsible manner and in

---

[222] Ibid.

[223] Ibid, 9.

[224] Fasterling (2017), pp. 242–243.

[225] Ibid.

line with the OECD Guidelines.[226] These cases provided concrete guidance on how companies can carefully manage the exit from their business relationships in order to minimise negative impacts and maintain their responsibility towards the affected rightsholders.

In the first case against Unilever, which was heard by the Dutch NCP, the issue of responsible engagement came to the fore when Unilever sold its shares in Marsavco, a company operating in the DRC.[227] Unilever's rationale for the sale was that following a strategic review, the company had identified its operations in the DRC as 'non-core' and economically unviable following a protracted civil war.[228] Although this decision was taken for business reasons, the Dutch NCP emphasised that responsible withdrawal under the OECD Guidelines involves more than just economic considerations.[229] Companies are expected to conduct a thorough risk assessment, considering relevant adverse impacts related to stakeholders, before divesting shares or property, especially in conflict-affected areas. In this case, the NCP was unable to determine whether Unilever had identified the human rights risks associated with the sale. However, the decision to sell shares in a conflict-affected area had serious consequences for workers, raising concerns about the company's compliance with the RBC.

The OECD Guidelines on responsible disengagement, updated in 2023, is more explicit on the obligations of companies when considering exiting a business relationship.[230] Companies are expected to prioritise ongoing risk mitigation efforts and consult meaningfully with rights holders before making a final decision to exit. The Guidelines emphasised that the divestment or exit should only be considered as a last resort if all attempts at risk mitigation have failed or if risk mitigation is not considered feasible due to the severity of the negative impact.[231] In addition, companies are required to consider the potential social, environmental and economic impact of their withdrawal. The Dutch NCP recommended that Unilever review and update its Responsible Engagement Policy to align with the strengthened expectations of the 2023 Guidelines.[232] This is an important reminder that responsible disengagement is not only about protecting business interests, but that the rights and welfare of affected stakeholders must also be considered, especially in vulnerable regions such as the DRC.

---

[226] NCP Denmark, Christian Juhl v. Bestseller A/S, Final Statement, 30 September 2022; NCP Australia, Publish What You Pay Australia v. Mallee Resources Limited, Final Statement, 2 August 2023; NCP Netherland 'Final Statement: NCP Specific Instance ATUMA v. Unilever' 7 May 2024.

[227] Ibid, NCP Netherland 'Final Statement: NCP Specific Instance ATUMA v. Unilever' 7 May 2024.

[228] Ibid, 18.

[229] Ibid.

[230] OECD Guidelines for Multinational Enterprises, Chapter 2: General Policies, Commentary paras 23 and 25.

[231] Ibid.

[232] NCP Netherland 'Final Statement: NCP Specific Instance ATUMA v. Unilever' 7 May 2024, 9.

Clearer examples are the cases of Mallee and Bestseller, who were operating in Myanmar. In the case against Mallee, which has already been analysed earlier in this book, the Australian NCP highlighted important considerations for disengagement under the OECD Guidelines.[233] The Guidelines provide for disengagement as a last resort when a company is unable to exert sufficient leverage over a third party to ensure respect for human rights. In this case, however, the withdrawal was not sought as part of a strategic escalation of measures to improve the human rights situation. Instead, Mallee's withdrawal was a reaction to a sudden and radical change in the government and security situation in Myanmar.[234] Despite this difference, the OECD Guidelines emphasise that regardless of whether divestment is a tool to exert leverage or a broader business decision to exit a difficult project, due diligence is still required. Companies are expected to 'consider the potential negative social and economic impacts of the decision to withdraw'.[235] In this case, the assessment of the human rights risks associated with divestment would have required a thorough understanding of the human rights record of the company to which Mallee divested. However, the information indicates that Mallee did not conduct a comprehensive due diligence associated with divesting to another company called WMM.[236] Instead, it relied on previous due diligence of the company and personal relationships with representatives of WMM. NCP viewed that while personal knowledge of individuals within the company can provide context, it is not a substitute for adequate HRDD.

In the case against Bestseller before the Danish NCP, the NCP emphasised that if, after conducting enhanced due diligence, a company concludes that the most responsible action is to terminate a partnership or cease doing business in a country, this decision must be taken in a responsible manner. The Danish NCP emphasised that companies must comply with domestic legislation, international labour standards and all applicable collective agreements, while ensuring transparency by explaining and documenting the reasons for their decision to relevant stakeholders.[237] In addition, the company should provide sufficient notice to affected parties, including suppliers, workers and neighbouring communities, before suspending or terminating the business relationship.[238] In this case, the Danish NCP emphasised not only the need to comply with legal standards, but also the crucial role of communication and transparency with affected communities during the withdrawal process, which further underlines the importance of careful consideration when deciding on withdrawal. This ensures that corporate decisions, particularly the

[233] NCP Australia, Publish What You Pay Australia v. Mallee Resources Limited, Final Statement, 2 August 2023

[234] Ibid, 30.

[235] Ibid, 28–30.

[236] Ibid, 35–36.

[237] NCP Denmark, Christian Juhl v. Bestseller A/S, Final Statement, 30 September 2022.

[238] Ibid, 12.

suspension or termination of partnerships, do not disproportionately affect vulnerable groups.

In addition to the cases where companies have withdrawn due to serious negative impacts on human rights and social instability in conflict zones, several examples have shown that financial institutions have to divest from projects that can contribute to significant negative impacts. One prominent case concerns a Danish financial institution where two NGOs filed a complaint with the Danish NCP which was previously analysed.[239] Although the NCP found that the institution had undertaken sufficient efforts to mitigate the damage, including attempts to leverage its influence, the financial institution eventually decided to withdraw from the project when these measures were not sufficient to remedy the damage.[240] This case can serve as an example of best practice. It shows how investors can responsibly mitigate the negative impact of their investments by actively seeking solutions and withdrawing if necessary.

A similar situation arose in the case against the BKW Group, in which the company was accused of violating the provisions of the OECD Guidelines on Chapter 2: General Policies and Chapter 4: Human Rights.[241] The accusations stemmed from BKW's minority stake in a wind power plant project in Norway, which entailed potential risks for the indigenous Sami communities. BKW claimed that it had carried out thorough due diligence prior to the investment and had taken the interests of the Sami community into account during the planning and approval phase of the project. Despite initial disagreements, the mediation process resulted in a written agreement. In this agreement, BKW committed to ensure that future projects potentially affecting indigenous communities include clear human rights expectations, such as FPIC. In addition, BKW committed to withdraw from projects if human rights compliance cannot be achieved or if violations continue to occur during project implementation.[242] This commitment to integrate human rights standards into business contracts—including withdrawal clauses in the event of continued non-compliance—underlines the investor's responsibility to exert its leverage and withdraw from harmful investments if necessary.

In the Rabobank case, the Dutch NCP made it clear that withdrawal is not always the best solution, even when a financial institution is accused of violating the OECD Guidelines.[243] Rabobank came under scrutiny for its connection to a palm oil project in Indonesia that raised concerns about human rights and environmental impacts. The NCP found that withdrawing financial support from institutions that adhere to the Roundtable on Sustainable Palm Oil (RSPO) principles would not necessarily be conducive to the SDGs in this case, although this is one of the options outlined

---

[239] NCP Denmark, Two NGOs v. Danish Financial Instittute, Final Statement, 19 June 2018.

[240] Ibid, 5–6.

[241] NCP Switzerland, Society for Threatened Peoples v. BKW Group, Final Statement, 26 August 2021.

[242] Ibid, 3.

[243] NCP Netherlands, Friends of Earth Europe and Friends of Earth Netherlands/Milieudefensie v. Rabobank, Final Statement, 15 January 2016.

in the OECD Guidelines.[244] Instead, the NCP emphasised that it is the responsibility of financial institutions to decide whether to address the identified negative impacts through continued engagement or divestment. The OECD Guidelines suggest that companies should consider potential social and economic impacts before deciding to exit.[245] The NCP also emphasised that withdrawal should be considered as a last resort, as it does not always lead to meaningful progress.[246] By maintaining engagement, financial institutions can work towards more sustainable outcomes and ensure they remain part of the solution, rather than simply cutting ties when problems arise.

2.4.2.5 Preliminary Conclusion

The analysis of OECD case law highlights the increasing responsibility of companies, including financial institutions, to proactively prevent and mitigate human rights abuses. A broad range of prevention and mitigation measures, guided by the UNGPs and the OECD Guidelines, have become essential tools in this effort. Whether through direct causation, contribution, or complex business relationships, companies are now expected to conduct thorough due diligence, assess risks, and implement effective mitigation strategies.

Given the complexity of negative impacts and the diversity of business relationships, this section examines how companies apply different risk mitigation approaches, with a particular focus on leveraging influence and responsible engagement. While a more detailed analysis of corporate actors will follow, this section provides a general overview of corporate responsibility in risk mitigation. This research marked that companies must move beyond superficial assessments. To conduct meaningful and effective due diligence, they should actively engage with business partners, strengthen their leverage, meaningfully involve stakeholders, monitor the effectiveness of risk mitigation measures, and ensure these efforts translate into tangible, positive outcomes.

---

[244] Ibid, 4.

[245] Ibid.

[246] Ibid.

2.5 Tracking and Monitoring the Effectiveness of Human Rights Measures

2.5.1 The Importance and Challenges of Tracking and Monitoring in Human Rights Due Diligence

Tracking and monitoring corporate responses to human rights abuses are critical components within the HRDD framework, ensuring that companies' actions are both effective and aligned with their human rights commitments. Despite its significance, tracking often receives less attention compared to other aspects of HRDD, such as risk assessment and reporting.[247] This section of the book explores the vital role of tracking and monitoring in HRDD, focusing on their importance in evaluating the effectiveness of corporate human rights policies and actions. It also addresses the challenges companies face in establishing robust tracking mechanisms, identifies best practices for improving these systems, and highlights the need for stronger regulatory oversight to ensure HRDD leads to meaningful human rights outcomes. Drawing on academic literature and practical examples from OECD case law, this analysis provides a detailed understanding of why tracking is essential, the barriers that limit its effectiveness, and how businesses can address these challenges.

Tracking and monitoring are integral to the success of HRDD because they allow companies to evaluate whether their actions are effectively addressing human rights risks.[248] According to the UNGPs, Principle 20, companies should not only assess human rights risks but also track the effectiveness of their responses to those risks.[249] This continuous evaluation process is necessary to ensure that corporate efforts are not merely performative but lead to substantive improvements in human rights conditions.[250] The Principle 20 emphasised that tracking should involve both qualitative and quantitative indicators and should draw on feedback from a wide range of sources, including internal audits, employee surveys, performance evaluations, and external stakeholders such as affected communities.[251] This multi-faceted approach ensures that companies can identify whether their policies are being properly implemented and whether improvements are being achieved over time. Moreover, the OECD Guidelines reinforce the importance of tracking by stating that due diligence goes beyond risk identification and assessment—it requires companies to act on their findings and continuously monitor the effectiveness of their actions.[252]

---

[247] Most articles regarding to the HRDD are less focused on tracking process.

[248] Wettstein (2022), pp. 153–154.

[249] UN Guiding Principles on Business and Human Rights, Principle 20.

[250] Ibid.

[251] Ibid.

[252] OECD Guidelines for Multinational Enterprises, commentary to the Chapter 2: General Policies, para 15, Commentary to the Chapter IV: Human Rights, para 50.

According to the UNDP, tracking is essential not only for ensuring that identified human rights issues are effectively addressed but also for assessing the impact and effectiveness of a company's responses.[253] Tracking is not a static process but a dynamic one that must adapt and evolve in tandem with the company's shifting business environment.[254] Despite its importance, tracking and monitoring in HRDD remain challenging for many businesses. One of the most significant challenges is the tendency for companies to engage in 'tick-box' exercises, where tracking is conducted primarily to meet regulatory requirements rather than to drive meaningful change.[255] In these cases, companies may track compliance with reporting obligations, such as disclosing human rights policies, without genuinely evaluating the impact of those policies on human rights outcomes. This superficial approach undermines the effectiveness of HRDD by prioritising form over substance.[256]

Another major challenge is the lack of standardised metrics for tracking human rights performance. While the UNGPs and the OECD Guidelines provide general principles for tracking, they do not offer precise definitions or methodologies for measuring effectiveness.[257] As a result, companies are often left to develop their own indicators, leading to inconsistencies in how human rights performance is tracked across different sectors and regions. For example, some companies may focus on tracking easily quantifiable metrics, such as the number of audits conducted or instances of non-compliance with labour standards, while neglecting more complex issues like the right to a living wage.[258]

Moreover, many companies rely on third-party social audits and certifications to assess human rights performance in their supply chains.[259] However, these audits have been widely criticised for offering only surface-level solutions. Justine Nolan and Nana Frishling pointed out that social auditing consumes up to 80% of ethical sourcing budgets but often fails to detect serious human rights violations, particularly when auditors are paid by the very buyers or suppliers they are meant to effectively assess.[260] This creates inherent conflicts of interest that undermine the reliability and independence of the audits. Also, Nolan and Frishling mentioned that auditors tend to focus their evaluations only on their direct suppliers—those with whom they have a direct contractual relationship. However, global supply chains are inherently structured with multiple layers of production. Limiting social audits to

---

[253] Sweden Sverige and UNDP 'Human Rights Due Diligence: An Interpretative Guide' 2022 https://www.undp.org/sites/g/files/zskgke326/files/2022-10/HRDD%20Interpretive%20Guide_ENG_Sep%202021.pdf#page=5.57 (accessed 31 January 2026).

[254] Ibid, 18.

[255] Wettstein (2022), pp. 152–153.

[256] Ibid.

[257] Bennet (2022), pp. 143–162; New York University, Centre for Business and Human Rights (2017) https://www.stern.nyu.edu/experience-stern/global/putting-s-esg-measuring-human-rights-performance-investors (accessed 31 January 2026).

[258] LeBaron (2021b), pp. 1–20 https://doi.org/10.1017/bhj.2020.32 (accessed 31 January 2026).

[259] LeBaron (2021a), pp. 156–178.

[260] Nolan and Frishling (2020), pp. 108–138.

first-tier suppliers merely push issues further down the chain, where they go unnoticed.[261] Moreover, many auditors and business and human rights consultants do not follow up with companies on how they address issues identified during inspections and monitoring.[262]

Despite these challenges, several best practices can help companies improve their tracking and monitoring systems. According to analysis by Lise Smit, Gabrielle Holly, McCorquodale, and Stuart Neely, a crucial step is to utilise various tools, including grievance mechanisms, to track HRDD performance. Moreover, it is essential to communicate and consult findings with external stakeholders rather than keeping them confined to internal and confidential channels.[263] Moreover, companies should adopt a commitment-based approach to HRDD, focusing on long-term engagement with stakeholders rather than short-term compliance with regulatory requirements. According to research by McCorquodale and Nolan, businesses to conduct effective HRDD to work collaboratively with stakeholders, including workers, local communities, and civil society organizations, to identify and address human rights risks in a meaningful way.[264] Rather than relying solely on top-down audits or internal assessments, companies should seek input from a diverse range of stakeholders, particularly those directly affected by their operations.[265]

In addition to stakeholder engagement, McCorquodale suggested in his book that companies should leverage technology to enhance their tracking capabilities.[266] Emerging technologies like blockchain offer potential for improving traceability and transparency in complex supply chains. Blockchain can create immutable records of transactions and movements within the supply chain, providing companies with a clear and verifiable trail of data on modern slavery risks.[267] However, companies must ensure that their data collection processes are robust and that they have systems in place to verify the accuracy of the information they receive.[268] McCorquodale also mentioned that enhancing the strength of trade unions and workplace representation offers a valuable strategy for improving monitoring and accountability.[269] Gaining direct visibility into on-the-ground working conditions, rooted in workers' experiences, also provides essential insights into effective ways

---

[261] Ibid, 123.

[262] Harrison (2023), pp. 1–31 https://wrap.warwick.ac.uk/id/eprint/174876/1/WRAP-harrison-hrdd-2023.pdf (accessed 31 January 2026).

[263] Smit et al. (2020), p. 220.

[264] McCorquodale and Nolan (2021), pp. 455–478, https://doi.org/10.1007/s40802-021-00201-x (accessed 31 January 2026).

[265] Ibid, 471–473.

[266] McCorquodale, *Business and Human Rights*, 170.

[267] Tambe and Tambay (2020), pp. 22–27. https://doi.org/10.1109/AI4G50087.2020.9311031 (accessed 31 January 2026).

[268] McCorquodale, *Business and Human Rights*, 170.

[269] Ibid.

to address and resolve issues.[270] Huib Huyse contended that trade unions often face challenges in engaging directly with suppliers or lead companies, particularly those with low public profiles and limited reputational risks.[271] To address labour violations effectively, trade unions utilise HRDD-related legislation and the OECD's NCP dispute mechanism to pressure lead firms into using their influence within the supply chain. Huyse further argued that mHRDD legislation serves as a powerful tool for trade unions and CSOs to drive companies to monitor their performance and address negative impacts comprehensively.[272] Echoing this perspective, Rachel Chambers and Anil Yilmaz Vastardis cautioned that without robust regulatory mechanisms to ensure the quality of human rights disclosures, tracking efforts risk becoming superficial compliance exercises that fail to address genuine human rights risks.[273]

To overcome these challenges in HRDD implementation, governments must take a more proactive role in monitoring compliance with HRDD laws and holding companies accountable for their human rights practices. The recently adopted CSDDD reinforces the need for such oversight, aiming to strengthen corporate accountability on human rights and environmental issues. Article 15 of the CSDDD mandated that companies regularly monitor the effectiveness of their due diligence efforts regarding their own operations, subsidiaries, and relevant business partners, aiming to address human rights and environmental impacts proactively. By requiring at least annual assessments—triggered sooner if significant changes or new risks arise—and basing them on both qualitative and quantitative indicators, the directive fosters a systematic, evidence-based approach to identifying and mitigating risks. This structured, ongoing monitoring approach is designed to prevent companies from treating due diligence as a one-time compliance exercise, instead pushing for continuous improvement through updated policies and mitigation measures. If rigorously enforced by Member States, Article 15 has the potential to drive a more adaptive, responsible approach to corporate due diligence that aligns with evolving real-world conditions.

---

[270] Huyse (2021), pp. 1–19 https://hiva.kuleuven.be/sites/researchchairdw/Reports/worker_centered_HRDD_EN (accessed 31 January 2026).

[271] Ibid, 4.

[272] Ibid, 14.

[273] Chambers and Yilmaz Vastardis (2021), pp. 323–366 https://chicagounbound.uchicago.edu/cjil/vol21/iss2/4 (accessed 31 January 2026).

2.5.2 *Case Studies: Lessons from OECD Case Law on Effective Monitoring and Tracking of Human Rights Performance*

As analysed earlier, tracking and monitoring are crucial components of HRDD. These elements enable companies to evaluate the effectiveness of their efforts and ensure that human rights risks are being adequately managed. However, despite their significance, tracking systems remain underdeveloped across many companies, leading to superficial assessments that fail to drive substantial change. While regulatory frameworks such as the UNGPs and the OECD Guidelines address these issues, the practical implementation and scholarly discourse often lack detailed attention to this critical stage of HRDD. The OECD case law provides valuable insights, with multiple cases addressing the monitoring aspect of due diligence. In approximately 12 instances, the NCPs analysed how companies conducted monitoring and tracking. These cases revealed both encouraging developments and persistent challenges. In several instances, the NCPs played an active role in facilitating dialogue between the parties, thereby improving monitoring mechanisms and ensuring that due diligence processes effectively track and mitigate adverse human rights impacts across company value chains.

In some cases, NCPs assessed a company's monitoring approach directly. For example, in the case against Moeller, the Danish NCP recommended that all companies regularly review their due diligence processes to ensure a systematic integration of risk-based approaches aligned with the OECD Guidelines.[274] This review should encompass all six steps of risk-based due diligence. Companies were also encouraged to consult the OECD's 2018 Due Diligence Guidance for Responsible Business Conduct for further guidance on improving their processes. Furthermore, the Danish NCP observed that while the company's practices had evolved since the submission of the complaint, its sustainability reports for 2021 and 2022 lacked clarity regarding the implementation of due diligence processes.[275] Specifically, it was unclear how Moeller's 'red-flag system' operated, and the NCP could not determine how the company identified and addressed potential or actual impacts, nor how it ensured follow-up on such issues.[276]

The Danish NCP also emphasised the importance of transparency and effective communication in due diligence processes. Referring to the OECD Due Diligence Guidance, it pointed out that companies should not only implement risk-based approaches but also communicate these efforts clearly to their stakeholders. One of the core suggestions is that companies like Moeller, should provide comprehensive information on the significant adverse impacts or risks they identify throughout

[274] NCP Denmark, Former Employees of the Joint Venture Douala International Terminal S.A. in Cameroun v. A.P. Moeller – Maersk A/S, Final Statement, 06 May 2024.

[275] Ibid, 27.

[276] Ibid, 26.

their operations.[277] This is not just about noting risks but also about sharing how these risks are being addressed and prioritised. This aligns precisely with what business and human rights scholars discussed regarding the effectiveness of tracking HRDD. Danish NCP further stressed that prioritisation should be guided by well-defined criteria, ensuring that the most serious issues are dealt with first.[278] Moreover, companies must go beyond identification and communicate the specific steps they are taking to prevent or mitigate these risks.[279] It is crucial for stakeholders to understand what actions have been taken, as well as the rationale behind them. In cases like Moeller, the lack of clarity on the steps taken undermines confidence in the company's ability to manage human rights risks effectively.

In addition to detailing actions, companies should also share expected timelines and benchmarks for improvements. Without these, stakeholders are left in the dark regarding when they might expect tangible changes. NCP noted that providing clear timelines and benchmarks enables stakeholders to hold companies accountable for their commitments, creating a sense of progression towards better practices. Furthermore, companies should outline how they plan to track the implementation and effectiveness of these measures. It is not enough to merely take action—there needs to be a system in place to monitor the outcomes, ensuring that the efforts are actually reducing the identified risks. The Danish NCP encouraged Moeller to disclose their monitoring processes to assure stakeholders that due diligence efforts are not just a box-ticking exercise but a meaningful part of their operational strategy. The absence of such detailed communication creates uncertainty about whether the company is genuinely addressing human rights concerns in its value chain.

In another case involving a Danish financial institution which was previously extensively analysed in this book, the Danish NCP acknowledged the company's robust monitoring and follow-up approach, setting a strong example of how financial actors can meaningfully implement HRDD. To clarify, the Danish financial institution maintained close communication and cooperation with its investee, Company A, throughout the term of its loan agreement. Upon identifying adverse impacts, the bank engaged in dialogue with Company A, resulting in a formal agreement to address the issues and regularly report back on progress made in mitigating the situation.[280] This ongoing engagement ensured that the financial institution did not merely act as a passive investor but took active steps to monitor human rights risks and manage them responsibly.

What further elevated this case was that the Danish Financial Institution's close engagement with CSOs and local stakeholders in the project area.[281] This level of interaction is critical in HRDD, as it provides a platform for affected communities to voice their concerns and allows companies to gain a more nuanced understanding

[277] Ibid, 28.

[278] Ibid.

[279] Ibid.

[280] NCP Denmark, Two NGOs v. Danish Financial Instittute, Final Statement, 19 June 2018.

[281] Ibid, 6–7.

of the local context. In many cases, CSOs and local stakeholders are the first to notice human rights issues arising from projects, and their involvement can lead to more informed and effective interventions. The fact that the Financial Institution sought out this engagement demonstrates its commitment to ensuring that human rights risks were being actively managed and mitigated at multiple levels. This case is regarded as a best practice example for investor responsibility in conducting HRDD and will be further analysed in Chap. 4 of this book, particularly in the section on investor responsibility. Additionally, Sect. 2.9 of this chapter will explore how meaningful HRDD can be conducted, drawing on the lessons from this case.

Moreover, in the case involving VINCI Airport, the French NCP pointed out the importance of robust monitoring processes within the company's HRDD framework, particularly in relation to workers' rights.[282] The NCP welcomed two key due diligence measures implemented by VINCI, including the initiation of an audit process aimed at identifying and addressing human rights risks.[283] The NCP highlighted that the audit could be significantly enhanced by involving an independent body, adding credibility to the assessment and ensuring that it was carried out objectively and impartially. By recommending that the audit be conducted by a third party, the French NCP reinforced the notion that robust monitoring should involve independent verification to provide transparency and build trust with external stakeholders. Moreover, the French NCP emphasised the importance of fostering meaningful dialogue between VINCI Airport and workers' representatives as part of the due diligence process. It recognised that monitoring human rights risks cannot be fully effective without the inclusion of those directly affected—in this case, the workers.

In the case against KiK Textilien, the German NCP similarly emphasised the need for comprehensive assessments as a critical part of effective HRDD.[284] Specifically, the NCP recommended that safety standards should be monitored continuously through both scheduled and unannounced inspections, ensuring that compliance is consistently maintained.[285] These assessments could be conducted either by local staff employed by the contractor or by external auditors, with the key requirement being that those conducting the checks are well-trained and reliable. By referring an unannounced audit, the NCP highlighted the importance of preventing companies from preparing for inspections, thus providing a more accurate picture of on-the-ground conditions. Furthermore, the German NCP stressed the importance of regularly informing corporate headquarters of the assessment results.[286]

Furthermore, effective complaint-based mechanisms are fundamental to ensuring that monitoring mechanisms in HRDD are meaningful and capable of

---

[282] NCP France, the International Trade Union Confederation (ITUC) and the Cambodian Labour Confederation v. VINCI Airports in Cambodia, Final Statement, 11 December 2018.

[283] Ibid, 6.

[284] NCP Germany, Uwe Kekeritz, Member of the German Bundestag v. KiK Textilien und Non-Food GmbH, Bönen (hereinafter "KiK"), C&A Mode GmbH & Co., Düsseldorf (hereinafter "C&A"), and Karl Rieker GmbH & Co. KG, Bodelshausen, Final Statement, November 2014.

[285] Ibid, 7.

[286] Ibid.

addressing human rights risks. In the case of the BTC Pipeline, the UK NCP highlighted the importance of local implementation of consultation and monitoring frameworks as part of HRDD.[287] While the overall BTC framework was considered to be in alignment with the OECD Guidelines, the UK NCP identified potential weaknesses in its execution at the local level, particularly in how complaints were handled.[288] The distinction made by the company between formal grievance mechanisms and other informal channels for raising complaints led to gaps in addressing local community concerns. In one specific region, this distinction contributed to significant delays and shortfalls in consultations with affected communities.[289] The UK NCP noted that for monitoring to be effective, it must be inclusive, ensuring that all voices, regardless of the form in which they are raised, are acknowledged and addressed in a timely manner.

Moreover, in two notable OECD cases—one handled by the Australian NCP and the other by the Swiss NCP—the OECD's case-handling mechanism was leveraged to significantly improve the companies' monitoring processes. For instance, also analysed earlier, in the case filed BWI against FIFA, the parties agreed to conduct joint labour inspections to monitor working conditions at FIFA World Cup related project sites.[290] Both FIFA and BWI recognised the importance of having a monitoring process that included the participation and representation of workers on the ground.[291] This agreement ensured that monitoring would not be a superficial exercise but would involve the active engagement of those directly affected by labour conditions. FIFA committed to using its leverage as far as permissible under domestic law to facilitate ongoing dialogue between BWI and the Supreme Committee, which oversees labour conditions on these sites. The MoU reached between the Supreme Committee and BWI on labour inspections was viewed as a positive outcome, signalling that joint efforts between corporate actors and labour representatives can lead to more effective monitoring processes.[292]

Similarly, in the case regarding the Cerrejón mine, the Swiss NCP facilitated important changes that strengthened the company's monitoring and engagement with local communities.[293] As part of the resolution, Cerrejón appointed an on-site Social Responsibility Manager and engaged an independent organisation to monitor the progress of its commitments, particularly in relation to addressing environmental and community concerns.[294] This independent oversight helped to ensure that Cerrejón's actions were properly evaluated and that improvements were tangible.

[287] NCP United Kingdom, Corner house et al., v. BTC Pipeline, Revised Final Statement, 22 February 2011.

[288] Ibid, 2.

[289] Ibid.

[290] NCP Switzerland, BWI v. FIFA, Final Statement, 2 May 2017, 3–4.

[291] Ibid, 3–6.

[292] Ibid, 4.

[293] NCP Switzerland, Individual v. Cerrejon Coal Mine, Columbia, Final Statement, 15 July 2009.

[294] Ibid, 6.

Furthermore, Cerrejón agreed to provide accurate and transparent environmental information to local communities, committing to engaging with them in a more meaningful way moving forward.[295]

Critically, both cases illustrated how the OECD NCP mechanism can be a powerful tool not just for resolving disputes but for strengthening corporate due diligence processes, particularly in monitoring of the implementation. In the case of FIFA, the inclusion of worker representation in the monitoring process highlighted the value of multi-stakeholder engagement, ensuring that those directly affected by labour conditions had a voice in how these conditions were assessed. This move towards joint inspections was a significant step forward in ensuring that monitoring is not merely top-down but incorporates input from the ground. On the other hand, the Cerrejón case demonstrated the importance of external, independent monitoring, which added credibility and transparency to the company's environmental and social commitments.

2.6 Communicating and Ensuring Transparency in Human Rights Policies

2.6.1 Importance of Transparent Communication: Building Trust with Stakeholders Through Public Reporting and Disclosure

The UNGPs stated that businesses must communicate effectively how they manage human rights impacts, highlighting the critical roles of transparency and accountability, particularly for those negatively affected by corporate actions.[296] Principle 21 of the UNGPs asserts that communication should reach the relevant audiences and provide sufficient detail to allow for a meaningful evaluation of the company's responses to human rights challenges.[297] These communications can take multiple forms, ranging from formal reports—such as human rights or corporate responsibility reports—to more informal methods, including social media updates. They may also involve direct stakeholder engagement, such as dialogue sessions, stakeholder meetings, or consultations.[298] This principle emphasises that transparency is not a one-size-fits-all approach but must be adapted to the nature of the audience and the severity of the impacts.

Similarly, the OECD Guidelines reinforce the expectation of HRDD and further promote transparency.[299] They urge businesses to disclose non-financial risks and

[295] Ibid.

[296] UN Guiding Principles on Business and Human Rights, Principle 21.

[297] Ibid.

[298] Ibid, Commentary to the Principle 21.

[299] OECD Guidelines for Multinational Enterprises, Chapter 3.

their impacts on employees and other stakeholders. The OECD Due Diligence Guidance goes further, stressing the importance of publicly sharing due diligence processes, findings, and actions.[300] This serves not only to help stakeholders evaluate a company's performance but also to build trust and foster collaboration in addressing and preventing future adverse impacts. The emphasis on transparency across both frameworks reflects a common understanding that open communication is essential for holding businesses accountable and driving change.

However, while these frameworks push companies towards greater transparency, the actual impact of such measures remains a subject of debate. Olga Martin-Ortega critiqued the reliance on transparency, noting that despite its centrality in the UNGPs and OECD Guidelines, it often leads to confusion when applied in due diligence processes.[301] Regulatory frameworks, such as the Duty of Vigilance Law and Modern Slavery Acts of the UK, Australia and Canada, often treat transparency as a catch-all solution for corporate accountability.[302] Yet, as she raised, important questions linger: Does transparency alone lead to accountability? Is it a voluntary practice, or should it be enforced as a binding obligation? These questions are crucial for understanding transparency's limitations, especially in global supply chains that are frequently designed to obscure harmful practices. Martin-Ortega also critiqued the over-reliance on transparency as a stand-alone tool, arguing that without accompanying accountability measures, transparency risks becoming superficial.[303]

This is clearly reflected in the implementation of non-financial reporting directives in the European Union and modern slavery legislation in the United Kingdom and Australia.[304] Despite these reporting obligations, the human rights records of many MNEs have not substantially improved, leading to widespread criticism.[305] Companies often disclose information to appear compliant without making meaningful changes to their operations or addressing the root causes of human rights abuses. McCorquodale, citing the Walk Free Foundation's report on asset managers, highlighted that fewer than one-third of UK asset management firms conducted any form of HRDD in their portfolio companies, despite being required to comply with the UK Modern Slavery Acts.[306] This lack of due diligence, coupled with inadequate or misleading public disclosures, creates a false appearance of compliance while allowing human rights violations to persist.[307] Further complicating the issue, McCorquodale highlighted the difficulties businesses face in communicating human rights risks due to fears of litigation or reputational damage.[308] For example,

[300] OECD Due Diligence Guidance, Section.5.1 and Q85.

[301] Martin-Ortega (2022), pp. 100–120.

[302] Ibid, 120.

[303] Ibid, 116.

[304] Ruehmkorf (2023), pp. 164–170.

[305] Ibid, 168.

[306] McCorquodale, *Business and Human Rights*, 172.

[307] Ibid.

[308] Ibid.

disclosing supply chain risks may expose companies to legal liabilities if their public statements are inconsistent with their actual efforts to address human rights issues.[309]

Bottom line, despite the proliferation of sustainability and human rights reporting over the past two decades, significant flaws remain in terms of quality, reliability, and comparability.[310] While the rise in reporting frameworks has brought greater attention to corporate responsibility, many reports fall short of providing meaningful insights or fostering genuine accountability. Issues such as selective transparency, lack of standardised metrics, and inconsistent third-party verification undermine the reliability and comparability of disclosures.[311] As a result, these reports often fail to drive substantive change, highlighting the need for stronger regulatory frameworks and standardized, independently verified reporting practices. Moreover, as highlighted by Martin-Ortega, communication and access to information extend beyond mere physical accessibility.[312] According to the OECD Guidelines and the Due Diligence Guidance, information must be presented in a manner that ensures it is understandable and disclosed in a timely fashion, using a format, language, and location that guarantee it reaches its intended audience and can be effectively utilised.[313]

The true intent of the UNGPs regarding reporting, transparency, and communication is more meaningful and nuanced. Buhmann provided a comparative analysis of the UNGPs and the EU Non-Financial Reporting Directive (NFRD), noting that while non-financial reports typically target external audiences, the UNGPs take a more comprehensive approach, prioritising communication with affected stakeholders, including those harmed by corporate actions.[314] According to the UNGPs, communication is integral to the entire HRDD process, not merely an after-the-fact accountability measure. In contrast to retrospective reporting, communication within the HRDD process takes a proactive stance, aiming to identify, prevent, or mitigate negative impacts before they escalate.[315] Moreover, communication within the HRDD framework should not be limited to formal reports. It should include direct engagement with affected stakeholders, such as in-person meetings or online discussions, to ensure ongoing accountability. This broader form of communication encourages continuous dialogue and builds trust, ultimately strengthening corporate responsibility.

Supporting this, some companies have reported positive outcomes from increased transparency. In empirical legal research conducted by several authors, semi-structured interviews were held with representatives from 10 companies to

---

[309] Ibid.

[310] Ruehmkorf (2023), p. 170.

[311] Ibid.

[312] Martin-Ortega (2022), p. 117.

[313] Ibid.

[314] Buhmann (2018), pp. 23–45 https://doi.org/10.1017/bhj.2017.24 (accessed 31 January 2026).

[315] Ibid.

understand how communication is implemented in practice.[316] One company shared that, despite initial internal resistance, publicly reporting on supply chain issues generated positive responses from stakeholders.[317] This, in turn, helped to educate internal teams and foster greater accountability within the organisation.[318] This example demonstrated that, when executed properly, transparency can drive internal improvements and build trust with external stakeholders.

In conclusion, while transparency remains a powerful tool for holding companies accountable, it is not sufficient on its own. For transparency to be effective, it must be part of a larger framework that includes genuine accountability mechanisms, continuous stakeholder engagement, and substantive corporate responsibility efforts. Without these elements, transparency risks becoming a hollow exercise that does little to protect affected rightsholders or address human rights risks meaningfully.

2.6.2 Case Studies: How Transparency in Human Rights Policies Has Strengthened Corporate Accountability in OECD Case Law

Communication is one of the most frequently emphasised steps in HRDD within OECD case law, receiving more extensive treatment compared to monitoring, prevention, and mitigation measures discussed in Sects. 2.4 and 2.5 of this chapter. In over 35 cases, NCPs have underlined the critical role of effective communication in the HRDD process, encompassing transparency and disclosure aligned with the OECD Guidelines. This includes references to Chapter 3 on Disclosure, as well as the communication responsibilities embedded within the risk-based due diligence framework of Chapter 3: General Policies and Chapter 4: Human Rights. In many cases, companies have fallen short in this area, prompting NCPs to issue general recommendations consistent with the OECD Guidelines. However, in some specific cases, NCPs have offered more detailed guidance to help companies enhance communication practices in the face of various challenges.

The analysis of corporate responsibility to disclose, communicate, and report on the HRDD process and findings in the OECD case law should be organised according to the different stakeholder groups, that companies are required to communicate with. As discussed above, companies should communicate with all relevant stakeholders, including workers, local communities, and any individuals affected by their business activities. In large number of cases under OECD NCP specific instances, the NCPs analysed and recommended companies how first they should communicate and disclose information with their own workers.

---

316 Smit et al. (2020), p. 963.

317 Ibid, 959.

318 Ibid, 954–955.

2.6.2.1 Communication with Workers

The first case to analyse involved a complaint filed by the Bank Workers Union of São Paulo against Itaú Unibanco S.A., a Brazilian MNE.[319] The Union alleged that Itaú Unibanco conducted mass layoffs starting in early 2011, specifically targeting older employees nearing retirement, and that it increased outsourcing practices, resulting in additional job losses. In response, the Brazilian NCP provided detailed guidance on how the company should communicate with employees, focusing on transparency and the type of information that employees are entitled to receive.[320]

The Brazilian NCP's recommendations emphasised that Itaú Unibanco should have voluntarily provided employees and their representatives with information enabling them to understand the company's structure, economic and financial outlook, employment trends, and anticipated operational changes, while respecting commercial confidentiality.[321] Additionally, the NCP advised the company to notify employees, their representatives, and government authorities of employment-impacting changes in advance, to mitigate adverse effects.[322] The NCP also emphasised the importance of fostering cooperation on shared interests. It noted that information on matters such as hiring and dismissal practices must be disclosed, and it encouraged the adoption of transparent policies to reduce staff turnover and support the relocation of workers who are dismissed. Lastly, the NCP urged Itaú Unibanco to ensure non-discriminatory practices in hiring, job assignment, compensation, promotion, and termination, aligning with relevant ILO conventions and recommendations on protecting older workers, maternity, and disability rights.[323] This case exemplifies how MNEs should communicate with employees on critical topics like organisational structure, financial health, employment changes, and non-discrimination practices, ensuring alignment with international labour standards. Specifically, the information about employment changes is essential for employees since it will adversely impact their livelihood so that they need to have information.

The Italian NCP addressed a similar issue in the case against Ball Beverage Packaging Italia, the Italian branch of the US-based MNE.[324] The company was accused of failing to provide adequate information to its employees regarding its sudden decision to close its San Martino sulla Marruccina plant.[325] After reviewing the case, the NCP highlighted that the closure would have a significant impact on the 70 employees at the plant and the surrounding community.[326] The NCP also

---

[319] NCP Brazil, The Trade Union Bank Workers Union of São Paulo, v. Itau-Unibanco Bank, Final Statement, 23 April 2013.

[320] Ibid, 2–3.

[321] Ibid, 3.

[322] Ibid.

[323] Ibid.

[324] NCP Chile, FIO-CGIL v. Ball Beverage Packaging, Initial Statement, 21 February 2019.

[325] Ibid.

[326] Ibid, 5.

noted that there was no evidence that Ball Beverage Packaging Italia had taken preventive measures to mitigate the risks associated with the plant's closure or to address the economic and social impacts on affected workers and the local area.[327] The NCP concluded that the issue was substantial and closely linked to the company's activities. Looking forward, the NCP recommended that Ball Beverage Packaging Italia involve all relevant workers, their representatives, and other stakeholders whenever making decisions regarding plant closures, reorganizations, or worker dismissals.[328] Additionally, the NCP advised that, in cases of closure or reorganisation, the company should promptly disclose information and conduct due diligence as outlined in the OECD Guidelines. This includes identifying, preventing, and mitigating any negative impacts on workers and other stakeholders, as well as providing an account of how these impacts are addressed.

Furthermore, there are other cases where NCPs have guided companies on how they should communicate with a stronger focus on the process itself. For example, the Belgian Minister of Enterprises filed a case to the Belgian NCP against the MNE Brink to determine whether it violated the OECD Guidelines, specifically the Employment Relations section.[329] This case centred on Brink's restructuring measures proposed in October 2010, following several years of negative financial results in Belgium. Brink communicated these measures to employee representatives at the end of October with a request for feedback by November 5, 2010.[330] In its analysis, the Belgium NCP highlighted that, although Brink did share information with employees, the response time given was unreasonably short. Additionally, the NCP noted that Brink's inadequate disclosure of economic and financial information impeded constructive social dialogue with employee representatives. This lack of transparency contravened the OECD Guidelines, which emphasises timely and open communication to foster trust and effective engagement between company and workers.[331]

The NCP further observed that the local board had limited bargaining power, especially during social mediation efforts, which hindered reaching a mutually acceptable solution. This imbalance demonstrated the need for mechanisms that strengthen the role of local boards and employee representatives in mediation processes.[332] In light of these findings, the NCP urged Brink to adhere to OECD Guidelines, specifically those advocating for transparent economic and financial disclosures and promoting constructive social dialogue. The NCP emphasised that even under challenging economic conditions, companies must uphold socially responsible business practices and meaningful consultations with social partners,

[327] Ibid, 5–6.

[328] Ibid, 6–7.

[329] NCP Belgium, Mr. Vincent Van Quickenborne, Minister for Enterprises v. Brink, Final Statement, 20 January 2011.

[330] Ibid, 2.

[331] Ibid.

[332] Ibid, 2–3.

reinforcing the importance of ethical conduct and strong worker engagement in responsible business operations.

One case that successfully exemplifies how companies can agree to communicate effectively with workers is the mediation between Sindicato de Trabajadores Compañía Minera Quebrada Blanca (Trade Union) and Teck Resources Chile Ltda. (Teck), facilitated by the Chilean NCP.[333] The case stemmed from the Trade Union's complaint regarding alleged violations by Teck in areas of labour relations, environmental practices, union rights, collective bargaining, and workplace health and safety at the Quebrada Blanca open-pit mine in Chile's Tarapacá region.[334] The Chilean NCP successfully facilitated mediation between the parties, resulting in an agreement. Teck committed to upholding workers' rights, particularly the right to freedom of association and collective bargaining. The company further agreed to foster fair, direct, and transparent communication with workers and their representatives. Furthermore, as a part of the agreement, the parties established mechanisms to strengthen communication channels, including a joint review process to assess the implementation of commitments, identify responsible actors, and set deadlines. The agreement formalised regular engagement through structured practices, such as monthly meetings between the trade union and senior HR management, where commitments, timelines, and monitoring mechanisms are jointly reviewed.[335] Additionally, quarterly presentations by the General Manager to union leaders and workers are now mandated, with feedback opportunities through mailboxes and other channels to enhance transparency and engagement. The agreement also included measures to raise awareness of complaint mechanisms on labour and harassment issues, complemented by training for union leaders and workers to ensure compliance with national regulations and internal policies. This case analysis highlights the importance of NCP-facilitated mediation in bridging gaps in effective engagement and addressing labour rights concerns between MNE and the rightsholders.

To sum up, these cases highlighted the necessity for companies to communicate and disclose relevant information in an adequate and timely manner to impacted stakeholders, including employees, especially during branch closures, mass layoffs, hiring practices, or outsourcing decisions. Across all cases, the NCPs emphasised the importance of transparent communication to mitigate potential negative impacts on workers and the value of good-faith engagement to build trust.

[333] NCP Chile, Quebrada Blanca Trade Union v. Teck, Final Statement, 7 February 2020.

[334] Ibid, 3.

[335] Ibid, 11–18.

2.6.2.2 Communication with Local Communities

Other NCP cases concerning corporate disclosure and communication frequently reiterate the importance of transparency with a wider range of stakeholders—extending beyond employees to include local communities, Indigenous Peoples, customers, and even the natural environment affected by corporate activities. In a notable case underscoring the importance of corporate communication with the public, Greenpeace filed a complaint with the Belgian NCP against Jan De Nul NV.[336] Greenpeace raised concerns over Jan De Nul's Sabetta Harbour project in the Russian Arctic, alleging that the company had failed to conduct thorough environmental due diligence, particularly regarding impacts on marine life and whale populations, and did not conduct environmental due diligence in line with the OECD Guidelines.[337]

In response, Jan De Nul hired a specialised firm to conduct an environmental assessment. However, the company withheld the findings from the public, citing confidentiality concerns. The NCP found that environmental information, by definition, does not constitute proprietary company data and, according to the OECD Guidelines, recommended that Belgian companies communicate potential environmental hazards to the public in a transparent manner to build trust, while respecting certain commercial and intellectual property rights.[338] Additionally, the NCP advised Jan De Nul to establish contacts with the International Union for Conservation of Nature to adopt best practices for detecting and mitigating risks to whales, such as turbulence, noise, and collision dangers. In connection with this case, the NCP plans to reach out to Belgian companies involved in ongoing phases of the Sabetta project.[339]

NCPs often recommend that companies publicly disclose accurate and timely information not only on their assessments and findings regarding potential and actual risks but also on their mitigation and preventive remedial actions. This is particularly essential in cases involving significant negative social, economic, and environmental impacts on local communities. In two cases filed with the Brazilian NCP against VALE S.A., the company was alleged to have violated the OECD Guidelines following the catastrophic Brumadinho dam failure in Minas Gerais on 25 January 2019.[340] These cases pointed out VALE's obligation to transparently disclose its remedial actions to the affected communities.

In the first case, property owners near the village of Pires claimed the dam collapse caused severe impacts, such as the halting of real estate developments, restricted property access due to increased traffic, and the contamination of the

[336] NCP Belgium, Greenpeace v. Jan De Nul NV, Final Statement, 24 November 2014.

[337] Ibid, 2.

[338] Ibid, 5.

[339] Ibid, 6.

[340] NCP Brazil, Carlos Cleber Guimarães Júnior and Carla de Laci França v.VALE S.A, Final Statement, 28 October 2021, NCP Brazil, Vila Solaris Hospedagens e Eventos, represented by Rogério Mário Ziviani Gomes v. VALE S.A, Final Statement, 5 May 2021.

Paraopeba River.[341] This contamination disrupted local economic activity and had profound social, economic, and psychological effects on the community. The second case involved allegations that VALE stopped paying agreed-upon rent in January 2020 and failed to provide compensation covering 'losses, moral damages, and lost profits' related to the suspension of activities at Vila Solaris.[342] Additionally, the complainants highlighted that the São Sebastião das Águas Claras business community was excluded from VALE's decision-making process and that no public information was provided regarding the risks posed by the B3 and B4 tailings dams.[343] Although this second case was resolved outside the NCP, both cases prompted the Brazilian NCP to issue recommendations urging VALE to adhere to OECD Guidelines and prioritize transparent communication with stakeholders.

The Brazilian NCP specifically recommended that VALE: (1) prepare and publish a report on the scope and effectiveness of its remedial measures at the individual, community, and societal levels; (2) disclose a list of national and international commitments relevant to the complaints, along with VALE's performance in relation to these commitments; and (3) conduct and publish a compliance diagnosis to assess how the company's governance aligns with OECD Guidelines.[344] These recommendations emphasised the importance of VALE maintaining open communication about its remediation efforts, ensuring that affected individuals and communities are informed and reassured about the steps taken to address both immediate and long-term impacts.

In numerous cases, NCPs have emphasised the essential need for effective communication with the local communities, particularly within the extractive industry, where operations often have adverse impacts on their human rights. NCPs frequently recommend that companies not only disclose their risk assessments and findings but also provide clear, timely, and accessible information on their mitigation efforts and preventive remedial actions.

The Canadian NCP, for instance, has addressed cases involving Endeavour Mining, China Gold, Barrick Gold, and Sun Peak, where mining activities led to significant socio-economic and environmental harm for local communities.[345] In the cases involving Endeavour Mining and Sun Peak, the NCP recommended that the companies enhance the transparency and the communication with the local communities.[346] Specifically, the NCP advised Endeavour Mining to publicly disclose actions taken in line with NCP recommendations, including specific health and safety measures at the Tabakoto mine, particularly those related to contractors'

---

341 Ibid, (Carlos Cleber Guimarães Júnior and Carla de Laci França), 4.

342 Ibid, (Vila Solaris), 3.

343 Ibid.

344 Ibid, 5.

345 NCP Canada, FENAME v. Endeavour Mining, Final Statement, 24 October 2017; NCP Canada, Individuals against Barrick Gold, Final Statement, 17 May 2024; United Tegaru Canada v. Sun Peak Metals Corp, Final Statement, 3 April 2024.

346 NCP Canada, FENAME v. Endeavour Mining, Final Statement, 24 October 2017.

activities on-site.[347] This recommendation highlighted the importance of transparency in occupational health and safety, especially regarding hazardous materials like lead, to reduce risks for both workers and nearby residents in the extractive industry.

However, the Canadian NCP has varied in its responses to the gravity of these impacts and in holding companies accountable. In the case of China Gold, accused of harming the environment and infringing on community rights in Tibet's Gyama Valley, the NCP imposed sanctions after China Gold refused to participate in mediation.[348] The sanctions rendered China Gold ineligible for official letters of support, commercial advocacy in foreign markets, and participation in government trade missions.[349] In other cases, such as Barrick Gold's, the NCP focused on recommendations rather than sanctions. Barrick Gold faced allegations of facilitating the killing of protestors by local security forces, but the NCP cited insufficient evidence due to limited investigation and did not substantiate some allegations.[350] Instead, the NCP advised Barrick Gold to consider disclosing more information on its engagement with government authorities regarding the 2021 resettlement and details of its relationship with local police and security forces, including any material support provided.[351] Additionally, the NCP encouraged Barrick Gold to engage with the local community to build awareness of the role of police in mine security, and to collaborate with local authorities in promoting respect for human rights in law enforcement activities related to the mine.

Other cases highlighted the importance of communication as a core element of risk-based due diligence in the extractive industry, crucial for maintaining transparency. In a case brought against Minera Candelaria with the Chilean NCP, the mining company was accused of causing continuous noise, pollution, and waste that significantly impacted the lives of the nearby local communities.[352] The case was closed when the company declined to participate in mediation; however, the NCP condemned the company's refusal, stating that it had missed an important opportunity to improve its relationship and build trust with the local communities by not engaging in dialogue. In its final statement, the NCP noted, 'Transparency lays the foundations for trust.'[353] It urged the company to create formal records of meetings and agreements with the community, approved by both parties, clearly detailing the issues discussed, commitments made, responsible officers, deadlines, and progress in fulfilling those commitments. This emphasis on transparency was echoed in the case against Shell by the Dutch NCP, where it highlighted the importance of making

---

[347] Ibid, para 35.

[348] NCP Canada, The Canada Tibet Committee v. China Gold International, Final Statement, 8 April 2015.

[349] Ibid, Analysis and Considerations.

[350] NCP Canada, Individuals v. Barrick Gold, Final Statement, 17 May 2024.

[351] Ibid, para 66.

[352] NCP Chile, A Group of 26 neighbours v. Minera Candelaria, Final Statement, 18 August 2022.

[353] Ibid, para 59, section IX.

information about corporate activities and their environmental impacts accessible to the public.[354] According to the Dutch NCP, transparency is essential for building public confidence and is most effective when paired with active consultation with stakeholders—including local communities and the wider public—thereby fostering long-term trust and mutual understanding on environmental issues.[355] The Dutch NCP further advised that enterprises should consider going beyond basic requirements in disclosing environmental information, setting a higher standard for open communication.

The French NCP, in proceedings involving the energy company Perenco, similarly emphasised the importance of communication with local communities in the extractive industry.[356] The NCP specifically recommended that Perenco disclose certain key information, advising that the company follow recommendations 1 to 4 of Chapter 3 of the OECD Guidelines, which cover the disclosure of financial, non-financial, and governance information.[357] To enhance Perenco France's Duty of Vigilance Plan and the Group's sustainability report, the NCP suggested including sector-specific standards—such as security, human rights, and environmental benchmarks—alongside objectives, indicators, and details on Perenco's due diligence mechanisms.[358] It also recommended that the Group publish both reports on its website for public access. These cases consistently reinforced the extractive industry's responsibility to actively communicate with local communities, especially regarding the social and environmental impacts of their operations, to build trust and foster long-term, and sustainable relationships.

Moreover, transparency is essential not only for companies in the extractive industry but also for those operating in conflict-affected areas. Companies in these regions must recognise the importance of effective communication with stakeholders, disclosing all relevant information about their potential involvement in human rights issues and their efforts to address them. This principle has been emphasised in the multiple OECD cases, including one against Mallee in the Australian NCP, a company operating in Israel under the Spanish NCP, and G4S operating in the OPT under the UK NCP.[359]

In some instances, NCPs have gone further, offering specific recommendations on stakeholder communication, such as ensuring that disclosed information is publicly accessible, free of financial barriers, and translated into local languages. This guidance has been highlighted in cases against PanAust in the Australian NCP,

---

[354] NCP Netherlands, Aminigboko Community v. the Shell Petroleum Development Company of Nigeria Limited and Shell Headquarters, Final Statement, 10 February 2023, 11.

[355] Ibid, 15.

[356] NCP France, ASF v. Perenco, Final Statement, 7 January 2022.

[357] Ibid, 8.

[358] Ibid.

[359] NCP Australia, Publish What You Pay Australia v. Mallee Resources Limited, Final Statement, 2 August 2023; NCP United Kingdom, LPHR v. G4S, Final Statement, March 2015; NCP Spain, Committee for Solidarity with the Arab Cause v. Spanish MNE, Final Statement (reclaimed), 6 October 2022.

Chevron in the Dutch NCP, Perenco in the French NCP, and ENRC in the UK NCP, underscoring the importance of making information easily accessible and understandable for local communities.[360]

In this section, OECD case law illustrated that companies—particularly those in the extractive industry or operating in conflict-affected areas—must maintain a high level of transparency and effective communication with local communities. This includes clearly conveying identified potential and actual risks and explaining the measures the company is taking to address them. NCPs emphasised that transparency in these interactions is essential for building and sustaining positive relationships with the affected local communities and the public, fostering trust, and ensuring long-term, cooperative engagement. NCPs also addressed that the information disclosed by companies must be detailed, easily understandable, and readily accessible to the public. This level of transparency ensures that local communities can fully grasp the potential and actual risks posed by corporate activities, as well as the steps being taken to address them.

2.7 Corporate Responsibility to Remediate: Grievance Mechanisms and Remedy

2.7.1 Corporate Responsibility to Remediate Human Rights Violations: Responsibilities under the UNGPs and OECD Guidelines

Under the UNGPs, Principle 22 and the OECD Guidelines, Chapter 2, Section 12 and Chapter IV, Section 6, companies have a proactive responsibility to remedy harms they have caused, or to engage in legitimate remediation processes for harms they have contributed to or are directly linked with.[361] Florencia S. Wegher Osci described this responsibility as positive and proactive, noting that in the OECD Due Diligence Guidance, remediation is an essential, integrated element of due diligence process.[362]

However, as discussed earlier in this book, mitigation and prevention measures, including leverage and disengagement actions by companies, can also be considered remedial approaches aimed at addressing and preventing adverse impacts, as

[360] NCP France, ASF v. Perenco, Final Statement, 7 January 2022; NCP Netherlands, FNV, ITF, PSI, IndustriALL Global Union v. Chevron Netherlands BV et al., Final Statement, 24 March 2022; NCP United Kingdom, Rights and Accountability in Development (RAID) v. ENRC, Final Statement, February 2016; NCP Australia, Project Sepik and Jubilee Australia Research Centre on behalf of Sepik River communities v. PanAust Limited, Final Statement, 3 October 2023.

[361] UN Guiding Principles on Business and Human Rights, Principle 22; OECD Guidelines for Multinational Enterprises, Chapter 2, Section 12 and Chapter IV, Section 6.

[362] Wegher Osci (2023), p. 172.

outlined in UNGPs Principle 19. In contrast, Principle 21 of the UNGPs emphasised that the need for companies to establish specific mechanisms for effective harm remediation.[363] Although the OECD Guidelines embed remediation responsibility in their six-step risk-based due diligence framework—especially in the final step—they lack an explicit requirement for a 'legitimate process' for remediation, as highlighted in the UNGPs.[364] The OECD Due Diligence Guidance recommends that when a company identifies it has caused or contributed to adverse impacts, it should, where possible, seek to restore affected persons to their original position, ensuring remediation aligns with the impact's scale and significance.[365]

The UNGPs use of the term 'legitimate process' in Principle 22 underlines the importance of establishing grievance mechanisms to provide or support remediation process. Newton argued that Principle 22 implies companies must either create their own grievance mechanisms or work with other mechanisms to fulfil this obligation.[366] Furthermore, Osci noted that 'remediation' in Principle 22 includes state-based judicial and non-judicial mechanisms as well as company-based grievance mechanisms.[367] Pillar 3 of the UNGPs highlighted that the operation of these mechanisms, with Principle 29 detailing how businesses should set up structures for remediation, requiring that these mechanisms be effective.[368] UNGPs Principle 31 sets out essential criteria for effective non-judicial grievance mechanisms, covering both state and non-state-based systems.[369] Newton described these criteria as a 'benchmark for designing, revising, or assessing a non-judicial grievance mechanism to ensure its practical effectiveness,' which requires a holistic approach to function well in practice.[370]

Many scholars, including Martijn Scheltema, Newton, McCorquodale, and Muchlinski, emphasised the advantages of effective grievance mechanisms, benefiting both victims and companies.[371] For victims, corporate grievance mechanisms (CGMs) offer practical advantages over judicial processes, such as faster resolution, lower costs, and cross-border accessibility. For companies, these mechanisms allow early, direct handling of grievances, helping prevent escalation and reducing potential harm. Newton highlighted that CGMs provide insights into complaint patterns and trends, which can improve human rights due diligence processes, allowing companies to adjust business practices accordingly.[372] Scheltema added that these

---

[363] UN Guiding Principles on Business and Human Rights, Principle 21.

[364] Ibid, Principle 22.

[365] The OECD Due Diligence Guidance, Section 6.2 and Q48-Q51.

[366] Newton, The Business of Human Rights: Best Practice and the UN Guiding Principles, 114.

[367] Wegher Osci (2023), p. 172.

[368] UN Guiding Principles on Business and Human Rights, Principle 29.

[369] Ibid, Principle 31.

[370] Newton (2019), p. 118.

[371] Scheltema (2023), pp. 222–229; Newton (2019), p. 118; McCorquodale, *Business and Human Rights*, 220–222, Muchlinski (2022), pp. 142–145.

[372] Ibid Newton (2019), p. 117.

mechanisms foster continuous learning, helping companies identify root causes of adverse impacts and promoting meaningful, effective dialogue between businesses and victims.[373]

However, scholars noted that few companies implement CGMs effectively, and even fewer address adverse impacts comprehensively. This may be due to companies' limited knowledge of how to operate these mechanisms effectively, as well as victims' lack of trust in mechanisms managed by the companies responsible for the harm. For example, Muchlinski questioned whether CGMs can truly provide fair, effective remediation, especially in weak governance zones where legal remedies are limited, potentially making these mechanisms the primary redress.[374] In countries with robust legal systems, however, these mechanisms can effectively complement judicial options, though they still may disadvantage local communities.

For CGMs to be genuinely effective, they must be accessible, gender-sensitive, and protect complainants from retaliation. Scheltema observed that even when operational, these mechanisms often fall short of providing full remediation, with compensation frequently limited to specific forms, like salary reimbursements.[375] McCorquodale highlighted some innovative approaches companies are adopting, such as smartphone apps linked to worker voice programs, which help educate community members on human rights and collect data. For example, the app might ask workers about their freedom to leave jobs or whether they need to pay their employers, aiding in addressing issues like forced labour.[376]

Despite progress, many companies still lack a full understanding of how to operate effective CGMs. According to the 2023 CHRB results, 91% of companies now offer grievance mechanisms for workers, and 76% for external stakeholders—an increase from 83% and 46% in 2017, respectively.[377] While the availability of these mechanisms is encouraging, CHRB notes that many still fall short in quality.[378] Currently, only 5% of companies in the CHRB 2023 report demonstrated efforts to foster trust among rightsholders, and just 10% show a commitment to rightsholder ownership, indicating a significant engagement gap.[379]

Encouragingly, the recently adopted CSDDD includes a dedicated article requiring covered companies to establish CGMs. Article 14 of the CSDDD mandates Member States to ensure companies provide a transparent, accessible complaint and notification mechanism, allowing affected persons, representatives, and civil society organisations to raise concerns about adverse impacts from the company's

---

373 Ibid Scheltema, 225.

374 Ibid Muchlinski, 143.

375 Ibid Scheltema, 226.

376 McCorquodale, *Business and Human Rights*, 223.

377 CHRB, Corporate human Rights Benchmark 2023 report, November 2023, 14, https://assets.worldbenchmarkingalliance.org/app/uploads/2024/03/2023_Corporate_Human_Rights_Benchmark__Insights_Report_13Mar2024.pdf (accessed 31 January 2026).

378 Ibid, 14–15.

379 Ibid, 14.

operations or supply chain.[380] It requires companies to protect complainants' identities, prevent retaliation, and respond to substantiated complaints with appropriate action. Complainants are also entitled to follow-up, explanations, and meetings with company representatives.[381] Companies may fulfil these obligations individually or collaboratively, without restricting complainants' rights to seek further legal or non-judicial remedies.[382] However, while article 12 of the CSDDD requires companies to engage stakeholders during due diligence processes like monitoring and risk assessment, it does not specify that stakeholders must be consulted on the effective operation of complaint and notification mechanisms.[383] Considering the CSDDD requirement on the establishment of the corporate based grievance mechanism, James Harrison, Mark Wielga, and Margarita Parejo warned that mHRDD laws could lead to a rise in ineffective corporate grievance mechanisms, creating a confusing and burdensome landscape for rightsholders.[384] They argued that effective monitoring is essential to distinguish well-functioning CGMs from ineffective ones and to raise standards across the board.[385]

In conclusion, while frameworks like the UNGPs, OECD Guidelines, and the CSDDD mark significant steps towards embedding effective grievance mechanisms and remediation responsibilities within corporate practices, achieving genuine accountability and trust will ultimately depend on companies' commitment to operationalise these mechanisms transparently and responsively, bridging gaps between policy intent and practical impact for affected communities.

2.7.2 Best Practices for Redress: Insights from OECD Case Law on Effective Corporate Grievance Mechanisms

Out of 394 cases, this research identified 32 in which NCPs addressed, in some form, how companies should fulfil their responsibility to remediate harms they caused, contributed to, or are associated with. As previously discussed in Sect. 2.4, very few cases found that a company directly caused harm—primarily in labour-related cases, such as those involving failure to recognise the right to collective bargaining. In most instances, NCPs concluded that companies may have contributed to the harm or, more commonly, were linked to it. Consequently, numerous cases emphasised how NCPs advise companies to cooperate in remediation efforts in line with the OECD Guidelines. For example, in cases involving TEPN with the Norwegian NCP and Shell and PvM with the Dutch NCP, the NCPs noted that,

[380] Corporate Sustainability Due Diligence Directive, Article 14.

[381] Ibid.

[382] Ibid.

[383] Ibid, Article 12.

[384] Harrison et al. (2024) https://doi.org/10.1093/jhuman/huae011 (accessed 31 January 2026).

[385] Ibid, 832.

because these companies were linked to the harms, they held a responsibility to cooperate in remediation efforts.[386] Additionally, the NCPs highlighted the need for these companies to leverage their influence on direct partners causing the harm to help provide remediation for victims.

In the case against TEPN involving the Samsung crane incident, the Norwegian NCP suggested that, although TEPN was not directly responsible, it could still facilitate remediation.[387] However, despite discussions, remediation did not ultimately occur. In contrast, other cases involving companies linked to harm through business relationships or investments—such as the case against ANZ with the Australian NCP and the case against Bralima Heineken with the Dutch NCP—led to financial compensation for victims, though only after the NCP proceedings had concluded.[388] These examples demonstrate that while NCPs can encourage companies to engage in remediation, the outcomes often depend on the willingness of companies to act beyond formal obligations, especially in cases where they are not the direct cause.

In these 32 cases, NCPs frequently evaluated CGMs—such as notification and complaint systems—for alignment with OECD Guidelines and the effectiveness criteria outlined in the UNGPs. A prominent example is the German NCP's case against Adidas, where complainants alleged that Adidas neglected its responsibilities under the OECD Guidelines by failing to address anti-union practices, layoffs, and wage issues at a subcontractor's factory in Indonesia, which was previously already discussed in this book.[389] In this case, the German NCP recommended that Adidas review its reporting and complaint channels, working with stakeholders (such as trade unions, workers, and business partners) to (1) identify obstacles that may deter individuals from using these channels and (2) explore ways to improve their effectiveness.[390] This case highlighted the NCP's role in assessing grievance mechanisms and providing actionable recommendations to enhance accessibility and effectiveness.

---

[386] NCP Norway, Samsung Heavy Industries Martin Linge Project Crane Accident Workers Support Team and Korean Transnational Corporations Watch v. Totalenergies E&P Norge As, Equinor Asa, Technip Energies N.V., Final Statement, 22 February 2023; NCP France, Unite Here v. Natixis/NGAM, Final Statement, 5 December 2017; NCP Netherlands, IUF v. Perfetti Van Melle, Final Statement, 15 June 2020; NCP Netherlands, Aminigboko Community v. the Shell Petroleum Development Company of Nigeria Limited and Shell Headquarters, Final Statement, 10 February 2023, 11.

[387] NCP Norway, Samsung Heavy Industries Martin Linge Project Crane Accident Workers Support Team and Korean Transnational Corporations Watch v. Totalenergies E&P Norge As, Equinor Asa, Technip Energies N.V., Final Statement, 22 February 2023; NCP France, Unite Here v. Natixis/NGAM, Final Statement, 5 December 2017.

[388] NCP Australia, Equitable Cambodia and Inclusive Development International on behalf of 681 Cambodian families v. Australian and New Zealand Banking Group (ANZ), Final Statement, 27 June 2018; NCP Netherlands, Former employees v. Bralima, Heineken, Final Statement, 18 August 2017.

[389] NCP Germany, SÜDWIND Institut, Sedane Labour Resource Centre (Lembaga Informasi Perburuhan Sedane, (LIPS"), Bogor (West Java, Indonesia), Clean Clothes Campaign v. Adidas, Final Statement, 14 March 2018. Furthermore, see section 2.4.2.1.3 C section of this chapter.

[390] Ibid, 14.

Another example involves the BTC Pipeline, reviewed by the UK NCP, where a complaint alleged that BTC exerted undue influence over regulatory frameworks, sought exemptions from social, labour, tax, and environmental laws, failed to contribute to sustainable development, inadequately consulted affected communities, and undermined the host government's ability to address environmental and safety risks.[391] In this case, the NCP identified weaknesses in BTC's consultation and monitoring processes, particularly due to BTC's distinction between formal grievance channels and informal complaints.[392] In one region, this approach led to inadequate consultations, resulting in the company's failure to address local security force intimidation against communities, thus undermining the grievance process.[393] The NCP concluded that BTC's actions in this region did not fully align with the Guidelines. In these cases, the NCPs sought to understand how CGMs operate and how they can be better aligned with the OECD Guidelines and the UNGPs.[394]

A notable example within the OECD case law showcasing effective grievance mechanisms is the complaint against Australian Laboratory Services (ALS).[395] ALS was accused of violating the rights of Malian laboratory workers, including the unjust dismissal of 135 workers, among them all union leaders.[396] The complaint further alleged that ALS mishandled workers' health concerns, which reportedly stemmed from exposure to hazardous substances such as lead in the workplace. In response to these allegations from one of the employees, the Australian NCP observed that ALS engaged constructively with the concerns raised, both internally and through external complaint mechanisms.[397] The notifier had initially flagged health and safety concerns through ALS's whistleblower hotline, which prompted senior ALS representatives to travel to Mali to contact the notifier directly.[398] Subsequently, ALS implemented several improvements, including translating geochemistry procedures and ensuring employees received their medical test results. ALS also actively participated in the Australian NCP's processes to address employment and health and safety issues. This case highlights ALS's proactive measures to prevent future incidents, with the company acknowledging that its Bamako site was not fully integrated into ALS's Health and Safety program until the end of 2008, despite being acquired in 2006.[399] Recognising the need for prompt alignment with group standards, ALS now enforces a 100-day integration program for all newly

[391] NCP United Kingdom, Corner house et al., v. BTC Pipeline, Revised Final Statement, 22 February 2011.

[392] Ibid, 17.

[393] Ibid.

[394] Ibid, 19.

[395] NCP Australia, Mr. Yacouba Traoré on behalf of the Former Employees Collective of the Australian Laboratory Services Mali SARL Laboratory Group v. Australian Laboratory Services (ALS), Final Statement, 8 March 2019.

[396] Ibid, 3.

[397] Ibid, 10–11.

[398] Ibid.

[399] Ibid, 13.

acquired sites.[400] This case illustrated the potential for companies to act swiftly on issues raised through their CGMs.

Similarly, the case against Walmart, reviewed by the Chilean NCP, highlighted Walmart's effective complaint notification mechanism.[401] A request for review was submitted to the Chilean NCP, alleging that Walmart had violated the Guidelines related to the Chapter 2: General Policies and 8: Consumer Interests.[402] The submission cited 'undue charges applied by the enterprise' as a key issue. The Chilean NCP commended Walmart for its willingness to address the issues raised and made several recommendations to enhance its approach.[403] Specifically, the NCP acknowledged the 'Supplier Ombudsman' mechanism, noting it as a good practice that serves as a formal and open channel for supplier complaints.[404] It recommended that this channel also support inquiries on contractual terms, thereby fostering ongoing dialogue with suppliers and reducing potential disputes. The NCP further advised periodic assessments of the mechanism, including supplier feedback, to ensure its effectiveness and incorporate necessary improvements. Additionally, the NCP recommended that Walmart consider incorporating staggered dispute settlement clauses or alternative dispute resolution mechanisms to provide third-party mediation if issues remain unresolved by the Supplier Ombudsman, without limiting access to legal or competition bodies.

In some instances, the NCP mediation process itself has facilitated the establishment or enhancement of grievance mechanisms between parties to address issues raised in complaints. Notably, three cases involving FIFA, BKW Group, and Syngenta illustrated this impact.[405] During NCP proceedings, the parties discussed the effectiveness of these companies' existing grievance mechanisms. In the cases of BKW Group and Syngenta, the NCPs recommended improvements to make the mechanisms more accessible and transparent, aligning with key criteria under the UNGPs. For BKW Group, it was highlighted that these mechanisms should also be accessible to indigenous groups and other potentially affected communities.

In the case against FIFA, filed by the BWI, both parties recognised the importance of FIFA's newly established Human Rights Advisory Board, created to advise FIFA's administration on various human rights issues, including those related to the World Cup.[406] BWI acknowledged that FIFA would invite a BWI representative to

---

[400] Ibid.

[401] NCP Chile, Arpal Spa v. Walmart, Final Statement, 20 May 2021.

[402] Ibid, 3–4.

[403] Ibid, 15.

[404] Ibid.

[405] NCP Switzerland, BWI v. FIFA, Final Statement, 2 May 2017; NCP Switzerland 'Final Statement: Specific Instance regarding BKW Group submitted by the Society for Threatened Peoples Switzerland' 26 August 2021; NCP Switzerland, Maharashtra Association of Pesticide Poisoned Persons, Pesticide Action Network India, Public Eye, European Centre for Constitutional and Human Rights, Pesticides Action Network Asia Pacific v. Syngenta AG, Final Statement, 16 June 2022.

[406] NCP Switzerland, BWI v. FIFA, Final Statement, 2 May 2017.

join this oversight body. Since 2017, the Advisory Board has been issuing recommendations to FIFA biannually. Additionally, the parties addressed the effectiveness of grievance mechanisms for workers involved in World Cup-related projects in Qatar, agreeing that some existing local procedures were inadequate and should be reviewed and improved. FIFA committed to addressing this matter further in a proposed meeting with the Supreme Committee and BWI in Doha.

Another example is the case involving Sjøvik AS, mediated by the Norwegian NCP, where the company was accused of disregarding the rights of the Saharawi people by investing in a Moroccan company allegedly infringing on Western Sahara's right to self-determination.[407] As part of the mediation outcome, Sjøvik committed to conducting an environmental and social impact assessment for its activities in line with OECD Guidelines.[408] For ongoing follow-up, Sjøvik also agreed to establish an internal grievance mechanism to address both internal and external concerns or suggestions for improvement.[409] This mechanism would be aligned with OECD Guidelines, appropriately scaled to the company's size, and designed to receive complaints from anyone affected by its operations.

Additionally, although outside of formal NCP proceedings, the NCP process helped facilitate an agreement that established a grievance mechanism in the case against G-Star International BV with the Dutch NCP.[410] This case involved G-Star's supplier, Fibres & Fabrics International (FFI), and its subsidiary, Jeans Knit Pvt. Ltd. (JKPL), concerning alleged violations of collective bargaining rights. The Dutch government offered to mediate between the NGOs, their internet providers, and FFI. Since the NCP procedure focused solely on the complaint against G-Star, and with G-Star's announcement to end its relationship with FFI, the NCP deferred to the Dutch government's mediation, led by Minister of State Ruud Lubbers, to address the remaining issues. Ultimately, the parties agreed to establish an 'ombudsman' in Bangalore, in cooperation with local Indian organizations and trade unions, to handle future complaints from FFI/JKPL employees.[411] Consequently, FFI withdrew all legal actions, and the complainants ended their campaigns against FFI/JKPL and G-Star. After productive consultations, G-Star resumed its commercial relationship with FFI, securing the employment of Indian workers. The complainants also withdrew their specific instance complaint against G-Star from the NCP process.[412] This case, with the support of the Dutch government, exemplifies one of the constructive outcomes possible through the NCP process, showcasing how effective mediation can yield long-term grievance mechanisms that benefit all parties involved.

---

[407] NCP Norway, Norwegian Support Committee for Western Sahara v. Sjøvik AS, Final Statement, 3 July 2013.

[408] Ibid, 5.

[409] Ibid.

[410] NCP Netherlands, Clean Clothes Campaign and Landelijke India Werkgroep (India Committee of the Netherlands, LIW) v. G-Star International BV, Final Statement, 6 April 2008.

[411] Ibid, 2.

[412] Ibid.

Furthermore, in cases such as the complaint against Rockwool with the Danish NCP, the NCP evaluated the company's actions through the lens of remedial responsibility.[413] Specifically, the Danish NCP acknowledged that Rockwool had documented improvements by addressing issues that arose during the project. NCP Denmark recognised Rockwool's efforts to rectify the situation by enhancing internal risk management processes concerning societal impacts, engaging with the local communities, and implementing voluntary measures to address community concerns.[414] The Danish NCP concluded that these measures qualify as acts of remedy in accordance with the OECD Guidelines.[415] Similarly, in the case against PvM, the Dutch NCP responded to a request from the IUF to elaborate on the concept of remedy. The NCP observed that the parties had not reached an agreement on whether child labour had occurred in PvM's factory.[416] Due to the limitations of the procedure, the NCP was unable to verify the existence of child labour with certainty. Nevertheless, the NCP emphasised that, under the OECD Guidelines, access to remedy is a responsibility for MNEs. Referring to the OECD Due Diligence Guidance, the NCP highlighted that 'the type of remedy or combination of remedies that is appropriate will depend on the nature and extent of the adverse impact and may include: […] educational programs... [and] measures to prevent future adverse impacts.'[417] The Dutch NCP noted positively that PvM had decided to phase out its relationship with Rahat Corporation, which had been identified as a complicating factor in this case. These cases illustrate how NCP assess companies' compliance with OECD Guidelines by identifying the types of actions that qualify as remedial responsibilities.

2.8 Engaging Stakeholders in Corporate Human Rights Responsibilities

2.8.1 Fostering Meaningful Engagement: Strategic Approaches to Collaboration Under the UNGPs and OECD Guidelines

Effective HRDD is fundamentally rooted in meaningful stakeholder engagement, where the term 'meaningful' takes on critical importance. The UNGPs embed the concept of meaningful stakeholder engagement (MSE) within their framework for due diligence process. Under Principles 17 and 18, companies are required to

413 NCP Netherlands, West Virginians for Sustainable Development v. Rockwool International A/S, Final Statement, 3 June 2021.

414 Ibid, 10.

415 Ibid, 11.

416 NCP Netherlands, IUF v. Perfetti Van Melle, Final Statement, 15 June 2020.

417 Ibid.

include stakeholder perspectives in their assessment of actual or potential adverse impacts—whether through their own operations or business relationships.[418] As Buhmann, Alberto Fonseca, Nathan Andrews and Giuseppe Amatulli stated, this mandate for engagement emphasises not merely legally mandated consultations but as clarified by the OHCHR, prioritises genuine dialogue, fostering a more inclusive and comprehensive approach to risk assessment.[419]

Scholars Claire Bright and Céline da Graça Pires highlighted that for companies mapping supply chain risks beyond Tier 1, it is essential to focus on dialogue and engagement with suppliers and sub-suppliers who present a higher risk to human rights.[420] This concept, centred on dialogue-based approach, is further reinforced in the OECD Guidelines and the OECD Due Diligence Guidance. The OECD Guidelines, Chapter 2, paragraph 16 instructed companies to engage substantively with relevant stakeholders or their legitimate representatives, ensuring that their insights are factored into activities that could significantly impact them.[421] Furthermore, Chapter IV's commentary paragraph 45 emphasised that companies should pay special attention to the unique needs of specific groups or individuals who may be particularly vulnerable to adverse impacts, such as human rights defenders or Indigenous Peoples.[422] However, both the UNGPs and the OECD Guidelines leave the concept of who qualifies as stakeholders open to interpretation; however, they place particular emphasis on women, human rights defenders, and Indigenous Peoples and other groups. The OECD Due Diligence Guidance for Meaningful Stakeholder Engagement in the Extractive Sector (OECD Guidance for MSE) emphasises that engaging with Indigenous Peoples and local communities constitutes an external stakeholder engagement, often demanding additional sensitivity and effort.[423] Companies must account for cultural and linguistic factors in communication and be mindful of community power dynamics, applying a gender-sensitive approach where relevant.[424]

Specifically, engagement with Indigenous communities requires companies to acknowledge certain key aspects: Indigenous governance structures, their rights to self-determination, their cultural and spiritual ties to land, the historical discrimination they have faced, and their distinct societal and legal positions.[425] These unique characteristics necessitate careful consideration in stakeholder engagement strategies to ensure respect for Indigenous People's rights and cultural heritage, as well

---

418 UN Guiding Principles on Business and Human Rights, Commentary to the Principles 17 and 18.

419 Buhmann et al. (2025), p. 8.

420 Bright and da Graça Pires (2023), p. 138.

421 The OECD Guidelines for Multinational Enterprises. Chapter 2: General Policies, Section 16.

422 Ibid, Chapter IV: Human Rights, Commentary para 45.

423 The OECD Due Diligence Guidance for Meaningful Stakeholder Engagement (MSE) in the Extractive Sector (OECD Guidance for MSE), OECD 2017, https://www.oecd.org/en/publications/2017/02/oecd-due-diligence-guidance-for-meaningful-stakeholder-engagement-in-the-extractive-sector_g1g65995.html> (accessed 31 January 2026).

424 Ibid, Annex B. Engaging with Indigenous Peoples.

425 Ibid.

as compliance with international and, in some cases, specific national legal protections. Extractive activities affecting the Indigenous groups should remain fully aware of these unique factors to foster truly meaningful engagement. In addition, beyond Indigenous Peoples, companies must also engage with other local communities. Edward Freeman and Prem S. Menghwar highlighted that the existence of numerous communities, many of which—such as Indigenous groups and those in rural or remote areas—face particular vulnerabilities.[426] They argue that there is no single, universal strategy that can effectively address the diverse needs of each community. Instead, tailored approaches are essential to address their unique concerns.[427] Each community requires a distinct approach, and understanding the internal power dynamics is crucial.[428] Moreover, it is necessary to consider the regulations and frameworks required to balance stakeholder power and promote sustainable outcomes.[429] Developing a deeper understanding of how organisations engage with their communities will strengthen our ability to support and sustain these communities effectively.[430] However, there is a notable lack of empirical and comprehensive research on this topic. Further studies are needed to examine the specific methods and practices companies employ, as well as the challenges, risks, and benefits associated with each approach.

When it comes to a particular focus on how to engage, MSE goes beyond simple communication; it requires companies to structure interactions in a way that ensures stakeholders feel genuinely valued and considered throughout both the process and outcome. Without this approach, impact assessments—and any subsequent corrective actions—will lack the comprehensive perspective needed to accurately identify and address risks. The 2023 update to the OECD Guidelines pointed out this by elevating MSE as not only integral to due diligence but, in some instances, 'a right in and of itself'.[431] Additionally, it emphasises that the level of engagement should correspond to the degree of impact on stakeholders.[432] Relevant stakeholders include individuals or groups potentially affected by the company's activities, such as local communities and others impacted by government or corporate actions. Moreover, the OECD Guidelines highlight the importance of recognising intersecting risks, particularly those affecting marginalised or vulnerable groups, to ensure a fully inclusive approach to stakeholder engagement.[433]

Looking from above, both the UNGPs and OECD guidance documents consistently highlighted the necessity of understanding risks and impacts from the affected

---

[426] Freeman and Menghwar (2024), pp. 43–55.

[427] Ibid, 52–53.

[428] Ibid.

[429] Ibid.

[430] Ibid.

[431] OECD Guidelines for Multinational Enterprises, Chapter 2: General Policies, commentary para 28.

[432] Ibid.

[433] Ibid.

individuals' perspective. Bright and da Graça Pires noted that HRDD under the UNGPs differs from traditional corporate due diligence by prioritising risks to people over risks to the business itself, emphasising the involvement of rights holders.[434] According to McCorquodale and Nolan, the effectiveness of HRDD hinges on robust stakeholder participation, where a defining measure of success is the ability to establish mechanisms for rights holders—such as workers and local communities—to question and influence corporate practices meaningfully.[435]

Recent mHRDD legislations increasingly draw on the definitions provided by the UNGPs and OECD Guidelines as authoritative frameworks for due diligence requirements. The newly adopted CSDDD exemplified this approach, incorporating specific articles that mandate meaningful stakeholder engagement within its due diligence process.[436] Article 13 of the CSDDD provides detailed guidance on when and how companies should engage stakeholders and Article 3.1 (n) defines the groups to be involved.[437] Article 13 requires companies to engage with stakeholders at critical stages of due diligence, such as during the gathering of information on actual or potential adverse impacts for the identification, assessment, and prioritization process as specified in Articles 8 and 9; in the development of prevention and corrective action plans, both standard and enhanced, as set out in Articles 10 and 11; in decision-making around terminating or suspending business relationships; in adopting appropriate remediation measures to address negative impacts under Article 12; and when creating qualitative and quantitative indicators for monitoring progress under Article 15.[438] When effective stakeholder engagement is not feasible, the Directive allows companies to consult credible experts who can provide insights into potential or actual adverse impacts. Additionally, companies are required to address any engagement barriers to ensure the process is meaningful, protecting participants from any form of retaliation by safeguarding confidentiality or anonymity where necessary.

The Directive's Article 3.1(n) extends the definition of 'stakeholders' to include not only the company's employees and their representatives but also those indirectly impacted by the company's activities, including communities, entities, and individuals affected by its operations, subsidiaries, and business partners.[439] This broader definition covers employees of business partners, trade unions, national human rights and environmental institutions, civil society organisations, and legitimate representatives of affected groups.

While the CSDDD highlighted the importance of comprehensive engagement by mandating a broad inclusion of voices throughout the due diligence process—requiring in-depth consultation and protections against retaliation to promote

---

434 Bright and da Graça Pires (2023), p. 139.

435 McCorquodale and Nolan (2021), pp. 474–475.

436 Corporate Sustainability Due Diligence Directive.

437 Ibid, Article 13.

438 Ibid, Article 15.

439 Ibid, Article 3.1(n).

transparency and accountability—it leaves stakeholder engagement out of CGMs. This omission limits the Directive's potential for fostering a fully aligned approach between corporate activities, human rights, and sustainability goals, though it does position stakeholder engagement as both a strategic and ethical priority. Furthermore, although the CSDDD attempts to incorporate various marginalised groups within its stakeholder framework, the limited material scope of the Directive ultimately excludes Indigenous Peoples and migrant workers from this definition, as previously discussed in this book.[440]

From a practical perspective, effectively implementing these principles presents significant challenges. Wettstein argued that, for stakeholder involvement to be genuinely impactful, companies must conduct on-the-ground human rights assessments, engaging directly with affected individuals to understand their concerns firsthand.[441] This critical task, however, is laden with obstacles: identifying true community representatives is complex, as communities often encompass diverse and sometimes conflicting interests.[442] Building trust among these varied groups is both essential and delicate, requiring ongoing and sensitive engagement to avoid setbacks. HRDD's stakeholder framework extends beyond local communities and individual workers to include CSOs, advocacy groups, suppliers, subcontractors, and the broader workforce. The OECD Guidelines, especially within the Chapter 8: Consumer Interests, broaden this concept further by including end-users and customers in the downstream supply chain.[443] This expansive network of stakeholders illustrates HRDD's complexity, where fostering genuine, trust-based engagement requires addressing the distinct needs and vulnerabilities of each group involved.

As HRDD practices evolve, companies are increasingly encouraged to focus on the most marginalised groups within their supply chains—those facing the highest risks of exclusion. However, a recent CHRB report highlighted a concerning gap: among the top 112 global companies, while 61% have implemented a human rights due diligence process, only 27% directly engaged with rightsholders.[444] CHRB contended that this shortfall raises questions about the true effectiveness of these efforts, as direct engagement with rightsholders is crucial for shaping meaningful HRDD practices that genuinely address human rights challenges.[445]

Companies that prioritise this level of engagement go beyond mere communication to foster an environment where stakeholder perspectives are genuinely valued. As conceptualised by Buhmann, Fonseca, Andrews, and Amatulli, 'meaningful' engagement is genuine, inclusive, process-driven, and technically sound, while 'engagement' itself implies a two-way, interactive, and adaptive dialogue that

---

[440] See Sect. 2.3 of this chapter.

[441] Wettstein (2022), pp. 162–163.

[442] Ibid.

[443] OECD Guidelines for Multinational Enterprises, Chapter 8: Consumer Interest, Sections 2, 3 and 4.

[444] CHRB, 2023 Corporate Human Rights Benchmark, 12.

[445] Ibid.

extends beyond one-off consultations.[446] When the concept of MSE is rigorously applied within HRDD, it transforms due diligence from a compliance measure into a proactive corporate culture that actively safeguards human rights and promotes responsible business practices.[447] The OECD case law further supports this commitment to MSE, as various NCP have advocated for and upheld meaningful stakeholder engagement in real-world cases, underscoring its critical role in driving ethical, rights-oriented business practices.

2.8.2 *Case Studies in Effective Stakeholder Engagement: Key Insights from OECD Case Law Across Industries*

The OECD case law placed significant emphasis on stakeholder engagement, with over 60 out of 394 cases examining and providing recommendations to companies on fostering MSE practices. These cases often delve into identifying which groups should be recognised as stakeholders, with various NCPs highlighting groups such as workers and Indigenous Peoples as essential stakeholders for companies to focus on meaningfully. In other cases, the OECD provides specific guidance on how companies should engage stakeholders, outlining concrete actions to ensure genuine involvement. The cases also assess the quality of existing stakeholder engagement efforts, evaluating whether a company's engagement approach can be deemed effective (See Fig. 2.3). Based on this extensive analysis, this section on stakeholder engagement in the OECD case law will be organised into three key subsections: defining the stakeholder, effective methods of engagement, and evaluating the effectiveness of stakeholder engagement.

2.8.2.1 Identifying Stakeholders

This subsection will focus on how NCPs have analysed and advised companies on identifying stakeholders, offering guidance on whom to prioritise for engagement and defining who qualifies as a stakeholder. The analysis will highlight NCP

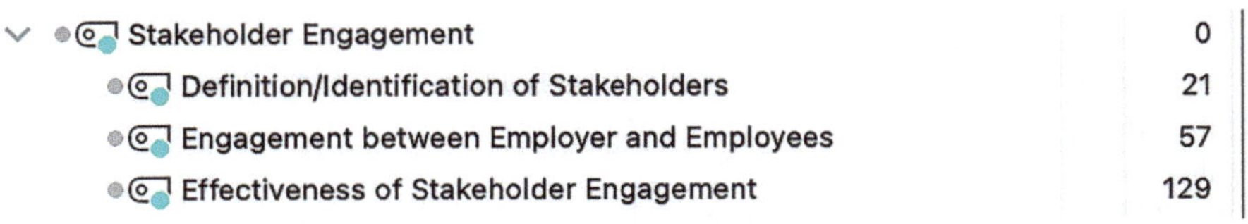

Fig. 2.3 Sub-codes of Parent code: Stakeholder engagement

[446] Buhmann et al. (2025), p. 11.

[447] Ibid, 11–12.

recommendations, particularly in cases underscoring the importance of targeted, meaningful engagement with those directly or indirectly affected by a company's operations. In the OECD case law, at least 12 cases specifically address these issues. A notable example is the case against VALE concerning the dam collapse, reviewed by the Brazilian NCP.[448] As previously analysed, in other related cases, the complainants, who owned property in the urban expansion area near the village of Pires, alleged that the failure of the Córrego do Feijão tailings dam led to significant impacts. These included material damages from (1) the halted negotiations on a real estate development, (2) increased vehicle flow that restricted property access, and (3) the discharge of mud into the Paraopeba River, which compromised the site's economic utility.[449] This incident affected the entire community, generating social, economic, and psychological challenges. In response, the NCP specifically recommended that VALE adopt a due diligence framework for stakeholder engagement that encompasses both broad and specific categories: those indirectly affected by the company's operations (such as relevant public, economic, and social entities at both national and international levels) and those directly impacted (including communities and individuals residing near the company's mining or production sites).[450] This case clearly demonstrated how all relevant stakeholders can be directly and indirectly affected by a company's operations.

This broad spectrum of potentially affected stakeholders was also emphasised in the case against Rockwool, reviewed by the Danish NCP.[451] In this case, the Danish NCP advised Rockwool not to restrict its identification of relevant stakeholders to those recognised under local legislation alone. Instead, the NCP recommended that Rockwool anticipate and include stakeholders who may be directly or indirectly affected by its activities throughout the entire project lifecycle.[452] This guidance was particularly relevant to Rockwool's manufacturing facility project in West Virginia, where the Danish NCP highlighted the importance of comprehensive stakeholder engagement beyond minimal legal requirements to address potential impacts more effectively.

When it comes to agriculture and extractive industries, which often involve large-scale projects impacting local communities, NCPs advise companies to adopt a broad stakeholder engagement approach. This includes recognising and consulting a wide range of stakeholders, as illustrated in cases handled by the French NCP against EDF and the COPAGEF Group, and the Canadian NCP against Imperial Metals, where similar guidance was provided.[453] In the EDF case, the case pertained

---

[448] NCP Brazil, A Group of Individuals v. VALE S.A, Final Statement, 5 May 2021.

[449] Ibid, 16.

[450] Ibid, 19.

[451] NCP Denmark 'Specific instance submitted by West Virginians for Sustainable Development regarding the activities of Rockwool International A/S and its subsidiary Rockwool 3 June 2021.

[452] Ibid, 8–9.

[453] NCP Canada, the Southeast Alaska Conservation Council (SEACC) v. Imperial Metals, Final Statement, 8 May 2020; NCP France, 14 Local Watch Committees ("Comités Riverains de Veille") and Centre of Actions for Life and Earth ("Centre d'Action pour la Vie et la Terre") v. COPAGEF,

to the development of a 252 MW wind farm project named 'Gunaa Sicarú,' managed by Eólica de Oaxaca, a Mexican subsidiary of EDF Renewables Mexico from the EDF Group.[454] The case focused on the adverse social and environmental impacts to the community of Unión Hidalgo, a municipality with approximately 12,000 residents, over 90% of whom are Zapotec, an Indigenous group formally recognised in Mexico.[455] The French NCP recommended that EDF engage with a broad spectrum of stakeholders, both supporters and those impacted by the project, including landowners, businesses, and local administrations.[456] It further stressed the importance of involving stakeholders who have claims to information access and consultation rights, particularly Indigenous communities. Specifically, the NCP highlighted the need to engage with the local Indigenous sub-community, represented by the 'community goods representative' within the community assembly ('asamblea de comuneros').[457]

In addition to advocating for a broad range of stakeholders, some NCPs have advised companies to engage not only with specific groups but with all relevant stakeholders potentially impacted by their operations. This was referred in several cases in Australian, Norwegian and Swiss NCPs. For example, in the Australian NCP case against ElectraNet, the company was accused of failing to engage with certain individuals affected by the construction of its electricity facilities.[458] Among these stakeholders were the Starkey family, who hold traditional custodial responsibilities over an aboriginal heritage site damaged by ElectraNet activities. While ElectraNet conducted stakeholder consultations with most affected parties, it did not engage with the Starkeys.[459] In response, the Australian NCP found that by excluding this group, ElectraNet had breached the OECD Guidelines, which mandate engagement with all relevant stakeholders.

A similar recommendation was made by the Norwegian NCP in the case against Intex Resources ASA and the Mindoro Nickel Project.[460] Here, the company was alleged to have violated the OECD Guidelines on several grounds: (1) inadequate consultations with Indigenous communities that contradicted the consent of the affected people, (2) alleged involvement in bribery to secure mining exploration permits, and (3) inadequate communication regarding the risk of severe environmental damage if the project proceeded.[461] In this case, the Norwegian NCP

SOMDIAA and SOSUCAM in Cameroon, Final Statement, 17 May 2022; NCP France, ProDESC v. EDF Group, Final Statement, 10 March 2020.

[454] Ibid case against EDF, 3.

[455] Ibid, 3–4.

[456] Ibid, 10–11.

[457] Ibid 13.

[458] NCP Australia, Andrew Starkey and Robert Starkey v. ElectraNet Pty Lt, Final Statement, 9 June 2021.

[459] Ibid, 21–22, para 61.

[460] NCP Norway, The Future In Our Hands (FIOH) v. Intex Resources ASA and The Mindoro Nickel Project, Final Statement, 30 November 2011.

[461] Ibid, 5.

emphasised that while the Guidelines do not set specific engagement standards, companies are expected to consider the views of all stakeholders at each stage of a project. It defined stakeholders as 'all those affected by the project,' which includes various project components such as the mine site, processing facilities, residual deposits, and transport routes by land and sea.[462] For stakeholders to make informed decisions on their support, they must have access to comprehensive information about these essential project aspects.[463]

Several other cases emphasised the importance of specific groups as vital stakeholders, with NCPs frequently highlighting workers as essential to meaningful corporate engagement. For instance, in the Chilean NCP case against Unilever, the NCP noted the company's acknowledgment of the irreplaceable role of the union as the representative body for workers.[464] In the end of the case, parties reached the agreement and in the agreement, Unilever affirmed its recognition of the union's role, extending this acknowledgment to union leaders, members, and the right of workers to associate with federations or entities chosen by the union.[465] The union, in turn, acknowledged that prior to the plant closures, it maintained a normal, positive relationship with the company, emphasising the essential nature of constructive engagement between the enterprise and its workers. Similarly, in the Norwegian NCP case regarding the Samsung Crane Accident, the workforce on the Martin Linge project was identified as a central stakeholder group and a valuable source of information for TEPN in assessing Samsung HI's activities.[466] The NCP highlighted the importance of engaging workers in identifying actual or potential adverse impacts, developing mitigation measures, and tracking the effectiveness of implemented actions. The complainants raised several issues affecting workers, including dangerous work orders, tight deadlines, and increased risks due to multi-level subcontracting, all pointing to the need for thorough engagement with the workforce to ensure safe and responsible operation.[467]

2.8.2.2 Approaches to Stakeholder Engagement

Approaches to stakeholder engagement vary significantly depending on the stakeholder group involved. In the OECD case law, the most common form of engagement highlighted is between employers and employees, with a strong emphasis on fostering meaningful communication and cooperation in workplace settings.

[462] Ibid 5–6.

[463] Ibid, 10–11.

[464] NCP Chile, CUT v. Unilever, Final Statement, 10 July 2020.

[465] Ibid, 17.

[466] NCP Norway, Samsung Heavy Industries Martin Linge Project Crane Accident Workers Support Team And Korean Transnational Corporations Watch v. Totalenergies E&P Norge As, Equinor Asa, Technip Energies N.V., Final Statement, 22 February 2023; NCP France, Unite Here v. Natixis/NGAM, Final Statement, 5 December 2017.

[467] Ibid, 18–19.

Comparatively, cases focusing on engagement with local communities, Indigenous Peoples, and women are less frequent. Given these trends, this subsection will explore stakeholder engagement strategies by dividing the discussion into two categories: engagement with workers and engagement with other stakeholder groups.

2.8.2.2.1 Engagement with Workers

Out of the 394 OECD cases, 37 specifically highlighted engagement between employers and employees. While Chap. 3 of this book examines corporate responsibility to respect workers' rights as seen in the OECD case law, this subsection focuses on effective and meaningful stakeholder engagement with workers, exploring how companies can fulfil their stakeholder engagement responsibilities. Many of these cases emphasised that NCPs advise companies to engage with employees meaningfully, which begins with recognising union rights and involving worker representatives in decision-making on matters that may impact them. This approach helps companies address both potential and actual negative impacts on employees through a cooperative framework.

Additionally, transparent information-sharing is crucial in these engagements. As discussed in Sect. 2.6.2.1 on communication as a part of due diligence process, effective communication with workers is crucial, especially when sudden changes in business activities, such as closures or layoffs, are anticipated. In such cases, timely and clear communication is not only a best practice but also a core element of meaningful engagement. This section builds on that foundation, focusing on engagement practices that go beyond mere information-sharing to foster a more collaborative and responsive relationship with employees. Numerous cases illustrate NCPs advising companies on effectively engaging with workers, extending this guidance not only to workers within a company's direct operations but also to those employed by its suppliers and subsidiaries. For instance, in the case against Brink, previously discussed, the NCP emphasised guidelines related to the Chapter V: Employment and Industrial Relations. The NCP observed that inadequate disclosure of economic and financial information hindered constructive social dialogue with employee representatives. Additionally, the NCP noted that the local board had limited bargaining power, particularly during the social mediation phase, which prevented it from reaching a solution acceptable to all parties involved.

In the case against Itaú Unibanco, the Brazilian NCP emphasised the importance of transparent and proactive information-sharing as a cornerstone of meaningful engagement between employers and employees.[468] The NCP highlighted that beyond situations involving sudden changes that directly impact employees' livelihoods, companies should maintain an open flow of information with their

---

[468] NCP Brazil, The Trade Union Bank Workers Union of São Paulo, v. Itau-Unibanco Bank, Final Statement, 23 April 2013.

workforce to support continuous engagement.[469] This involves voluntarily providing workers and their representatives with essential information for effective negotiations on working conditions, helping them to fully understand the company's structure, financial status, and employment trends, while safeguarding the commercial confidentiality.

Additionally, NCP further accentuated the value of cooperation on mutual interests, advising companies to engage with workers and their representatives on matters such as hiring, firing, and workforce relocation.[470] The aim is to develop a collaborative and transparent policy framework that can reduce turnover and support dismissed workers in finding new placements. Lastly, the NCP stressed a commitment to non-discrimination in all employment terms and practices, from hiring and job assignments to compensation and retirement, in line with international labour standards, including key ILO Conventions and Recommendations on worker protections.[471] Overall, the Brazilian NCP's guidance in this case illustrates a comprehensive approach to MSE that goes beyond immediate business needs, fostering an environment where workers are respected, informed, and integrated into the company's decision-making processes.

Some cases also highlight effective ways to engage with workers on critical topics like working conditions. In the case against Drummond International in Colombian NCP, the complainants alleged that the company had breached the OECD Guidelines by failing to recognise collective bargaining rights and neglecting due diligence responsibilities to address negative health and safety impacts of the workers.[472] Although mediation did not result in an agreement, the Colombian NCP recommended that the company engage directly with workers to address these issues, particularly around health and safety conditions and collective bargaining rights. The Colombian NCP suggested several specific actions, including collaboration between the company and the union to develop a self-care program aimed at building a safety-oriented culture at the workplace.[473] It further recommended that the company and the union strengthen existing communication channels, with monthly and quarterly check-ins focused on the needs of sick and disabled workers. The NCP also advised Drummond to continue its commitment to comprehensive human rights training for all employees, with active participation from the union encouraged.[474] These recommendations highlighted the need for continuous, structured engagement to promote safer working conditions, support employee wellbeing, and uphold collective bargaining rights.

---

[469] Ibid, 3.

[470] Ibid, 2–3.

[471] Ibid.

[472] NCP Colombia, Sindicato de Trabajadores Enfermos y Discapacitados del Sector Minero (SINTRADEM) And the Federación General el Trabajo CGT Seccional Cesar (CGT) v. Drummond Ltd., Final Statement, November 2018.

[473] Ibid, 13.

[474] Ibid.

The importance of worker engagement is strongly emphasised in the Norwegian NCP case concerning the Samsung Crane Accident, where the NCP recommended that companies ensure MSE with workers, actively including their voices throughout the due diligence process.[475] This is particularly essential in high-risk industries, such as shipyards and oil and gas, where workers are critical stakeholders. A similar focus on worker engagement appears in the Norwegian NCP case against NBIM, filed by the IUF, concerning gender-based harassment within the McDonald's food chain.[476] This case also highlighted the need for inclusive and proactive engagement between employer and employees. The NCP specifically mentioned that OECD Guidelines describe stakeholder engagement as an interactive, two-way process of meaningful communication.[477] NCP advised companies to continually assess whether their business model, organisational structure, incentive systems, training programs, and broader company culture effectively incorporate sustainable business practices, including those related to Gender-Based Violence and Harassment (GBVH). Furthermore, the agreement between the parties after the mediation process included the statement that 'workers, as 'key' stakeholders reliant on the company for their livelihood, should be integrally involved in these sustainability efforts.[478] Engaging workers through channels like collective bargaining can be instrumental in ensuring the successful and sustainable implementation of these practices.'[479] This case also explores the role of investors in engaging with the workers of investee companies, serving as a strong example of how investors can take responsibility and actively participate in MSE between companies and the workers.

There are also cases that demonstrate how parent companies can effectively engage with workers across their subsidiaries. Large MNEs like Just Eat, Ikea, and Teleperformance, which operate branches worldwide, bear the responsibility of actively engaging with local workers to ensure they fully enjoy their rights as employees. This is particularly challenging given the diverse regulatory environments and cultural contexts across different countries. One effective strategy, highlighted in these cases, is the facilitation of unionisation for all workers and active engagement with worker representatives to assess and address potential risks to their rights and well-being.

The Ikea case provides a clear example. The Dutch NCP recommended that Ikea's local branches in the U.S., Portugal, and Ireland continue constructive dialogue with unions to develop practical solutions that align with globally

[475] NCP Norway, Samsung Heavy Industries Martin Linge Project Crane Accident Workers Support Team And Korean Transnational Corporations Watch v. Totalenergies E&P Norge As, Equinor Asa, Technip Energies N.V., Final Statement, 22 February 2023; NCP France, Unite Here v. Natixis/NGAM, Final Statement, 5 December 2017.

[476] NCP Norway, Trade Unions IUF, EFFAT-IUF, SEIU And UGT v. Norges Bank Investment Management (NBIM), Final Statement, 22 April 2022.

[477] Ibid, 4.

[478] NCP Norway, Agreement between IUF, EFFAT-IUF, SEIU and UGT v. NBIM, Agreement, 9 March 2022.

[479] Ibid, 2.

agreed-upon principles.[480] For instance, in the US, the NCP advised local parties to work towards a practical arrangement for union access to the workplace, ensuring that workers' rights to representation are respected.[481] The NCP similarly encouraged ongoing dialogue in Portugal to further implement these global principles and advised the parties in Ireland to strengthen efforts to establish constructive communication channels.[482] The case concluded successfully with an agreement between the parties, in which Ikea committed to upholding union rights and facilitating effective communication with employees. This agreement mandates that local arrangements define conditions for meaningful union access and effective interaction with workers, with Ikea supporting all unions equally and showing no favouritism.

2.8.2.2.2 Engagement with External Stakeholders, Including the Local Communities and Indigenous Peoples

The first part of this section discussed the challenges in current international regulations and literature review companies face when engaging with external stakeholders, including Indigenous Peoples and various local communities. Scholars emphasised that numerous factors must be considered. For instance, for the Indigenous Peoples, this includes their unique relationship with nature and the land, while for local communities, it is essential to understand internal power dynamics and the cultural factors. Chapter 3 of this book will examine corporate responsibility more broadly in respecting Indigenous Peoples and local communities within the OECD case law. However, this section focuses specifically on the responsibility of companies to engage with these groups in a meaningful and effective way across OECD case law.

In several instances within OECD case law, NCPs have evaluated how companies engage with Indigenous Peoples and local communities, with a particular focus on the requirement for FPIC. While FPIC is a fundamental standard in interactions with Indigenous communities, many companies lack a clear understanding of how to implement it effectively. The case of PanAust, reviewed by the Australian NCP, exemplifies these challenges.[483] The Australian NCP advised PanAust that, to obtain FPIC, the company must communicate transparently with all relevant Indigenous communities regarding the potential impacts of its projects and the steps it will take to mitigate them.[484] In the proposed Sepik Development Project of the case, the materials attached with complaint examined suggested that, if the project moves

[480] NCP Netherlands, Building and Wood Workers International (BWI) et al., v. IKEA Holding B.V, Final Statement, 25 April 2023.

[481] Ibid, 9.

[482] Ibid, 8.

[483] NCP Australia, Project Sepik and Jubilee Australia Research Centre on behalf of Sepik River communities v. PanAust Limited, Final Statement, 3 October 2023.

[484] Ibid, 42.

forward, it would significantly affect certain Indigenous groups in ways that necessitate FPIC.[485] This includes communities that could face relocation, land or resource inundation due to the dam, storage of hazardous materials on their land, or other threats to their cultural survival. NCP further noted that FPIC is inevitably essential when impacts reach a 'significant' level—such as proximity to the mine, dam, or facilities, or when cultural survival is at risk.[486]

A second key issue highlighted by the Australian NCP is the importance of language in communication. For informed consent to be genuinely achieved, companies must engage Indigenous communities in a language they fully understand. The NCP identified this as a critical improvement area for PanAust, as Tok Pisin—a widely used language in the region—may not be understood by all affected communities.[487] PanAust acknowledged the linguistic and cultural diversity of the project area, implying that effective FPIC would require engagement in languages and cultural contexts relevant to each community. However, the NCP emphasised that simple translation is insufficient, noting that relying solely on Tok Pisin and English may not be adequate for meaningful FPIC.[488] PanAust indicated that where Tok Pisin is not understood, they use volunteer interpreters from local villages to translate discussions into local dialects.[489] Nevertheless, the NCP underlined that merely providing materials in Tok Pisin or English does not meet FPIC requirements in communities unfamiliar with these languages. This highlights the need for communication strategies that fully support informed consent. Furthermore, the Australian NCP cautioned that if PanAust cannot effectively implement and achieve FPIC, the project should not proceed. This case shows the critical importance of genuine, culturally aware engagement with Indigenous communities in line with FPIC principles.

Similarly, the case against Vedanta for its alleged failure to address the negative environmental and social impacts on local indigenous people in India reflects similar findings regarding engagement with indigenous communities.[490] In this case, the UK NCP analysis highlighted Vedanta's inadequate engagement with the Indigenous population concerning its proposed bauxite mine in the Niyamgiri Hills, Orissa, India.[491] Upon reviewing the case, the NCP found no evidence that Vedanta had made meaningful efforts to communicate with these communities, especially considering literacy barriers that prevented many locals from understanding or responding to written notices.[492] Vedanta's 2002 environmental impact assessment revealed low literacy rates in Orissa, with rates below 20% in the area surrounding the

[485] Ibid 41, Paras 116–117.

[486] Ibid.

[487] Ibid 42, para 120.

[488] Ibid 35, paras 96–97.

[489] Ibid.

[490] NCP United Kingdom, Survival International v. Vedanta, Final Statement, 25 September 2009.

[491] Ibid, para 10–11.

[492] Ibid, para 64–65.

mine.[493] Despite this, Vedanta did not use alternative communication methods, leaving the Dongria Kondh community largely uninformed and unconsulted about the project's potential impacts on their traditional way of life.[494] This lack of accessible communication fell short of the OECD Guidelines, which require companies to provide adequate, timely, and accessible communication with affected communities, especially regarding environmental and social impacts. Furthermore, the UK NCP emphasised recommendations from the experts that suggest using diverse communication methods, including local languages, to ensure consultations are accessible to indigenous communities.[495] By failing to adopt this model, the UK NCP concluded that Vedanta disregarded essential guidelines for meeting the specific needs of Indigenous Peoples like the Dongria Kondh.

In addition to focusing on Indigenous Peoples, many OECD cases emphasised the importance of companies engaging effectively with local communities. This means companies should take a comprehensive, multi-dimensional approach to MSE. First, they need to gain a thorough understanding of the cultural and historical background of the land and people, which allows them to better identify and address potential impacts. This knowledge is essential for developing approaches that honour and align with community heritage and values. One case against a French MNE at the French NCP illustrated this point.[496] The case, filed by an Australian individual representing his family, claimed that the family's assets were confiscated in Central Europe starting in 1939.[497] This family owned an Austrian holding company that in turn owned a Polish company with industrial operations in Upper Silesia. Although the industrial activities ceased in 1933, and the site was converted into a marketplace, the family retained ownership of the land, and the plant located there. In 2007, a Polish subsidiary of the French MNE acquired the property, and the complainant questioned the company's due diligence during this acquisition, requesting financial compensation through NCP mediation.[498] After NCP analysing the case, it questioned whether, beyond standard registry checks, the MNE had consulted local sources, such as the municipality, to gather additional historical context of the land.[499] The company responded that it had relied on official land records, which, to its knowledge, were accurate and legal. However, the NCP raised concerns about the lack of engagement with municipal authorities, which could have enriched the company's understanding of the property's history and mitigated potential disputes.

Secondly, in cases involving community impact, companies must prioritise clear and comprehensive communication to capture and address community concerns effectively. Building on the previous cases, the Dutch NCP's review of Shell

---

[493] Ibid,

[494] Ibid, 66.

[495] Ibid, 73–75.

[496] NCP France, A foreign national v. a French MNE in Poland, Final Statement, 30 June 2022.

[497] Ibid, 3.

[498] Ibid.

[499] Ibid, 6.

Exploration indicated the importance of providing comprehensive information to local communities affected by the Corrib Gas project.[500] The NCP advised that Shell should not merely meet the minimal legal requirements for information disclosure but should exceed them to ensure that communities are fully informed.[501] This approach is essential for fostering a MSE between companies and the local communities, as encouraged by Chapter V, Paragraph 2 of the OECD Guidelines. In this case, the NCP assessed whether the Consortium involved in the Corrib Gas project had engaged the public in genuine dialogue. Information from the Department of Communications, Energy, and Natural Resources helped to clarify the extent of Shell's interactions with the community.[502]

Furthermore, the NCP emphasised that transparent and thorough disclosure of information about the project's activities and environmental impacts is a crucial means of building public confidence.[503] This is most effective when it not only provides necessary details but also actively invites input from stakeholders, including local residents and the broader public. Such engagement promotes a foundation of trust and understanding, particularly on shared environmental concerns. Thus, the NCP ultimately suggested that companies consider going beyond basic disclosure requirements to facilitate long-term, cooperative relationships with communities impacted by their operations.[504] Third, it is essential to establish a robust, two-way communication channel that goes beyond isolated instances of information sharing. Such a channel should promote ongoing dialogue, built on trust, and facilitate continuous, open feedback from both sides.

The case against ENRC in the UK NCP illustrates the consequences of failing to meet the above standards. The UK NCP found a significant lapse in ENRC's obligations to maintain effective communication with stakeholder communities like Lenge after acquiring interests in Africo and Comide.[505] ENRC was expected to put in place clear communication channels to keep the local communities informed about developments affecting them and to provide a means for these communities to voice their concerns or grievances.[506] However, the NCP's findings indicated that these mechanisms were absent. RAID, an advocacy group, provided evidence of repeated but unsuccessful attempts by both community members and RAID to raise issues with ENRC.[507] Although ENRC claimed it had engaged in discussions with some community representatives, it failed to provide requested documentation to verify

[500] NCP Netherlands, Final Statement of the Irish and Netherlands National Contact Points (NCPs) on the notification dated 21st August, 2008 concerning the Corrib Gas project, pursuant to the OECD Guidelines for Multinational Enterprises, 30 July 2010.

[501] Ibid, 15–16.

[502] Ibid.

[503] Ibid.

[504] Ibid, 15.

[505] NCP United Kingdom, Rights and Accountability in Development (RAID) v. ENRC, Final Statement, February 2016.

[506] Ibid, Key Summary.

[507] Ibid, paras 68–70.

these interactions, citing confidentiality concerns. The UK NCP argued, however, that confidentiality should not extend to withholding information critical to stakeholder transparency and accountability.[508] The NCP further emphasised the urgency of establishing strong, continuous communication with the Lenge community, given their close proximity to the Comide concession and a history of tensions in the area.[509] Evidence of four riots by artisanal miners between 2007 and 2011 signalled underlying issues and unrest within the community. This background highlights ENRC's responsibility to address Lenge's concerns directly to prevent adverse effects from Comide's activities. By failing to build and maintain effective communication channels and by neglecting to engage meaningfully with Lenge on critical issues, the UK NCP concluded that ENRC had not met its obligations under Chapter 2, Paragraph 14 of the OECD Guidelines.

Finally, an effective engagement strategy fundamentally depends on a well-structured and accessible complaint mechanism. For instance, in the case of Imperial Metals, the Canadian NCP emphasised the necessity of a responsive and respectful complaint system as an essential area for improvement.[510] The NCP recommended that the company's stakeholder engagement strategy should explicitly outline processes for identifying relevant communities and engaging them in consultations, providing information, and involving them in a dispute resolution mechanism for submitting complaints. Furthermore, maintaining sincerity within communication channels and grievance mechanism is critical for trust-building.[511] In cases involving POSCO International and SK E&C, the Korean NCP highlighted the importance of companies clearly and honestly explaining their actions, impacts, compensation, and grievance processes to affected communities.[512]

2.8.2.3 Effectiveness in Meaningful Stakeholder Engagement

MSE requires inclusivity, two-way communication, timeliness, transparency, responsiveness, and continuity, as set out in the OECD Guidelines.[513] Several NCPs have evaluated and advised companies on how to uphold these principles in practice. Achieving inclusivity, for instance, necessitates the involvement of all relevant stakeholders throughout the process. This was evident in the case brought by WVSD against Rockwool International A/S, reviewed by the Danish NCP. As discussed earlier in this book, Rockwool was accused of failing to conduct adequate risk-based due diligence during the planning and construction of a mineral wool manu-

---

[508] Ibid.

[509] Ibid, para 82.

[510] NCP Canada, SEACC v. Imperial Metals Corporation, Final Statement, 08 May 2020.

[511] Ibid, para 35.

[512] NCP Denmark 'West Virginians for Sustainable Development (WVSD) v. Rockwool International AS, Final Statement, 3 June 2021.

[513] OECD Guidelines, Commentary on Chapter 2: General Policies, para 28.

facturing plant in Jefferson County, West Virginia. Notably, the company was alleged to have neglected to provide stakeholders with meaningful opportunities to participate during key planning and decision-making stages.[514] The Danish NCP found that Rockwool did not meet the OECD Guidelines' standards for engaging relevant stakeholders, especially for projects with significant local impact.[515]

Initially, Rockwool's approach lacked inclusivity and transparency, as the company did not fully identify and involve all relevant stakeholders, and several major decisions were made with limited input. Upon recognising these deficiencies, Rockwool implemented corrective measures, such as enhancing community outreach and holding public meetings. Additionally, the company developed a 'Community Engagement Manual' to set standards for future engagement and social due diligence.[516] While these steps demonstrated Rockwool's commitment to improvement, they also indicated the need for proactive and genuine engagement from the outset. As the Danish NCP highlighted, stakeholder engagement is not merely a compliance formality; it is central to responsible business conduct. MSE enables companies to mitigate risks, build trust, and make more informed decisions by integrating diverse perspectives.[517] The Rockwool case serves as a reminder that companies must go beyond formalistic gestures and authentically involve stakeholders in planning and decision-making to align with OECD Guidelines.

Another case demonstrating the importance of trust-based MSE involved Statkraft and the Jijnjevaerie Saami village, assessed by the Swedish NCP. This case examined whether Statkraft complied with the OECD Guidelines, which advise companies to 'develop and apply effective self-regulatory practices and management systems that foster confidence and mutual trust.'[518] A central issue raised by the Saami village was the absence of structured, predictable, and transparent communication with Statkraft.[519] The NCP emphasised that enterprises, particularly when working with Indigenous communities, should establish effective communication channels that consider any administrative limitations faced by those communities.[520] Communication difficulties during the reindeer herding season and inadequate documentation of the Saami village's perspectives led to confusion and trust issues. The NCP suggested that Statkraft could have improved transparency by clarifying how it considered the village's input in its decisions.[521]

Additional obstacles, such as limited telecommunication infrastructure in certain regions, demanded greater patience and understanding from both parties. As the

---

[514] NCP Denmark, WVSD v. Rockwool, Final Statement, 3 June 2021, 4.

[515] Ibid, 10.

[516] Ibid, 11.

[517] Ibid.

[518] NCP Sweden, Jijnjevaerie Saami village v. Statkraft SCA Vind AB, Final Statement, 10 February 2016.

[519] Ibid, 3.

[520] Ibid, 16.

[521] Ibid.

NCP noted, Statkraft could have streamlined the process by attending meetings with fully authorised representatives or by engaging an independent third party to support meeting planning and documentation. Although Statkraft made adjustments to its plans based on feedback from the Saami village, the village felt its views were still inadequately reflected. Ultimately, while Statkraft did not breach OECD Guidelines, the NCP identified areas where improved communication could have strengthened mutual trust.

A further case involved Victoria Oil and Gas PLC (VOG) and its Logbaba gas project in Cameroon, where the UK NCP identified failures in their responsibility towards stakeholder engagement.[522] According to the OECD Guidelines, effective engagement relies on two-way communication and good faith from all participants, with companies expected to establish systems that foster trust with local communities.[523] The UK NCP found that VOG's engagement process lacked accessibility and inclusivity, as materials were not translated into local languages, consultation periods were too brief, and Platform Meetings were cancelled without notice.[524] Although the complainants argued that public consultations did not meet with Cameroonian legal standards, the NCP clarified that its role was to assess compliance with OECD Guidelines rather than local law. Concluding that VOG had not fully adhered to the Guidelines, the NCP recommended that VOG adopt self-regulatory practices to foster trust, provide more opportunities for stakeholder input, and address the broader implications of inadequate engagement for human rights, environmental, and labour concerns.

The UK NCP's focus on building trust between companies and communities is echoed in the multiple cases, including those against GCM Resources PLC (GCM), Vedanta, and ENRC. In the GCM case, the company's plans to develop a mine in Phulbari, Bangladesh, were criticised for disregarding the community rights, with inadequate community engagement and trust-building cited as breaches of the OECD Guidelines.[525] While GCM initially implemented self-regulatory practices that met international standards, the company's communication strategies suffered significant gaps.[526] Documents were not translated into local languages, responses to opposition were easily misinterpreted, and direct engagement with the community was either non-existent or minimal for extended periods. These issues contributed to community distrust and hindered open dialogue.

The NCP acknowledged GCM's intent to limit community engagement due to concerns about escalating violence and a lack of clarity from the Bangladeshi

[522] NCP United Kingdom, Association des Habitants de Ndogpassi 1, 2 et 3 [Ndogpassi 1, 2 and 3 Residents Association] (AHN) and Cercle de Bon Voisinage de Logmayangui [Logmayangui Good Neighbours Circle] (CBVL) v. Victoria Oil and Gas PLC, Final Statement, 20 January 2023.

[523] Ibid, Conclusion section.

[524] Ibid.

[525] NCP United Kingdom, International Accountability Project and World Development Movement v. GCM Resources PLC, Final Statement, November 2014.

[526] Ibid, paras 48–50.

government.[527] However, the NCP concluded that relying solely on national government advocacy was insufficient for building trust. As a result, GCM's limited communication and engagement practices breached Chapter 2, Paragraph 7 of the OECD Guidelines from August 2006 to 2012. This series of cases highlighted the importance of genuine, two-way communication and trust-building in stakeholder engagement. The NCP's recommendations consistently highlighted that proactive, culturally aware engagement strategies are fundamental to responsible corporate conduct and to maintaining a constructive relationship with communities impacted by corporate activities.

In conclusion, these cases illustrate that maintaining effective MSE goes beyond compliance and technical consultation; it requires building trust, fostering open communication, and demonstrating respect for local perspectives and cultural nuances. The NCPs' findings across Rockwool, Statkraft, VOG, and GCM emphasised that companies must proactively engage with communities in a way that is transparent, inclusive, and responsive to their needs. Adherence to these principles not only aligns with the OECD Guidelines but also strengthens companies' social license to operate, mitigates potential conflicts, and enhances decision-making by incorporating diverse viewpoints.

2.9 Evaluating the Effectiveness of Human Rights Due Diligence

2.9.1 Effectiveness Analysis within Human Rights Due Diligence

Analysing the effectiveness of HRDD is essential to ensure that businesses not only comply with international standards but also genuinely prevent and mitigate adverse human rights impacts. Effective HRDD goes beyond merely completing procedural steps; it requires an integration of multiple factors that collectively determine how well a company can uphold human rights throughout its operations and supply chains. Key drivers identified in the literature include strong leadership commitment, integration into corporate culture, a risk-based approach, MSE, transparency, continuous improvement, and the access to effective remedy.[528]

James Harrison argued that HRDD's impactfulness hinges on moving beyond superficial compliance to incorporate robust, participatory, and transparent processes.[529] He emphasised that transparency, external verification, and independent monitoring are vital for credible HRDD, proposing that HRDD closely aligns with HRIA

---

[527] Ibid.

[528] Wettstein (2022), p. 165.

[529] Harrison (2023), pp. 27–28.

practices.[530] Meaningful HRDD, he contended, should include rigorous consultation and evidence-based assessment to genuinely address human rights concerns.[531] In support of this perspective, Riccardo Torelli, Simona Fiandrino, and Francesco Scarpa discussed the role of corporate governance in bolstering HRDD.[532] Their research highlighted the positive influence of corporate governance structures, such as board diversity and sustainability committees, which enhance HRDD's effectiveness by fostering a culture of accountability and stakeholder engagement.[533] Their study underlines that corporate leadership commitment must extend beyond policy statements to operational practices, ensuring comprehensive HRDD efforts that address human rights impacts substantively.[534]

Additionally, Nolan and McCorquodale emphasised on HRDD's proactive role in mitigating business-related human rights abuses, positioning it as a tool to identify, assess, and address potential and actual adverse impacts within operations and supply chains.[535] Their analysis pointed out the importance of legislative support, like the French Duty of Vigilance Law, which mandates HRDD compliance and holds companies accountable for human rights impacts across their operations.[536] However, they noted that HRDD effectiveness can be inconsistent, often relying on varying levels of corporate compliance and enforcement mechanisms.[537] They also emphasised the critical role of stakeholder engagement, stressing that involving affected rights holders, such as employees and local communities, leads to more meaningful and impactful HRDD outcomes.[538] The authors further cautioned against over-reliance on social audits, which may inadequately address deep-rooted human rights issues, and highlight the need for HRDD to be viewed as a human-rights-centred approach rather than merely a risk management tool.

For HRDD to be truly effective, corporations must embed human rights considerations deeply within their governance structures, corporate culture, and operational processes. This includes fostering strong leadership and governance, where executives and board members prioritise human rights, aided by mechanisms such as sustainability committees and diverse boards that align governance with social responsibility goals. Transparency and accountability are equally critical, as open communication about HRDD policies and impacts builds trust among stakeholders. MSE is foundational, allowing companies to develop proactive strategies informed by the insights of affected communities and employees. Continuous improvement is

---

[530] Ibid.

[531] Ibid, 29.

[532] Torelli et al. (2024), p. 1280 https://onlinelibrary.wiley.com/doi/epdf/10.1002/csr.3001 (accessed 31 January 2026).

[533] Ibid, 1281.

[534] Ibid, 1289.

[535] McCorquodale and Nolan (2021), p. 475.

[536] Ibid, 471–472.

[537] Ibid, 473.

[538] Ibid.

also essential, requiring companies to monitor, adapt, and refine HRDD practices in response to evolving risks and regulatory standards, such as the CSDDD. Lastly, integrating HRDD into a company's core culture ensures that human rights considerations inform every business decision, enhancing the depth and authenticity of due diligence practices.

In conclusion, effective HRDD is achieved when companies go beyond minimal compliance, aiming instead for transformative, human-rights-centred corporate responsibility. By embedding HRDD into their governance, culture, and operations, companies can foster meaningful change that not only meets regulatory requirements but also upholds the dignity and rights of individuals throughout their supply chains.

2.9.2 Insights from OECD Case Law on the Effectiveness of Human Rights Due Diligence

Analysis of OECD case law revealed how NCPs assessed companies' human rights and environmental due diligence practices for adequacy and effectiveness. Two significant cases—the French NCP's reviews of Socapalm and DIAM International Group—provide valuable insights into the challenges and expectations surrounding corporate compliance with OECD Guidelines.[539] In the case of Socapalm, a Cameroon-based palm oil company, the French NCP examined allegations of environmental and social adverse impacts resulting from the company's extractive business activities.[540] The Socapalm case showed the critical elements required for effective HRDD, highlighting both initial failings and areas of progress.

At the outset, Socapalm failed to integrate environmental and social risks into its governance and decision-making processes, leading to harmful air and water emissions that severely impacted local communities. The company's oversight in addressing these risks until harm had occurred exemplified the consequences of inadequate governance structures and insufficient planning. The French NCP also identified deficiencies in Socapalm's 'dialogue platforms', which lacked transparency and failed to ensure meaningful consultation with affected communities. This absence of MSE is contrary to the OECD Guidelines, which emphasised the importance of inclusive, timely, and accessible stakeholder consultation in identifying and addressing human rights and environmental risks. In response to the NCP proceedings, Socapalm introduced a Quality, Health, Safety, and Environment (QHSE) programme in 2011. This initiative represents a shift towards more effective HRDD practices, incorporating critical elements such as training employees in

[539] NCP France, Birlesik Metal against DIAM International, Final Statement, 14 May 2019; NCP France, group of four non-governmental organisations (NGOs) and associations from Cameroon, France and Germany v. SOCAPALM, Bollore Group, Report, 3 June 2013.

[540] Ibid, 1.

environmental management, hazardous materials handling, and accident prevention. Chapter VI of the OECD Guidelines mandated such training as an essential for RBC. Furthermore, the QHSE programme aimed to enhance governance by integrating certifications and compliance measures, supported by the Bolloré Group, under the NCP's monitoring.

The Socapalm case demonstrated that effective HRDD requires more than reactive measures. Proactive due diligence involved continuous assessment of risks, comprehensive strategies for risk prevention, and robust systems for integrating environmental and human rights considerations into decision-making. Additionally, accessible feedback mechanisms and meaningful engagement with all stakeholders are essential to building trust and ensuring accountability. Governance structures must prioritise transparency and accountability at every stage, with clear lines of responsibility for identifying and mitigating adverse impacts.To sum up, the Socapalm case serves as a learning opportunity for the implementation of effective HRDD. It highlighted the need for companies to adopt systematic approaches that incorporate RBC governance, thorough due diligence steps, and MSE. Moreover, in this case, French NCP highly noted that while the QHSE programme marked progress, sustained and ongoing improvements remain necessary for Socapalm to fully meet the expectations of effective HRDD.[541]

The French NCP also evaluated the HRDD measures of DIAM International Group, a mid-sized MNE headquartered in France with subsidiaries worldwide, including Turkey. DIAM manufactured counter displays for luxury and cosmetics brands. The NCP's assessment focused on the company's adherence to the OECD Guidelines, particularly concerning workers' rights to freedom of association, collective bargaining, and representation at its Turkish subsidiary.[542] The case centred on a 2017 labour dispute that revealed significant shortcomings in DIAM's HRDD framework. While DIAM implemented several measures in response—including engagement with the union Birleşik Metal-İş and the introduction of due diligence processes—these steps were found by the NCP to be inadequate. Although the company partially mitigated the adverse impacts, it failed to establish meaningful social dialogue, thereby falling short of fully meeting the expectations set out in the OECD Guidelines. The NCP further highlighted DIAM's absence of a proactive and systematic mechanism for safeguarding workers' rights, indicating a reactive rather than preventive approach to labour-related risks.[543]

Taken together, the DIAM and Socapalm cases illustrated the core elements of effective HRDD and expose the limits of reactive, piecemeal approaches. In both instances, failure to embed human rights and environmental considerations into corporate governance, decision-making, and MSE led to adverse impacts and incomplete remediation. In Socapalm, insufficient environmental safeguards and weak stakeholder consultation resulted in serious harm to local communities. DIAM,

---

[541] Ibid, 13.

[542] NCP France, Birlesik Metal v. DIAM International, Final Statement, 14 May 2019.

[543] Ibid, 10.

likewise, lacked a proactive mechanism to ensure social dialogue and protect workers' rights, addressing issues only after they arose. Both cases demonstrate the necessity of proactive risk identification, continuous monitoring, and meaningful engagement with affected stakeholders.

2.10 Preliminary Conclusion

This chapter provided an in-depth analysis of the role of NCPs in evaluating and guiding companies' HRDD practices, with a strong emphasis on aligning these practices with the UNGPs and the OECD Guidelines. The chapter was organised according to the six steps of risk-based due diligence outlined in the OECD Guidelines, inclusion of other essential components like MSE and effective implementation of HRDD. It highlighted the corporate responsibility to proactively (but not reactively) identify, prevent, and mitigate potential harms, thereby assessing the overall effectiveness of HRDD frameworks in practice. As the core chapter of this book, it aimed to answer the central question of how NCPs elaborate on corporate responsibilities related to human and environmental rights, emphasising companies' fundamental responsibility to implement effective due diligence processes. Each section within this chapter focused on one of the six due diligence steps, first exploring recent developments in international human rights law and soft policy regulations. Here, the analysis drew from scholarship, policy discussions, and legislative efforts to capture how these steps are being defined, debated, and refined. The review of BHR scholarship reveals persistent concerns regarding the uneven and often superficial implementation of HRDD across diverse sectors and corporate actors, particularly financial institutions. Although the UNGPs and the OECD Guidelines provide a foundational framework, substantial gaps remain in defining what *effective* HRDD entails in practice. The lack of universally accepted criteria for evaluating the quality, depth, and outcomes of corporate due diligence processes makes it difficult to distinguish between genuine human rights responsibility and mere procedural or reputational compliance. As many scholars emphasised, effective HRDD must go beyond formal reporting: it should tackle the structural and root causes of harm and meaningfully reach the affected rightsholders at the ground level, ensuring that their voices, needs, and lived experiences shape both risk assessment and remediation.

A closer reading of OECD NCP case law demonstrates that, while NCPs play an important role in advancing more participatory and continuous models of HRDD, their capacity to drive substantive change is limited by structural and normative constraints embedded in the OECD Guidelines. These constraints are evident in what the reports both reveal and leave unsaid. They often highlight critical issues—for example, the neglect of vulnerable communities or the absence of effective complaint-handling mechanisms—but rarely go beyond surface-level diagnosis. This is particularly the case where the Guidelines fail to provide clear direction, such as in matters involving gender-specific harms or intersectional vulnerabilities.

Despite these shortcomings, different types of NCP intervention do emerge in the research analysis. In some cases, the reports serve primarily to expose practical deficiencies, such as corporate neglect of the rights and perspectives of marginalised groups. In others, NCPs seek to refine the meaning of substantive HRDD requirements, as seen in varying interpretations of FPIC between, for instance, the Dutch and Australian NCPs. Elsewhere, the emphasis is procedural, with NCPs facilitating mediation processes that enable companies to assume a norm-shaping role through negotiated outcomes. There are also instances where the focus turns to the responsibilities of specific corporate actors, such as the Danish NCP's scrutiny of Danish financial institutions engagement with mining company—itself a vivid illustration of how investors can be implicated in human rights risks in extractive sector.

This diversity of NCP interventions demonstrate both their potential and their limitations. On the one hand, NCPs can help bridge the divide between corporate commitments and real-world outcomes—shedding light on neglected risks, catalysing corrective measures, and generating sectoral learning. On the other, their influence is often circumscribed by the parameters of the OECD Guidelines, which remain underdeveloped in key areas such as responsiveness to specific human rights, intersectionality, and enforceability. As a result, NCP reports can appear fragmented, even cautious, lacking the normative depth required to fully guide companies in addressing complex human rights challenges.

Ultimately, this analysis suggests that while NCPs can be catalysts for improved HRDD practice, their current mandate is not sufficient to ensure consistent, rights-based outcomes. Strengthening the normative content of the OECD Guidelines—particularly with regard to group-specific risks and gendered harms—would give NCPs the tools they need to drive deeper and more sustained corporate accountability. These insights lay the foundation for the next chapter, which explores how HRDD must be adapted to different sectoral contexts and rights-specific concerns, especially when the stakes are highest for marginalised or structurally vulnerable groups.

References

Cases

UK Supreme Court, Vedanta Resources PLC and another (Appellants) v Lungowe and others (Respondents).

Legislations

Australia. *Modern Slavery Act 2018 (Cth)*. No. 153. Canberra: Federal Register of Legislation, 2018.
Fighting Against Forced Labour and Child Labour in Supply Chains Act (S.C. 2023, c. 9) 11 May 2023.
Germany. *Act on Corporate Due Diligence Obligations in Supply Chains (Lieferkettensorgfaltspflichtengesetz, LkSG)*. 22 July 2021.
The Government of Norway 'Act relating to enterprises' transparency and work on fundamental human rights and decent working conditions (Transparency Act).
The Swiss Federal Council. '*Ordinance on Due Diligence and Transparency in relation to Minerals and Metals from Conflict-Affected Areas*' (DDTrO) of 3 December 2021.
United Kingdom. *Modern Slavery Act 2015*. c. 30.

Documents

OECD (2017) Due Diligence Guidance for Meaningful Stakeholder Engagement (MSE) in the Extractive Sector (OECD Guidance for MSE). OECD, https://www.oecd.org/en/publications/2017/02/oecd-due-diligence-guidance-for-meaningful-stakeholder-engagement-in-the-extractive-sector_g1g65995.html. Accessed 31 Jan 2026
OECD (2018) OECD Due Diligence Guidance for Responsible Business Conduct. p 60. https://www.oecd.org/en/publications/oecd-due-diligence-guidance-for-responsible-business-conduct_15f5f4b3-en.html. Accessed 31 Jan 2026
OECD (2023) OECD guidelines for multinational enterprises on responsible business conduct. OECD Publishing
UN General Assembly, United Nations Declaration on the Rights of Indigenous Peoples: resolution / adopted by the General Assembly, A/RES/61/295, 2 October 2007; UN General Assembly, UN Declaration on Human Rights Defenders, A/RES/53/144, 8 March 1999
UN General Assembly, International Convention on the Protection of the Rights of All Migrant Workers and Members of their Families, A/RES/45/158, 18 December 1990, UN "Convention on the Elimination of All Forms of Discrimination against Women." 1988 Treaty Series 1249: 13
United Nations (2011) Guiding principles on business and human rights: implementing the United Nations "Protect, Respect and Remedy" framework. United Nations, New York and Geneva

Bibliography

Bennet E (2022) The efficacy of voluntary standards, sustainability certifications and ethical labels. In: Marx A, Van Glaster G, Wouters J, Otteburn K, Lica D (eds) Research handbook on global governance, business and human rights. Edward Elgar Publishing, pp 143–162
Bernaz N (2013) Enhancing corporate accountability for human rights violations: is extraterritoriality the magic potion? J Bus Ethics 117:493–511. https://doi.org/10.1007/s10551-012-1531-z. 10 April 2019 UKSC/2017/0185 https://www.supremecourt.uk/cases/uksc-2017-0185#judgment-details. Accessed 31 Jan 2026
Bonnitcha J, McCorquodale R (2017) The concept of 'due diligence' in the UN guiding principles on business and human rights. Eur J Int Law 28(3):899–919

Bright C, da Graça Pires C (2023) Guiding Principle 18: human rights impact assessment. In: Choudhury B (ed) The UN guiding principles on business and human rights: a commentary. Edward Elgar Publishing, pp 138–146

Buhmann K (2018) Neglecting the proactive aspect of human rights due diligence? A critical appraisal of the EU's non-financial reporting directive as a pillar one avenue for promoting pillar two action. Bus Hum Rights J 3(1):23–45. https://doi.org/10.1017/bhj.2017.24. Accessed 31 Jan 2026

Buhmann K, Fonseca A, Andrews N, Amatulli G (2025) The Routledge handbook on meaningful stakeholder engagement. Routledge

CCC, ECCHR (2022) Public Eye and SOMO 'Legislating Human Rights Due Diligence: Respecting Rights or Ticking Boxes?' A Briefing Paper, January 2022. https://www.ecchr.eu/fileadmin/Publikationen/PublicEye_Report_Respecting-Rights_1-22.pdf#page=2.26. Accessed 31 Jan 2026

Chambers R, Yilmaz Vastardis A (2021) human rights disclosure and due diligence Laws: the role of regulatory oversight in ensuring corporate accountability. Chic J Int Law 21(2):323–366. https://chicagounbound.uchicago.edu/cjil/vol21/iss2/4. Accessed 31 Jan 2026

CHRB, Corporate human Rights Benchmark 2023 report, November 2023, 14, https://assets.worldbenchmarkingalliance.org/app/uploads/2024/03/2023_Corporate_Human_Rights_Benchmark__Insights_Report_13Mar2024.pdf. Accessed 31 Jan 2026

Edward F, Menghwar PS (2024) Chapter 2: Stakeholder theory and communities. In: Buhmann K, Fonseca A, Andrews N, Amatulli G (eds) The Routledge handbook on meaningful stakeholder engagement. Routledge, pp 43–55

Fasterling B (2017) Human rights due diligence as risk management: social risk versus human rights risk. Bus Human Rights J 2(2):225–247

Ford J, Nolan J (2020) Regulating transparency on human rights and modern slavery in corporate supply chains: the discrepancy between human rights due diligence and the social audit. Aust J Hum Rights 26(1):20–29. https://ssrn.com/abstract=3612492. Accessed 31 Jan 2026

Global Business Initiative (GBI) Making Policy Commitment. https://gbihr.org/business-practice-portal/making-a-policy-commitment. Accessed 31 Jan 2026

Götzmann N (2017) Human rights impact assessment of business activities: key criteria for establishing a meaningful practice. Bus Human Rights J 2(1):87–108

Harrison, J (2023) Human rights due diligence: challenges of method, power and competition' Centre for Human Rights in practice' Working Paper, University of Warwick, pp 1–31. https://wrap.warwick.ac.uk/id/eprint/174876/1/WRAP-harrison-hrdd-2023.pdf. Accessed 31 Jan 2026

Harrison J, Wielga M, Parejo M (2024) In search of effective corporate grievance mechanisms: can mandatory due diligence laws be a progressive force? J Human Rights Pract 16(3):819–835. https://doi.org/10.1093/jhuman/huae011. Accessed 31 Jan 2026

Human Rights Watch (2023) Bangladesh: Social Audits Shortchange Workers: Shahidul Islam's Killing Underscores Heightened Risks for Independent Unions. 14 September 2023 https://www.hrw.org/news/2023/09/14/bangladesh-social-audits-shortchange-workers>. Accessed 31 Jan 2026

Huyse H (2021) Towards Worker-Centred Human Rights Due Diligence (HRDD)' Research supported by ACV-CSC in the framework of the research chair Decent Work and the SDGs. KU Leuven Policy Brief, pp 1–19. https://hiva.kuleuven.be/sites/researchchairdw/Reports/worker_centered_HRDD_EN. Accessed 31 Jan 2026

Kanis BE (2015) Business, human rights, and due diligence: an approach for contractual integration. In: Martin J, Bravo KE (eds) The business and human rights landscape: moving forward, looking Back. Cambridge University Press, pp 413–441

Law 2017-399 of March 27, 2017 on the Duty of Vigilance of Parent Companies and Contracting Companies., Respect International 'French Corporate Duty of Vigilance Law (English Translation)' https://respect.international/french-corporate-duty-of-vigilance-law-english-translation/. Accessed 31 Jan 2026

LeBaron G (2021a) A market in deception? Ethically certifying exploitative supply chains. In: LeBaron G, Pliley JR, Blight DW (eds) Fighting modern slavery and human trafficking: history and contemporary policy. Cambridge University Press, pp 156–178

LeBaron G (2021b) Wages: an overlooked dimension of business and human rights in global supply chains. Bus Human Rights J 6(1):1–20. https://doi.org/10.1017/bhj.2020.32. Accessed 31 Jan 2026

Mares R (2024). The Unintended Consequences of Mandatory Due Diligence: the Importance of Supportive Measures in the EU Corporate Sustainability Due Diligence Directive. 13 June 2024 Https://Verfassungsblog.De/Csddd-The-Unintended-Consequences-Of-Mandatory-Due-Diligence/. Accessed 31 Jan 2026

Mares R (2018) Human rights due diligence and the root causes of harm in business operation' A textual and contextual analysis of the guiding principles on business and human rights. Northeastern Univ Law Rev 10(1):1–71

Martin-Ortega O (2022) Transparency and human rights in global supply chains: from corporate-led disclosure to a right to know. In: Marx A, Van CG, Wouters J (eds) Research handbook on global governance, business and human rights. Edward Elgar Publishing Limited, pp 100–120

McCorquodale R, Nolan J (2021) The effectiveness of human rights due diligence for preventing business human rights abuses. Netherlands Law Rev 68: 455–478. https://doi.org/10.1007/s40802-021-00201-x. Accessed 31 Jan 2026

McCorquodale R, Blanco-Vizarreta C (2023) Guiding principle 17: human rights due diligence. In: Choudhury B (ed) The UN guiding principles on business and human rights: a commentary. Edward Elgar Publishing, pp 126–136

Meyer N, Patz C (2024) Dividing the Indivisible: Human Rights under the EU Corporate Sustainability Due Diligence Directive. VerfassungBlog, 1 June 2024 https://verfassungsblog.de/dividing-the-indivisible-human-rights-under-the-eu-corporate-sustainability-due-diligence-directive/, https://doi.org/10.59704/a61ef927af06b44f. Accessed 31 Jan 2026

Muchlinski P (2022) Advanced introduction to business and human rights: Elgar Advanced Introductions. Edward Elgar Publishing

Natour F, Pluess JD (2013) How to conduct an effective human rights impact assessment. BSR Blog 19 March 2013 Https://Www.Bsr.Org/En/Blog/How-To-Conduct-An-Effective-Human-Rights-Impact-Assessment. Accessed 31 Jan 2026

Neglia M (2023) Principle 16: policy commitment. In: Choudhury B (ed) The UN guiding principle on business and human rights: a commentary. Edward Elgar, pp 118–125

New York University, Centre for Business and Human Rights 'Putting the S in ESG: Measuring Human Rights Performance for investors' 2017. https://www.stern.nyu.edu/experience-stern/global/putting-s-esg-measuring-human-rights-performance-investors. Accessed 31 Jan 2026

Newton A (2019) The business of human rights: best practice and the UN Guiding Principles. Taylor Francis Publishing

Nolan J, Frishling N (2020) Human rights due diligence and the over reliance on social auditing in supply chains. In: Deva S, Birchall D (eds) Research handbook on human rights and business. Edward Elgar Publishing, pp 108–138

Olsen T, Rehbein K, Snelson-Powell A, Westermann-Behaylo M (2022) Human rights in the oil and gas industry: when are policies and practices enough to prevent abuse? Bus Soc 61(6):1512–1557

Osci FSW (2023) Guiding principle 22: remediation. In: Choudhury B (ed) The UN guiding principles on business and human rights: a commentary. Edward Elgar, pp 171–177

Ripley M (2020) Getting beyond Tier 1: using a systems approach to improve working conditions in global supply chains. ILO The Lab October 2020 Https://Www.Ilo.Org/Sites/Default/Files/2024-05/Wcms_759213.Pdf#Page=3.05. Accessed 31 Jan 2026

Ruehmkorf, Andreas. 'Guiding Principle 21: communication of human rights impacts' in The UN guiding principles on business and human rights: a commentary edited by Barnali Choudhury, 164–170. Elgar Commentaries 2023

Ruggie JG, Sherman JF III (2017) The concept of 'due diligence' in the UN guiding principles on business and human rights: a reply to Jonathan Bonnitcha and Robert McCorquodale. Eur J Int Law 28(3):921–928

Scheltema M (2023) Guiding Principle 29: non-state-based grievance mechanisms: role of business. In: Choudhury B (ed) The UN guiding principles on business and human rights' a commentary. Edward Elgar, pp 222–229

Schilling-Vacaflor A (2021) Integrating human rights and the environment in supply chain regulations. Sustainability 13(17):1–15. Https://Www.Mdpi.Com/2071-1050/13/17/9666. Accessed 31 Jan 2026

Sherman JF III (2012). Are there risks knowing and showing? BSR Human Rights Working Group 22 October 2012, Shift https://shiftproject.org/wp-content/uploads/2012/10/Sherman_risksknowingshowing2012.pdf. Accessed 31 Jan 2026

Sherman JF III (2020) 'Beyond CSR: the story of the UN guiding principles on business and human rights' corporate responsibility initiative, Harvard Kennedy school. Working Paper March 2020:1–41 https://www.hks.harvard.edu/sites/default/files/centers/mrcbg/files/CRI_AWP_71.pdf#page=11.17. Accessed 31 Jan 2026

Shift (2013) Using Leverage in Business Relationships to Reduce Human Rights Risks, November 2013 https://shiftproject.org/wp-content/uploads/2013/11/Shift_leverageUNGPs_2013.pdf. Accessed 31 Jan 2026

Smit L, Holly G, McCorquodale R, Neely S (2020) Human rights due diligence in global supply chains: evidence of corporate practices to inform a legal standard. Int J Hum Rights 25(6):945–973

Stoop N, Verpoorten M, van der Windt P (2018) More legislation, more violence? The impact of Dodd-Frank in the DRC. PLoS One:1–19. https://journals.plos.org/plosone/article?id=10.1371/journal.pone.0201783. Accessed 31 Jan 2026

Sweden Sverige and UNDP (2022) Human Rights Due Diligence: An Interpretative Guide. https://www.undp.org/sites/g/files/zskgke326/files/2022-10/HRDD%20Interpretive%20Guide_ENG_Sep%202021.pdf#page=5.57. Accessed 31 Jan 2026

Tambe P, Tambay P (2020) Reducing Modern Slavery Using AI and Blockchain. In: 2020 IEEE / ITU International Conference on Artificial Intelligence for Good (AI4G), Geneva, Switzerland, pp 22–27, https://doi.org/10.1109/AI4G50087.2020.9311031. Accessed 31 Jan 2026

Tamir I, Zoen S (2017) Human rights impact assessments in a brazil land conflict: towards a hybrid approach. Bus Human Rights J 2(2):371–377. https://doi.org/10.1017/bhj.2017.16. Accessed 31 Jan 2026

Taylor MB (2020) Chapter 5: human rights due diligence in theory and practice. In: Deva S, Birchall D (eds) Research handbook on human rights and business. Edward Elgar Publishing, pp 88–107

The International Peace Information and Service (IPIS) insights on Due Diligence in Mineral Sourcing Regulating responsible sourcing of 3TG minerals: Comparative analysis of Section 1502 of the US Dodd-Frank Act and the EU Conflict Minerals Regulation, lessons learned and risks for implementation, Antwerp, 20 December 2019

Torelli R, Fiandrino S, Scarpa F (2024) Value-enhancing drivers of corporate governance in improvinghuman rights due diligence. John Wiley and Sons 32(1):1280

Wettstein F (2022) Business and human rights: ethical, legal, and managerial perspectives. Cambridge University Press

Wood S (2012) The case for leverage-based corporate human rights responsibility. Bus Ethics Q 22(1):63–98

Wörsdörfer M (2015) The equator principles and human rights due diligence—towards a positive and leverage-based concept of corporate social responsibility. Philos Manag 14:193–218. https://doi.org/10.1007/s40926-015-0014-6. Accessed 31 Jan 2026

Websites

Corporate Human Rights Benchmark. https://www.worldbenchmarkingalliance.org/corporate-human-rights-benchmark/. Accessed 31 Jan 2026

Chapter 3
Clarifying Corporate Human Rights Responsibilities in Specific Contexts Through OECD Case Law

3.1 Introduction

As discussed, Chap. 2 of this book serves as the core chapter, illustrating how NCPs elaborate on corporate responsibilities for human rights and environmental due diligence in alignment with the international BHR framework. However, the analysis of OECD case law reveals that human rights risks are diverse and often context-specific, involving different vulnerable groups, unique situations, and distinct concepts. This diversity in risk profiles indicates that a one-size-fits-all approach to HRDD is insufficient. Instead, corporate HRDD practices need to be tailored and customised to effectively address the specific risks associated with each company's actions and operating environment. The findings from the OECD case law highlighted that for HRDD to be truly effective, it must be responsive to the particular vulnerabilities and contextual factors that arise in different cases. For instance, risks related to workers' rights, Indigenous People's rights, or environmental impacts may require distinct approaches, given their unique implications for different groups and settings.

Thus, this chapter examined various cases within the OECD case law, identifying seven distinct areas in which corporate HRDD responsibilities must be adapted to address specific issues (Fig. 3.1. Sub-codes of Parent code: Corporate responsibilities in specific contexts). These areas reflect a range of critical concerns, from the need for MSE in Indigenous communities to implementing grievance mechanisms that account for cultural sensitivities. Based on this analysis, Chap. 3 is organised into six sections, each dedicated to one of these unique issues. In each section, the book first explored current developments under international human rights law and soft regulations, examining how scholars, policymakers, and legislators are defining and conceptualising corporate responsibilities in these specific contexts. This includes analysing recent guidelines, policy discussions, and legal interpretations

O. Davaanyam, *Conceptualising the Corporate Human Rights and Environmental Responsibilities*, Interdisciplinary Studies in Human Rights 17,
https://doi.org/10.1007/978-3-032-21430-0_3

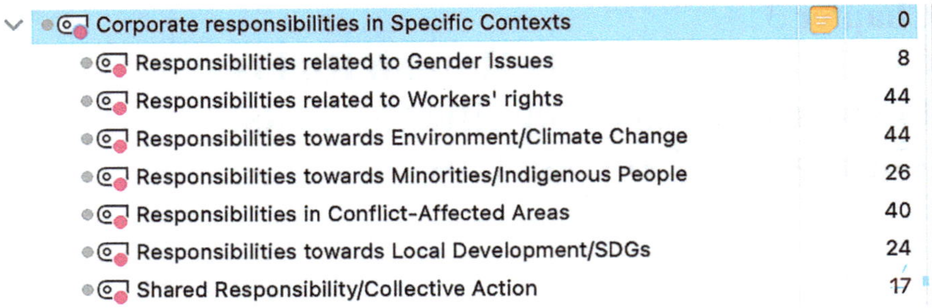

Fig. 3.1 Sub-codes of Parent code: Corporate responsibilities in Specific Contexts

that shed light on how due diligence requirements are evolving to meet each specific emerging human rights challenges.

The second part of each section then delves into OECD case law, drawing insights from real cases to illustrate how NCPs have interpreted and advised companies on these specific responsibilities in practice. By examining these cases, the book offers a nuanced perspective on how theoretical principles of HRDD are applied in diverse, real-world situations, providing valuable guidance for companies seeking to meet their human rights obligations. Ultimately, this chapter demonstrated that effective HRDD is not merely about adhering to general standards but about adapting those standards to address the unique risks that arise in different corporate contexts. By providing an in-depth analysis of OECD case law, this book aims to offer a practical roadmap for companies, scholars, and policymakers, highlighting the importance of a flexible, context-sensitive approach to HRDD responsibilities.

3.2 Corporate Human Rights Responsibility for Group Rights

The first and most essential aspect of corporate human rights due diligence is its ability to respond effectively to the distinct issues and risks faced by various vulnerable groups, including women, Indigenous Peoples, and workers, with particular attention to the rights of migrant workers. Each of these groups faces unique challenges that demand a tailored approach within due diligence practices. For example, Indigenous communities may face unique challenges, such as the risk of losing access to traditional lands and cultural heritage, which impacts not only their identity but also their economic and social stability.[1] Women in these communities might face compounded issues, dealing not only with discrimination and unequal treatment in the workplace but also with the impacts of cultural dislocation. Migrant

[1] OECD Guidance for MSE, Annex B. Engaging with Indigenous Peoples.

workers often encounter vulnerabilities tied to precarious legal status, language barriers, and limited access to support systems; for migrant women, these risks may be heightened by gendered expectations, limited protections, and the threat of exploitation.[2] These overlapping factors demonstrate how intersecting identities amplify the risks and challenges faced by marginalised groups.[3]

This section explores how companies can adapt their HRDD processes to address the specific needs of each group, ensuring that risks are not only identified but also managed in a way that respects the unique rights and circumstances of each. By implementing group-specific strategies, companies can make their due diligence efforts more meaningful and impactful, ultimately contributing to more equitable outcomes. It is also important to note that other vulnerable groups, such as children, people with disabilities, the elderly, and certain migrant populations, are relevant to corporate human rights considerations. However, these groups are not analysed in detail within this book due to the limited number of OECD cases available, which restricts the ability to draw comprehensive conclusions about best practices in these areas.

3.2.1 Corporate Human Rights Responsibility for Gender Issues

3.2.1.1 Corporate Responsibility to Respect Women's Rights: A Critical Evaluation Within International Business and Human Rights Frameworks

Despite extensive international treaties like the Convention on the Elimination of All Forms of Discrimination Against Women (CEDAW), there are critical gaps and ambiguities in how international law addresses women's rights within the business sector.[4] Many countries have ratified these treaties, yet few have effectively translated them into laws or policies that mandate corporate accountability on gender-specific issues.[5] This lack of clarity allows businesses to operate without robust

[2] Ibid, Annex C. Engaging with Women.

[3] Ibid, 101–102.

[4] UN General Assembly, *Convention on the Elimination of All Forms of Discrimination Against Women*, UNTS, 1249, 13, 18 December 1979, https://www.refworld.org/legal/agreements/unga/1979/en/13757 (accessed 31 January 2026).

[5] As of April 2022, 189 countries have committed to the CEDAW Convention and its obligations. Nevertheless, according to the International Centre for Research on Women, 50% of women worldwide are at risk of experiencing sexual harassment, violence, or discrimination in the workplace during their lifetime.

guidelines for protecting women's rights, especially in high-risk industries and conflict zones, where these protections are most needed.[6]

The UNGPs and the OECD Guidelines incorporate principles from CEDAW and other human rights agreements, yet their approach to women's rights is inconsistent and often lacks concrete requirements.[7] For instance, while the UNGPs emphasise non-discriminatory practices and address some gender issues, they rely on general recommendations rather than enforceable standards. This leads to ambiguity: Principles like 3, 7, and 12 suggest that states guide businesses on gender issues, address gender-based violence, and respect the rights of vulnerable groups, but they don't specify how these measures should be implemented or monitored.[8] Without stronger legislative commitments, these principles remain largely aspirational and fail to offer clear protections for women and girls in industries prone to exploitation.

The OECD Guidelines similarly lack precision regarding gender issues.[9] While the guidelines address general human rights responsibilities, they do not explicitly mention women's rights or detail the unique risks women face in business settings.[10] The recently updated version of the OECD Guidelines also failed to address gender issues more thoroughly. Gender is briefly mentioned in a single paragraph that advises companies to consider those at high risk of adverse impacts, but this minimal reference lacks actionable guidance.[11] This vagueness leaves companies to interpret gender-related responsibilities at their discretion, often resulting in inadequate protections for women in sectors with high female participation, such as apparel and agriculture.[12] Although the OECD Due Diligence Guidance introduces more detailed suggestions for integrating gender into corporate practices—such as collecting gender-disaggregated data and establishing gender-sensitive grievance mechanisms—its impact is limited by its non-binding nature.[13] Companies are encouraged but not required to adopt these practices, leading to inconsistent application and continued gender-based disparities in supply chains.[14]

[6] Quiroz and Seitz (2021), https://corporatejustice.org/news/corporate-accountability-whats-gender-got-to-do-with-it/ (accessed 31 January 2026).

[7] Corsi (2021), pp. 321–322.

[8] UN Guiding Principles on Business and Human Rights, Commentary to Principles 3, 7 and 12.

[9] The OECD Guidelines provide limited guidance on adopting a gender-sensitive or intersectional approach. Under Chapter IV: Human Rights, commentary paragraph 45, they briefly mention that MNEs should pay special attention to the rights and needs of women. However, this reference lacks detailed elaboration or a framework for implementing such an approach in practice.

[10] OECD (2020), https://mneguidelines.oecd.org/mneguidelines/Responsible-Business-Conduct-and-Gender.pdf.

[11] OECD Guidelines for Multinational Enterprises, para 45 of the Commentary to the Chapter IV: Human Rights.

[12] OECD Due Diligence Guidance, Section 2.2.i.

[13] Ibid.

[14] Grosser (2021), pp. 1624–1637.

Critics, including Jessica Lynn Corsi, highlighted that the UNGPs' approach to women's rights remains narrow and incomplete.[15] Corsi argued that the UNGPs primarily address sexual violence in conflict settings, failing to recognise the broader structural and workplace-related gender-based violence affecting women worldwide.[16] This limited framing creates an impression that gender-based violence is an exceptional issue, not an everyday concern. Additionally, Corsi, along with Simons and Handl, pointed out that the UNGPs' prioritisation of 'core' rights over gender-specific rights undermines an intersectional perspective, relegating women's rights to a 'secondary status' within international law.[17] By categorising women's rights as supplementary rather than essential, the UNGPs weaken protections and fail to align with international human rights law, which views women's rights as integral to universal human rights.[18] Moreover, as observed by Kristiansson and Götzmann and echoed by Kate Grosser, the inadequate integration of feminist perspectives into the UNGPs results in limited focus on the rights of women and girls during their implementation, particularly within NAPs on BHR.[19]

In response to these gaps, the WGBHR launched a project in 2017 to explore the gender dimensions of the UNGPs.[20] The resulting 2019 report offers businesses guidance on upholding the 'protect, respect, and remedy' principles in relation to women's rights. It introduces a three-step change process for implementing the UNGPs, which includes 'gender-responsive assessment, gender-sensitive measures, and gender-transformative remedies'.[21] Yet, this guidance remains non-binding, and its impact is diluted by its reliance on voluntary corporate compliance. Scholars like Sara Seck and Penelope Simons argued that this report also overlooks the larger role of neoliberal capitalism, which drives exploitative practices and reinforces global power imbalances.[22] Without addressing how capitalism perpetuates gender inequality, the report stops short of fostering meaningful change, leaving systemic vulnerabilities in place.

Emerging human rights laws also reflect these ambiguities. The CSDDD, for instance, has been criticised for failing to incorporate CEDAW or directly address the gendered impacts of the corporate abuses. Likewise, Australia's 2018 Modern Slavery Act, though requiring due diligence on exploitation risks in supply chains, does not address gender differences in these risks.[23] This lack of a gender perspective in legislation leaves women's experiences in supply chains overlooked, per-

---

[15] Corsi (2021), pp. 322–323; Simons and Handl (2019), p. 113.

[16] Ibid.

[17] Handl et al. (2022), p. 220.

[18] Ibid.

[19] Grosser (2021), pp. 1626–1627.

[20] UN WGBHR (November 2017a), https://www.ohchr.org/sites/default/files/Documents/Issues/Business/GenderConsultation30.11.17.pdf (accessed 31 January 2026).

[21] UN Human Rights Council (23 May 2019b).

[22] Seck and Simons (2019), pp. 1–6. https://utppublishing.com/doi/10.3138/cjwl.31.1.01a.

[23] Vijeyarasa (2020), pp. 74–92.

petuating gender inequalities and allowing businesses to sidestep accountability.[24] Had these laws mandated gender-sensitive due diligence and required gender-specific data collection, they could have set a standard for gender-responsive legislation.

In terms of the gender-transformative remedies, as introduced by the WGBHR, marks a shift toward integrating a gender perspective into the UNGPs.[25] Aleydis Nissen argued that this approach emphasises the need for preventive, redressive, and deterrent measures that challenge patriarchal norms and the unequal power dynamics fuelling gender-based violence, discrimination, and stereotypes.[26] Effective gender-transformative remedies require a nuanced, intersectional approach that recognises the specific ways women are disproportionately affected by corporate practices and broader social structures.[27] Feminist scholars argued that a deeper reimagining of dispute resolution is needed to incorporate gender perspectives, proposing that judicial decisions reflect substantive equality and correct power imbalances.[28] Some OECD NCP cases, particularly those involving women's working conditions, labour discrimination, difficulties in unionising, directly impact issues in gender, business and human rights, revealing the systemic nature of gendered disparities. This need for 'gender-transformative' remediation reflects a call for more coherent, accessible, and standardised gender-sensitive practices within international human rights frameworks, challenging existing power structures and promoting a more inclusive approach to corporate accountability.[29]

Handl, Seck and Simons strongly advocated for an intersectional approach to addressing the gender-based impacts of corporate activities, arguing that such an approach requires businesses to consider the diverse identities and vulnerabilities of affected women, girls, and people of various gender identities.[30] Adopting intersectionality means that businesses must not only identify all potentially affected groups but also understand how their activities differently impact individuals facing multiple forms of oppression and discrimination.[31] This includes recognising the ongoing influence of colonialism and its legacies, which continue to shape power dynamics and economic inequalities globally.[32] From a critical perspective, Seck and Simons challenged the traditional, often simplistic view of gender impact assessments in BHR frameworks. They emphasised that intersectionality demands a deeper, more nuanced analysis that goes beyond gender alone to account for how race, class,

---

[24] Ibid.

[25] Grosser (2021), pp. 1626–1627.

[26] Nissen (2020), https://aleydisnissen.com/gallery/publicationsp-Inthelongrun_Cambridge_Nissen_2.pdf (accessed 31 January 2026).

[27] Ibid.

[28] Ibid.

[29] Osci (2023), p. 176.

[30] Handl et al. (2022), pp. 207–208.

[31] Corsi (2021), pp. 322–323.

[32] Handl et al. (2022), pp. 212–213.

ethnicity, and historical injustices intersect to shape unique experiences of harm. Implementing such an approach would require businesses to undertake gender-responsive HRDD processes that can capture these layered impacts and address them meaningfully.[33]

This intersectional approach poses significant implications for both states and corporations. For states, it raises questions about their regulatory and enforcement roles in ensuring that businesses adopt comprehensive, intersectional HRDD practices.[34] For corporations, it demands a shift from a 'one-size-fits-all' approach to HRDD toward practices that are adaptable to the specific needs of marginalised communities. This shift necessitates not only structural adjustments but also a re-evaluation of corporate responsibility, as businesses would need to engage with impacted communities and relevant organisations in meaningful, and inclusive ways. In essence, BHR scholarship faces the task of defining and operationalising intersectional HRDD in both theory and practice. This approach could offer critical insights into how businesses can better respect human rights by acknowledging and addressing the complex realities of those most vulnerable to corporate harms.[35] However, achieving this requires moving beyond theoretical commitments to intersectionality and establishing practical, enforceable guidelines that embed these principles within corporate governance and accountability frameworks.

In conclusion, the UNGPs, OECD Guidelines, and other related frameworks, while progress toward gender equity, remain vague and non-binding, often failing to address the capitalist structures that underpin gender inequality in global value chain. These international laws and frameworks lack clear, enforceable standards, relying on voluntary compliance rather than rigorous accountability. To achieve real gender equity, BHR frameworks must adopt binding, intersectional policies that explicitly address the complex economic and social systems that sustain global gender-based oppression. Without such measures, international law will continue to fall short, leaving women's rights in the business context inadequately protected.

3.2.1.2 Gender Equality Under Human Rights Due Diligence: Lessons from OECD Case Law

Out of 394 cases, only 7 explicitly address corporate responsibility in mitigating gender-based negative impacts. These cases generally discuss the responsibilities of companies to tackle issues such as sexual discrimination, workplace harassment, and the adverse impacts on women in local and Indigenous communities. However, they often lack depth, likely due to the absence of gender-specific guidelines within the OECD framework. Nonetheless, some of these cases highlighted a clear need

[33] Ibid, 216.

[34] Ibid, 216–218.

[35] Seck and Simons (13 April 2020) https://digitalcommons.schulichlaw.dal.ca/ialawrbc/1/ (accessed 31 January 2026).

for companies to address gender-related impacts, providing explicit guidance on how to do so effectively.

The first case concerns the submission against Tosyalı Iron and Steel Senegal S.A. before the Turkish NCP, which brought to light serious gender-specific concerns, especially the adverse effects of the company's operations on local women's livelihoods, socio-economic security, and human rights.[36] The complaint from Lumiere Synergie pour le Développement (LSD) and the Fisher Women Association of Bargny highlighted the conflict between Tosyali's industrial activities and the established livelihoods of over 1500 women in fish processing.[37] Although the OECD Guidelines require companies to consider the human rights of all affected rightsholders, Tosyalı's response reveals a clear absence of gender-sensitive due diligence. The company failed to assess or acknowledge the differentiated impacts its operations may have on women, particularly in relation to their socio-economic roles and vulnerabilities. Moreover, the case reflects broader environmental justice concerns: the construction on the Khelcom site has disrupted the local ecosystem and undermined women's livelihood activities, yet no proactive, participatory impact assessment was undertaken to identify, prevent, or mitigate these harms.[38] Although the company has engaged in an environmental and social impact assessment (ESIA) after beginning their operations, this reactive measure failed to account fully for the women's displacement and the potential and actual socio-economic losses they faced. The proposal to relocate these women to an alternative site has seen delays and disagreements.[39]

Based on the final statement, the company's engagement strategy, coordinated with Senegalese authorities, appears to have been predominantly top-down and insufficiently responsive to the rightsholders' needs.[40]

From a procedural perspective, the Turkish NCP encountered substantial obstacles in facilitating the resolution of the case. These included persistent difficulties in maintaining contact with the complainants and continued disagreements between the parties regarding the resettlement arrangements and associated contractual terms. The final statement further noted that the NCP's role was constrained by limited engagement from both sides, reducing its involvement to periodic requests for updates rather than enabling sustained dialogue or meaningful mediation.[41] Additionally, the NCP lacked the authority to comprehensively assess the situation in terms of compliance with the OECD Guidelines.

---

[36] NCP Turkey, "Lumiere Synergie pour le Developpement" and "l'Association des femmes transformatrices de poissons de Bargny Guèdj (Khelcom)" v.Tosyalı Iron And Steel Senegal S.A, Initial Statement, 27 August 2021.

[37] Ibid, 1.

[38] Ibid, 1–2.

[39] Ibid.

[40] NCP Turkey, "Lumiere Synergie pour le Developpement" and "l'Association des femmes transformatrices de poissons de Bargny Guèdj (Khelcom)" v.Tosyalı Iron And Steel Senegal S.A, Initial Statement, 16 August 2023.

[41] Ibid, 3.

The second case concerns Barrick Gold's operations in Papua New Guinea and the complaint filed by PLOA, ATTA, and MiningWatch Canada against the Porgera Joint Venture (PJV).[42] The complainants alleged serious human rights abuses, including sexual violence by security personnel, forced evictions, and the destruction of homes and farmland.[43] These violations expose a systemic failure in the company's HRDD responsibilities, particularly in identifying and preventing gender-based violence and ensuring effective grievance mechanisms. From a gender perspective, the case reveals how women bear the brunt of such harms—facing physical violence, trauma, and economic displacement—highlighting the absence of a gender-responsive HRDD framework. Environmental justice issues further compound these harms: PJV's waste disposal and emissions reportedly polluted local water and air, undermining both ecosystems and livelihoods. The company's lack of transparency in environmental monitoring and reporting reflects a deeper accountability gap, restricting affected communities' access to environmental information and participation in decision-making processes essential to remedy and trust-building.

While the Canadian NCP–as characterised by its operatively voluntary and non-adjudicative nature–was structurally inhibited from ruling on the most severe allegations, including rape and other forms of gender-based violence, it nevertheless concluded its specific instance procedure with notable procedural successes in the form of a mediated agreement. The agreement included commitments by the company to implement an action- plan jurisdictionally spanning the provision of mitigation-enhæcing infrastructure (e.g. potable water systems), health risk assessments, strengthened grievance mechanisms, and a framework addressing violence against women.[44]

However, the formal categorisation of the case as 'successfully concluded' obscures material deficiencies in the NCP's engagement with the substantive allegations. The final statement issued by the Canadian NCP is conspicuously silent regarding both the legal gravity and the gendered nature of the reported violations. It neither articulates the seriousness of the allegations nor delineates the corresponding corporate responsibility to remedy such harms in accordance with the OECD Guidelines and the UNGPs. This analytical and normative vacuum effectively divests the proceedings of their potential to develop jurisprudential guidance on gender-responsive HRDD. Moreover, the NCP's failure to address—or request transparency regarding—steps taken by the company to substantiate or remedy serious gender-based violations reflects a broader institutional reluctance to engage with systemic human rights abuses beyond procedural compliance. In doing so, the NCP arguably undermines the interpretative authority of its own mandate and

[42] NCP Canada, The Porgera Landowners Association (PLOA), a Papua New Guinean association, and the Akali Tange Association (ATA), a Papua New Guinean NGO, assisted by Mining Watch Canada (MWC), a Canadian NGO v. Porgera Gold Mine in Papua New Guinea, Barrick Gold, Final Statement, 16 January 2014.

[43] Ibid, 6. Initial statement.

[44] Ibid, 7. Mediation.

neglects an opportunity to advance legally coherent, gender-responsive standards for corporate conduct within the OECD system.

The cases involving TÜV Rheinland AG, APG Asset Management, and Chanel Korea provide more substantive insights into how MNEs approach the complex challenge of addressing gender-based violence and harassment (GBVH) in the workplace. In particular, the Chanel Korea case is instructive, as it highlighted the overarching corporate responsibility to prevent, address, and remedy workplace GBVH and related human rights violations.[45] The Korean NCP received a complaint from the Chanel Korea Branch of the Department Store Sales and Service Workers' Union, alleging multiple violations by Chanel Korea. These included sexual harassment claims, denial of trade union rights, refusal to provide essential information for collective bargaining, violations of labour standards (such as forced holiday work), discriminatory treatment of union members, and mandatory work during the COVID-19 pandemic. The NCP organised a form of a mediation committee facilitated dialogue between the parties. As part of the mediated agreement, Chanel Korea committed to the 'Better Workplace for Women' project and established internal procedures for reporting and addressing GBVH at workplace.[46]

In this case, the company responded to the OECD NCP process by disclosing further information about its internal procedures for investigating and reporting workplace GBVH, following consultations with the complainant.[47] While the publicly available details remain limited, the case nevertheless demonstrates the constructive potential of deceptive—as voluntary and non-binding—NCP proceedings to induce corporate improvements: Chanel Korea committed to develop formal GBVH policies and initiate staff training programmes. Notably, the company's decision to begin targeted due diligence on GBVH only materialised after its engagement with the complainant during mediation. This reflects not only the NCP's capacity to promote corporate behavioural change, but also exposes a significant compliance gap—namely, the absence of gender-responsive HRDD measures prior to the complaint. The Chanel Korea case therefore exemplifies both the value and the limitations of the NCP process in advancing workplace protections against GBVH while simultaneously underscoring the need for more systematic, preemptive integration of gender-specific due diligence within corporate policy frameworks.

The TUV Rheinland case highlighted the limitations and responsibilities of social audits and risk assessments in ensuring workplace compliance with OECD Guidelines, especially regarding gender issues in high-risk sectors like the textile industry in Bangladesh.[48] Complainants argued that TÜV India's social audit failed to meet OECD Guidelines, particularly concerning risks related to GBVH, child

[45] NCP Korea, Chanel Korea Branch of the Department Store Sales and Service Workers' Union against Chanel Korea YH, Final Statement, 19 December 2023.

[46] Ibid, 8.

[47] Ibid.

[48] NCP Germany, European Center for Constitutional and Human rights et al. against TUV Rheinland, Final Statement, 26 June 2018.

labour, and forced labour, raising critical questions about the effectiveness of social audits in protecting vulnerable workers.[49] A central concern raised by the German NCP in the TÜV Rheinland case was the disconnect between the audit findings and the root causes linked to the local industry and working environment. Although TÜV India's audit report did not identify instances of GBVH or labour exploitation, the complainants argued that this outcome stemmed not from an absence of risk, but from the audit's inadequate assessment methodology. In particular, the audit failed to account for sector-specific and gender-specific vulnerabilities that are well-documented within the regional textile and garment industry. This highlights a systemic limitation of conventional social auditing: a narrow, checklist-based approach risks producing 'clean' reports while overlooking embedded structural harms, thereby weakening the credibility and preventive function of corporate due diligence.[50]

This disconnect indicated a significant challenge in workplace audits: while existing standards form the foundation, they may lack the depth needed to address specific social risks, particularly those affecting vulnerable groups including women. Complainants suggested improvements, such as using more female auditors, engaging trade unions more directly, and conducting off-site or anonymous interviews.[51] These measures could enable a more gender-sensitive approach, considering nuanced, often concealed forms of discrimination and harassment faced by women. The German NCP acknowledged that auditing firms cannot single-handedly enact structural changes in corporate responsibility without involvement from various stakeholders, including standards-setters, procurement officers, and civil society organisations.[52] The case highlighted that merely meeting existing audit standards is insufficient in high-risk sectors; collaborative efforts are needed to refine standards, making audits more comprehensive and transparent.

The case against APG Asset Management, reviewed by the Dutch NCP, emphasised the growing recognition of investors' responsibilities to address GBVH in the workplace, especially within industries like fast food.[53] This case sets a precedent by highlighting the role of investors in driving gender-responsive practices within their portfolio companies. The complaint emphasised the importance of APG adopting a gender-responsive lens in its investment assessments, expanding the scope of RBC to include social and gender-specific factors.[54] The agreement reached between APG, and the complainants outlines key commitments to enhance gender sensitivity in APG's investment practices. First, the exchange of information on APG's RBC policies and the prevalence of GBVH in the fast-food industry reflected a proactive

[49] Ibid, 4–5.

[50] Ibid.

[51] Ibid, 12–13.

[52] Ibid, 13.

[53] NCP Netherland, 4 Trade Unions (IUF, EFFAT-IUF, SEIU, UGT) v. APG Asset Management, 'Follow up of the Final Statement, 21 December 2023.

[54] Ibid, 2.

approach to identifying risk areas within APG's investments.[55] Second, the development of a shared understanding of standards on GBVH and the call for effective, publicly available policies illustrated the parties' recognition of the need for transparency and accountability.[56] The agreement also underlined the value of MSE, particularly with workers, in formulating policies and training programs, acknowledging that those affected by GBVH must be involved in creating effective solutions.

The roadmap for further cooperation demonstrated APG's commitment to embedding a gender-based perspective in its policies through continuous learning and development. Additionally, the roadmap emphasised developing indicators and data sets, industry engagement guidance, and internal documentation on GBVH, which would provide APG with concrete tools to measure and monitor gender-related risks across its investment activities. This case exemplified how investors can take meaningful steps toward integrating gender considerations into policies and operational frameworks, setting a model for the financial sector in advancing gender equity within corporate practices.

Taken together, these cases expose persistent structural gaps in how MNEs and financial institutions conceptualise and operationalise their responsibilities regarding GBVH and other gendered human rights risks. Across all cases, a common pattern emerges: corporate compliance tends to remain limited to baseline standards, while the gendered dimensions of harm—particularly in high-risk sectors such as extractives, manufacturing, and global supply chains—continue to be marginalised or entirely overlooked. The selective visibility of gender in corporate due diligence demonstrates that existing practices are not merely incomplete, but structurally ill-equipped to detect, prevent, or remedy GBVH and related violations. Although the involvement of certain NCPs has proven instrumental in prompting dialogue, disclosing internal procedures, and encouraging incremental policy reform, these interventions also reveal the limits of reactive, case-by-case engagement. The cases highlighted the urgent need for companies to embed gender-responsive due diligence as a *systemic* and *anticipatory* obligation, rather than a remedial response triggered only by complaints. More broadly, they point to the necessity of integrating gender-transformative standards within the architecture of BHR frameworks—including the OECD Guidelines, sector-specific guidance, and financial sector policies—so that gender is not treated as an 'add-on,' but as a core element of RBC.

[55] Ibid.

[56] Ibid, 2–3.

3.2.2 *Corporate Responsibility to Respect Labour Rights Under Current Business and Human Rights Regulations: A Critical Analysis*

3.2.2.1 Examining Corporate Responsibility to Respect Workers' Rights Under Current Business and Human Rights Regulations

Labour rights, a cornerstone of BHR, encounter substantial challenges within the contemporary global economy. Neoliberal policies, prioritising deregulation and unrestricted capital flows, have weakened worker protections, leading to a sharp increase in precarious and informal employment that now affects over 60% of the global workforce.[57] Moreover, the expansion of global commodity chains—which drive nearly 80% of international trade—has shifted much of the industrial labour base to the Global South, where around 70% of the world's industrial workforce is now concentrated.[58] Although these workers are essential to global production across industries like construction, automotive, and high-tech manufacturing, they continue to experience severe wage disparities and harsh working conditions.[59] Such inequities highlight a critical flaw in the global economic structure, where the labour contributions of workers in these regions are undervalued and undercompensated. The precarious nature of these conditions weakens workers' ability to exercise essential rights, like freedom of association and collective bargaining, which are vital for fair labour standards. Although BHR frameworks formally recognise labour rights, their practical impact is limited due to weak enforcement mechanisms and territorial restrictions, which are often ineffective against transnational business practices.[60] This lack of enforceability allows corporations to exploit regulatory gaps, undermining the labour protections that these frameworks aim to uphold.[61]

International labour rights are enshrined in prominent global frameworks, including the Universal Declaration of Human Rights (UDHR), the International Covenant on Civil and Political Rights (ICCPR), and the International Covenant on Economic, Social, and Cultural Rights (ICESCR), as well as various regional instruments.[62] However, fragmented implementation of these standards leads to inconsistent

---

[57] Cornell (2019), pp. 43–57; Torkington (4 June 2024), https://www.weforum.org/stories/2024/06/what-is-the-informal-economy/ (accessed 2 February 2026).

[58] Deva and Pushkar (2024). https://doi.org/10.1093/oso/9780198889755.003.0006 (accessed 2 February 2026).

[59] For example, see BHRRC 'Fiji: 34 Bangladeshi workers allegedly subject to exploitative working conditions & "inhumane treatment" at Pacific General Builders; incl. co comment' 2 November 2024 https://www.business-humanrights.org/en/latest-news/fiji-34-bangladeshi-workers-allegedly-subject-to-exploitative-working-conditions-inhumane-treatment-at-pacific-general-builders-incl-co-comment/ (accessed 2 February 2026).

[60] Landau and Howe (2022), pp. 466–491.

[61] Novitz (2022), pp. 231–252.

[62] Articles 4, 23 and 24 of the Universal Declaration of Human Rights and Articles 6, 7 and 8 of the International Covenant on Economic, Social and Cultural Rights.

protections, especially in countries where enforcement is weak or where attracting corporate investment takes precedence over labour rights.[63] The International Labour Organization (ILO) has set nearly 200 conventions that address minimum wages, working hours, workplace safety, and protection from harassment.[64] Despite the ILO's comprehensive system for labour rights, enforcement remains a significant challenge. The ILO's supervisory bodies, such as the Committee of Experts on the Application of Conventions and Recommendations (CEACR) and the Committee on Freedom of Association (CFA), are tasked with monitoring compliance through independent reviews and recommendations.[65]

However, these bodies lack direct enforcement power, which means they rely heavily on member states' voluntary compliance.[66] As a result, countries and transnational corporations may ignore ILO standards without immediate legal or financial repercussions, weakening the effectiveness of these conventions and diminishing protections for workers, especially in industries with exploitative practices. For example, the CEACR provides periodic technical evaluations and encourages states to adopt labour standards but cannot impose sanctions for non-compliance.[67] This reliance on moral authority limits its impact, especially in jurisdictions prioritizing economic flexibility over labour rights. Similarly, while the CFA addresses violations related to the right to unionize, its influence is primarily through recommendations and public reports rather than enforceable penalties.[68]

While the ILO has established many 'international labour standards' over the past century, some are seen as especially important. In 1998, the ILO introduced the Declaration on Fundamental Principles and Rights at Work, highlighting four key areas to protect human rights at work worldwide, including freedom of association, the elimination of forced and child labour, and non-discrimination.[69] The UNGPs draw their normative foundation from two primary international frameworks: the International Bill of Human Rights and the ILO Declaration on Fundamental Principles and Rights at Work.[70] The UNGPs provide a framework for companies to address human rights issues, drawing from international human rights and labour standards. A central component is HRDD, a proactive process that enables companies to identify, prevent, and address human rights risks associated with their operations. This approach is especially important in global supply chains and regions with inconsistent labour standards, helping companies manage risks and reduce negative impacts on workers and communities.

---

[63] Nicolas (2022), pp. 421–438.

[64] ILO List of Conventions https://normlex.ilo.org/dyn/nrmlx_en/f?p=NORMLEXPUB:12000:0::NO:::. accessed 10 October 2024.

[65] ILO (2019) https://www.ilo.org/sites/default/files/wcmsp5/groups/public/@ed_norm/@normes/documents/publication/wcms_730866.pdf#page=4.10 (accessed 2 February 2026).

[66] Ibid, 35–46.

[67] Ibid, 17–32.

[68] Ibid, ILO (1949) (No. 98), pp. 83–86.

[69] ILO Declaration on Fundamental Principles and Rights at Work (18 June 1998).

[70] UN Guiding Principles on Business and Human Rights, Principle 12 and its Commentary.

The OECD Guidelines reinforce the UNGPs by establishing HRDD as a standard practice, offering a six-step framework to help companies fulfil their human rights responsibilities.[71] This framework incorporates key ILO conventions, supporting a business model based on accountability, transparency, and ethical practices. Chapter VI of the OECD Guidelines, focused on Employment and Industrial Relations, outlines core labour rights and encourages companies to comply with standards that go beyond national labour laws, ensuring protections that align with international principles.[72]

However, these frameworks, despite referencing core labour standards like those in the 1998 ILO Tripartite Declaration of Principles concerning Multinational Enterprises and Social Policy (ILO MNE Declaration), often fail to outline specific actions required from corporations. For example, while the ILO MNE Declaration urges companies to take 'immediate and effective measures' to combat forced labour, it provides little actionable guidance, allowing corporations broad discretion in interpreting their obligations. These voluntary frameworks have inspired numerous private regulatory initiatives, commonly called 'multi-stakeholder initiatives,' which attempt to turn corporate human rights obligations into practice. Such initiatives often involve private commitments to improve labour conditions in supply chains and address labour rights abuses through codes of conduct. However, the scope and enforcement of these initiatives vary greatly, resulting in inconsistent labour rights protections.[73] The voluntary nature of the UNGPs and the OECD Guidelines means their effectiveness largely depends on corporate goodwill or, in some cases, enforcement through national law, leading to uneven practices and limited accountability.

The limitations of national labour legislation often fail to fully address the realities of transnational business activities, especially when developing countries prioritise economic gains over human rights and decent work standards. This leaves many workers without adequate protections. Additionally, many workers migrate abroad in search of better income, but due to limited labour protections in some host countries, they are at higher risk of exploitation, including forced labour and poor working conditions.[74]

However, governments are beginning to respond with mandatory regulations to hold MNEs accountable both domestically and internationally. Starting with California's Transparency in Supply Chains Act, countries are increasingly implementing laws that require MNEs to adhere to labour rights standards.[75] The

---

[71] OECD Guidelines for Multinational Enterprises, Chapter IV: Human Rights.

[72] Ibid, Chapter VI.

[73] Baumann-Pauly et al. (2017), pp. 771–787. https://doi.org/10.1007/s10551-016-3076-z (accessed 2 February 2026).

[74] Migration Data Portal (12 June 2024) *https://www.migrationdataportal.org/themes/labour-migration#:~:text=According%20to%20the%20latest%20available,force%20(ILO%2C%20 2021)* (accessed 2 February 2026).

[75] The California Transparency in Supply Chains Act https://oag.ca.gov/sites/all/files/agweb/pdfs/sb657/resource-guide.pdf (accessed 2 February 2026).

legislations, such as UK, and Australia's Modern Slavery Acts, Canada's Child Labour and Forced Labour Act, Switzerland's Ordinance on Minerals and Child Labor, the Netherlands' Child Labour Due Diligence Act, the Duty of Vigilance Law, and LkSG, mandates that companies align with ILO standards, especially in preventing child and forced labour.[76] These laws represent a significant shift toward mHRDD, requiring companies to adopt responsible practices that go beyond voluntary guidelines.

Anne Lafarre and Bas Rombouts argued that mHRDD requirements are increasingly recognised as an effective approach for ensuring that companies address human rights risks in their global value chains, particularly for fundamental labour standards that are often under strain.[77] Such legislation aims to narrow the gap between corporate leaders who already prioritize these standards and laggards who have yet to take adequate action. However, they noted that it is crucial that mHRDD legislation is carefully crafted to minimise potential negative impacts, such as excessive administrative burdens on smaller businesses or unintended shifts in labour practices that could harm workers in certain regions.[78] Furthermore, empirical evidence studied by the scholars suggested that French Duty of Vigilance Law has had a positive impact by compelling companies previously lagging in human rights practices to improve their commitment to sustainable business models.[79] This law has effectively pushed these companies to integrate workers' rights and other human rights into their operations, contributing to better protections within their supply chains. Such outcomes suggested that well-designed mHRDD laws can be instrumental in promoting widespread corporate accountability and fostering a more consistent adherence to labour rights across industries.

The recent adoption of the CSDDD reinforces the commitment to respect labour rights, mandating companies to address a broad range of core labour rights within their value chains.[80] These regulations encompass critical protections, including workers' rights, safe working conditions, and bans on child and forced labour, holding companies accountable for upholding these standards across all operations and suppliers.[81] The CSDDD has the potential to enhance corporate responsibility for labour rights by promoting robust and meaningful HRDD. The CSDDD advocates for comprehensive measures, including third-party verification, contractual assurances, and potentially even financial and non-financial support to help suppliers

[76] Modern Slavery Act UK; Modern Slavery Act Australia; Fighting Against Forced Labour and Child Labour in Supply Chains Act; (Wet zorgplicht kinderarbeid) Child Labour Due Diligence Act Official Gazette of the Kingdom of the Netherlands, 24 October 2019, 401 https://zoek.officielebekendmakingen.nl/stb-2019-401.html (accessed 2 February 2026); Germany. The Act on Corporate Due Diligence Obligations in Supply Chains (Lieferkettensorgfaltspflichtengesetz, LkSG) 22 July 2021 and Duty of Vigilance Law.

[77] Lafarre and Rombouts (2020), pp. 1–17.

[78] Ibid, 17.

[79] Ibid.

[80] Corporate Sustainability Due Diligence Directive.

[81] Ibid, Annex, Part I.

meet labour standards.[82] Additionally, it requires businesses to engage actively with relevant stakeholders, including their own employees as well as workers within their supply chains. This engagement can help ensure that labour rights impacts are addressed transparently and collaboratively, leading to a more responsible approach to managing labour conditions across global value chains.

However, gaps remain: many endorsing countries—including all EU member states—have not ratified the International Convention on the Protection of the Rights of All Migrant Workers and Members of Their Families.[83] This omission leaves migrant workers, who are disproportionately vulnerable to forced labour, trafficking, and other abuses, without adequate protections. Additionally, the proposed EU Regulation to prohibit products made with forced labour within the Union market overlooked the specific risks faced by migrant workers, even though they represent a significant portion of forced labour victims globally.[84] This oversight means that one of the most vulnerable groups in the global workforce remains insufficiently protected, highlighting a critical need for policies that explicitly address the unique challenges faced by migrant labourers. In 2023 alone, the BHRRC recorded 613 instances of human rights abuses involving migrant workers.[85] Although they are key stakeholders in the global labour market, their protections are routinely neglected.

One of the key advancements in the CSDDD is its inclusion of contract workers, as well as workers throughout the supply chain, within its scope.[86] Contract workers, while often performing similar roles to permanent employees, are frequently excluded from essential protections, with employers avoiding responsibility for their working conditions, health and safety, insurance, and severance benefits.[87] By explicitly covering contract workers along with permanent employees, the CSDDD aims to address these disparities, extending critical labour protections to a broader segment of the workforce. This inclusion is a notable step toward ensuring that all workers, regardless of their contract type, benefit from responsible labour practices under the directive.

The urgent need for corporate accountability is highlighted by high-profile cases that revealed the severe consequences of inadequate labour protections. Incidents

---

[82] Ibid, Articles 10 and 11.

[83] International Convention on the Protection of the Rights of All Migrant Workers and Members of Their Families.

[84] EU, Regulation of the European Parliament and of the Council on prohibiting products made with forced labour on the Union market and amending Directive (EU) 2019/1937, https://data.consilium.europa.eu/doc/document/PE-67-2024-INIT/en/pdf(accessed 2 February 2026).

[85] BHRRC 'Migrant workers in global supply chains' https://www.business-humanrights.org/en/big-issues/labour-rights/migrant-workers-in-global-supply-chains/ (accessed 2 February 2026).

[86] Recital 27 of the Corporate Sustainability Due Diligence Directive, which states that temporary agency workers, other workers in non-standard forms of employment, as well as seasonal workers, should be included in the employee thresholds.

[87] ILO (1998) https://webapps.ilo.org/public/english/standards/relm/ilc/ilc86/rep-vadd.htm (accessed 2 February 2026).

such as the Ali Enterprises factory fire in Pakistan, the Rana Plaza collapse in Bangladesh, and lawsuits against major tech companies accused of benefiting from child labour in the Democratic Republic of the Congo highlighted the devastating impact of unsafe working conditions and corporate negligence.[88] These cases accentuate the necessity for businesses to proactively protect labour rights across their supply chains, including ensuring safe working environments, fair wages, prevention of forced labour, protection against child exploitation, and non-discrimination. However, enforcing these responsibilities remains complex, especially in industries with complex global supply chains, where accountability is often diluted, such as in the global construction sector, which has faced labour abuse allegations within its migrant and weak legal protection.[89] While voluntary frameworks have increased awareness and spurred some corporate accountability efforts, they fall short of providing effective labour rights protections in the absence of enforceable mechanisms. The lack of binding requirements, combined with limited oversight and ambiguous guidance, allows corporations to treat labour rights as aspirational rather than obligatory. This flexibility results in significant disparities in how businesses address labour rights, particularly in sectors reliant on informal and vulnerable labour forces.[90]

While frameworks such as the UNGPs, the OECD Guidelines, and ILO MNE Declaration established a baseline for corporate responsibility in labour rights, their voluntary nature severely undermines their effectiveness. Vulnerable groups—particularly contract workers—remain excluded from core ILO conventions, leaving them unprotected. Even when guidance exists, weak implementation diminishes its impact. Binding regulations with clear standards and robust accountability measures are essential to transform these frameworks from aspirational to enforceable. In this context, the recently adopted CSDDD marks a promising development by imposing legally binding HRDD obligations across value chains and including contract and supply-chain workers. Whether it can bridge the gulf between voluntary principles and enforceable standards—and genuinely improve labour protections worldwide—remains to be seen.

3.2.2.2 Advancing Fair Labour Practices: OECD Case Law Insights

Many specific instances reviewed by the OECD NCPs involve labour rights violations. Our research on OECD case law revealed that at least 107 cases addressed collective bargaining rights violations, with an additional 112 cases also relating to

[88] For example, Kelly (16 December 2019), https://www.theguardian.com/global-development/2019/dec/16/apple-and-google-named-in-us-lawsuit-over-congolese-child-cobalt-mining-deaths (accessed 12 November 2024); Clean Clothes Campaign 'Justice for the Ali Enterprises victims' https://cleanclothes.org/campaigns/past/ali-enterprises#:~:text=What%20happened%3F,windows%20and%20locked%20exit%20doors (accessed 2 February 2026).

[89] Segall (2022), pp. 358–379.

[90] Jovanovic (2021), p. 358.

labour rights breaches, some overlapping cases with the previous 107 cases. These violations primarily occur in developing countries, where MNEs are involved through various business relationships. This pattern highlighted the significant impact MNEs can have on labour conditions abroad, especially in developing countries where rule of law and human rights protections are weak. It emphasised the need for increased oversight and accountability in global supply chains to uphold fundamental labour standards. Of these cases, 31 were specifically examined within OECD case law to analyse corporate responsibilities toward workers' rights, focusing on how they should meet their responsibilities effectively. This focused review by NCPs is essential for defining corporate responsibilities and guiding MNEs in effectively addressing labour rights within their operations and business partnerships.

Most OECD cases focused on the corporate responsibility to recognise workers' rights to collective bargaining. These cases emphasised the significance of such rights and assessed how MNEs align their practices with the OECD Guidelines and the ILO Conventions. For instance, in the case against Teck before the Chilean NCP, Teck was recommended to respect workers' right to collective bargaining, and required to engage with workers and their union representatives transparently and meaningfully, upholding applicable labour laws and the labour rights under the OECD Guidelines.[91] Similarly, in the case against Accor at the French NCP, the NCP indicated that Accor should respect workers' rights to form or join trade unions and to recognise these unions for collective bargaining purposes.[92] The NCP highlighted Accor's responsibility to engage in constructive negotiations with union representatives and to foster cooperation on the issues of mutual interest.[93] These examples illustrated how NCPs uphold workers' collective bargaining rights as fundamental, urging MNEs to foster transparent, collaborative, and respectful labour rights due diligence.

Furthermore, there are other cases that shows the importance of MNEs' practices are consistently aligned with international labour standards across diverse jurisdictions. In the case against Teleperformance in French NCP, a MNE with over 50 branches worldwide, the NCP emphasised the need for the company to promptly recognise union rights and engage meaningfully with workers' representatives and unions.[94] The NCP underlined that unions play a crucial role in enabling effective due diligence responsibilities, particularly during crises like the COVID-19 pandemic, where health and other worker impacts are magnified.[95] This statement shows the importance of unions in promoting transparency, addressing workers' concerns, and safeguarding health and safety in challenging times.

---

[91] NCP Chile, Quebrada Blanca Trade Union v. Teck, Final Statement, 7 February 2020.

[92] NCP France, IUF v. Accor Group, Final Statement, 11 December 2012.

[93] Ibid, 3.

[94] NCP France, UNI Global Union v. Teleperformance, Final Statement, 5 July 2021.

[95] Ibid, 1.

Several cases addressed the connection between union rights and meaningful engagement with workers, as analysed in the Sects. 2.6.2.1 and 2.8.2.2 of this research on corporate responsibility for worker engagement. NCPs in cases involving companies such as Itaú Unibanco, Starbucks, and Unilever, reviewed by the Chilean and Brazilian NCPs, have emphasised the critical role of unions in representing workers and the importance of engaging with them as key stakeholders.[96] This approach is viewed as essential for respecting workers' rights and ensuring transparent communication channels between corporations and their employees. Furthermore, in the case against KiK Textiles, the German NCP emphasised the importance of trade union involvement in the due diligence process, particularly in delivering worker training on health and safety issues.[97] Such initiatives illustrated how union engagement contributes to empowering workers with knowledge about their rights and helps companies maintain ethical standards in line with OECD guidelines. Furthermore, NCP cases consistently highlight that effective communication through trade unions enhances both the meaningfulness and impact of worker engagement, empowering workers in negotiations.

It is also worth noting that in several cases, including those involving Starbucks and Atos Group reviewed by the Chilean and French NCPs, the NCP mechanism became an important leverage tool for unions to negotiate with multinational companies.[98] These proceedings resulted in transnational union agreements that extended representation and protections to hundreds—and in some instances thousands—of workers. While these outcomes demonstrate the potential of NCPs to facilitate large-scale collective bargaining, they also expose a structural limitation: such advances depend not on binding obligations, but on companies' voluntary cooperation. The cases therefore indicate both the enabling role of NCPs in strengthening labour rights across borders and the persistent fragility of relying on a non-mandatory mechanism to secure durable corporate accountability.

Many of these cases focus on corporate responsibility to address negative impacts on workers, particularly regarding health and safety conditions. For example, in the case against ALS brought before the Australian NCP, previously reviewed in the OECD case law, the NCP emphasised the responsibilities outlined in the OECD Guidelines.[99] In its final statement, the NCP highlighted that the OECD Guidelines require companies to take adequate measures to ensure occupational health and safety, including providing effective training and implementing safety practices for

[96] See the Sects. 2.6.2.1 and 2.8.2.2 of this chapter.

[97] NCP Germany, Uwe Kekeritz, Member of the German Bundestag, v. KiK Textilien and Non-Food GmbH, C&A Mode GmbH & Co., and Karl Rieker GmbH & Co.KG, Final Statement, 04 November 2014.

[98] NCP France, Intersyndicate Atos v. Atos Group, Final Statement, 15 December 2022; NCP Chile, the Starbucks Coffee Chile S.A. Workers' Union, the Central Unitaria de Trabajadores (CUT) v. Starbucks Coffee Chile S.A, Final Statement, 18 May 2015.

[99] NCP Australia, Mr. Yacouba Traoré on behalf of the Former Employees Collective of the Australian Laboratory Services Mali SARL Laboratory Group v. Australian Laboratory Services (ALS), Final Statement, 8 March 2019.

handling hazardous materials. Additionally, the Guidelines expect companies to monitor their practices, establish processes for raising concerns, and address any adverse impacts from their operations.

The NCP assessed ALS's compliance with these requirements, particularly its implementation of health and safety programmes, including worker training and the use of safety equipment. It also evaluated ALS's internal compliance programme, which mandates regular reporting from on-site management, supported by a regional management framework to ensure oversight and consistency across locations. As a result, the NCP was satisfied with ALS's compliance with the OECD Guidelines, particularly its monitoring and enforcement of health and safety standards, as well as its swift and adequate response to the complaint.

In several cases, the treatment of contract workers highlighted broader implications for workers' rights within the framework of the OECD Guidelines. The issue of contract and subcontracted workers in the South Korean shipbuilding industry, as highlighted in the case regarding Samsung Crane Accident exemplifies broader challenges in worker protections within global supply chains.[100] The fatal accident at Geoje Shipyard revealed systemic risks stemming from multi-layer subcontracting, a widespread practice in the industry. This approach allows large corporations like Samsung Heavy Industry to outsource certain functions and, unfortunately, many of the associated risks, to third-tier subcontractors. This practice often results in temporary and subcontracted workers receiving lower pay, less training, limited health and safety protections, and exclusion from the prime contractor's occupational accident insurance.[101] The case showed a recurring issue in supply chains: the diffusion of accountability, which dilutes responsibility for safety and other essential protections. Multi-tier subcontracting, as seen in this case, allows primary contractors to sidestep direct responsibility for health and safety compliance. Consequently, subcontracted workers face significantly higher risks, with data showing that 80% of shipyard fatalities involve subcontracted employees. This setup leaves subcontracted workers as some of the most vulnerable within these high-risk industries.[102]

The South Korean Ministry of Employment and Labour, along with the Korean NCP, has emphasised that prime contractors like Samsung bear primary responsibility for overseeing risk factors and ensuring subcontractor safety measures.[103] The OECD's Due Diligence Guidance aligns with this, recommending that companies facing systemic industry issues collaborate across sectors, engage governments, and

[100] NCP Norway, Samsung Heavy Industries Martin Linge Project Crane Accident Workers Support Team and Korean Transnational Corporations Watch v. Totalenergies E&P Norge As, Equinor Asa, Technip Energies N.V., Final Statement, 22 February 2023; NCP France, Unite Here v. Natixis/NGAM, Final Statement, 5 December 2017.

[101] Ibid, 25.

[102] Workers Support Team and KTNC Watch (20 March 2019), pp. 9–10; The Korea Bizwire (7 September 2018), http://koreabizwire.com/outsourced-risk-80-of-shipyard-deaths-involve-subcontractors/123980 (accessed 2 February 2026).

[103] Ibid 25.

support existing safety initiatives.[104] In response to this, Samsung prepared mid- and long-term safety improvement plans, and the Korean NCP suggested that the company should take an industry-wide initiative alongside other major actors and the government to enhance safety standards.[105]

Also, the case against VINCI Airport, reviewed by the French NCP, highlighted the complexities surrounding contract worker rights more specific way, particularly in cases of long-term temporary employment. VINCI was accused of using contract workers as 'disguised employment' for over 5 years without transitioning them to full-time status, a practice that can allow companies to avoid providing full benefits, insurance, and other protections typically afforded to permanent employees.[106] During mediation, VINCI denied the allegations of 'disguised employment'—a practice in which contract workers are kept on successive temporary contracts rather than being offered permanent roles—yet conceded to audit the temporary agencies involved, implicitly acknowledging weaknesses in its oversight mechanisms. Additionally, VINCI proposed specific criteria for granting permanent positions to long-term contract workers, responding to a key request from the complainants. While the NCP approved these criteria, tensions persisted, especially as complainants withheld the names of affected workers, which prevented VINCI from assessing individual cases. This case shows the potential of NCP-facilitated mediation to introduce reforms addressing exploitative employment practices. However, it also illustrates the limitations when parties are unwilling or unable to reach the agreement, due to the fear of retaliation and sensitive information. However, by setting criteria for tenure conversion, VINCI made strides toward greater protection towards the contract workers, that could be reflected in the future BHR frameworks.

Additionally, the case against Holcim, reviewed by the Swiss NCP, raised similar concerns about contract workers' rights but concluded with more concrete outcomes.[107] The Swiss NCP facilitated dialogue that led to notable improvements for contract workers, including local negotiations on fair compensation schemes and a proposed skills-assessment program.[108] Additionally, Holcim addressed specific payment issues by compensating 26 former employees for unpaid wages over a period of 39–40 months.[109] This case illustrated how a structured dialogue facilitated by the NCP can result in meaningful steps to improve conditions for contract workers. Throughout the NCP proceedings, some progress was made in addressing

---

[104] OECD, OECD Due Diligence Guidance, Section 3.2(d).

[105] NCP Norway, Samsung Heavy Industries Martin Linge Project Crane Accident Workers Support Team and Korean Transnational Corporations Watch against Totalenergies E&P Norge As, Equinor Asa, Technip Energies N.V., Final Statement, 22 February 2023; NCP France, Unite Here v. Natixis/NGAM, Final Statement, 5 December 2017, 26.

[106] NCP France, the International Trade Union Confederation (ITUC) and the Cambodian Labour Confederation against VINCI Airports in Cambodia, Final Statement, 11 December 2018.

[107] NCP Switzerland, Pragatisheel Cement Shramik Sangh (PCSS) v. Holcim India and Holcim Group, Final Statement, 18 December 2014.

[108] Ibid, 6.

[109] Ibid.

contract workers' conditions, such as initiating local discussions on fair compensation schemes, considering a skill assessment for contract workers in skilled or semi-skilled roles, and proposing a salary and benefits framework.[110] Despite these efforts, certain issues remained unresolved, such as disagreements over bonus payments, with the company opting to distribute silver coins as a symbolic gesture instead. These outcomes illustrated a partial but significant recognition of contract workers within the OECD Guidelines framework, highlighting both the potential and limitations of these standards in improving the employment conditions for them.

Furthermore, in a case reviewed by the UK's NCP, a UK-based investment company was accused of failing to oversee its Cameroonian subsidiary, which allegedly withheld a worker's documents and failed to pay his salary and retirement benefits in 2014.[111] The UK company, having acquired a majority stake that year, claimed it had no role in the subsidiary's daily operations. Nonetheless, the situation highlighted parent companies' responsibility for their subsidiaries' labour practices, even when direct management involvement is disputed. Although the NCP considered the worker's complaint legitimate, it concluded that the dispute fell outside the scope of the OECD Guidelines, categorising it as an individual matter involving trade union rights and anti-discrimination. This narrow interpretation significantly limited the investigation. As organisers noted, the UK NCP ultimately failed to address the substance of the claim, avoiding a meaningful assessment of the company's responsibility toward the individual worker.

In preliminary conclusion, the analysis of OECD case law on workers' rights reveals a broader interpretation of corporate responsibility than that set out in the OECD Guidelines and the UNGPs. The cases demonstrate that companies are expected not only to comply with health and safety standards, but also to uphold collective bargaining rights, strengthen social protections for contract workers, and ensure effective grievance mechanisms. Cases such as VINCI and Holcim show that the strategic use of long-term contract work to avoid granting full employment benefits constitutes a harmful practice incompatible with RBC. Similarly, the Samsung-related cases underlined that MNEs operating in high-risk sectors have a heightened responsibility to guarantee safe working conditions across their entire value chain, including for subcontracted labour.

---

[110] Ibid, 6–7.

[111] NCP United Kingdom, An individual in Cameroon against UK-based MNE, Initial Statement, June 2016.

3.2.3 Corporate Human Rights Responsibility for Minorities and Indigenous Peoples

3.2.3.1 Corporate Responsibility to Protect Minority and Indigenous Rights Under International Business and Human Rights Standards

The international legal landscape offers foundational protections for Indigenous Peoples and minority rights through frameworks like the ILO Convention 169, the United Nations Declaration on the Rights of Indigenous Peoples (UNDRIP) and the UN Declaration on the Rights of Persons Belonging to National or Ethnic, Religious, and Linguistic Minorities (UN Declaration on Minorities).[112] Indigenous Peoples, encompassing communities with unique cultural identities, ancestral ties to specific lands, and governance systems distinct from national frameworks, and minority groups, including ethnic, religious, and linguistic populations, are each protected by these rights frameworks.[113] Both Indigenous Peoples and minority groups face heightened risks of displacement, cultural erasure, and exploitation when their rights intersect with corporate activities, particularly in industries such as resource extraction, infrastructure, and development that impact their territories, natural resources, and cultural heritage.[114]

The ILO Convention No. 169, UNDRIP as well as the UN Declaration on Minorities establish the responsibility of states, rather than corporations, to protect, promote, and fulfil Indigenous peoples and minority communities' rights. However, as Kendyl Salcito argued that these frameworks also implicitly acknowledge the role of corporate actors in infringing upon these rights, particularly when it comes to the exploitation of natural resources.[115] ILO 169, for instance, provides safeguards against forced labour, workplace discrimination, and labour trafficking, issues often associated with agricultural and industrial expansion onto Indigenous lands.[116] Key articles within ILO 169 address forced recruitment, labour trafficking, and the displacement of Indigenous Peoples for natural resource 'exploration or exploitation.'[117] Similarly, the UNDRIP reaffirmed these protections by calling for FPIC in projects affecting the Indigenous People's lands and explicitly protecting

---

[112] International Labour Organization (ILO) (27 June 1989), https://www.refworld.org/legal/agreements/ilo/1989/en/19728 (accessed 2 February 2026); UN General Assembly (2 October 2007), https://www.refworld.org/legal/resolution/unga/2007/en/49353 (accessed 2 February 2026) (UNDRIP); UN Declaration on the Rights of Persons Belonging to National or Ethnic, Religious and Linguistic Minorities General Assembly Resolution A/RES/47/135, 18 December 1992 https://www.ohchr.org/en/instruments-mechanisms/instruments/declaration-rights-persons-belonging-national-or-ethnic (accessed 2 February 2026).

[113] Wettstein (2023), p. 92.

[114] Ibid, 92–93.

[115] Salcito (2023b), pp. 295–313.

[116] Ibid, 296.

[117] Ibid.

Indigenous territories from hazardous materials affected their rights and environment. The UN Declaration on Minorities also affirms the rights of minority groups to be free from all forms of discrimination and to participate effectively in all decision-making processes at national and regional levels concerning their communities and regions.[118]

Despite these protections, the implementation of both frameworks remains limited. The ILO 169 has only been ratified by 23 countries, and while UNDRIP has broader international endorsement, it remains largely non-binding.[119] This lack of enforceable mechanisms weakens the frameworks in the face of corporate violations, especially in countries with weak regulatory systems. Globally, Indigenous Peoples and minority communities are disproportionately impacted by corporate activities that often disregard their social, environmental, and cultural rights.[120] Industrial and agricultural projects frequently encroach upon Indigenous lands, leading to exploitative labour practices, environmental degradation, and cultural erosion.[121] Adding to this, the gendered and intersectional dimensions associated with Indigenous women, alongside the unique challenges faced by mobile Indigenous populations with nomadic lifestyles, add layers of complexity to addressing their rights and needs.[122] Addressing these issues requires intersectional approaches that account not only for gendered forms of marginalisation but also for the mobility and land-based identities of nomadic communities, thereby intensifying the complexity of inclusive policymaking.

The UNGPs and the OECD Guidelines place a crucial emphasis on corporate responsibility to respect Indigenous Peoples and minorities rights, especially when states fail to uphold these rights.[123] This responsibility is operationalised through due diligence processes that require companies to actively assess and mitigate human rights impacts. Importantly, businesses are expected to verify whether national laws align with the international standards (like ILO Convention 169) and to ensure that affected Indigenous and minority groups are genuinely involved in the

---

[118] United Nations Declaration on the Rights of Indigenous Peoples (UNDRIP), Article 17(2).

[119] ILO '30th anniversary of the Indigenous and Tribal Peoples Convention, 1989 (No. 169)' 30 January 2019 https://www.ilo.org/resource/30th-anniversary-indigenous-and-tribal-peoples-convention-1989-no-169#:~:text=169%20has%20been%20ratified%20by,indigenous%20and%20tribal%20peoples%20worldwide (accessed 2 February 2026).

[120] For example, see Salcito (2023a), pp. 265–270.

[121] See 'BHRRC 'Brazil: Indigenous communities in Pará say they were not consulted by the government about carbon credit contracts with multinationals' 5 November 2024 https://www.business-humanrights.org/en/latest-news/brazil-indigenous-communities-in-par%C3%A1-say-they-were-not-consulted-by-the-government-about-carbon-credit-contracts-with-multinationals-2/ (accessed 2 February 2026).

[122] Tapias Torrado (2020), pp. 29–44; University of Oxford (8 October 2024), https://www.ox.ac.uk/news/2024-10-08-new-report-spotlights-urgent-issues-faced-mobile-indigenous-populations (accessed 2 February 2026).

[123] UN Guiding Principles on Business and Human Rights, Principle 12; OECD Guidelines for Multinational Enterprises, Chapter IV: Human Rights, commentary para 45.

decisions affecting their territories, resources, livelihood and rights.[124] Additionally, Černič highlighted that the NAPs on BHR and the Legally Binding Instrument on BHR (LBI) include specific protections for Indigenous Peoples' rights and reflect growing global efforts to enhance corporate accountability toward Indigenous and minority communities.[125]

However, the UNGPs' and the OECD Guidelines non-binding nature grants companies' considerable flexibility, which can lead to inconsistent interpretations of what constitutes adequate protection. Without enforceable obligations, many companies may view their responsibilities toward these groups as discretionary, which contributes to the 'hierarchy of human rights' criticism.[126] This critique, as expressed by feminist and TWAIL scholars, argued that categorising certain rights as optional or secondary reinforces a perception that rights specific to Indigenous people, minorities, and vulnerable groups are not as universally essential as others.[127] This implicit bias risks marginalising these groups further by treating their rights as 'special interests' rather than fundamental rights, despite the guidance for corporations to engage in due diligence process and empowerment.[128] The lack of binding enforcement in the UNGPs thus creates a paradox: while companies are expected to go beyond national shortcomings to uphold these rights, the flexibility in interpretation often leads to insufficient protections. This gap demonstrates the critique that the UNGPs and the OECD Guidelines, in their current form, may inadequately ensure the universal application of human rights, particularly for marginalised groups.

Furthermore, a central tenet for safeguarding Indigenous People's rights within these frameworks is the principle of FPIC.[129] Rooted in the ILO 169 and further solidified by the UNDRIP, FPIC mandates that Indigenous communities must provide consent before any operations that could impact their lands, resources, or cultures begin.[130] The FPIC is also relevant to minority rights, as many minority communities reside in vulnerable areas where corporate activities threaten their lands and resources.[131] Each element of FPIC—'Free,' 'Prior,' 'Informed,' and 'Consent'—demands authentic and responsible actions from both states and corporations. BHR frameworks such as the UNGPs, the OECD Guidelines, and the ILO MNE Declaration have significantly raised awareness of Indigenous and minority rights. These frameworks set clear expectations: corporations must respect human

[124] The UN Working Group on Business and Human Rights, Report on business-related impacts on the rights of indigenous peoples, 6 August 2013, A/68/279.

[125] Černič (2020), p. 350.

[126] McCorquodale (2024), p. 50.

[127] Ibid.

[128] Ibid.

[129] Bhatt (2021), pp. 455–480.

[130] ILO 169.

[131] Lewis (October 2012) https://minorityrights.org/app/uploads/2024/01/download-1157-corporate-responsibility-to-respect-the-rights-of-minorities-and-indigenous-peoples.pdf#page=14.61 (accessed 2 February 2026).

rights in all circumstances, while states retain the primary responsibility to protect these rights. In this context, FPIC acts as a crucial mechanism, enabling states to protect Indigenous rights while obligating corporations to respect them.

The OECD Guidelines, which reference the UNDRIP, call on companies to respect all internationally recognised human rights, specifically including Indigenous Peoples' rights, and to address any human rights harms they may cause.[132] These guidelines empower stakeholders to demand that companies avoid contributing to or causing harm to Indigenous rights and require that companies address and remediate any such harm. FPIC is central to this approach, with the OECD's due diligence guidance offering practical advice on its application. Additionally, companies are encouraged to take preventive steps to avoid or mitigate harms to Indigenous rights when they are directly linked to the business's operations.

Further guidance on FPIC implementation is offered by the International Finance Corporation (IFC), which incorporated FPIC principles into its Sustainability Framework in 2012 through the revision of Performance Standard 7 (PS7).[133] The IFC Performance Standards, in turn, influence the Equator Principles, which also incorporated FPIC in their revised draft.[134] However, challenges arise in applying these standards, as shown in a recent BSR mining project in the Philippines. Here, BSR encountered difficulties due to vague legislation, which offered broad guidelines but lacked a clear, approved process for obtaining FPIC. This ambiguity disadvantaged both the company, and the stakeholders involved.[135] In the absence of a defined process, companies needed significant time and resources to develop an approach to FPIC that was acceptable to stakeholders. The requirement to formalise the consent process meant that companies had to communicate both the benefits and costs of the project to all relevant stakeholders early in the project lifecycle. Achieving true informed consent, rather than merely consulting, required additional time, expertise, and resources.[136] Finally, the project's social investment requirements also affected FPIC implementation. In this case, government influence on the allocation of investment funds sometimes overshadowed the community's interests.[137]

---

[132] OECD Watch 'The OECD Guidelines and Indigenous Peoples' https://www.oecdwatch.org/oecd-ncps/the-oecd-guidelines-for-mnes/what-is-in-the-oecd-guidelines/the-oecd-guidelines-and-indigenous-peoples/#:~:text=You%20can%20use%20the%20OECD,and%20informed%20consent%20(FPIC) (accessed 2 February 2026).

[133] The IFC's Sustainability Framework consists of policy on environmental and social sustainability, performance standards, and access to information policy, 31 December 2011, https://www.ifc.org/en/insights-reports/2012/publications-policy-sustainability-2012 (accessed 2 February 2026).

[134] Equator Principles, June 2006. Please note: The IFC's revised Performance Standards apply to the Equator Principles Framework that also take effect as of January 1, 2012, www.equatorprinciples.com/resources/equator_principles.pdf (accessed 2 February 2026).

[135] Business for Social Responsibility (September 2012) https://www.bsr.org/reports/BSR_Engaging_With_FPIC.pdf#page=6.09 (accessed 2 February 2026).

[136] Ibid, 12.

[137] Ibid, 12–13.

Deanne Kemp and John R Owen also argued that the application of FPIC faces significant challenges in areas where the recognition of rights is crucial but the supporting legal and social structures are weak.[138] For FPIC to be effective in protecting Indigenous People's rights and reducing risks for mining companies, certain conditions are necessary, including a solid regulatory framework, a functional land tenure system, and the capacity of companies to manage FPIC's complexities. In jurisdictions lacking these supports, the risks associated with initiating an FPIC process may outweigh the intended benefits for Indigenous communities.[139] Kemp and Owen noted that the compatibility of FPIC with local legal frameworks is a critical factor.[140] For instance, Australia's Native Title Act gives Indigenous groups a procedural right to negotiate over mining projects but lacks a veto power, limiting the extent to which FPIC can be genuinely implemented. In countries where Indigenous People's rights are unrecognised, as seen in Papua New Guinea, one-time consent processes may be invalid or threaten state sovereignty, exposing Indigenous communities to potential harassment if they assert their rights in oppressive political environments.[141]

Without consistent state support, companies may leave Indigenous communities vulnerable by suspending or abandoning FPIC processes due to market volatility or divestment, as frequent in the mining sector. The engagement process must ensure meaningful inclusion, which depends on understanding local decision-making structures. As argued by Kemp and Owen, poorly managed FPIC processes risk reinforcing exclusion within communities, as illustrated by the Argyle diamond mine case in Australia, where the exclusion of Indigenous women from early consultations led to cultural and rights violations.[142]

Considering above analysis, for corporate responsibility in Indigenous Peoples and minority rights to move from voluntary commitment to meaningful action, binding regulations with explicit standards and accountability mechanisms are essential. The international community and regulatory bodies must prioritise enforceable requirements that compel companies to consistently uphold Indigenous Peoples and minority rights, ensuring these protections go beyond the goodwill of individual corporations. However, the recent progress in binding legislation on corporate responsibility for human rights and environmental protection has been disappointing when it comes to safeguarding the rights of Indigenous Peoples and minorities. The EU Deforestation-Free Products Regulation (EUDR) missed a critical opportunity to provide meaningful protections for indigenous communities.[143]

---

[138] Kemp and Owen (2017), pp. 163–169.

[139] Ibid, 166.

[140] Ibid.

[141] Ibid.

[142] Ibid, 166–167.

[143] Regulation (EU) 2023/1115 of the European Parliament and of the Council of 31 May 2023 on the making available on the Union market and the export from the Union of certain commodities and products associated with deforestation and forest degradation and repealing Regulation (EU) No 995/2010 (Text with EEA relevance) PE/82/2022/REV/1.

The recently adopted CSDDD has also proven to be disappointing, as it does not include the UN Declaration on the Rights of Indigenous Peoples (UNDRIP), ILO Convention No. 169, or the UN Declaration on the Rights of Minorities in the list of international treaties that companies must adhere to.[144] However, under the due diligence responsibilities, corporations are required to engage effectively with local communities, which can include Indigenous peoples and minorities.

In conclusion, while frameworks like ILO 169, UNDRIP, the UNGPs, and the UN Declaration on Minority Rights have laid essential groundwork for protecting Indigenous Peoples and minority rights, their lack of enforceability and specific, actionable guidance limits their impact on corporate practices. To achieve meaningful and consistent corporate accountability, binding regulations with clear, enforceable standards that protects these vulnerable groups are crucial. Advancing beyond aspirational principles, a robust BHR framework should ensure that Indigenous Peoples and minority communities have genuine, enforceable protections, enabling them to preserve control over their lands, cultures, and futures within a globalized economy that increasingly intersects with corporate interests.

3.2.3.2 Indigenous Peoples and Minority Rights Within Human Rights Due Diligence: Perspective from the OECD Case Law

Of the 394 cases analysed in this research, at least 36 involved issues related to FPIC, land grabbing, and the rights of Indigenous Peoples, while at least 7 cases explicitly mentioned the rights of minority groups. This shows the recurring challenges faced by Indigenous Peoples and minority communities in safeguarding their rights against corporate activities that adversely affect their lands and resources. However, within this OECD case law research, a focused analysis of 15 specific cases has been conducted, where NCPs provided detailed guidance on how companies should comply with the OECD Guidelines and other international standards to respect minority and Indigenous Peoples' rights, particularly in implementing FPIC.

First and foremost, a clear example taken from OECD case law is the case against PanAust in the Australian NCP.[145] In this instance, the Australian NCP explored how companies should implement FPIC and respect Indigenous Peoples' rights under the OECD Guidelines. The Australian NCP emphasised that for projects like PanAust's Sepik Development Project, which significantly impacts Indigenous groups, obtaining FPIC is essential.[146] It clarified that FPIC is not merely about acquiring government permits or licenses; rather, it requires genuine consent from Indigenous Peoples who could be substantially affected by the project.[147] This

[144] Corporate Sustainability Due Diligence Directive, Recital 33; Meyer and Patz (2024).

[145] NCP Australia, Project Sepik and Jubilee Australia Research Centre on behalf of Sepik River communities v. PanAust Limited, Final Statement, 3 October 2023.

[146] Ibid, 3.

[147] Ibid, 35 and paras 96 and 97.

underlined that corporate actions should not bypass the importance of direct community engagement. The NCP noted that while PanAust acknowledged the need for FPIC, the company lacked sufficient documentation to demonstrate that its consultation processes met international standards. The NCP recommended that PanAust establish clear procedures aligned with these standards to ensure FPIC is treated as a prerequisite rather than a flexible requirement.[148] This would involve specific measures to communicate project impacts transparently and in local languages accessible to the relevant Indigenous communities, ensuring that these communities can make informed decisions.

A critical point emphasised by the NCP in this case was the distinction between general stakeholder engagement and rights-holder obligations under the OECD Guidelines. Indigenous communities, as one of the rightsholders, require a more comprehensive consultation process than other stakeholders. This distinction reinforces the company's duty to prioritise Indigenous People's rights, not merely as a social responsibility but as a legal and moral obligation under the international law. Furthermore, the NCP pointed out that compensating Indigenous communities as an alternative to obtaining FPIC is inconsistent with the OECD Guidelines.[149] Compensation alone cannot replace the need for consent, as FPIC involves the right of communities to participate actively in decisions affecting their lands and resources. NCP's stance emphasised that companies should avoid using monetary compensation as a substitute for meaningful, consent-based engagement. In conclusion, Australian NCP's recommendations to PanAust included implementing internal procedures to ensure FPIC is obtained before project commencement, involving independent third-party facilitators in consultations, ensuring that consultations address community concerns thoroughly (including environmental impact assessments and dam safety analyses), and maintaining an ongoing dialogue with Indigenous communities throughout the project lifecycle. The findings in this case reinforce the expectation under the OECD Guidelines that companies rigorously uphold Indigenous Peoples and minority rights and avoid interpreting FPIC obligations as optional or substitutable by other forms of engagement.

The cases involved Shell Petroleum Development and Salini Impregilo in Dutch and Italian NCPs offer supplementary insights and alternative interpretations of corporate responsibility to implement FPIC and respect Indigenous People's rights, building on the findings in the case against PanAust handled by the Australian NCP. As stated earlier, in the case against PanAust, the Australian NCP underlined the company's direct responsibility to ensure FPIC for projects impacting Indigenous People's traditional lands and emphasised that FPIC is not merely procedural but requires companies to seek and secure Indigenous communities' genuine consent. The Australian NCP recommended PanAust implement specific FPIC protocols and involve communities directly in decision-making. This interpretation places a clear

[148] Ibid, 42 and para 120.

[149] Ibid, para 98–99, and 117.

responsibility on companies to proactively embed FPIC into project planning as a continuous process rather than a one-time approval.

The Shell Petroleum Development case, overseen by the Dutch NCP, highlighted the complexities introduced when a company operates within a joint venture.[150] Shell declined the NCP's offer for mediation, citing its partnership limitations, which impacted its leverage to fully engage with FPIC processes or to cooperate with remediation. The Dutch NCP criticised this stance, stressing that the company still had a responsibility to exercise due diligence and maintain transparency with affected communities, regardless of joint venture constraints.[151] The Dutch NCP suggested that Shell should use its position to influence joint venture partners toward meaningful community engagement and uphold its commitments in line with the OECD Guidelines. This interpretation introduces an important nuance to the OECD Guidelines by underscoring corporate leverage and responsibility toward Indigenous Peoples within complex corporate structures. While the NCP issued some strong statements in ist final statement, Shell's refusal to engage meaningfully in the process ultimately limited the case's potential to advance stronger normative expectations on parent-company accountability toward Indigenous and other marginalised communities.

In the case against Salini Impregilo, managed by the Italian NCP, the interpretation shifted again due to the company's role as a subcontractor on the Gibe 3 dam project.[152] Salini argued that consultation responsibilities lay with the Ethiopian government, which commissioned the project. However, the Italian NCP clarified that Salini, despite its contractual role, still had a responsibility to uphold Indigenous People's rights under the OECD Guidelines.[153] The Italian NCP advised that Salini should exercise leverage on the Ethiopian authorities to support FPIC implementation effectively, thus suggesting that corporations in subcontractor roles cannot fully defer responsibility to governments and must independently ensure human rights due diligence. This interpretation expands the PanAust case's findings, reinforcing that even companies not in full control of a project must actively promote FPIC and Indigenous People's rights where possible, reflecting a broader scope of responsibility within complex project frameworks. Together, these cases illustrated how NCPs adapt the OECD Guidelines to different operational contexts. While the PanAust case emphasised a company's direct responsibility in implementing FPIC, the Shell and Salini cases add layers of accountability for corporations operating in joint ventures or as subcontractors. These cases collectively affirm that companies must respect Indigenous People's rights regardless of business structure or operational role, using all available influence to uphold FPIC standards and ensure meaningful community involvement in decisions affecting their lands and resources.

---

[150] NCP Netherlands, Aminigboko Community v. the Shell Petroleum Development Company of Nigeria Limited and Shell Headquarters, Final Statement, 10 February 2023.

[151] Ibid, 9.

[152] NCP Italy, Survival International Italia v. Salini Impregilo S.p.A, Final Statement, 8 June 2017.

[153] Ibid, 4–5.

Furthermore, the case against EDF in French NCP, it showed NCP's guidance on implementing FPIC, emphasising that companies should proactively engage with Indigenous Peoples beyond simply adhering to national consultation procedures.[154] The French NCP advised that while EDF Renewables followed Mexico's state-led Indigenous consultation process, it should have extended its due diligence by initiating meaningful engagement with the Zapotec community from an earlier project stage.[155] This includes informing and consulting all stakeholders, particularly in culturally significant or complex contexts where state processes may not fully capture the community's needs and concerns. Additionally, the French NCP recommended establishing a CSR committee dedicated to community and Indigenous stakeholder engagement. Furthermore, the NCP noted that EDF failed to conduct comprehensive due diligence from the outset of the project to thoroughly assess land tenure rights belonging to Indigenous Peoples. It emphasised that relying solely on domestic legal checks on land ownership was insufficient, as it failed to account for the cultural heritage inherently tied to the land. Although the final statement provided a strong analysis, it lacked enforceable actions requiring EDF to address the harms its project has inflicted on Indigenous Peoples. Furthermore, the French NCP failed to recognise that corporate responsibility is separate from state responsibility. Companies have their own obligation to consult with Indigenous Peoples in accordance with FPIC standards, regardless of the state's duty to do so.

The principle that FPIC is not a one-time agreement but requires continuous engagement was emphasised in case against Statkraft, handled by the Norwegian and Swedish NCP.[156] This case concerned Statkraft's wind power development in the traditional reindeer herding grounds of the Jijnjevaerie Saami village, where the Saami community raised concerns about the project's impact on their cultural and economic livelihood. The NCPs acknowledged that while Statkraft had complied with Swedish law, obtained the necessary permits, and conducted FPIC in line with the OECD Guidelines, the consultation process could have been more effective in ensuring meaningful engagement. They emphasised that genuine consultation should provide Indigenous Peoples with more legal empowerment to promote and protect their rights. The NCP underlined further that companies must engage Indigenous communities meaningfully, in ongoing, substantive dialogue beyond mere legal compliance, treating FPIC as a continuous and dynamic process rather than a one-time requirement.

The NCPs recommended that Statkraft establish structured, transparent communication channels with the Saami village to enhance mutual trust and facilitate genuine engagement.[157] Building on cases such as PanAust and Salini, where the emphasis was on direct consent or leveraging influence over state-led projects, and

[154] NCP France, ProDESC v. EDF and EDF Renewables, Final Statement, 10 March 2020.

[155] Ibid, 13.

[156] NCP Sweden, Jijnjevaerie Saami village v. Statkraft SCA Vind AB, Final Statement, 10 February 2016.

[157] Ibid, 15.

similar to the case against EDF, this instance highlighted the critical importance of sustained, trust-based dialogue, even when formal legal processes have been followed. Additionally, the Swedish NCP advised Statkraft to consider appointing an independent third party to facilitate the FPIC process, ensuring structured meeting management and documentation.[158]

OECD cases consistently expose a fundamental misunderstanding of FPIC by both companies and states, who treat it as a one-off procedural step rather than a sustained, iterative process of consent. The cases further confirm that corporations cannot hide behind the state's duty to consult: they hold an independent responsibility to respect Indigenous People's rights, particularly when states prioritise extractive profits over community consent. Yet the NCP system itself often reinforces these gaps. In the Statkraft and EDF cases, benefit-sharing—an essential component of Indigenous People's rights—was either marginalised or ignored entirely. The French NCP went further by failing to assert that FPIC must be conducted by companies directly, rather than outsourced to state processes that routinely exclude Indigenous voices. In doing so, NCPs missed a key normative opportunity: to clarify that meaningful engagement, ongoing consent, and equitable benefit-sharing are not optional add-ons but core corporate obligations. Instead, these cases reveal the structural limits of a system still reluctant to confront power imbalances between corporations, states, and Indigenous Peoples.

As for minorities, the cases against Mallee Resources overseen by the Australian NCP and the case against UBS under the Swiss NCP provided insights into how NCPs analyse corporate responsibility concerning minority rights, particularly through due diligence and business relationships. In the case against Mallee Resources case, the Australian NCP emphasised the company's responsibility to conduct comprehensive HRDD, especially given Myanmar's political instability and risks to local communities, including the risks associated with minorities.[159] The NCP criticised Mallee for not consulting adequately with affected stakeholders, which included minority groups, before divesting from its Myanmar mining project.[160] This oversight resulted in risks of human rights violations post-divestment, particularly impacting Myanmar's ethnic minorities, who might face heightened conflict and displacement risks. The Australian NCP's analysis addressed that companies should prioritise risks related to marginalised groups including minorities within due diligence, ensuring disengagement strategies minimise harm to these groups.

In case against UBS, the Swiss NCP assessed UBS's investment links to Hikvision, a Chinese company implicated in surveillance activities targeting Uyghur and Turkic minorities.[161] The NCP identified UBS's indirect relationship with

[158] Ibid, 3.

[159] NCP Australia, Publish What You Pay Australia v. Mallee Resources Limited, Final Statement, 2 August 2023.

[160] Ibid 33, para 122.

[161] NCP Switzerland, Society for Threatened People v. USB Group AG, Final Statement, 20 January 2021.

Hikvision as a potential link to human rights abuses, urging UBS to implement more robust due diligence on its investment choices, particularly regarding passive investments.[162] The NCP highlighted that financial institutions must consider the human rights impacts their investment portfolios might have on minority communities and ensure transparency and accountability, especially when connected to sensitive contexts like Xinjiang Uyghur and Turkic minorities.

Both cases illustrated that the OECD Guidelines expect companies to uphold minority rights by conducting thorough, context-specific due diligence and adopting accountability measures. The Australian and Swiss NCPs emphasised that corporate responsibilities extend beyond direct actions to include examining how business relationships and investments may affect minority groups, especially in high-risk regions. This approach stresses the principle that corporations are required to integrate minority rights considerations systematically throughout their risk assessment and decision-making processes, in accordance with international human rights standards. Nevertheless, the limited number of NCP statements addressing corporate obligations toward minority groups reveals a significant normative and practical gap. Both NCPs and companies frequently overlook the distinct vulnerabilities of minorities within human rights due diligence processes, thereby perpetuating their marginalisation within corporate accountability frameworks.

3.3 Corporate Human Rights Responsibility for Environmental Damage: Exploring Corporate Environmental Due Diligence Responsibilities

3.3.1 Corporate Environmental Responsibility Under Global Human Rights Frameworks

As environmental degradation and climate change continue to escalate, the global community increasingly recognises the essential role of corporate environmental responsibility within the broader human rights framework.[163] The interconnection between environmental health and human rights has led to significant regulatory advancements, signalling an evolving understanding that environmental protection is not just an ethical concern but a fundamental human right. This shift is seen in

[162] Ibid, 6.

[163] For example, see Milieudefensie v. Royal Dutch Shell [2021] C/09/571932 / HA ZA 19-379 (by 2030 RDS must reduce greenhouse gas emissions across its own operations and from the oil it produces by 45 percent) https://climatecasechart.com/non-us-case/milieudefensie-et-al-v-royal-dutch-shell-plc/ (accessed 2 February 2026).

recent resolution from the UN General Assembly, which affirm the right to a clean, healthy, and sustainable environment.[164]

Despite these developments, corporate compliance with environmental standards within human rights frameworks remains inconsistent and often inadequate.[165] Corporations wield significant influence over environmental outcomes, yet the integration of environmental considerations into BHR discourse has historically been fragmented and 'piecemeal'.[166] This section explores how corporate environmental responsibility is defined, advocated, and regulated within global human rights frameworks. By examining existing policies, treaties, and principles, it seeks to illuminate both the progress made and the challenges that remain in creating a cohesive, enforceable structure that ensures corporations play a constructive role in safeguarding both human rights and the environment.

Initially, environmental and human rights discourses developed independently within BHR frameworks, with limited overlap. Stephen Turner argued that international human rights law and international environmental law are distinct branches that do not naturally align in shaping corporate decision-making.[167] This separation stems from their unique historical and technical developments, each producing different institutions and priorities.[168] Referencing Bantekas's view, Martin-Ortega and her colleagues argued that human rights law—predating environmental law—is centred on principles of dignity, equality, and liberty, rooted in solidarity and focused on human relationships. In contrast, international environmental law is guided by principles such as precaution, prevention, and the polluter pay principle, with an emphasis on limiting harm to other states or the global commons.[169] This divergence highlights the difficulty in creating a cohesive framework that can effectively address both corporate human rights impacts and environmental degradation.

Despite this, the link between the environment and human rights is gradually recognised, scholars are pushing for these issues to be addressed within a unified framework. In his report on human rights obligations related to a safe, clean, healthy, and sustainable environment, Special Rapporteur emphasised that, under the UNGPs, businesses have a clear responsibility to avoid causing or contributing to adverse human rights impacts through environmental harm.[170] This includes

---

[164] UNGA 'The human right to a clean, healthy and sustainable environment' Resolution adopted by the General Assembly on 28 July 2022, A/RES/76/300.

[165] Martin-Ortega and Dehbi (2022), p. 18 https://www.mdpi.com/2071-1050/14/11/6596 (accessed 2 February 2026).

[166] Ibid, 2.

[167] Turner (2021), p. 1.

[168] Ibid.

[169] Martin-Ortega and Dehbi (2016), pp. 263–264.

[170] UN. Special Rapporteur on human rights and the environment 'Policy Brief No. 3: Essential elements of effective and equitable human rights and environmental due diligence legislation, A policy brief by David R. Boyd, UN Special Rapporteur on human rights and the environment, and Stephanie Keene, Independent Consultant, International Human Rights Lawyer, June 2022, 9.

addressing such impacts when they occur and taking proactive measures to prevent or mitigate harm directly linked to their operations, products, or business relationships.[171] Companies are expected to comply with environmental laws, issue policy commitments to respect human rights via environmental protection and conduct human rights due diligence processes—such as impact assessments—to identify, prevent, mitigate, and account for their environmental impacts on human rights, as well as enable remediation where needed. However, many scholars argued that the UNGPs lack clarity in defining the responsibilities of corporations and states in managing environmental harm.[172] For example, while the Commentary on Principle 18 of the UNGPs suggests that businesses assess how environmental impacts affect rights holders, the guidelines do not provide a comprehensive framework for corporate responsibility toward the environment.[173] In contrast, the OECD Guidelines have a dedicated environmental chapter requiring businesses to conduct thorough environmental assessments and avoid environmental harm across key areas such as climate change, biodiversity loss, pollution, and waste management.[174] Although these guidelines outline various environmental impacts, the specific responsibilities of corporations in fulfilling their human rights and environmental due diligence obligations in integrated unified way remain ambiguous.[175]

In response, scholars have begun to explore the intersection of human rights obligations with environmental and climate responsibilities within the BHR context. Chiara Macchi and Nadia Bernaz, for instance, argued that although the UNGPs and OECD Guidelines do not explicitly address climate change, this omission does not exempt corporations—especially financial institutions—from climate-related responsibilities.[176] Martin-Ortega and her colleagues acknowledged that their work is shaping both theoretical and practical approaches to embedding environmental stewardship into corporate frameworks.[177] Macchi, in particular, advocates for integrating environmental and climate impacts into human rights due diligence, calling for a mandatory human rights and environmental due diligence (mHREDD) approach and the concept of climate due diligence as a necessary step forward.[178]

The call for a more unified approach is reflected in recent initiatives, including the drafting of LBI on BHR and the recent adoption of the CSDDD. The LBI's second draft acknowledges the connection between environmental and human rights by defining 'environmental rights' as rights that, if violated, would constitute human rights abuses, and the last Updated Draft formally includes the right to a

[171] Ibid.

[172] Dehbi and Martin-Ortega (2023), pp. 927–928.

[173] UN Guiding Principles on Business and Human Rights, Commentary to the Principle 18.

[174] OECD Guidelines, Chapter VI: Environment.

[175] Dehbi and Martin-Ortega (2023), pp. 928–929.

[176] Macchi and Bernaz (2021), pp. 1–2.

[177] Martin-Ortega and Dehbi (2022), p. 16.

[178] Macchi (2021), pp. 93–119.

clean, healthy, and sustainable environment.[179] Similarly, the CSDDD combines human rights and environmental risks into a unified requirement for companies to address these impacts throughout their supply chains.[180] Many scholars view the CSDDD as a significant step in integrating human rights and environmental considerations into corporate accountability, despite criticisms of its selective scope, such as the exclusion of plastic waste.[181]

Martin-Ortega and Dehbi, however, argued that while mHREDD laws in countries like France, Germany, and Norway, as well as across the EU, represent progress from previous voluntary measures, they lack strong foundations for effectively holding corporations accountable.[182] Key shortcomings include limited coverage of human rights and environmental issues and insufficient remediation options for affected communities. These gaps could perpetuate corporate impunity, which mHREDD aims to combat. Furthermore, they advocated that, to build a more robust mHREDD framework, future legislations should emphasise an integrated approach that addresses both human rights and environmental harms more comprehensively. This involves not only addressing direct human rights impacts from environmental harm but also considering broader environmental protection needs for vulnerable groups in the Global South. Additionally, stronger collaboration between home and host states and active enforcement by public bodies are essential for ensuring effective corporate accountability.

However, as I have argued elsewhere, efforts to integrate environmental and human rights due diligence need to recognise that environmental due diligence requires different approaches due to its unique impacts.[183] The OECD Guidelines treat these areas separately, with Chapter VI on the environment focusing on risk assessment, measurable objectives, the precautionary principle, mitigation measures, and ongoing monitoring. While some of these processes overlap with human rights due diligence, environmental issues—such as air and water pollution or climate change—are often global and diffuse, whereas human rights violations typically have direct, localized impacts on specific communities.

---

[179] Open-ended intergovernmental working group on transnational corporations and other business enterprises with respect to human rights (OEIGWG) Second draft of the Legally Binding Instrument to Regulate, in International Human Rights Law, the Activities of Transnational Corporations and Other Business Enterprises 6 August 2020 https://www.ohchr.org/sites/default/files/Documents/HRBodies/HRCouncil/WGTransCorp/Session6/OEIGWG_Chair-Rapporteur_second_revised_draft_LBI_on_TNCs_and_OBEs_with_respect_to_Human_Rights.pdf (accessed 2 February 2026); OEIGWG Updated draft legally binding instrument to regulate, in international human rights law, the activities of transnational corporations and other business enterprises, July 2023 https://www.ohchr.org/sites/default/files/documents/hrbodies/hrcouncil/igwg-transcorp/session9/igwg-9th-updated-draft-lbi-clean.pdf (accessed 2 February 2026).

[180] Corporate Sustainability Due Diligence Directive, Recital 16.

[181] Rouas et al. (10 June 2024) https://verfassungsblog.de/from-paper-to-practice-csddd-implementation (accessed 2 February 2026).

[182] Dehbi and Martin-Ortega (2023), pp. 927–928.

[183] Mohamadieh and Davaanyam (20 March 2025), p. 9.

Recent reports emphasised that environmental due diligence should be intersectional and prioritise Indigenous Peoples and other rights holders, combining scientific evidence with traditional knowledge to prevent environmental harm.[184] Merging environmental and human rights due diligence into a single framework risk creating a 'one-size-fits-all' approach that overlooks their specific requirements. For instance, addressing carbon emissions demands long-term strategies and technical data, while tackling human rights issues like child labour requires immediate action and direct stakeholder involvement.

In conclusion, while significant progress has been made in recognising the link between human rights and environmental responsibility within corporate frameworks, there remains a pressing need to clarify how these due diligence obligations can be effectively integrated into a single, cohesive process. Current BHR frameworks, such as the UNGPs and OECD Guidelines, often address human rights and environmental responsibilities separately, reflecting the distinct nature of their impacts. Environmental harms are typically global and diffuse, requiring long-term strategies and technical approaches, while human rights issues often demand immediate, localized actions. Without a clear, tailored approach, attempts to unify these areas risk creating a generalized framework that may fail to adequately address the unique requirements of each. To build an effective integrated framework, future legislation should ensure comprehensive coverage of both human rights and environmental impacts, prioritise the needs of vulnerable communities, particularly in the Global South, and foster stronger collaboration between home and host states. Only with a clearly defined, intersectional, and enforceable approach can corporations be held truly accountable for their impacts on both people and the planet.

3.3.2 OECD Case Law Perspectives on Corporate Environmental Due Diligence Responsibilities

This research on OECD case law has primarily focused on corporate responsibility for environmental harm and climate change. Of the total NCP cases, over 160 allege environmental harm and related human rights impacts on local communities. This section covers 28 cases in which NCPs assessed how companies addressed environmental concerns and conducted environmental due diligence. Covering the period from 2011 to 2024, the cases reviewed encompass a wide range of sectors, with the extractive industries most prominently represented, though matters arising in sectors such as marketing and finance are also addressed. This section focuses on the issues of environmental harm and corporate environmental due diligence, while the

[184] UN Human Rights Council 'Expert seminar on the responsibility of business enterprises to respect the human right to a clean, healthy and sustainable environment Report of the Special Rapporteur on the issue of human rights obligations relating to the 55. of a safe, clean, healthy and sustainable environment, David R. Boyd' 2 January 2024 UN Doc A/HRC/55/41, para 66.

subsequent section will provide a more thorough analysis of corporate responsibilities in relation to climate change.

While most NCP cases address environmental harm through its effects on human rights, only a limited number recognise environmental damage as a standalone issue grounded in environmental norms. Two Belgian NCP cases—both filed by Greenpeace—concerned Dredging International (Dhamra Port, India) and Jan De Nul NV (Sabetta Harbour, Russian Arctic), focusing on biodiversity loss rather than direct human rights violations.[185] The complaints alleged failures to conduct adequate environmental assessments and to apply the precautionary principle in ecologically sensitive areas. A similar focus on biodiversity arose in the Norwegian NCP case against Cermaq, where the company's aquaculture operations were linked to fish disease and ecological risks.[186] That case concluded with a joint agreement acknowledging the need for precautionary, sustainable resource use, and Cermaq's commitment to comply with international environmental standards. In all three cases, complainants relied on Chapter VI(4) of the OECD Guidelines, which reflects the precautionary principle by requiring companies to take preventive measures even in the absence of full scientific certainty.[187] These cases demonstrate that corporate environmental responsibility under the Guidelines may be invoked independently of human rights impacts, affirming that environmental harm constitutes a distinct basis for corporate accountability.

Drawing on the OECD Guidelines' Environmental chapter, many NCPs, including Brazilian, French, Dutch and Finnish NCPs have analysed and recommended that companies conduct thorough assessments of their environmental impacts on local communities. A first example is the case against Shell, where the Dutch NCP highlighted the general standards on company's environmental responsibilities under the OECD Guidelines.[188] Specifically, it cited the Guidelines from the Disclosure chapter, stating that MNEs must timely and accurately disclose information on their activities and related issues, particularly environmental information for workers and stakeholders.[189] They are also expected to maintain high standards in non-financial disclosures, such as environmental and social reporting. Furthermore, NCP recommended to Shell that, in accordance with the Environment chapter, MNEs should provide adequate, measurable, and timely information on potential health, safety, and environmental impacts, engage in meaningful communication

---

[185] NCP Belgium, Greenpeace v. Jan De Nul NV, Final Statement, 24 November 2014; NCP Belgium, Greenpeace India v. Dredging International, Final Statement, 11 March 2011.

[186] NCP Norway, Norwegian Society for the Conservation of Nature/Friends of the Earth Norway and Forum for Environment and Development (Forum) v. Cermaq ASA, Final Statement, July 2011.

[187] Ibid, 4–5.

[188] NCP Netherlands, Aminigboko Community v. the Shell Petroleum Development Company of Nigeria Limited and Shell Headquarters, Final Statement, 10 February 2023.

[189] Ibid, 11.

and consultation with affected communities, and conduct environmental impact assessments when significant impacts are anticipated.[190]

Additionally, MNEs are required to establish contingency plans to prevent, mitigate, and manage serious environmental and health damage. In this case, Shell was criticised for failing to disclose an environmental impact assessment, neglecting to communicate with the community on issues like groundwater contamination, and declining to mitigate oil pollution in 2010, such as by providing portable drinking water. Notably, the same expectations applied under the previous (2000) version of the OECD Guidelines, underscoring the longstanding importance of these responsibilities.[191] This case highlighted that corporate environmental responsibility includes several key aspects, such as providing timely and adequate environmental information to all relevant stakeholders, consulting with them effectively, conducting thorough and comprehensive environmental impact assessments, and establishing contingency plans to prevent effectively the potential environmental harms.

A similar analysis can be derived from the case against Bracell Bahia Specialty Cellulose S.A. in the Brazilian NCP which addressed the corporate responsibility to uphold environmental standards as outlined in the OECD Guidelines.[192] In this case, Bracell was accused of failing to respect property boundaries, unauthorised access, and inadequately managing environmental impacts associated with its eucalyptus plantation operations. The Brazilian Ministry of Environment, acting as an authority in the case, argued that Bracell had not fulfilled its obligations to provide sufficient information about its activities' environmental impacts, which compromised both disclosure and environmental responsibilities under the OECD Guidelines.[193]

The Ministry emphasised the importance of companies conducting environmental impact assessments, engaging in transparent communication with local communities, and ensuring that their operations do not harm local ecosystems or infringe on property rights.[194] This case emphasises the growing expectation that corporations must go beyond conducting environmental due diligence; they must also uphold the rights and boundaries of local communities through transparent and accountable practices. The Bracell case served as an illustration of corporate environmental responsibility under the OECD Guideline, highlighting the important integration of HREDD. This interconnected approach ensured that companies not only mitigate environmental impacts but also respect and protect the rights of affected communities, underlining the necessity of effective due diligence that addresses the connection between these two issues.

Another case that emphasised the effective integration of the HREDD is the case against Nordex SE, a German wind turbine manufacturer, filed with the German

---

[190] Ibid, 12.

[191] Ibid, 11.

[192] NCP Brazil, Izabel Lopes Soares da Silva, represented by José Reinaldo Soares da Silva v. Bracell Bahia Specialty Cellulose S.A, Final Statement, 14 December 2021.

[193] Ibid, 7–8.

[194] Ibid, 8–9.

NCP, that centred on allegations of inadequate corporate environmental due diligence.[195] The complaint, submitted by an individual in Turkey, claimed that Nordex had failed to conduct proper due diligence for its role as a supplier of wind turbines to a wind energy project in Turkey. Key issues included a lack of public consultation, the absence of an environmental impact assessment, and failure to ensure safe transport and installation of the turbines, as well as neglecting to assess potential impacts on local property rights and environmental conditions. The German NCP facilitated a mediation process, leading to Nordex's commitment to strengthen its 'gate process' for evaluating due diligence prior to signing supply agreements.[196] Nordex agreed to review relevant permits, assess environmental and social impacts, including effects on biodiversity, noise, and land rights, and to ensure adequate consultation with affected communities.[197] This case highlighted the critical importance of comprehensive corporate environmental due diligence aligned with OECD Guidelines, especially for companies engaged in large-scale infrastructure projects with significant environmental and social impacts. It underlined that effective environmental due diligence must go beyond simply assessing environmental risks; it must also address the impacts on local communities and ecosystems, integrating both human rights and environmental considerations.

Adding to this, in the case against Pöyry Plc brought before the Finnish NCP, in where the company was accused of failing to address environmental impacts on local communities related to the Xayaburi hydropower project in Laos, NCP analysed the corporate environmental responsibility in detail. The Finnish Ministry of the Environment became directly involved in this case. The Ministry argued that the OECD Guidelines should apply broadly, even to companies without a permanent presence in the country where their activities have an impact.[198] It stated that companies like Pöyry have a duty to prevent adverse impacts that are directly linked to their operations through business relationships, even if they do not cause them directly. As a leading expert in hydropower, Pöyry, according to the Ministry, should have leveraged its influence to delay the dam's construction until essential environmental studies were completed.[199] Key concerns included the dam's potential impact on fish migration, sediment movement, flood risk, erosion, ecosystem services, biodiversity, and local housing. The Ministry emphasised the importance of transparency and consultation with local communities in Laos and the broader Mekong region, given the project's significant impact on these populations.[200] It requested that Pöyry provide further information on its engagement with affected communities, highlighting that such stakeholder involvement was crucial in this context. This

---

[195] NCP Germany, Mr. Dominic Whiting v. Nordex SE, Final Statement, 31 August 2016.

[196] Ibid, 3.

[197] NCP Finland, the Siemenpuu Foundation, Friends of the Earth Finland, and 13 other NGOs v. Pöyry Plc and the Xayaburi hydropower project, Final Statement, 10 June 2013.

[198] Ibid, 1.

[199] Ibid, 2.

[200] Ibid.

case stressed the responsibility of companies to use their influence to ensure that contractual partners adhere to environmental standards and the crucial need of stakeholder engagement in the HREDD.

In contrast, although not directly comparable, the Nuon Energy case before the Dutch NCP indicated the principle of corporate independent responsibility. The Dutch NCP made it clear that companies cannot shift environmental responsibility to states. It rejected Nuon's argument that such obligations lie primarily with the host government, emphasising instead that companies must independently assess and address the environmental risks associated with their operations, regardless of the host state's role.

Furthermore, the case involving Copagef, Somdiaa, and their subsidiary Sosucam centres on allegations that the companies failed to adequately address environmental and human rights impacts associated with its sugar production activities in Cameroon.[201] Local communities alleged that Sosucam's operations led to significant environmental degradation, including water and soil pollution from the use of chemicals and fertilisers, which directly impacted their living conditions. The complainants also raised concerns about inadequate stakeholder engagement, asserting that Sosucam did not provide sufficient information or consult with communities potentially affected by these environmental risks.[202] Additionally, there were claims that Sosucam had exerted pressure on community representatives who sought to voice these issues.

The French NCP addressed these allegations, emphasising the critical role of corporate environmental due diligence in managing the social and environmental impacts of agro-industrial activities. Noting that Sosucam's most recent social and environmental impact assessments were conducted in 2012 and 2017, the NCP recommended that a new impact assessment be carried out promptly to reflect current environmental and climate-related challenges. This recommendation aligns with OECD Guidelines, specifically Chapter VI: Environment, which outlines the need for businesses to assess and mitigate their environmental impacts continually. In response to alleged pollution risks, the NCP also recommended regular monitoring of surface and groundwater quality, expanding beyond preventive measures limited to the sugar plant's water usage.[203] The NCP stressed that the results of these studies should be made transparent to affected communities, given the direct implications for their health and livelihoods. Additionally, it was recommended that health authorities be involved in the consultation process to ensure that public health concerns are adequately addressed. The NCP's recommendations stressed a comprehensive approach to human rights and environmental due diligence (HREDD), highlighting the importance of continuous impact assessment, stakeholder engagement, and the integration of findings into sustainable development policies.

[201] NCP France, 14 Local Watch Committees ("Comités Riverains de Veille") and Centre of Actions for Life and Earth ("Centre d'Action pour la Vie et la Terre") v. COPAGEF, SOMDIAA and SOSUCAM in Cameroon, Final Statement, 17 May 2022.

[202] Ibid, 4.

[203] Ibid, 14.

Also, in this case, French NCP played a crucial role in monitoring and evaluating the effectiveness of duty of vigilance plans of respondent companies by assessing whether companies are adequately implementing these plans to prevent and mitigate adverse environmental and human rights impacts, providing recommendations, and facilitating dialogue between companies and affected communities to ensure compliance with OECD Guidelines as well as the Duty of Vigilance Law.

A further notable example that illustrated the vital importance of MSE in HREDD is the complaint against Intex Resources and the Mindoro Nickel Project (MNP) brought before the Norwegian NCP.[204] This case highlighted the critical need for strong corporate environmental due diligence, particularly in high-impact sectors like mining. The Norwegian NCP stressed that mineral and metal extraction requires not only comprehensive assessments of direct and indirect environmental impacts but also transparent and inclusive communication with local communities, including Indigenous Peoples. Guiding frameworks such as the OECD Guidelines, IFC Performance Standards, and the Global Reporting Initiative emphasise proactive stakeholder engagement and the provision of clear, accessible information on environmental, health, and safety risks.[205] In this case, Intex Resources was found to have fallen short of these standards, with the NCP concluding that the company's practices failed to meet international expectations for corporate environmental responsibility.

While Intex conducted an impact assessment for the MNP, the Norwegian NCP identified significant gaps in the assessment and its disclosure. The analysis did not adequately address critical environmental and social risks, nor did it outline comprehensive management and monitoring plans. Additionally, Intex failed to effectively share detailed information, such as technical reports, impact studies, maps, and other materials necessary for stakeholders to evaluate the safety and environmental soundness of the project. This lack of accessible information limited affected groups' ability to understand and assess potential environmental consequences, particularly in relation to sensitive issues like siltation, flood risks, and health impacts on the Mindoro community.

Furthermore, the Norwegian NCP recommended that Intex undertake a more extensive environmental impact assessment, complemented by proactive stakeholder consultations in line with the IFC Performance Standards.[206] This would involve making non-technical summaries of findings available in local languages, organising consultations with NGOs and civil society groups, and providing thorough technical analysis to substantiate key environmental issues. The NCP upheld allegations from FIOH that Intex's environmental information was incomplete and found that its failure to offer timely and transparent communication with affected communities constituted a breach of Chapter VI of the OECD Guidelines. This case

[204] NCP Norway, The Future In Our Hands (FIOH) v. Intex Resources ASA and The Mindoro Nickel Project, Final Statement, 30 November 2011.

[205] Ibid, 46.

[206] Ibid, 45–46.

highlights the need for companies to not only conduct rigorous environmental assessments but also to ensure that the resulting information is accessible and understandable to those impacted. Intex's approach demonstrates a critical lesson: environmental due diligence in resource extraction is not only about assessing risks but also about building trust and accountability through meaningful stakeholder engagement and transparency.

Furthermore, corporate HREDD is particularly critical for parent companies, as they bear a significant responsibility to ensure that their subsidiaries adhere to environmental standards, especially in high-impact sectors like agro-industry. In the case of Socapalm and its parent company, the Bolloré Group, the French NCP emphasised the need for Bolloré to not only implement comprehensive environmental policies but also actively monitor and support Socapalm's compliance with OECD Guidelines.[207]

This case underlined how parent companies can play a vital role in fostering environmental responsibility, demonstrating that parent companies' responsibility extends beyond policy creation to include continuous oversight, guidance, and support for subsidiaries. To enhance awareness and effectiveness in environmental due diligence, parent companies must embed practices such as regular training, transparent communication, and ongoing risk assessment across all levels of their operations. The NCP's recommendations in this case pointed to specific areas for improvement, such as integrating environmental impacts into decision-making and fostering a proactive approach to environmental management. In this case, Socapalm was found lacking in considering environmental impacts, but the NCP expressed optimism that Bolloré's support for Socapalm's Quality, Health, Safety, and Environment (QHSE) program could address these gaps.[208] Additionally, NCP highlighted the importance of training employees in environmental management, including safe handling of hazardous materials and accident prevention. By enhancing employee knowledge and awareness through targeted training, Socapalm can ensure a more engaged and responsible workforce.

This section examined several cases in detail, demonstrating that environmental assessments must be deeply integrated with social considerations, particularly the rights and impacts on local communities. This integration requires identifying all relevant stakeholders, including Indigenous Peoples and other vulnerable groups, and recognising their connection to the environment and land. The integration of human rights and environment into due diligence as HREDD is therefore essential. Effective HREDD hinges on meaningful stakeholder engagement, which must be at the core of the process. Numerous cases reveal that companies often fail to implement effective HREDD due to inadequate engagement with local communities. In some instances, state authorities responsible for environmental oversight participated in NCP proceedings and provided guidance to companies on conducting

[207] NCP France, Birlesik Metal v. DIAM International, Final Statement, 14 May 2019; NCP France, group of four non-governmental organisations (NGOs) and associations from Cameroon, France and Germany v. SOCAPALM, Bollore Group, Report, 3 June 2013.

[208] Ibid, 12–13.

effective HREDD. However, these cases also highlight a lack of clarity regarding how state authorities monitored corporate activities prior to allegations being raised. Additionally, OECD case law explored the responsibilities of various types of companies—whether suppliers, contractors, or parent companies—to proactively implement HREDD. Despite their differing roles, all are obligated to conduct thorough and effective HREDD in alignment with international standards.

3.4 Corporate Human Rights Responsibility Concerning Climate Change

3.4.1 Corporate Responsibility for Climate Impact Under International Law

The impacts of climate change are becoming increasingly apparent, intensifying the need for accountability from both states and corporations. International organisations are actively linking human rights with climate change, recognising that climate change impact and the environmental degradation pose a serious threat to fundamental rights. Recently, the UN Human Rights Committee, in its General Comment No. 36 on Article 6 of the International Covenant on Civil and Political Rights (ICCPR), stated that 'environmental degradation, climate change, and unsustainable development constitute some of the most pressing and serious threats to the ability of present and future generations to enjoy the right to life.'[209]

Corporate responsibility for climate change, particularly in the fossil fuel industry, is gaining significant attention. A landmark study revealed that just ninety companies, primarily in the oil, gas, and coal sectors, are responsible for two-thirds of historical greenhouse gas (GHG) emissions driving climate change.[210] Chevron alone accounts for 3.5% of these emissions.[211] The Paris Agreement, an international treaty adopted in 2015 under the United Nations Framework Convention on Climate Change (UNFCCC), aims to limit global warming to well below 2 °C above pre-industrial levels, with an aspirational target of 1.5 °C.[212] Although it does not explicitly address corporations, the Agreement's temperature targets provide a crucial benchmark for guiding corporate emissions reduction efforts.

Regarding the contexts of the business contribution to the GHG emissions, climate-related lawsuits against both states and companies are on the rise. A recent

[209] UN. Human Rights Committee, 'General Comment No. 36 on Article 6 of the International Covenant on Civil and Political Rights, on the Right to Life', CCPR/C/GC/36 (3 September 2019), para 62.

[210] Heede (2014), pp. 229–241.

[211] Ibid.

[212] Conference of the Parties, Adoption of the Paris Agreement, Dec. 12, 2015; U.N. Doc FCCC/CP/2015/L.9/Rev./1 (Dec. 12, 2015).

and notable example is the case against Shell in the Dutch courts, which demonstrated the shared responsibility of states and private actors in addressing climate change.[213] Although Shell won the appeal, the court's ruling emphasised that the fight against climate change is a collective responsibility, extending beyond states to corporations.[214] The court highlighted that companies whose products significantly contribute to climate change, and who possess the means to help combat it, are obligated to do so in the interests of all inhabitants of the planet—even in the absence of explicit public law requirements.[215] In its judgment, the court referenced the OECD Guidelines and the UNGPs, frameworks to which Shell has committed, as a basis for this corporate responsibility to mitigate climate-related harm.[216]

Although the UNGPs do not explicitly mention climate change, they aim to address all negative human rights impacts resulting from business activities. As Wettstein argued, this scope implicitly includes human rights impacts linked to corporate contributions to climate change.[217] In contrast, the 2023 update to the OECD Guidelines explicitly emphasised climate change, marking a significant advancement in corporate responsibility towards climate change.[218] The updated Guidelines underlined that climate change and biodiversity are critical areas for businesses to address, with far-reaching implications. Chap. VI: Environment of the updated Guidelines emphasised the critical role of MNEs in addressing global, regional, and local environmental challenges, particularly climate change.[219] It provides a broad, non-exhaustive list of potential environmental impacts associated with business activities, including climate change, biodiversity loss, ecosystem degradation, deforestation, pollution, and hazardous waste management.[220] The chapter underlined the need for enterprises to conduct risk-based due diligence to identify, assess, and mitigate adverse environmental impacts.[221] Climate considerations feature prominently, with the Guidelines encouraging enterprises to adopt circular economy approaches and use international commitments and scientific evidence as benchmarks for environmental responsibility.[222] The text aligns with key international frameworks, including the Rio Declaration, the 2030 Agenda for Sustainable Development, the UN Framework Convention on Climate Change, and the Paris Agreement, reinforcing the Guidelines' foundation in established environmental

---

[213] Climate Case Chart 'Milieudefensie Et Al. V. Royal Dutch Shell Plc.' https://climatecasechart.com/non-us-case/milieudefensie-et-al-v-royal-dutch-shell-plc/ (accessed 2 February 2026).

[214] Ibid.

[215] Nollkaemper (2024), https://verfassungsblog.de/shell-milieudefensie-climate-litigation/, DOI: https://doi.org/10.59704/dd77504c9eae2abd (accessed 2 February 2026).

[216] Ibid.

[217] Wettstein (2023), pp. 348–363.

[218] Aristova et al. (2024), pp. 505–525 https://doi.org/10.1017/S0020589324000125 (accessed 2 February 2026).

[219] OECD Guidelines for Multinational Enterprises, Chapter VI: Environment.

[220] Ibid, Section 1.

[221] Ibid, Sections 1–3.

[222] Aristova et al. (2024), p. 507.

principles and goals.[223] Scholars affirmed that it also acknowledged corporate responsibility to contribute to a 'just transition' and aligns the Guidelines with the Paris Agreement of 2015.[224]

As for the climate integration to the due diligence, the updated OECD Guidelines, building on the UNGPs, explicitly integrate climate risks within corporate human rights responsibilities, pushing companies HRDD responsibilities to align with global climate goals.[225] This framework encourages the climate due diligence concept that consists of science-based targets, transparency, significant emissions reductions, and a fair transition to sustainable practices.[226] Scholars predicted that this emphasis on climate accountability will lead to more cases from civil society, adding to climate litigation efforts.[227] As Macchi noted, emerging cases illustrate an evolving concept of climate due diligence, where companies assess climate risks, integrate them into planning, and communicate transparently.[228]

However, according to the New Climate Institute's Corporate Climate Responsibility Monitoring 2023, many companies are struggling to keep up with regulatory developments.[229] In a review of 24 major MNEs, their total reported GHG emissions for 2019—including upstream and downstream (scope 3) emissions—were around 2.2 $GtCO_2e$, equivalent to 4% of global GHG emissions in that year.[230] Despite these companies presenting themselves as climate leaders, only a minority demonstrated replicable good practices. Most climate strategies are plagued by vague commitments, reliance on questionable offsetting plans, and exclusions in emissions scopes.[231] Furthermore, the report addressed that 15 of the 24 companies analysed show low or very low integrity in their climate strategies, indicating that their commitments fall short of the leadership they profess.[232] Although these companies are intended to serve as role models, close scrutiny revealed that many climate pledges lack the substance needed to achieve meaningful climate leadership.

A recent report by the Special Rapporteur on hazardous substances and waste highlighted concerns about industries like fossil fuels, chemicals, mining, and plastics promoting misleading climate solutions, engaging in disinformation, and downplaying their human rights and environmental impacts.[233] In response, the Special

[223] OECD Guidelines for Multinational Enterprises, commentary para 70.

[224] Aristova et al. (2024), p. 507.

[225] Ibid, 518–522.

[226] Ibid.

[227] Macchi (2021), pp. 93–119. https://doi.org/10.1017/bhj.2020.25 (accessed 2 February 2026).

[228] Ibid.

[229] New Climate Institute (23 February 2023) https://newclimate.org/resources/publications/corporate-climate-responsibility-monitor-2023 (accessed 2 February 2026).

[230] Ibid.

[231] Ibid.

[232] Ibid.

[233] UN HRC 'The toxic impacts of some proposed climate change solutions: Report of the Special Rapporteur on the implications for human rights of the environmentally sound management and

Rapporteur on human rights and climate change called on digital platforms and media companies to combat misinformation, avoid climate washing, and provide accurate, evidence-based information on climate change and human rights.[234] This approach aims to foster a trustworthy and diverse information ecosystem that empowers civil society in global climate action.

The recent adoption of the CSDDD aimed to accelerate corporate responsibility for climate change. Article 22 requires companies, including ‘regulated financial undertakings,’ to develop and implement climate transition plans aligned with the Paris Agreement’s 1.5 °C goal and the EU’s climate neutrality target.[235] These plans must include time-bound, science-based targets, decarbonization strategies, investment details, and oversight roles, with progress reviewed annually.[236] Furthermore, disclosure obligations under Article 22 align with the Corporate Sustainability Reporting Directive (CSRD) and European Sustainability Reporting Standards (ESRS), ensuring companies that report under these frameworks meet the adoption requirement.[237] While the Directive represents a significant step toward integrating climate action into corporate governance, its focus on obligation of conduct rather than obligation of result and the optional nature of Scope 3 emission targets weakens its potential impact.[238] Addressing these gaps will be crucial to ensure the Directive supports the EU’s climate goals and the Paris Agreement’s objectives effectively.

Adding to this, critics argued that climate due diligence alone falls short of true accountability, particularly in high-emission industries.[239] Effective corporate climate accountability should address not only future risks but also past harms, especially for vulnerable communities disproportionately affected by climate change. Julia Dehm’s concept of ‘red lines’ for fossil fuels proposes setting thresholds beyond which further fossil fuel development is prohibited.[240] This would prevent new fossil fuel projects and reflect a stronger commitment to climate mitigation, recognising that combating climate change requires both emissions reduction and a fundamental shift from fossil fuel dependence.[241]

There is also a growing call for reparations, urging corporations to address the social and environmental harm they have caused, especially in communities

---

disposal of hazardous substances and wastes, Marcos Orellana’ UN Doc A/HRC/54/25, 13 July 2023 para 5.

[234] UN HRC ‘Report of the Special Rapporteur on the promotion and protection of human rights in the context of climate change: Access to information on climate change and human rights; 18 July 2024 UN Doc A/79/176, para 64–71.

[235] Corporate Sustainability Due Diligence Directive, Article 21.

[236] Ibid.

[237] Corporate Sustainability Due Diligence Directive, Article 22.

[238] Kinda et al., Complementarity of the Legally Binding Instrument on Business and Human Rights and the EU Corporate Sustainability Due Diligence Directive, 7.

[239] Dehm (2023), pp. 151–179, https://doi.org/10.1017/bhj.2023.30 (accessed 2 February 2026).

[240] Ibid, 170–172.

[241] Ibid.

disproportionately impacted by climate change.[242] This approach centred on restorative justice, with corporations supporting adaptation and resilience efforts in affected regions, integrating climate-related human rights as part of a broader commitment to social and economic justice. Wettstein also highlighted the concept of corporate climate 'retrospective responsibility,' where businesses are held accountable for past actions contributing to climate-induced harm.[243] This framework suggested that companies should not only focus on preventing future impacts but also actively counteract damage resulting from their historical practices.

In summary, evolving standards around corporate climate responsibility require a multifaceted approach that goes beyond voluntary frameworks. Integrating concept of climate due diligence with binding limits on fossil fuel expansion, enhanced transparency in reporting, and reparations for impacted communities can help corporations align with human rights and environmental goals. Ultimately, enforceable standards on emissions, corporate influence, and reparative actions are essential for shifting corporate behaviour towards a sustainable and equitable climate future.

3.4.2 Addressing Corporate Climate Responsibility: OECD Case Law Approaches

As analysed by Aristova and her colleagues, up to 2024, 14 notable cases explicitly addressed corporate climate responsibility.[244] These cases were resolved through NCP mediation procedures at different times, mostly before the 2023 update of the OECD Guidelines, which explicitly include climate change provisions. Additionally, some of these cases were initiated before landmark international agreements, such as the Paris Agreement, which set globally recognised climate targets. Notably, the majority of these 14 cases concentrated on holding investors and fossil fuel companies accountable for contributing to the climate change through their activities, underscoring the increasing scrutiny of financial stakeholders' roles in exacerbating environmental harm. Furthermore, only a few cases explored the concept of climate due diligence as an integral aspect of companies' broader risk-based due diligence frameworks. This indicates an evolving but still nascent understanding of corporate responsibilities in addressing climate-related risks.

Early complaints addressing corporate climate responsibility, such as the case against Vattenfall in the German NCP and the case against Statoil ASA in the Norwegian NCP, were both dismissed.[245] These decisions reflected the limited guidance on emissions reductions in the 2011 OECD Guidelines and the absence of the

242 Ibid, 176–178.

243 Wettstein (2023), p. 355.

244 Aristova et al. (2024), p. 507.

245 NCP Germany, Greenpeace v. Vattenfall, Summary, 15 March 2010; NCP Norway, Norwegian Climate Network v. Statoil, Initial Statement, 28 November 2011.

2015 Paris Agreement to establish a clear international framework on climate action. For example, in the Statoil ASA case, the Norwegian NCP acknowledged the significant environmental risks posed by the oil sands industry, stating: 'the challenge of climate change is daunting, and the risks of major emissions and cumulative environmental consequences from the oil sands industry are significant.'[246] However, the NCP concluded that the complaint primarily targeted Canada's policy to permit oil sands development rather than Statoil's specific conduct within that framework. The NCP emphasised that the complaint did not allege violations of international instruments or national regulations by Statoil itself, as required by the OECD Guidelines.[247] The Norwegian NCP further clarified that for a complaint to fall within its mandate, it must demonstrate a breach of the OECD Guidelines by the specific company in question.[248] It determined that addressing this complaint would not meaningfully contribute to the purpose and effectiveness of the Guidelines. Instead, the NCP noted that complaints should focus on detailed violations of the Guidelines by the company involved, rather than critiquing an industry or sector as a whole.

Public expectations have shifted significantly, recognising the private sector's critical role in achieving climate goals. Since the Paris Agreement and the growing awareness of the private sector's contributions to climate change, complaints have increasingly targeted fossil fuels and financial institutions (FIs). Notable examples include cases against ING in the Dutch NCP, ANZ in the Australian NCP, and Japanese banks Mizuho, SMBC, and MUFG in the Japanese NCP for financing high-emission projects.[249] Similarly, the Polish NCP addressed a complaint against PZU for insuring coal plants. As Aristova and her colleagues addressed, these cases highlighted the rising focus on 'financed emissions' and the imperative to align financial flows with the goals of the Paris Agreement.[250]

Cases against ING and ANZ illustrated the evolving climate responsibilities of FIs under the OECD Guidelines.[251] In the ING case, the dialogue centred on the bank's efforts to measure and publish emissions, set measurable climate targets, and align its lending portfolio with the Paris Agreement. ING highlighted its methodologies, such as Paris Agreement Capital Transition Assessment of european

[246] NCP Germany, Greenpeace v. Vattenfall, Summary, 15 March 2010.

[247] Ibid.

[248] NCP Norway, Norwegian Climate Network v. Statoil, Initial Statement, 28 November 2011.

[249] NCP Netherlands, Oxfam Novib, Greenpeace Netherlands, BankTrack and Friends of the Earth Netherlands (Milieudefensie) v. ING, Final Statement, 19 April 2019; NCP Australia, Friends of Earth v. ANZ Group, Final Statement, 15 December 2021; NCP Japan, Market Forces v. SMBC, MUFG and Mizuho, Fiunal Statement, 15 January 2021.

[250] NCP Poland, Development Yes v. PZU Group, Final Statement, 26 July 2019; Aristova et al., Corporate Climate Change Responsibilities under the OECD Guidelines for Multinational Enterprises, 515.

[251] NCP Netherlands, Oxfam Novib, Greenpeace Netherlands, BankTrack and Friends of the Earth Netherlands (Milieudefensie) v. ING, Final Statement, 19 April 2019; NCP Australia, Friends of Earth v. ANZ Group, Final Statement, 15 December 2021.

financial markets and institutions (PACTA), to assess and steer financed emissions, particularly in high-carbon sectors. Despite progress, complainants raised concerns about reliance on Carbon Capture and Storage, prompting ING to advocate for alternative scenarios, reflecting its adaptability.[252] ING's 2018 commitment to align its portfolio with the Paris Agreement's 'well-below 2 degrees' goal marked a significant step toward climate action. The further dialogue emphasised the broader role of FIs in driving climate action and the need for tailored methodologies to address diverse lending portfolios. The Dutch NCP stressed that ING must align its impact with national and international climate commitments, highlighting the Paris Agreement as a critical benchmark.[253] However, the case also revealed the challenges of applying pre-2023 OECD Guidelines to contemporary climate expectations.

In contrast, the Australian NCP's approach to the ANZ case, though addressing similar concerns, acknowledged the bank's high level of engagement with climate issues.[254] The NCP argued that ANZ had fulfilled its obligations under the Guidelines, noting the lack of clear climate standards within the pre-2023 text. The NCP emphasised the need for updated Guidelines to reflect modern expectations of corporate responsibility.

Aside from FIs, several cases highlighted the corporate climate responsibilities mostly in agriculture extractive industries. The Legalità per il clima on behalf of 45 individuals and Italian CSOs against Cremonini S.p.A. highlighted human rights concerns linked to climate damage but lack detailed arguments establishing clear connections between the alleged climate harm and human rights impacts.[255] The first complaint focused on intensive livestock farming, which the complainants argue is a major source of methane, carbon dioxide, and other air pollutants contributing to climate change. They claim that companies involved in this sector violated OECD Guidelines by failing to conduct proper risk assessments, thereby neglecting their responsibility to respect human rights and address environmental risks. The second complaint targeted ENI, alleging that the company's industrial fossil fuel extraction and marketing plans have significant global climate repercussions.[256] The complainants argue that ENI's refusal to provide a comprehensive analysis of the

[252] NCP Netherlands, Oxfam Novib, Greenpeace Netherlands, BankTrack and Friends of the Earth Netherlands (Milieudefensie) v. ING, Final Statement, 19 April 2019.

[253] Ibid, 6.

[254] NCP Australia, Friends of Earth v. ANZ Group, Final Statement, 15 December 2021.

[255] NCP Italy, The Legalità per il clima on behalf of 45 individuals and Italian CSOs v. Cremonini S.p.A, 1 March 2022, (Pending) https://climatecasechart.com/wp-content/uploads/non-us-case-documents/2021/20211206_15717_points-of-claim.pdf(accessed 2 February 2026); Aristova et al. (2024), p. 516.

[256] NCP Italy, Rete Legalità Per Il Clima (Legality For Climate Network) and others v. Eni, 14 February 2022, (Pending) https://climatecasechart.com/non-us-case/rete-legalita-per-il-clima-legality-for-climate-network-and-others-v-eni/#:~:text=the%20complaint%20alleges%20that%20eni,company's%20activities%3b%20(iii)%20the (accessed 2 February 2026).

climate risks associated with its activities violates multiple provisions of the Guidelines, including those concerning human rights and environmental protection.

Additionally, there has been increasing scrutiny of corporate climate disclosures and the risk of greenwashing. For instance, a case against BP in the UK NCP raised concerns over advertising campaigns that overstated the company's renewable energy initiatives while downplaying its broader contributions to climate harm.[257] Client Earth's complaint was initially deemed material and substantiated but was later discontinued after BP withdrew the advertisements and pledged not to replace them. Similarly, a more recent case in the UK NCP against Drax Group plc questioned the accuracy of claims regarding the climate-friendliness of burning woody biomass for power generation.[258] The NCP found all but one of the allegations to be material and substantiated in its initial assessment, with the final statement still pending.

Lastly, scholars have identified the case against FCA Italy (Stellantis NV) as a pertinent example of a just transition-related issue, illustrating the human rights challenges inherent in the shift toward a low-carbon economy.[259] The complaint, filed with the Italian and subsequently the Dutch NCP, raises concerns about potential human rights violations in cobalt mining operations, which provide essential resources for electrification and decarbonization strategies.[260] The complainants sought transparency and accountability measures, including risk mitigation frameworks, supplier accountability mechanisms, and reparative actions for affected communities.[261] While the case does not directly address emissions reduction, it highlights the broader human rights implications of climate action and underlines the importance of embedding equity and inclusivity in the transition to sustainability. The resolution of this case by the Dutch NCP, which remains pending, will be a critical development in shaping the discourse on just transition and corporate accountability.

In conclusion, the analysis of OECD case law up to 2024 highlighted the evolving nature of corporate climate responsibility and the challenges in addressing these issues within the framework of the OECD Guidelines. Early cases, assessed under the 2011 Guidelines, faced limitations in addressing climate-specific obligations due to the lack of clear international frameworks like the Paris Agreement. As a result, many complaints, particularly those involving fossil fuel companies and financial institutions, emphasized the accountability of investors and financiers for their contributions to climate change but often lacked enforceable standards. The growing focus on 'financed emissions' and corporate responsibility for climate due diligence reflects a shift in public expectations, with notable cases like ING and

[257] NCP United Kingdom, ClientEarth v. BP, Initial Statement, 16 June 2020.

[258] Ibid, Conclusion section.

[259] Aristova et al. (2024), pp. 518–519; NCP Netherlands, Italian CSOs v. Stellantis NV and Stellantis Italy, Initial Statement, 13 February 2023, OECD Watch (Pending) https://www.oecd-watch.org/complaint/italian-csos-vs-stellantis-nv-and-fca-italy/ (accessed 2 February 2026).

[260] Ibid, 2.

[261] Ibid, 3–4.

ANZ illustrating the increased scrutiny of financial institutions' roles in aligning their practices with global climate goals.[262] However, these cases also revealed the difficulty of reconciling outdated standards with modern expectations of corporate accountability. Similarly, cases targeting agricultural and extractive industries, such as those against ENI and Rete Legalità, show the need for companies to integrate climate risk assessments into their broader due diligence frameworks.

Moreover, the emergence of complaints concerning greenwashing and just transition issues, exemplified by cases against BP and Stellantis, further demonstrates the intersection of climate responsibility with human rights, transparency, and equity. These cases indicated the imperative for companies to not only reduce emissions but also ensure that their sustainability efforts are inclusive and socially responsible. With the introduction of the 2023 OECD Guidelines, which provide clearer directives on climate-related responsibilities, there is an opportunity to better address the complexities of corporate climate accountability. However, the effectiveness of these updates will depend on their implementation and the ability of NCPs to bridge past gaps in oversight. The pending resolution of cases like Stellantis will serve as critical benchmarks for the evolving discourse on corporate climate responsibility and the just transition, shaping the future of sustainable and equitable business practices.

3.5 Corporate Human Rights Responsibility in Conflict-Affected and High-Risk Areas

3.5.1 Corporate Duties in High-Risk Areas Under Business and Human Rights Frameworks

MNEs operating in developing regions face significant human rights challenges, especially in conflict-affected and high-risk areas. In such environments, their presence can unintentionally worsen or prolong severe human rights violations, exacerbating vulnerabilities and contributing to instability.[263] The international BHR framework, including the UNGPs and the OECD Guidelines, acknowledges the complexities faced by companies in these regions, highlighting how their operations can adversely affect communities and even fuel conflict.[264] Importantly, these frameworks recognised that conflict situations are context-dependent, with legal and ethical implications varying based on the specific circumstances and environments. The definition of 'conflict-affected high-risk areas' has expanded over time.[265] It now

[262] Aristova et al. (2024), pp. 523–524.

[263] Van Ho (2020), pp. 379–401.

[264] UN Guiding Principles on Business and Human Rights, Commentary to the Principles 7 and 19; OECD Guidelines for Multinational Enterprises, Chapter IV: Human Rights, para 45.

[265] Buriakovska and Davaanyam (2025), pp. 30–31.

encompasses not only active war zones but also fragile states with histories of violence and latent potential for future conflicts.[266] In such contexts, MNEs bear a 'heightened responsibility' to implement rigorous HRDD and adopt conflict-sensitive strategies that prioritise human rights and peacebuilding.[267] These obligations require companies to go beyond traditional compliance and actively engage in mitigating risks to vulnerable populations.

Under the BHR framework, the UNGPs and the OECD Guidelines, heightened human rights due diligence (hHRDD) is critical in conflict-affected areas.[268] These frameworks emphasise the heightened vulnerability of affected communities and the risk that MNEs may unintentionally exacerbate conflicts through their operations. However, there are instances where MNEs have been accused of intentionally contributing to conflict, as exemplified by the Lafarge case, where deliberate actions by the company were alleged to have fuelled violence.[269] This shows the importance of robust hHRDD to prevent both inadvertent and deliberate corporate contributions to conflict and human rights abuses. Consequently, companies are explicitly warned that, they must, at a minimum, assess and mitigate their connection to the aggressor state's war efforts. This is critical, as involvement in armed conflict—whether through direct contribution, indirect support, or mere linkage to conflict dynamics—equates to complicity in human rights abuses under international norms.[270]

To address these risks, both the UNGPs and the OECD Guidelines require MNEs to mitigate adverse human rights impacts directly linked to their operations, even when they are not the primary cause of harm. This mitigation process is guided by the principle of proportionality, ensuring that the level of HRDD aligns with the severity and scope of the risks present in the business's operating environment. This proportional approach becomes particularly significant in conflict zones, where the potential for harm is magnified.[271]

Conflict-affected areas pose distinct obstacles to the effective implementation of HRDD. Although the UNGPs affirm the state duty to assist businesses in meeting their human rights responsibilities in such contexts, and the OECD Due Diligence Guidance provides sector-specific steps—particularly for the extractive industries—practical implementation remains limited.[272] For instance, while the OECD guidance suggested mapping key actors and ensuring supply chain transparency, it falls

---

[266] Ibid, 30.

[267] OHCHR (6 June 2014), p. 9; Graf and Andrea (2017), pp. 109–133.

[268] UN Guiding Principles on Business and Human Rights, Principles 7 and 17; OECD (2016). https://doi.org/10.1787/9789264252479-en (accessed 2 February 2026).

[269] 'Lafarge lawsuit (re complicity in crimes against humanity in Syria)', *Business & Human Rights Resource Centre*, https://www.business-humanrights.org/en/lafarge-lawsuit-re-complicity-in-crimes-against-humanity-in-syria (accessed 2 February 2026).

[270] Aparac (2020), pp. 270–275.

[271] Nagaivska and Uvarova (2024), pp. 315–320.

[272] OECD, OECD Due Diligence Guidance for Responsible Supply Chains of Minerals from Conflict-Affected and High-Risk Areas, Third Edition, OECD Publishing, Paris. https://doi.org/10.1787/9789264252479-en (accessed 2 February 2026).

short of providing comprehensive, actionable steps for broader conflict contexts.[273] This gap in practical guidance leaves MNEs navigating a complex environment without clear frameworks for effective conflict-sensitive HRDD.

Furthermore, the decision to withdraw from conflict affected areas to avoid exacerbating harm introduces additional dilemmas. Both the UNGPs and OECD Guidelines discourage abrupt corporate withdrawal, as it may harm affected communities and destabilise the region further.[274] Instead, they advocate for responsible, well-considered engagement that balances potential positive influence with the risks of perpetuating harm.[275] However, when positive influence is unattainable, responsible disengagement becomes necessary. Unfortunately, clear guidance on executing such disengagement is insufficient, creating significant challenges for MNEs. This highlights the pressing need for more detailed and actionable best practices to guide corporate conduct in conflict-affected areas.

Also, both UNGPs and OECD Guidelines underlined the importance of victim-centred reparations in conflict zones.[276] Companies are encouraged to adopt sensitive, inclusive approaches that apply a ‘conflict lens’ to address the unique vulnerabilities of affected populations. This requires a deep understanding of regional dynamics, peace agreements, and state policies, as well as a commitment to ensuring that the voices of marginalized groups are central to decision-making processes.[277] Such an approach ensures that HRDD goes beyond basic compliance with international humanitarian law (IHL) and actively contributes to preventing violence. Despite the strong conceptual foundation provided by the UNGPs and the OECD Guidelines, translating these principles into actionable strategies remains a significant challenge for businesses.[278] hHRDD stands apart from traditional HRDD by focusing on a deeper understanding of the operational context, especially in conflict-affected areas.[279] However, the lack of specificity in current frameworks often leaves companies uncertain about how to effectively implement hHRDD in these complex environments.

To bridge these gaps, the UNDP and the WGBHR have issued guidance that delineates the distinctions between hHRDD and traditional HRDD.[280] This guidance

---

[273] Ibid.

[274] OECD (2017b), https://mneguidelines.oecd.org/global-forum/2017-GFRBC-Session-Note-Responsible-Disengagement.pdf (accessed 2 February 2026).

[275] Ibid.

[276] Buriakovska and Davaanyam (2025), pp. 32–33.

[277] Ibid.

[278] Nagaivska and Uvarova (2024), p. 320.

[279] Ibid.

[280] UN Working Group on Business and Human Rights (WGBHR) (2020), ‘Business, Human Rights and Conflict-Affected Regions: Towards Heightened Action’ 21 July 2020 UN Doc A/75/212′, UN Doc A/75/212; United Nations Development Programme (UNDP) and WGBHR ‘Heightened Human Rights Due Diligence for Business in Conflict-Affected Contexts: A Guide’ 2022 https://www.undp.org/publications/heightened-human-rights-due-diligence-business-conflict-affected-contexts-guide (accessed 2 February 2026).

provides actionable steps for businesses to better understand the unique contexts in which they operate. Scholars emphasised that while traditional HRDD focuses on identifying and mitigating general human rights risks, hHRDD requires a nuanced comprehension of conflict dynamics.[281] The UNDP's 2022 guidance elaborates on this approach, highlighting that hHRDD involves identifying conflict flashpoints, potential triggers, and the underlying forces driving violence.[282] By proactively addressing these risks, businesses can minimize their contributions to violence and play a role in supporting peacebuilding efforts.

Central to a conflict-sensitive HRDD approach is meaningful stakeholder engagement.[283] This process demands that companies prioritise inclusivity, ensuring that the voices of affected communities, particularly the most vulnerable groups, are heard and integrated into decision-making. MSE not only addresses immediate concerns but also fosters trust and collaboration between businesses and communities. Beyond active conflict affected areas, the WGBHR guidance addresses the importance of post-conflict engagement. Businesses are advised to contribute to reconciliation, address past human rights abuses, and support sustainable recovery efforts.[284] These post-conflict activities require careful planning and adaptation to the unique circumstances of each scenario, ensuring that corporate actions align with broader goals of justice and stability.

3.5.2 *Human Rights Due Diligence in Conflict-Affected Areas: OECD Case Law Insights*

The OECD framework offers valuable insights into evolving corporate responsibility, especially for MNEs in conflict-affected regions. This section examines heightened corporate HRDD responsibilities in the OECD case law, focusing on how these responsibilities are applied in practice. Under OECD case law research, 15 NCP cases, focused on corporate responsibilities in conflict affected areas across Myanmar, DRC, and the Occupied Palestinian Territory (OPT). These cases demonstrated how business can uphold human rights through heightened due diligence, proactive stakeholder engagement, and responsible exits when operating in conflicting environments. This analysis offers insights into implementing HRDD and meeting human rights obligations amid conflict-related challenges.

OECD case law demonstrated that even before the adoption of the 2011 UNGPs and the revision of the OECD Guidelines to include a dedicated chapter on human rights, discussions about corporate responsibility in conflict-affected areas were

[281] Nagaivska and Uvarova (2024), pp. 315–316.

[282] United Nations Development Programme (UNDP) and WGBHR (2022).

[283] Ibid.

[284] WGBHR, 'Business, Human Rights and Conflict-Affected Regions: Towards Heightened Action', UN Doc A/75/212, 21 July 2020.

already underway. Cases such as Chemie Pharmacie Holland BV in Dutch NCP and DAS Air in the UK NCP highlighted the importance of robust due diligence for companies operating in such high-risk contexts. For instance, in 2005, the NGO RAID lodged a complaint with the UK NCP against DAS Air, alleging the company transported coltan from the DRC during a period of intense conflict.[285] The complaint specified that DAS Air conducted flights between the DRC and Uganda from 1998 to 2001, despite airspace closures due to the conflict. DAS Air claimed ignorance of the minerals' conflict-related origins. However, the UK NCP found this assertion implausible, given DAS Air's extensive presence and operations across Africa. The UK NCP ultimately concluded that DAS Air had violated the OECD Guidelines by failing to contribute to sustainable development, neglecting to respect human rights, and not promoting ethical corporate practices among its business partners.[286] These cases underlined that corporate responsibility in protecting human rights and upholding ethical standards in high-risk areas was an emerging area of focus even before the formalisation of the UNGPs and the OECD Guidelines' human rights sections. They highlight an evolving recognition of the need for businesses to conduct due diligence and adopt practices that align with international standards, particularly in conflict-affected regions.

Post-UNGPs adoption, cases increasingly required explicit policies from businesses in conflict zones. For example, the UK NCP case against JCB, where products were allegedly used in property demolitions in Palestinian territories, stressed that businesses in complex settings need clear human rights commitments.[287] The complaint asserts that JCB's products and machinery were utilised in the demolition of Palestinian properties and structures linked to settlements. In response, the UK NCP emphasised that when operating in complex environments, especially in human rights high-risk or conflict-affected areas, businesses must explicitly commit to respecting human rights.[288] A clear commitment to respecting and recognising human rights by businesses provides clarity to employees, suppliers, stakeholders, and customers about their position. Similarly, the Danish NCP's case against Bestseller reinforces the necessity of a proactive, conflict-sensitive approach to HRDD, particularly with attention to evolving risks in Myanmar.[289]

Additional cases highlighted the necessity for hHRDD that goes beyond the baseline requirements outlined in the UNGPs and OECD Guidelines. These examples stressed the critical importance of conflict-sensitive approaches and robust risk assessments in conflict-affected areas, demonstrating how companies must integrate comprehensive due diligence practices into their organizational structures to effectively navigate complex environments. For instance, in a case involving Mallee Resources Limited brought before the Australian NCP, Publish What You Pay

[285] NCP United Kingdom, RAID v. DAS Air, Final Statement, 17 July 2008.

[286] Ibid, 2–3.

[287] NCP United Kingdom, LPHR v. JCB, Final Statement, 12 November 2021.

[288] Ibid, 10. Conclusions.

[289] NCP Denmark, Christian Juhl v. Bestseller, Final Statement, 30 September 2022.

Australia alleged the company failed to conduct adequate due diligence and disengaged irresponsibly from its operations in Myanmar.[290] The Australian NCP emphasised that the effectiveness of hHRDD depends on a solid foundation of general HRDD. It noted that if the company had conducted thorough HRDD prior to and throughout its engagement with BJV, it would have been better equipped to respond to the challenges posed by the Myanmar military coup, in alignment with the OECD Guidelines. This stresses the need for companies operating in conflict-affected areas to embed comprehensive human rights practices proactively, enabling them to adapt and intensify their efforts in response to evolving conflict situations.

Similarly, in a case brought before the Danish NCP against Bestseller, the complainants alleged that Bestseller maintained ties with suppliers linked to the Myanmar military, potentially contributing to conflict financing.[291] The Danish NCP, using same approach consistent with the Australian NCP, examined Bestseller's risk assessments at three stages: before its investment in Myanmar in 2014, during its operational phase from 2014 to 2019, and after the military coups in 2019. Unlike Mallee Resources, Bestseller demonstrated a consistent and evolving commitment to HRDD. It prioritised addressing risks associated with the conflict, documented comprehensive due diligence processes, and tailored its approaches to the changing conflict landscape in Myanmar.[292]

For example, Bestseller's practices included conducting detailed investigations, commissioning third-party audits, using self-assessment forms, and engaging with suppliers, multi-stakeholder initiatives, external experts, and local and international stakeholders.[293] The Danish NCP commended Bestseller's ability to adapt to the dynamic risk environment, balancing efforts to mitigate adverse impacts with fostering income generation and promoting positive industry development in Myanmar. The Danish NCP also highlighted the importance of embedding RBC within corporate governance. For instance, critical decisions, such as entering the Myanmar market and halting new supplier onboarding, were made and communicated at the highest levels of Bestseller's management.

These cases collectively illustrate that hHRDD must be dynamic, context-specific, and deeply integrated into an corporate's operations and decision-making processes. Effective conflict-sensitive due diligence requires companies to draw on diverse information sources, maintain active stakeholder engagement, and continuously refine their strategies to address the evolving risks of conflict. Furthermore, they highlighted the role of responsible business behaviour at the managerial level, ensuring that ethical considerations and human rights priorities are central to corporate strategy and operations in high-risk areas. MSE is essential in conflict affected areas, as it enables businesses to understand local dynamics and build trust. Cases

---

[290] NCP Australia, Publish What You Pay v. Mallee Resources Limited, Final Statement, 2 August 2023.

[291] NCP Denmark, Christian Juhl v. Bestseller, Final Statement, 30 September 2022.

[292] Ibid, 5.

[293] Ibid, 10.

highlighted the importance of engaging a broad array of stakeholders, from local communities to NGOs. Previously analysed case against Bestseller, Danish NCP assessed that the company effectively engaged with stakeholders to analyse Myanmar's socio-political landscape.[294] Such engagement facilitates informed decision-making, particularly in areas with high human rights risks.

MSE is also critical for identifying potential abuses and ensuring that affected voices are heard. The case against Telenor, presented to the Norwegian NCP, centres on whether Telenor could reasonably have anticipated and mitigated the risk of its ICT infrastructure, such as communication towers, being misused by the military to perpetrate genocide against minority groups. This case highlighted the critical role of proactive human rights due diligence, particularly in conflict-affected areas.[295] The Norwegian NCP concluded that while the specific risk of Telenor's towers being exploited for such atrocities might have been unforeseeable initially, the company could have identified this potential misuse if it had engaged in robust stakeholder consultations and conflict-sensitive risk assessments. According to the NCP, MSE—conducted both prior to and during the escalation of the conflict—would have enabled Telenor to gain a deeper understanding of the evolving political and social dynamics, including the military's potential misuse of communication infrastructure.[296]

Thus, this case illustrated a broader principle: even in scenarios where risks are not immediately apparent, businesses operating in high-risk or conflict affected areas have a heightened responsibility to engage with local stakeholders, including CSOs, affected communities, and human rights experts. Such engagement provides critical insights into contextual risks and helps companies identify potential vulnerabilities in their operations.

The recent case brought before the Norwegian NCP highlighted the complexities businesses face when operating in regions with histories of human rights violations. CSOs have accused Aker ASA and Aker BP ASA of breaching OECD Guidelines by merging with Lundin Energy Norway AS, a company allegedly involved in gross human rights abuses in Sudan during a military campaign between 1997 and 2003.[297] This campaign, aimed at securing oil fields, led to the violent displacement of 160,000 people and 12,000 casualties, with extensive documentation from NGOs and ongoing criminal proceedings against Lundin executives in Sweden. The complainants argued that the merger diminishes Lundin's resources, potentially preventing victims from receiving adequate compensation.[298] They also claim that the merger was conducted without consulting affected communities or NGOs representing victims, ignoring their perspectives and further marginalizing them. The

[294] Ibid.

[295] NCP Norway, Committee Seeking Justice for Alethankyaw v. Telenor ASA, Final Statement, 29 August 2022.

[296] Ibid, 12–13.

[297] NCP Norway, Eight civil society organisations from South Sudan, Norway, Sweden, and the Netherlands v. Aker BP ASA and Aker ASA, Initial Statement, 27 February 2023.

[298] Ibid,

NCP highlighted the importance of responsible merger practices, a victim-centred approach, and stakeholder engagement, particularly in conflict-affected areas. It has emphasised that the 'right to effective remedy' is a fundamental human right and that mergers and acquisitions should not obstruct this right.[299] As the connection between due diligence and victims' right to remedy remains underexplored in NCP practices, the Norwegian NCP has decided to address the case.

Another essential component of hHRDD is responsible disengagement, a critical aspect of corporate accountability for human rights and environmental protection in conflict-affected areas. Responsible disengagement has become a recurring focus in OECD case law, underscoring its importance as part of a company's ethical responsibilities. A prominent example highlighting the significance of responsible disengagement is the case involving Mallee Resources brought before the Australian NCP.[300] The complainant alleged that Mallee Resources irresponsibly withdrew from its operations in Myanmar without conducting adequate HRDD to assess or address the adverse impacts of its departure. The Australian NCP concluded that Mallee Resources failed to sufficiently evaluate or mitigate potential human rights consequences resulting from its disengagement, whether the company directly caused, contributed to, or was linked to these harms. The Australian NCP emphasised that human rights due diligence is especially critical during disengagement in conflict-affected settings.[301]

According to the OECD Guidelines, disengagement should be treated as a last resort, only pursued after exhausting all options to leverage business partners to uphold human rights. In this case, Mallee Resources' divestment appeared to be a reaction to sudden political and security changes in Myanmar rather than a strategic and responsible exercise of leverage. Nonetheless, the NCP highlighted that companies, regardless of context, are obligated to assess the social and economic repercussions of their disengagement and mitigate harm to affected communities.

The principles of responsible disengagement were reinforced in a case involving Bestseller, reviewed by the Danish NCP. If Bestseller were to disengage from its operations in Myanmar, the Danish NCP advised that the company must conduct a comprehensive and enhanced risk assessment. This assessment should be evidence-based and informed by current evaluations of social and economic risks tied to withdrawal.[302] The Danish NCP acknowledged Bestseller for demonstrating a proactive approach to due diligence, emphasising that disengagement must be planned carefully to avoid exacerbating vulnerabilities in conflict-affected regions.[303] Key to Bestseller's approach was ongoing stakeholder engagement and a commitment to balancing withdrawal with harm mitigation. This demonstrated that responsible

[299] NCP Norway, PAX and others v. Aker BP ASA and Aker ASA, Final Statement, 18 June 2025, paras 5 and 6.

[300] NCP Australia, Publish What You Pay v. Mallee Resources Limited, Final Statement, 2 August 2023.

[301] Ibid, 37.

[302] NCP Denmark, Christian Juhl v. Bestseller, Final Statement, 30 September 2022.

[303] Ibid, 11–12.

disengagement is not merely a reactive measure, but a strategic process guided by ethical considerations and a deep understanding of local dynamics.

Contrasting the positive examples of responsible disengagement are cases where companies failed to uphold their obligations, leading to significant harm and missed opportunities to address corporate accountability in conflict-affected areas. For instance, Heineken's mass layoffs in the DRC, reviewed by the Dutch NCP, resulted in severe social repercussions due to insufficient due diligence and a lack of meaningful stakeholder engagement.[304] Similarly, cases involving Coca-Cola and Boeing brought to the US and Canadian NCPs illustrated missed opportunities for addressing heightened responsibilities in conflict settings. Specifically, in the first case against Coca-Cola, the company was accused of unfairly dismissing four employees from its DRC branch. While the US NCP acknowledged the challenging circumstances faced by the complainants, it dismissed the case, asserting that employment disputes involving a local DRC company fell outside its jurisdiction, despite the broader human rights implications within a conflict-affected environment.[305] In the second case, Boeing was accused of transporting products to Saudi Arabia that were allegedly used in Yemen in ways that adversely affected civilian populations.[306] The US NCP rejected the case outright, citing concerns that intervening in such matters could be perceived as inappropriate interference in another country's domestic affairs, which it argued would undermine the effectiveness of the OECD Guidelines.[307] These examples demonstrate the critical need for stronger mechanisms within the NCP system to address corporate responsibilities in conflict-affected areas. By rejecting cases with far-reaching human rights implications, NCPs risk diminishing their role in holding companies accountable and advancing the OECD Guidelines' objectives in high-risk environments.

In conclusion, the OECD case law provided critical insights into the evolving landscape of corporate accountability in conflict-affected regions. These cases emphasise that hHRDD is not a static requirement but a dynamic, context-sensitive process that demands proactive stakeholder engagement, robust risk assessments, and responsible decision-making. Whether through responsible disengagement, as seen in the Mallee Resources and Bestseller cases, or through avoiding complicity in human rights violations, such as in the Telenor and Aker ASA cases, the principles of hHRDD highlight the importance of responsible corporate behaviour in high-risk environments. These examples emphasise the need for businesses to embed human rights considerations into their core strategies, ensuring that their actions align with international standards and mitigate harm to vulnerable communities.

---

[304] NCP Netherlands, Former employees v. Bralima, Heineken, Final Statement, 18 August 2017.

[305] NCP United States, Formed employees v. Coca Cola, Final Statement, 21 December 2022.

[306] NCP United States, European Centre for Democracy and Human Rights et al. v. the Boeing Company and Lockheed Martin Corporation, Final Statement, 18 November 2016.

[307] Ibid, 9–10.

3.6 Corporate Responsibility to Contribute to the Sustainable Development Goals

3.6.1 Aligning Corporate Activities with the SDGs Under International BHR Framework

MNEs are uniquely positioned to play a transformative role in achieving the UN SDGs by 2030.[308] As key drivers of global economic activity, innovation, and investment, MNEs shape not only markets but also the social and environmental landscapes of the regions they operate in.[309] Recognising this critical role, the OECD Guidelines explicitly mandate that businesses contribute to economic, environmental, and social progress, thereby fostering sustainable development. This mandate is not merely aspirational; it constitutes a clear directive for MNEs to embed sustainability into their operations, investments, and strategic frameworks. Chapter 2 of the OECD Guidelines, General Policies, Section A.1, highlights this expectation, explicitly stating that corporations must contribute to economic, environmental, and social progress with a view to achieving sustainable development.[310] The accompanying commentary in paragraph 3 reinforces this directive, emphasising that there must be no contradiction between the activities of MNEs and the principles of sustainable development.[311] These guidelines highlight the intrinsic links between corporate decision-making and governance with the economic, social, and environmental progress for advancing SDGs.

By embedding this responsibility into the OECD Guidelines, the framework moves beyond the concept of the 'responsibility to respect' outlined in the UNGPs.[312] The UNGPs primarily focus on a passive duty to avoid and prevent harm, emphasising the need for businesses to respect human rights and mitigate negative impacts. In contrast, the OECD Guidelines call for an active and positive engagement with the objectives of sustainable development, requiring businesses to go beyond compliance and harm mitigation to make meaningful contributions to global progress.[313] This evolution from a reactive to a proactive approach emphasises a paradigm shift in how business responsibilities are framed.[314] However, some scholars argued that the interplay between the UNGPs and the SDGs reflects a broader vision where MNEs are expected to not only respect rights but also actively create value for

---

[308] UNGA (21 October 2015) UN Doc A/RES/70/1 https://documents.un.org/doc/undoc/gen/n15/291/89/pdf/n1529189.pdf (accessed 2 February 2026).

[309] Business and Sustainable Development Commission (January 2017) https://sustainabledevelopment.un.org/content/documents/2399BetterBusinessBetterWorld.pdf#page=99.09 (accessed 2 February 2026).

[310] OECD Guidelines for Multinational Enterprises, Chapter 2: General Policies, section A.1.

[311] Ibid, Commentary para 5 to the Chapter 2: General Policies.

[312] UN Guiding Principles on Business and Human Rights, Principle 13.

[313] Ibid, Deva (2021), pp. 1–22.

[314] Ibid, 9–10.

society.[315] This alignment transforms the role of businesses from being mere participants in global markets to becoming pivotal agents of sustainable development, integrating these objectives into their core ethos and operations. Businesses are expected to internalise global sustainability standards, such as human rights, labour rights, environmental stewardship, and governance principles, into their operations.[316] However, as Wettstein noted, the SDGs, unlike the UNGPs, do not specifically require any particular responsibility from businesses.[317]

Also, Katerina Akestoridi argued that by requiring MNEs to comply with international human rights standards under the UNGPs, the UNGPs inherently advocate for the SDGs.[318] This is because the strong interconnection between the SDGs and human rights establishes a robust normative foundation for integrating sustainability into business operations. Over 90% of the 169 SDG targets align with international human rights instruments and labour conventions, demonstrating the inseparability of development goals and human rights principles.[319] For example, rights such as access to food, water, health, and education, as outlined in the ICESCR, align with SDGs 1–4 and 6, while SDG 8 on decent work is supported by International Labour Organization conventions on child and forced labour.[320] Indeed, Shift also added that, by respecting human rights throughout their value chains and partnerships, businesses not only comply with the UNGPs but also contribute meaningfully to the realisation of the SDGs, reinforcing the intrinsic link between human rights and sustainable development.[321]

However, achieving this alignment requires businesses to address significant challenges, particularly the pervasive issue of short-termism and the potential conflict with their economic interests.[322] Deva contended that the SDGs and other sustainability policies often encourage companies to view compliance with human rights as an opportunity to advance their economic goals.[323] He further added that this approach is problematic, as prioritising economic interests over genuine human rights promotion undermines the core purpose of these initiatives.[324] Indeed, also in practice, pressure from investors focused on immediate financial gains often undermines long-term strategies that prioritise sustainable growth and respect for human rights. Thus, the SDGs cannot replace a company's due diligence obligations but

315 Wettstein (2023), p. 350; Business and Sustainable Development Commission (2017), p. 97.

316 Wettstein (2023), p. 350.

317 Ibid, 350–351.

318 Akestoridi (2021), pp. 87–88.

319 Filskov and Feiring (2018) https://www.humanrights.dk/sites/humanrights.dk/files/media/dokumenter/sdg/hr_and_2030_agenda-web_2018.pdf (accessed 2 February 2026).

320 Ibid, 4.

321 Shift (November 2016).

322 UN WGBHR 'Taking stock of investor implementation of the UN Guiding Principles on Business and Human Rights' Addendum report of the Working Group on the issue of human rights and transnational corporations and other business enterprises, A/HRC/47/39/Add.2, June 2021.

323 Deva (2021), pp. 9–10.

324 Ibid.

should complement them as a framework for identifying risks and opportunities for positive impact. Instead of this, the UNGPs can act as a catalyst, encouraging businesses to transition from a 'do no harm' approach to one that actively seeks to 'do good' by addressing social and environmental needs.[325] While the macro-level implementation of SDGs remains a state responsibility, companies are expected to link their activities to broader sustainable development outcomes, ensuring their actions contribute to global goals while upholding human rights as a foundational principle.[326]

However, corporate contributions to the SDGs remain significantly inadequate, with a wide gap between stated commitments and actual implementation. The WGBHR has noted that investor-driven pressures, particularly for short-term financial returns, often undermine meaningful progress toward sustainable development.[327] To address this accountability deficit, initiatives like the WBA have been established to assess and measure corporate alignment with the SDGs. For example, the WBA's 2022 ranking evaluated global FIs on their investments in low-income countries and support for SMEs to address economic inequality.[328] Alarmingly, only 2% of these institutions reported investments aligned with these critical goals, starkly highlighting the gap between corporate intentions and impactful action.[329]

This discrepancy indicates the need for stronger regulatory frameworks and governance mechanisms. Current international development paradigms, as highlighted in the OECD case law research, suggest that voluntary initiatives alone are insufficient. Instead, businesses must be incentivised—and where necessary, compelled—to align their operations with the SDGs. This includes adopting robust due diligence mechanisms to identify, prevent, and address negative impacts while proactively seeking opportunities to contribute to sustainable development.

The integration of HRDD as outlined in the UNGPs, is a critical step in this direction. By embedding respect for human rights into their operations, MNEs can ensure that their activities not only avoid harm but also actively promote well-being, equity, and sustainability. Enhanced due diligence frameworks, advocated by Buhmann, Jonas Jonsson and Mette Fisker, that combine human rights considerations with environmental and social assessments provide a pathway for businesses to align more closely with the SDGs.[330] The recent adoption of the CSDDD highlights the corporate role in achieving the SDGs. It mandates companies operating in the internal market to address and mitigate adverse human rights and environmental impacts across their operations and supply chains, while ensuring access to justice

---

[325] Buhmann et al. (2019a) https://www.emerald.com/insight/content/doi/10.1108/cg-01-2018-0030/full/html (accessed 2 February 2026).

[326] Wettstein (2023), p. 351.

[327] WGBHR, Taking stock of investor implementation of the UN Guiding Principles, 5.

[328] World Benchmarking Alliance (WBA) (2021) *Financial System Benchmark Methodology*.

[329] WBA, Financial System Benchmark 2022 report, key findings, https://www.worldbenchmarkingalliance.org/publication/financial-system/ (accessed 2 February 2026).

[330] Buhmann et al. (2019a), p. 399.

for affected parties.[331] Adding to this, the shift from compliance-driven approaches to transformative corporate sustainability is evident in the growing emphasis on integrating SDGs into business strategies. This shift requires companies to adopt a broader perspective that goes beyond the immediate financial returns of their operations.

Reviewing both BHR and CSR literatures, scholars affirmed that businesses are now increasingly expected to engage with SDGs as active partners, contributing to systemic changes that foster inclusive and sustainable growth. Many CSR scholars increasingly advocate for the 'triple bottom line' framework, which evaluates corporate performance through three interconnected pillars: people, planet, and profit.[332] This approach emphasised the need for balanced and comprehensive contributions to sustainable development, integrating economic, social, and environmental priorities. However, significant progress is still required.[333] The ongoing discussions about aligning business practices with SDG achievement call for a fundamental rethinking of the role of businesses in development. Rather than remaining passive beneficiaries of favourable conditions, businesses are expected to actively contribute to development by minimising negative impacts and maximising positive contributions. As Wettstein highlighted, while the WGBHR has advanced discussions on the intersection of SDGs and business, few governments and actors fully recognise the role of SDGs in shaping BHR regulatory frameworks.[334] Only a few countries have integrated SDGs into their NAPs on Business and Human Rights, highlighting a critical gap in aligning corporate practices with global development goals.[335] While the link between SDGs and corporate human rights responsibility must be strong to contribute meaningfully to broader impact, human rights must be at the core of these efforts. This ensures that corporate actions not only support economic growth but also promote social and environmental justice in a comprehensive and equitable manner.

3.6.2 Achieving the SDGs in Corporate Practice: Perspectives from OECD Case Law

OECD case law research offers valuable insights into how businesses navigate the challenges of sustainable development. Of the 394 cases reviewed, 18 specifically examined the role of corporate responsibility in contributing to SDGs within local

---

[331] Corporate Sustainability Due Diligence Directive, Recital 16.

[332] Księżak and Fischbach (2017), pp. 96–110.

[333] Ibid, 107.

[334] Wettstein (2023), p. 352; UN WGBHR 'The Business and Human Rights Dimension of Sustainable Development: Embedding "Protect, Respect and Remedy" in SDGs Implementation' Geneva, 30 June 2017 https://www.ohchr.org/sites/default/files/Documents/Issues/Business/Session18/InfoNoteWGBHR_SDGRecommendations.pdf (accessed 2 February 2026).

[335] Ibid, Wettstein (2023), p. 352.

development contexts. These studies primarily focused on extractive and agricultural companies, analysing how their activities impact local economies, employment, and development in the host countries. In some of these cases, NCPs also assessed whether corporate decisions and actions align with SDG principles. The findings highlighted a need to strengthen existing regulations governing MNEs, particularly regarding human rights and environmental responsibilities, to better align corporate actions with SDG objectives.

A notable example is the case brought against Rockwool International before the Danish NCP, which highlighted the importance of aligning corporate social and environmental impact assessments with the SDGs.[336] The case emphasised that these assessments should prioritise the effects of corporate activities on people, the environment, and society. However, based on the submitted documents by the company, the Danish NCP concluded that Rockwool failed to conduct risk-based due diligence in compliance with the OECD Guidelines during the initial phases of its manufacturing facility project. Instead, the company employed a transactional due diligence approach, focusing narrowly on risks to the company itself rather than identifying potential adverse impacts on stakeholders, as required by the OECD Guidelines. Additionally, the Danish NCP found that company failed to provide meaningful opportunities for relevant stakeholders to voice their concerns during the planning and decision-making stages of the project.[337] This case highlights the imperative for businesses to prioritise the risks and needs of affected rightsholders while adopting comprehensive, risk-based due diligence practices to ensure alignment with the OECD Guidelines and the SDGs.

Also, the cases involving Kinross Gold in the Brazilian NCP and Minera Candelaria in the Chilean NCP emphasised the potential for MNEs to act as catalysts for sustainable and inclusive development in the regions where they operate.[338] In the case of Minera Candelaria, the Chilean NCP emphasised the OECD Guidelines' expectation that enterprises contribute positively to economic, social, and environmental progress while minimising challenges arising from their operations.[339] The NCP noted that companies must respect internationally recognised human rights and actively promote sustainable development in the regions where they operate.[340] The NCP stressed that an enterprise with Canadian and Japanese capital—countries known for high compliance standards—should demonstrate similar conduct in the host country. This expectation involves applying higher standards from their home countries when those standards exceed and are compatible with the host country's national laws and regulations. By doing so, companies can further their positive contributions to the sustainable development of the host country.

---

336 NCP Denmark 'West Virginians for Sustainable Development (WVSD) against Rockwool International AS, Final Statement, 3 June 2021.

337 Ibid, 11.

338 NCP Brazil, Association of Neighborhoods v. Kinross Gold, Final Statement, 21 December 2016.

339 NCP Chile, A Group of 26 neighbours v. Minera Candelaria, Final Statement, 18 August 2022.

340 Ibid, 20–21.

This case shows the dual responsibility of MNEs to avoid harm and actively foster progress toward sustainable development, reflecting the SDG principles. As for the case of Kinross Gold, reviewed by the Brazilian NCP, focused on the company's relationship with local communities near its mining operations.[341] The NCP recommended that Kinross provide clear and transparent information to local residents about current and future activities that might affect the socio-economic aspects of their lives.[342] This approach aims to foster trust between the company and the affected population in Paracatu, which is crucial for ensuring that corporate operations contribute to inclusive and sustainable local development.

Furthermore, the cases concerning Perenco and the Bolloré Group, as reviewed by the French NCP, offer detailed insights into corporate influence on local sustainable development and their responsibilities in align with the SDGs.[343] In the case against Perenco, the company was accused of neglecting social and environmental risks to local communities in Kébili, Tunisia in their subsidiary mining operations. The French NCP highlighted Perenco's responsibility to contribute positively to local sustainable development.[344] It recommended that the company must prioritise employing local workers and investing in skills development in collaboration with worker representatives and government authorities. Furthermore, the NCP encouraged Perenco to improve transparency by providing stakeholders in Tunisia with detailed information on the direct and indirect impacts of its activities on employment and the economy, specifically differentiating the roles of subcontractors.[345] The case underlined the critical role of MNE for the local employment and capacity-building to enhance the sustainable development at the local level.

The case against Socapalm, a subsidiary of the Bolloré Group, revolved around the company's impact on local communities in Cameroon, particularly concerning resettlement and access to livelihoods.[346] The French NCP found that while Socapalm's activities aligned with Cameroon's national economic development policies, they made minimal contributions to the development of local communities. Displaced residents who lost their homes and livelihoods received inadequate compensation, and employment opportunities were scarce.[347] The NCP also noted that Socapalm failed to sufficiently engage with local communities to foster capacity-building initiatives as required under the OECD Guidelines.[348] While Socapalm did

---

[341] NCP Brazil, Association of Neighborhoods of v. Kinross Gold, Final Statement, 21 December 2016.

[342] Ibid, 11.

[343] NCP France, ASF and IWATCH v. Perenco, Final Statement, 26 July 2021; NCP France, group of four non-governmental organisations (NGOs) and associations from Cameroon, France and Germany against SOCAPALM, Bollore Group, Report, 3 June 2013.

[344] NCP France, ASF and IWATCH v. Perenco, Final Statement, 26 July 2021, 12.

[345] Ibid, 12.

[346] NCP France, group of four non-governmental organisations (NGOs) and associations from Cameroon, France and Germany v. SOCAPALM, Bollore Group, Report, 3 June 2013.

[347] Ibid, 10.

[348] Ibid.

support human capital development by establishing educational and vocational training institutions on its plantations, these efforts did not fully address the socio-economic needs of local communities, leaving significant gaps in employment and development support.

Despite these shortcomings, the cases also highlighted opportunities for improvement. In Perenco's case, the NCP encouraged greater transparency and stakeholder collaboration to align corporate actions with SDG goals. Similarly, as part of the mediation process, the Bolloré Group acknowledged its responsibilities and committed to improvements, including implementing a QHSE program and enhancing the living conditions of Socapalm workers and local communities.[349] These efforts reflect a gradual shift toward integrating BHR and SDG principles into corporate governance. Together, these cases addressed the critical need for MNEs to prioritise HRDD that not only addresses risks to people but also considers their needs. Similar to the case against Socapalm, in the case against ENRC, the UK NCP addressed concerns about the prolonged resettlement of the Kisankala community, which adversely affected their social and environmental rights.[350] The NCP found that delaying resettlement contradicted the Guidelines' requirements to promote sustainability and advised ENRC to consider and mitigate the negative impacts of such delays on affected communities.[351]

Moreover, the cases against the Spanish MNE and Holcim illustrated critical gaps in MNE's contributions to local employment and sustainable development.[352] In Guatemala, the Spanish NCP noted that while the Spanish MNE claimed economic benefits from its dam project, most jobs were limited to the construction phase, with no lasting impact, and independent sources criticized its socio-economic management. Similarly, in India, Holcim subsidiaries were accused of neglecting local hiring, adversely affecting livelihoods through environmental degradation, and failing to prioritise community well-being. Both cases highlighted the need for MNEs to adopt long-term local employment strategies, ensure independent verification of their socio-economic claims, and align their operations with the SDGs, particularly those focused on decent work (SDG 8), reducing inequalities (SDG 10), and sustainable communities (SDG 11).

The case against ArcelorMittal Liberia, brought before the Luxembourg NCP, also addressed the needs of local communities when conducting effective HRDD.[353] This approach should integrate human rights and sustainable development principles. A key concern highlighted in the case was the lack of tangible benefits for local communities from the project, despite its significant social and environmental impacts. In this case, ArcelorMittal negotiated a 25-year concession agreement with

---

[349] Ibid, 10–11.

[350] NCP United Kingdom, RAID v. ENRC, Final Statement, February 2016.

[351] Ibid, 14.

[352] NCP Spain, Alliance for Solidarity v. Spanish MNE in Guatemala, 19 December 2019.

[353] NCP Luxembourg, Friends of Earth Europre and Sustainable Development Institute of Liberia v. ArcelorMittal Liberia, Final Statement, 1 March 2024.

the Government of Liberia to operate an iron ore mine in Nimba. As part of the agreement, the company committed to paying $75 million over the concession period, including annual instalments of $3 million into the County Social Development Fund (CSDF). These funds were intended to benefit communities in the areas affected by the company's operations. According to the Terms of Reference for the CSDF, 20% of these annual contributions should directly benefit communities most impacted by the company's activities. However, the Luxembourg NCP noted significant discrepancies between the quality and completion of development projects and the expectations of local communities.[354] These gaps led to increased frustration and distrust in the government. This demonstrates that inadequate planning and execution of community-focused initiatives can exacerbate social dissatisfaction and erode public trust.

The NCP emphasised the critical need for affected communities to directly benefit from development funds to ensure equitable and inclusive outcomes. Specifically, guaranteeing that at least 20% of the CSDF serves these communities is vital for promoting equity, addressing core community needs, and fostering social cohesion. Moreover, in this case, the NCP and the company discussed initiatives such as constructing health facilities and providing technical and managerial training for Liberians as part of the company's responsibilities for the project.[355] These initiatives reiterate the importance of aligning corporate human rights responsibilities with the SDGs, particularly those related to health (SDG 3), quality education (SDG 4), and reducing inequalities (SDG 10).

This case highlighted the necessity for MNEs, like ArcelorMittal, to integrate the needs and benefits of local communities into their HRDD processes and stakeholder engagement strategies. Embedding local priorities and rights-based approaches into these frameworks ensures that corporate operations contribute meaningfully to sustainable development while respecting international human rights standards. More broadly, this case implies that MNEs have a fundamental responsibility to ensure their operations in host countries actively support the development and well-being of local communities, aligning their efforts with the SDGs to create positive social and economic impacts. Conversely, neglecting these considerations risks exacerbating social tensions, undermining community relations, and jeopardizing the viability of corporate operations in the affected regions.

In conclusion, the cases examined expose persistent gaps in the operationalisation of regulatory frameworks governing MNEs. Although the OECD Guidelines offer a normative baseline for responsible and sustainable business conduct, their practical implementation remains uneven and frequently inadequate. The findings reinforce earlier observations that corporate responsibility must extend beyond a passive 'responsibility to respect' towards more active forms of contribution, engagement, and accountability in local development processes. Achieving this shift requires enhanced transparency, meaningful and continuous engagement with

[354] Ibid, 8.

[355] Ibid, 5.

affected communities, and genuinely inclusive stakeholder participation to ensure that corporate activities correspond to local priorities rather than external corporate agendas.

3.7 Corporate Shared and Collective Responsibilities

3.7.1 Human Rights Challenges in Global Supply Chains: Embracing the Concept of Shared Responsibility

Global supply chains pose significant human rights challenges, largely due to a misalignment between the transnational nature of economic activities and the predominantly national scope of regulatory frameworks. While production processes and the laws facilitating them operate across borders, the regulations designed to protect people, and the planet remain confined within national jurisdictions.[356] This regulatory gap creates vulnerabilities, enabling systemic issues such as labour rights violations, environmental degradation, and the exploitation of marginalised populations.[357] Over the years, high-profile incidents have brought these issues into sharp focus. For instance, the Nike labour scandals of the 1990s revealed exploitative working conditions in Southeast Asia, while the Rana Plaza factory collapse in 2013 exposed fatal safety shortcomings in Bangladesh's garment sector.[358] These cases highlighted how intense downward pressure on costs in global supply chains externalises social and environmental harms to local communities, particularly in low-income countries.

Furthermore, the global supply chain is fraught with systemic issues that extend beyond isolated incidents, including forced labour, unsafe working conditions, and widespread human rights violations across production, distribution, and disposal stages. For example, the extraction of conflict minerals often involves severe labour exploitation, while the improper handling and disposal of electronic waste (e-waste) result in significant ecological and human harm.[359] These challenges highlight the interconnected and pervasive nature of supply chain impacts, necessitating a paradigm shift in accountability. This systemic failure is exacerbated by 'governance gaps' identified in international law, particularly within the context of globalisation.[360] The increasing power of MNEs, combined with the diminishing regulatory

---

[356] Buhmann et al. (2019b), pp. 337–345.

[357] Ibid, 338.

[358] Collier and Hernandez (23 July 2022) https://www.lemonde.fr/en/summer-reads/article/2022/07/23/the-nike-saga-winning-at-all-costs_5991163_183.html (accessed 2 February 2026); ILO (April 2023) https://webapps.ilo.org/infostories/en-GB/Stories/Country-Focus/rana-plaza#intro (accessed 2 February 2026).

[359] Amnesty international (2016) https://www.amnesty.org/en/wp-content/uploads/2021/05/AFR6231832016ENGLISH.pdf (accessed 2 February 2026).

[360] Wettstein (2015), p. 164.

capacity of national governments, has created a landscape where corporate human rights violations frequently go unaddressed and unnoticed. As Ruggie noted, these gaps enable corporations to exploit the lack of oversight, underscoring the urgent need for robust mechanisms to hold non-state actors accountable.[361] Bridging these governance gaps requires a collective effort to realign global supply chain operations with principles of sustainability and human rights.

The UNGPs emphasise the 'Protect, Respect, and Remedy' framework, outlining distinct responsibilities for states and corporations. States are tasked with protecting human rights through laws and enforcement, while corporations are required to respect those rights through due diligence and the mitigation of adverse impacts. However, as Wettstein concerned, the rigid separation of roles in this framework has raised questions about its adequacy in addressing the collaborative nature of human rights challenges in supply chains.[362] Furthermore, as Yossi Dahan and others argued, human rights violations in global supply chains are rarely the result of actions by a single entity.[363] Instead, they are the cumulative outcomes of interconnected activities by multiple actors—lead firms, suppliers, contractors, and subcontractors.[364] This reality necessitates a shift from viewing responsibilities as isolated to recognizing them as shared and interdependent. Shared responsibility calls for a collaborative approach where states, businesses, and civil society work together to address systemic issues while maintaining their distinct roles.

Wettstein identifies a significant lacuna in the SRSG's three-pillar framework, noting its limited recognition of the capacity of businesses to contribute proactively to collective problem-solving. He contends that the UNGPs largely frame corporate positive obligations—often described as the 'responsibility to fulfil'—as a potential encroachment upon state authority, premised on the concern that such responsibilities could dilute state accountability and erode public governance functions.[365] He argued that the current international framework, from both normative and empirical perspectives, cannot function effectively without rethinking corporate positive responsibilities to go beyond merely respecting rights, including considering issues like silent complicity. Additionally, as Nolan and Taylor pointed out, the traditional categories of responsibility—respect, fulfil, and protect—are often ambiguous and inadequate when applied to the realisation of certain rights, particularly economic and social human rights. Respect, in this context, involves more than simply avoiding human rights violations; it also requires proactive, positive actions.[366]

---

361 John Ruggie 'Protect Respect and Remedy: A Framework for Business and Human Rights' UN Doc A/HRC/8/5 http://www.reports-and-materials.org/sites/default/files/reports-and-materials/Ruggie-report-7-Apr-2008.pdf(accessed 2 February 2026).

362 Wettstein (2015), p. 174.

363 Dahan et al. (2023), p. 1025.

364 Ibid, 1026.

365 Wettstein (2023), pp. 202–203.

366 Ibid, 203; Nolan and Taylor (2009), pp. 443–451 https://link.springer.com/article/10.1007/s10551-009-0295-6 (accessed 2 February 2026).

In another article, Wettstein also argued that the UNGPs give little attention to the potential for corporations to enhance state capacities and accountability through effective collaboration.[367] The role businesses could play in supporting and promoting responsible regulatory frameworks and public policies, as well as contributing to the provision of public goods and services without replacing state functions, remains underexplored.[368] True collaboration involves corporations working alongside governmental agencies and other institutions, with corporate responsibility aimed at complementing and strengthening—rather than substituting—state responsibility.[369]

Dahan and others have argued that addressing shared responsibility requires innovative, collaborative approaches that harness the unique strengths of different stakeholders.[370] Similarly, the World Economic Forum's Shared Responsibility in Supply Chains highlighted that the 'shared responsibility' model is designed to tackle the root causes of severe and persistent human rights risks, such as weak governance and unsustainable upstream business practices.[371] This model calls for collective action, leveraging the influence and resources of key actors in global supply chains, including multinational corporations, national suppliers, governments (both in developed and developing countries), international financial and labour organisations, workers and trade unions, civil society, private philanthropic organisations, and development agencies that play vital roles in public-private partnerships.[372]

Wettstein suggested that current examples show that corporations, in particular, can contribute positively by supporting and advocating for responsible public policies and regulatory frameworks. This entails working in collaboration with states—not to replace state responsibilities, but to complement them.[373] Examples of effective collaborative models include multi-stakeholder initiatives like the Global Framework Agreements and Transnational Industrial Relations Agreements conducted between MNEs and the global union organisations.[374] These initiatives bring together businesses, governments, and civil society to establish and enforce ethical practices across supply chains, fostering more sustainable and equitable outcomes in textile industry.

To achieve truly effective shared responsibility, it is essential to consider all relevant factors and customise the model to fit specific contexts. Iris Young's 'social connection model of responsibility' introduced four parameters—power, privilege,

---

367 Wettstein (2015), pp. 174–175.

368 Wettstein (2012), pp. 155–184.

369 Ibid, 178–179.

370 Dahan et al. (2023), pp. 1029–1034.

371 World Economic Forum (2015) https://www3.weforum.org/docs/WEF_GAC_Supply_Chains_%20A_New_Paradigm_2015.pdf#page=21.05 (accessed 2 February 2026).

372 Wettstein (2012), p. 178.

373 Dahan et al. (2023), pp. 1028–1029.

374 Ibid.

interest, and collective ability—that distribute political responsibility for addressing systemic issues like sweatshop conditions.[375] Building on this idea, Dahan and others proposed a more detailed framework with five key principles for assigning and discharging responsibilities among different actors, which includes, connectedness, contribution, benefit, capacity and the power.[376] The principle of connectedness highlights moral obligations arising from special relationships between individuals or groups.[377] Contribution focuses on the responsibility tied to an agent's direct or indirect role in causing harm.[378] Benefit asserts that those who gain from injustice have a moral duty to address it.[379] Capacity emphasises that responsibility should align with an individual's or institution's ability to remedy harm without incurring excessive costs.[380] Finally, power recognises that structural power dynamics within shared practices shape the degree of responsibility.[381] This comprehensive framework accentuates the importance of a collaborative and tailored approach to address systemic injustices effectively.

The various models and concepts proposed by the scholars above emphasise that corporate responsibility must extend beyond merely respecting rights. Corporations need to actively contribute to and collaborate with states and other stakeholders to address systemic issues in global supply chains, particularly through industry-wide initiatives, as demonstrated in various existing examples. However, implementing shared responsibility in practice remains highly challenging. A major obstacle lies in the unequal distribution of power within supply chains. Lead firms often exert significant pressure on suppliers to cut costs and meet strict production deadlines, forcing suppliers into precarious situations where exploitative labour practices may become a survival strategy. To address this imbalance, empowering suppliers through fair contracts, financial support, and capacity-building initiatives is essential. These measures can help to uphold labour rights and workplace safety without undermining suppliers' competitiveness. Progress in this area is reflected in the recent adoption of the CSDDD, which requires MNEs to assist smaller suppliers in addressing human rights and environmental risks.[382] This support includes both financial and non-financial measures such as training, audits, and contract assurance. However, the practical implementation of these measures remains uncertain and complex.

---

[375] Ibid, Iris Young (2009).

[376] Ibid, 1029–1034.

[377] Ibid, 1029

[378] Ibid, 1030–1031.

[379] Ibid, 1031–1032.

[380] Ibid, 1032.

[381] Ibid, 1032–1033.

[382] Corporate Sustainability Due Diligence Directive, Articles 10 and 11.

3.7.2 Collaborative Approaches Under the OECD Case Law

There are at least 12 cases in which the NCPs and companies have reflected on the concept of collective and shared responsibility in addressing human rights and environmental risks. While the previous section focuses on why shared responsibility is essential in the context of global supply chains, it does not delve deeply into how this principle is applied in practice from a pragmatic standpoint. These 12 cases, though not exhaustive, provide valuable insights into the ways companies can operationalise shared responsibility. They highlighted specific scenarios and circumstances in which collaboration between companies and stakeholders can take place to address these risks effectively. By examining these cases, it becomes possible to identify practical approaches for companies to work together, share accountability, and integrate stakeholder input in managing human rights and environmental challenges. Although the analysis may not offer a comprehensive or in-depth guide, it may serve as a foundational analysis for understanding the conditions under which shared responsibility can be implemented and the strategies companies might employ to fulfil their human rights and environmental responsibilities collaboratively with other entities.

For example, in the case against PWT Group, the company was held accountable for failing to address labour safety and health conditions at its supplier, New Wave Style Ltd., located in the Rana Plaza building in Dhaka, Bangladesh.[383] The building collapsed on April 24, 2013, killing over 1100 people and injuring more than 2000. This case highlighted the critical role of shared responsibility in tackling systemic human rights and safety risks within global supply chains. In this case, Danish NCP emphasised the necessity of collective efforts in conducting risk-based inspections, including assessments of structural and building safety.[384] When such inspections are organised by industry-wide or collaborative organisations, they ensure that responsibility is shared among multiple stakeholders rather than being the sole burden of individual companies. The NCP also recommended utilising shared frameworks like the UN Global Compact and the CSR Compass to establish consistent standards and tools for due diligence, thereby fostering collective accountability. PWT Group's membership in the Accord on Fire and Building Safety in Bangladesh further demonstrated shared responsibility in practice.[385] The Accord's independent inspection program and collective oversight enable companies to work together to improve safety and accountability throughout their supply chains.

Moreover, cases handled by NCPs, such as those against WWF, FIFA, and Bestseller, addressed the concept of shared responsibility in addressing some challenging human rights issues. In the WWF case, the organisation was accused of failing to obtain FPIC from the Baka people when supporting the establishment of

[383] NCP Denmark, Clean Clothes Campaign Denmark and Active Consumers v. PWT Group, Final Statement, 17 October 2016.

[384] Ibid, 2.

[385] Ibid, 7.

protected areas in Cameroon.[386] Both parties agreed to measures that enhanced transparency in FPIC procedures, supported the Baka's land rights, and developed mechanisms to prevent abuse.[387] These actions required the active involvement of all relevant actors—local communities, state authorities, and CSOs—in upholding the rights of Indigenous Peoples. The responsibility to respect FPIC does not rest solely with operating companies; NPOs working in those regions also bear responsibility to ensure FPIC is fully respected and not undermined in practice.

Similarly, the case against FIFA, which was detailed earlier in this book, focused on labour rights violations of migrant workers involved in constructing facilities for Qatar's World Cup.[388] In this case, the NCP and both parties recognised the importance of capacity building and emphasised collaboration among contractors, workers, and local authorities to improve workplace safety and labour conditions.[389] This case further highlighted the shared responsibility approach as a model for addressing systemic labour rights challenges, particularly in countries reliant on large numbers of migrant workers. A key limitation of this research is that NCP recommendations in the analysed statements rarely provide sufficient detail on how the proposed actions are to be implemented, allocated among responsible actors, or assessed in practice. This lack of operational clarity significantly limits the ability to conceptualise shared responsibility in a meaningful way. Nonetheless, the statements still indicate, at least at a general level, the types of measures that may be expected from companies and other stakeholders, even if they fall short of enabling a deeper evaluation of how such responsibilities are to be concretely realised.

As for good practice, the Bestseller case exemplified how shared responsibility can be effectively implemented in the conflict-affected areas.[390] The Danish NCP commended Bestseller for its proactive measures during the Rohingya crisis in Myanmar. The company collaborated with other businesses operating in Myanmar to increase leverage on government actions, temporarily suspended onboarding of new suppliers to mitigate risks, and later resumed operations with stricter due diligence processes.[391] Specifically, with respect to collaborative efforts, Bestseller convened different meetings with other companies operating in the same region to discuss the identified human rights concerns, gather additional data, and coordinate a joint approach for engaging with state authorities on these issues. This cases show the examples of how some collective action among corporations to positively influence government decision-making towards the human rights and highlighted the importance of engaging communities to address risks in such contexts.

Moreover, cases involving FIs like UBS, ING, and Rabobank demonstrated the potential for shared responsibility to address human rights and environmental risks

[386] NCP Switzerland, Survival International v. WWF, Final Statement, 21 November 2017.

[387] Ibid, 5.

[388] NCP Switzerland, BWI v. FIFA, Final Statement, 2 May 2017.

[389] Ibid, 5.

[390] NCP Denmark, Christian Juhl v. Bestseller, Final Statement, 30 September 2022.

[391] Ibid, 7.

in the investment activities. In the case against UBS, the Swiss NCP mediated a dialogue between UBS and the STP regarding UBS's alleged ties to Hangzhou Hikvision Digital Technology, implicated in human rights violations.[392] The parties discussed UBS's HRDD, particularly its potential linkage to the adverse impacts in its passive investment activities and agreed on future engagement through regular meetings to enhance the inclusion of ESG criteria in the passive investment. UBS expressed that it is committed to leading industry initiatives, though no consensus was reached on making its due diligence process more robust with disengagement clauses.[393] The Swiss NCP emphasised the importance of continued collaboration and progress reporting to implement it within the FIs in passive investment as shared goals effectively.

Similarly, cases involving ING and Rabobank highlighted the critical need for FIs to adopt a shared responsibility approach, working collaboratively with other FIs, companies, and other stakeholders to conduct effective HRDD and address risks related to their investment activities.[394] The Dutch NCP in the case against Rabobank, which highlighted significant challenges in the palm oil sector, such as deforestation, environmental degradation, air pollution, and land expropriation.[395] Rabobank's participation in the Roundtable on Sustainable Palm Oil (RSPO) was acknowledged as a positive step toward a multi-stakeholder approach to systemic issues. However, the NCP emphasised that collaboration through initiatives like RSPO does not relieve FIs of their individual responsibility to conduct HRDD.[396] Rabobank was urged to develop its own due diligence policies to ensure it leverages its position to influence clients and mitigate risks in its supply chain.

In the case against ING, the NCP similarly emphasised the necessity for FIs to conduct shared responsibility in HRDD through collaboration with multi-stakeholder initiatives like RSPO.[397] While ING's involvement in such initiatives was seen as a positive step, the NCP reminded that the institution retains direct responsibility for ensuring its HRDD processes are thorough and aligned with the OECD Guidelines.[398] ING was encouraged to evaluate the quality of collaborative initiatives to ensure they incorporate robust mechanisms for addressing risks and improving outcomes. These cases highlighted that while shared responsibility among FIs, companies, and stakeholders is essential to tackle systemic challenges in high-risk industries, it must be complemented by strong, individual HRDD processes within each institution to ensure comprehensive risk mitigation and accountability.

---

392 NCP Switzerland, STP v. UBS Group, Final Statement, 20 December 2021.

393 Ibid, 4–5.

394 NCP Netherlands, Friends of the Earth Europe and Friends of the Earth Netherlands/Milieudefensie—Rabobank, Final Statement, 15 January 2016.

395 Ibid, 2.

396 Ibid, 4.

397 NCP Netherlands, Milieudefensie/Friends of the Earth Netherlands, WALHI/Friends of the Earth Indonesia and SDI/Friends of the Earth Liberia v. ING, Final Statement, 7 April 2022.

398 Ibid, 8.

Another case that highlighted the shared responsibility of FIs is the one against ABP/APG, accused of failing to conduct adequate HREDD related to its investment in a steel plant in Odisha, India.[399] Several NGOs—including Lok Shakti Abhiyan, KTNC Watch, Fair Green and Global Alliance, among others—submitted a specific instance to the Korean, Norwegian, and Dutch NCPs. The complaint alleged breaches of the OECD Guidelines by the South Korean company POSCO, the Dutch pension fund ABP and its pension administrator APG, as well as the Norwegian Government Pension Fund Global. In this case, the Dutch NCP, working jointly with the Norwegian and Korean NCPs, was mandated to facilitate dialogue between the parties in order to address the social and environmental harms affecting local communities and to clarify the respective responsibilities of the corporate actors involved, including the financial institutions.[400] In the NBIM case before the Norwegian NCP, the final statement made clear that merely acknowledging human rights risks is insufficient: NBIM is expected to *cooperate with other entities precisely for the purpose of enhancing its leverage over its investee company*. The NCP stressed that NBIM's responsibility is not limited to passive ownership but requires proactive coordination with other shareholders to increase collective pressure on POSCO to address the harms raised by affected communities.[401] By recommending that NBIM form coalitions with other investors, the NCP implicitly treated cooperation not as a voluntary gesture of goodwill but as a necessary strategy to overcome the limits of individual influence. The NCP further pointed out that NBIM should use shareholder voting, targeted dialogue, and clear human rights expectations to compel portfolio companies to adopt policies, conduct due diligence, and provide or cooperate in remediation.[402] Importantly, the recommendation that NBIM diversify its monitoring tools and information sources—especially beyond Global North datasets—exposed a structural gap in how investors assess risk, and highlighted that *effective leverage depends on meaningful engagement with those most affected, not on distant or generic reporting frameworks*.

The role of companies in multi-stakeholder initiatives as part of shared responsibility has been analysed in cases such as those against Mylan and KiK, handled by the Dutch and German NCPs respectively. In the case against Mylan, a pharmaceutical company accused of distributing rocuronium bromide used in lethal injections, the Dutch NCP emphasised the importance of a multi-stakeholder approach in fostering the wider application of due diligence within the pharmaceutical sector.[403] The NCP encouraged pharmaceutical companies to collaborate with distributors, human rights organisations, and other stakeholders to prevent the misuse of medicines in lethal injections. Furthermore, the NCP urged Mylan to share the outcomes

---

[399] NCP Netherlands, Lok Shakti Abhiyan, KTNC Watch, Fair Green and Global Alliance, Forum for Environment and Development v. ABP/APG, Final Statement, 18 September 2013.

[400] Ibid, 4.

[401] Ibid, 46.

[402] Ibid, 47.

[403] NCP Netherlands, Bart Stapert v. Mylan, Final Statement, 11 April 2016.

of its due diligence measures with other companies in the sector to strengthen collective efforts and set an example of responsible practices.[404]

Similarly, in the case against KiK Textilien, connected to the Rana Plaza disaster, the German NCP highlighted the value of multi-stakeholder initiatives in promoting sustainability within the textile sector.[405] The NCP noted that KiK's involvement in such initiatives enabled the sharing of expertise among stakeholders, critical evaluations of procurement practices, and improvements in CSR measures.[406] The participation of trade unions and CSOs in these initiatives was identified as key to ensuring credible and transparent improvement processes. These cases collectively demonstrate how multi-stakeholder approaches, as a form of shared responsibility, can enhance due diligence, foster collaboration, and drive meaningful change in high-risk sectors.

Another notable case that highlighted corporate shared responsibility is the case against IKEA, which addresses the shared accountability between a parent company and its subsidiary.[407] While both the parent and subsidiary have their own individual responsibilities, the Dutch NCP emphasised that parent companies must also share accountability for the human rights risk management of their subsidiaries.[408] This dynamic indicates the importance of a shared responsibility approach within corporate structures. Although the parent company's responsibility for its subsidiary's human rights practices will be discussed in greater detail in Chap. 4 of this book, it is important to highlight here that this case demonstrates a clear example of shared responsibility in corporate governance. The analysis of various NCP cases demonstrates the critical importance of collaborative and shared responsibility in addressing human rights and environmental risks across diverse sectors. From global supply chains and investment activities to corporate governance structures, these cases highlight the need for multi-stakeholder engagement and shared accountability among companies, FIs, CSOs, and the governments. Whether through collective efforts to enhance labour safety, address environmental degradation, or implement robust HRDD, these cases reiterated that shared responsibility is essential for tackling systemic challenges effectively. Collaborative frameworks, such as the Accord on Fire and Building Safety in Bangladesh, RSPO, and industry-specific initiatives, provide valuable tools for companies and stakeholders to align their efforts and leverage collective influence to promote sustainability and human rights compliance.

Admittedly, due to the limited detail and analytical depth provided in the NCP statements, the concept of corporate shared responsibility remains only partially developed. While the cases do not offer a comprehensive legal articulation of how

---

[404] Ibid, 5.

[405] NCP Germany, Uwe Kekeritz, Member of the German Bundestag, v. KiK Textilien und Non-Food GmbH, C&A Mode GmbH & Co., and Karl Rieker GmbH & Co. KG, Final Statement, 28 October 2013.

[406] Ibid, 8-9.

[407] NCP Netherlands, BWI et al., v. Inter IKEA Holding B.V, Final Statement, 25 April 2023.

[408] Ibid, 3.

such responsibility should be operationalised or distributed among actors, they nonetheless *signal an emerging normative direction* in corporate accountability discourse. The statements hint at a gradual shift from isolated corporate obligations towards more integrated forms of cooperation among parent companies, subsidiaries, and financial institutions. Although these references are often framed in general or voluntary terms, they reveal an implicit expectation that collaboration should serve to *enhance leverage and mutual accountability*, rather than merely demonstrate goodwill. Thus, even in their brevity, these cases provide early indications of how shared responsibility may evolve into a more structured legal and procedural concept within global supply chains.

3.8 Preliminary Conclusion

This chapter has provided a comprehensive exploration of corporate human rights responsibilities in various contexts, emphasising their complexity and the increasing need for businesses to tackle systemic challenges through proactive human rights-based approaches. By examining corporate responsibilities across key areas—such as group rights (including women's rights, workers' rights, and the protection of minorities and Indigenous Peoples), environmental sustainability, climate change, and operations in conflict-affected areas—it becomes clear that corporations bear complex human rights and environmental responsibilities. The integration of HRDD frameworks and insights drawn from OECD case law illustrated the practical implications of these responsibilities. Whether advancing gender equality, ensuring decent work practices, safeguarding environmental integrity, or contributing to the SDGs, the analysis underlined the necessity of aligning corporate activities with international human rights and environmental law. This chapter highlighted that addressing the broad spectrum of rights and environmental issues requires HRDD processes to be tailored to the specific risks, needs, and unique vulnerabilities of diverse rights-holders, demonstrating that there is no universal formula for effective HRDD. Instead, the cornerstone of effective due diligence lies in the MSE, enabling companies to customise their approaches to the contexts and groups affected.

This chapter further interrogated the intersection between climate and environmental risks and HRDD, arguing that the prevailing separation of these domains within corporate practice is conceptually flawed and normatively unsustainable. The analysis demonstrates that climate and environmental harms are not merely parallel concerns but structurally embedded within the very conditions that give rise to human rights impacts. Accordingly, HRDD that fails to integrate climate and environment related risks is, by definition, incomplete. The cases reviewed illustrate that environmental and climate due diligence must be treated as an inherent component of HRDD rather than an optional or secondary layer of risk management. The chapter also critiques the persistent framing of corporate responsibility as predominantly individualised, highlighting instead the necessity of shared and collective responsibility models. Addressing climate change and large-scale environmental degradation requires legal and institutional architectures capable of allocating responsibility across multiple actors—corporations, states, financial institutions, and CSOs—rather than defaulting to fragmented or voluntary commitments. While OECD NCP case law offers instructive examples of emerging practice, it also reveals the normative limitations of current frameworks, which continue to accommodate corporate discretion rather than impose binding obligations.

In conclusion, the evolution of corporate human rights responsibility necessitates a shift from a minimalist 'do no harm' posture toward a legally and ethically grounded responsibility to contribute to systemic solutions. Such a reorientation requires not only compliance with existing standards but the development of enforceable mechanisms that embed long-term accountability, ecological integrity, and equitable responsibility-sharing within corporate governance. Without this shift, the rhetoric of 'sustainability' risks functioning as a discursive shield rather than a jurisprudential advance.

References

Cases

Milieudefensie v. Royal Dutch Shell [2021] C/09/571932 / HA ZA 19-379 (by 2030 RDS must reduce greenhouse gas emissions across its own operations and from the oil it produces by 45 percent) https://climatecasechart.com/non-us-case/milieudefensie-et-al-v-royal-dutch-shell-plc/ (accessed 2 February 2026)

Legislations

Australia. Modern Slavery Act 2018

California. California Transparency in Supply Chains Act, 2015

Canada. Fighting Against Forced Labour and Child Labour in Supply Chains Act, 2021

Conference of the Parties, Adoption of the Paris Agreement, Dec. 12, 2015; U.N. Doc FCCC/CP/2015/L.9/Rev/1 (Dec. 12, 2015)

European Parliament and Council of the European Union. *Regulation (EU) 2023/1115 of the European Parliament and of the Council of 31 May 2023 on the Making Available on the Union Market and the Export from the Union of Certain Commodities and Products Associated with Deforestation and Forest Degradation and Repealing Regulation (EU) No 995/2010 (Text with EEA Relevance)*. PE/82/2022/REV/1. Official Journal of the European Union, 31 May 2023. https://eur-lex.europa.eu/legal-content/en/txt/?uri=celex%3a32023r1115

European Union. Regulation of the European Parliament and of the Council on prohibiting products made with forced labour on the Union market and amending Directive (EU) 2019/1937.https://data.consilium.europa.eu/doc/document/PE-67-2024-INIT/en/pdf (accessed 2 February 2026)

France. Duty of Vigilance Law, 2017 (Loi sur le devoir de vigilance)

Germany. *Act on Corporate Due Diligence Obligations in Supply Chains (Lieferkettensorgfaltspflichtengesetz, LkSG)*. 22 July 2021

ILO. *Right to Organise and Collective Bargaining Convention,* 1949 *(No. 98).* Costa Rica
ILO (1989) Indigenous and tribal peoples convention, no. 169. International Labour Organization, Geneva. https://www.ilo.org/dyn/normlex/en/f?p=1000:12100:0::no::p12100_instrument_id:312314
International Labour Organisation (ILO) (27 June 1989) *C169 - Indigenous and Tribal Peoples Convention, 1989,* No.169, https://www.refworld.org/legal/agreements/ilo/1989/en/19728. Accessed 2 Feb 2026)
Netherlands (24 October 2019) *Child Labour Due Diligence Act (Wet zorgplicht kinderarbeid). Official Gazette of the Kingdom of the Netherlands,* 401. https://zoek.officielebekendmakingen.nl/stb-2019-401.html. Accessed 2 Feb 2026
The Swiss Federal Council. '*Ordinance on Due Diligence and Transparency in relation to Minerals and Metals from Conflict-Affected Areas'* (DDTrO) of 3 December 2021
United Kingdom. Modern Slavery Act 2015. c. 30
United Nations. General Assembly. *Convention on the Elimination of All Forms of Discrimination Against Women.* UNTS 1249:13, 18 December 1979
United Nations. General Assembly. *Declaration on the Rights of Persons Belonging to National or Ethnic, Religious and Linguistic Minorities.* A/RES/47/135, 18 December 1992. https://www.ohchr.org/en/instruments-mechanisms/instruments/declaration-rights-persons-belonging-national-or-ethnic (accessed 2 February 2026)

Documents

Equator Principles Framework that also take effect as of January 1, 2012. www.equatorprinciples.com/resources/equator_principles.pdf (accessed 2 February 2026)
ILO (18 June 1998a) *Declaration on Fundamental Principles and Rights at Work*
ILO. 'Monitoring compliance with international labour standards: The key role of the ILO Committee of Experts on the Application of Conventions and Recommendations' 2019a Geneva https://www.ilo.org/sites/default/files/wcmsp5/groups/public/@ed_norm/@normes/documents/publication/wcms_730866.pdf#page=4.10. Accessed 2 Feb 2026
International Finance Corporation (2012) IFC sustainability framework. International Finance Corporation, Washington, D.C.. https://www.ifc.org/wps/wcm/connect/7c5bc4804a2790ac8de4f56b4bb34f32/IFC_Sustainability_Framework_2012.pdf?MOD=AJPERES&CVID=jkW0ekA. Accessed 2 Feb 2026
OECD (2016) OECD due diligence guidance for responsible supply chains of minerals from conflict-affected and high-risk areas, 3rd edn. OECD Publishing, Paris. https://doi.org/10.1787/9789264252479-en. accessed 2 Feb 2026
OECD (2017a) OECD due diligence guidance for meaningful stakeholder engagement in the extractive sector. OECD Publishing, Paris. https://www.oecd.org/content/dam/oecd/en/publications/reports/2017/02/oecd-due-diligence-guidance-for-meaningful-stakeholder-engagement-in-the-extractive-sector_g1g65995/9789264252462-en.pdf (accessed 2 Feb 2026)
OECD (2017b) Session Note—Responsible disengagement, Global Forum on Responsible Business Conduct, https://mneguidelines.oecd.org/global-forum/2017-GFRBC-Session-Note-Responsible-Disengagement.pdf. Accessed 2 Feb 2026
OECD (2020) Responsible business conduct and gender. OECD. https://mneguidelines.oecd.org/mneguidelines/Responsible-Business-Conduct-and-Gender.pdf
OEIGWG (July 2023) Updated draft legally binding instrument to regulate, in international human rights law, the activities of transnational corporations and other business enterprises, https://www.ohchr.org/sites/default/files/documents/hrbodies/hrcouncil/igwg-transcorp/session9/igwg-9th-updated-draft-lbi-clean.pdf. Accessed 2 Feb 2026

Office of the High Commissioner for Human Rights (OHCHR) (6 June 2014) *Mandate of the Working Group on the Issue of Human Rights and Transnational Corporations and Other Business Enterprises*, 'Statement on the Implications of the Guiding Principles on Business and Human Rights in the Context of Israeli Settlements in the Occupied Palestinian Territory,' https://www.ohchr.org/en/statements/statement-implications-guiding-principles-business-and-human-rights-context-israeli. Accessed 2 Feb 2026

Open-Ended Intergovernmental Working Group on Transnational Corporations and Other Business Enterprises with Respect to Human Rights (OEIGWG) (6 August 2020) *Second Draft of the Legally Binding Instrument to Regulate, in International Human Rights Law, the Activities of Transnational Corporations and Other Business Enterprises*. https://www.ohchr.org/sites/default/files/Documents/HRBodies/HRCouncil/WGTransCorp/Session6/OEIGWG_Chair-Rapporteur_second_revised_draft_LBI_on_TNCs_and_OBEs_with_respect_to_Human_Rights.pdf. (accessed 2 Feb 2026)

United Nations (1948) Universal declaration of human rights

United Nations. General Assembly (1966) *International Covenant on Economic, Social, and Cultural Rights*. Treaty Series 999 (December): 171

United Nations (2 October 2007) General Assembly. 2007. *United Nations Declaration on the Rights of Indigenous Peoples: General Assembly Resolution*, A/RES/61/295, https://www.refworld.org/legal/resolution/unga/2007/en/49353. accessed 13 Nov 2024) (UNDRIP)

United Nations (7 April 2008) Human Rights Council. *Eighth Session, Agenda Item 3: Promotion and Protection of All Human Rights, Civil, Political, Economic, Social, and Cultural Rights, Including the Right to Development. Protect, Respect and Remedy: A Framework for Business and Human Rights*. Report of the Special Representative of the Secretary-General on the Issue of Human Rights and Transnational Corporations and Other Business Enterprises, John Ruggie. UN Doc A/HRC/8/5

United Nations (2011) Guiding principles on business and human rights: implementing the United Nations "protect, respect and remedy" framework. United Nations, New York and Geneva

United Nations (6 August 2013a) Working Group on Business and Human Rights, *Report on Business-Related Impacts on the Rights of Indigenous Peoples*, A/68/279

United Nations (6 August 2013b) Working Group on Business and Human Rights, *Report on Business-Related Impacts on the Rights of Indigenous Peoples*, A/68/279

United Nations (November 2017a) Working Group on Business and Human Rights. *The Gender Lens to the UN Guiding Principles on Business and Human Rights*. https://www.ohchr.org/sites/default/files/Documents/Issues/Business/GenderConsultation30.11.17.pdf. accessed 2 Feb 2026

United Nations (30 June 2017b) Working Group on Business and Human Rights, *The Business and Human Rights Dimension of Sustainable Development: Embedding "Protect, Respect and Remedy" in SDGs Implementation'* Geneva, https://www.ohchr.org/sites/default/files/Documents/Issues/Business/Session18/InfoNoteWGBHR_SDGRecommendations.pdf. Accessed 2 Feb 2026

United Nations (3 September 2019a) Human Rights Committee, 'General Comment No. 36 on Article 6 of the International Covenant on Civil and Political Rights, on the Right to Life', CCPR/C/GC/36

United Nations (23 May 2019b) Working Group on Business and Human Rights. *Gender Dimensions of the Guiding Principles on Business and Human Rights*. A/HRC/41/43

United Nations (21 July 2020) Working Group on Business and Human Rights, *Business, Human Rights and Conflict-Affected Regions: Towards Heightened Action*, UN Doc A/75/212

United Nations (June 2021) Working Group on Business and Human Rights. *Taking stock of investor implementation of the UN Guiding Principles on Business and Human Rights* Addendum report of the Working Group on the issue of human rights and transnational corporations and other business enterprises, A/HRC/47/39/Add.2

United Nations. General Assembly. *The human right to a clean, healthy and sustainable environment* Resolution adopted by the General Assembly on 28 July 2022, A/RES/76/300

United Nations. Human Rights Council. Expert seminar on the responsibility of business enterprises to respect the human right to a clean, healthy and sustainable environment Report of the Special Rapporteur on the issue of human rights obligations relating to the 55. of a safe, clean, healthy and sustainable environment, David R. Boyd' 2 January 2024a UN Doc A/HRC/55/41

United Nations (18 July 2024b) Human Rights Council. *Report of the Special Rapporteur on the promotion and protection of human rights in the context of climate change: Access to information on climate change and human rights.* UN Doc A/79/176

United Nations Development Programme and Working Group on Business and Human Rights (2022) *Heightened Human Rights Due Diligence for Business in Conflict-Affected Contexts: A Guide.* https://www.undp.org/publications/heightened-human-rights-due-diligence-business-conflict-affected-contexts-guide (accessed 2 Feb 2026)

United Nations. General Assembly (21 October 2015) *Transforming our world: the 2030 Agenda for Sustainable Development: Resolution adopted by the General Assembly on 25 September 2015*, UN Doc A/RES/70/1 https://documents.un.org/doc/undoc/gen/n15/291/89/pdf/n1529189.pdf (accessed 2 February 2026)

Bibliography

Akestoridi K (2021) The role of business in international development and the attainment of the sustainable development goals. In: Bantekas I, Stein MA (eds) Cambridge companion to business and human rights law. Cambridge University Press, pp 86–114

Amnesty international (2016) This Is What We Die For' Human Rights Abuses in the Democratic Republic of the Congo Power The Global Trade In Cobalt. https://www.amnesty.org/en/wp--content/uploads/2021/05/afr6231832016english.pdf. Accessed 2 Feb 2026

Aparac J (2020) Business and armed non-state groups: challenging the landscape of corporate (un) accountability in armed conflicts. Bus Human Rights J 2(5):270–275

Aristova E, Higham C, Higham I, Setzer J (2024) Corporate climate change responsibilities under the OECD guidelines for multinational enterprises. Int Comp Law Q 73(2):505–525

Bantekas Oette L (2016) International human rights law and practice. Cambridge University Press

Baumann-Pauly D, Nolan J, van Heerden A et al (2017) Industry-specific multi-stakeholder initiatives that govern corporate human rights standards: legitimacy assessments of the fair labor association and the global Network initiative. J Bus Ethics 143:771–787

Bhatt K (2021) Innovative contractual remedies with indigenous peoples. In: Bantekas I, Stein MA (eds) The Cambridge companion to business and human rights law. Cambridge University Press, pp 455–480

Boyd DR, Keene S (June 2022) *Policy Brief No. 3: Essential Elements of Effective and Equitable Human Rights and Environmental Due Diligence Legislation, A policy brief by David R. Boyd, UN Special Rapporteur on Human Rights and the Environment, and Stephanie Keene, Independent Consultant, International Human Rights Lawyer*, https://www.ohchr.org/sites/default/files/2022-06/PolicyBrief_3_HREDD_June2022.pdf (accessed 2 Feb 2026)

Buhmann K, Jonsson J, Fisker M (2019a) Do no harm and do more good too: connecting the SDGs with business and human rights and political CSR theory. Good Governance 19(3):1–22. https://www.emerald.com/insight/content/doi/10.1108/cg-01-2018-0030/full/html (accessed 2 Feb 2026)

Buhmann K, Taylor M, Giuliani E (2019b) Editorial—business and human rights in global value chains. Compet Chang 23(4):337–345

Buriakovska K, Davaanyam O (2025) Analysing heightened corporate human rights responsibilities in the context of OECD case law. In: Davaanyam O, Krajewski M (eds) Exploring corporate human rights responsibilities in OECD case law. Springer Nature, pp 27–50

Business & Human Rights Resource Centre, Lafarge Lawsuit (Re Complicity in Crimes Against Humanity in Syria) https://www.business-humanrights.org/en/lafarge-lawsuit-re-complicity-in-crimes-against-humanity-in-syria (accessed 2 Feb 2026)

Business and Human Rights Resource Centre (5 November 2024a) 'Brazil: Indigenous communities in Pará say they were not consulted by the government about carbon credit contracts with multinationals'. https://www.business-humanrights.org/en/latest-news/brazil-indigenous-communities-in-par%C3%A1-say-they-were-not-consulted-by-the-government-about-carbon-credit-contracts-with-multinationals-2/ (accessed 2 February 2026)

Business and Human Rights Resource Centre (2 November 2024b) 'Fiji: 34 Bangladeshi workers allegedly subject to exploitative working conditions & "inhumane treatment" at Pacific General Builders; incl. co comment'. https://www.business-humanrights.org/en/latest-news/fiji-34-bangladeshi-workers-allegedly-subject-to-exploitative-working-conditions-inhumane-treatment-at-pacific-general-builders-incl-co-comment/ (accessed 2 February 2026)

Business and Human Rights Resource Centre. 'Migrant workers in global supply chains' https://www.business-humanrights.org/en/big-issues/labour-rights/migrant-workers-in-global-supply-chains/ (accessed 2 February 2026)

Business and Sustainable Development Commission (January 2017) 'Better Business Better World: The report of the Business & Sustainable Development Commission'. https://sustainabledevelopment.un.org/content/documents/2399BetterBusinessBetterWorld.pdf#page=99.09 (accessed 2 February 2026)

Business for Social Responsibility (September 2012) Engaging With Free, Prior, and Informed Consent. https://www.bsr.org/reports/BSR_Engaging_With_FPIC.pdf#page=6.09 (accessed 2 February 2026)

Černič JL (2020) Business and indigenous peoples' human rights. In: Deva S, Birchall D (eds) Research handbook on human rights and business. Edward Elgar Publishing, pp 335–353

Collier E, Hernandez A (23 July 2022) 'The Nike saga: Winning at all costs' Le Monde. https://www.lemonde.fr/en/summer-reads/article/2022/07/23/the-nike-saga-winning-at-all-costs_5991163_183.html (accessed 2 February 2026)

Cornell AB (2019) Labour rights. In: Ewing A (ed) Teaching business and human rights handbook. Teaching Business and Human Rights Forum, pp 43–57

Corsi JL (2021) Gender, Business and Human Rights. In: Bantekas I, Stein MA (eds) The Cambridge companion to business and human rights law. Cambridge University Press, pp 308–329

Dahan Y, Lerner H, Milman-Sivan F (2023) Shared responsibility and labor rights in global supply chains. J Bus Ethics 182(4):1025–1040

Dehbi F, Martin-Ortega O (2023) An integrated approach to corporate due diligence from a human rights, environmental, and TWAIL perspective. Governance Regulation 17(4):927–928

Dehm J (2023) Beyond climate due diligence: fossil fuels, 'red lines' and reparations. Bus Human Rights J 2(8):151–179. https://doi.org/10.1017/bhj.2023.30. (accessed 2 February 2026)

Deva S (2021) From 'business or human rights' to 'business and human rights': what next? In: Deva S, Birchall D (eds) Research handbook on business and human rights. Edward Elgar Publishing, pp 1–21

Deva S, Pushkar A (2024) A global south perspective on labour rights and supply chains for a post-growth world. In: Bueno N, ter Haar B, Zekic N (eds) Labour law utopias: Post-Growth & Post-Productive Work Approaches. Oxford University Press, pp 90–115

Filskov N, Feiring B (2018) Human rights and the 2030 agenda for sustainable development: lessons learned and next steps. Danish Institute for Human Rights, pp 1–54. https://www.humanrights.dk/sites/humanrights.dk/files/media/dokumenter/sdg/hr_and_2030_agenda-web_2018.pdf. accessed 2 Feb 2026

Graf A, Andrea IFF (2017) Respecting human rights in conflict regions: how to avoid the 'conflict spiral. Bus Human Rights J 2(1):109–133

Grosser K (2021) Gender, business and human rights: academic activism as critical engagement in neoliberal times. Gend Work Organ 28(4):1624–1637

Handl MN, Seck SL, Simons P (2022) Gender and Intersectionality in business and human rights scholarship. Bus Human Rights J 7(2):201–225

Heede R (2014) Tracing anthrophonic carbon dioxide and methane emissions to fossil fuel and cement products. Climate Change 122:229–241

Clean Clothes Campaign 'Justice for the Ali Enterprises victims' https://cleanclothes.org/campaigns/past/ali-enterprises#:~:text=What%20happened%3F,windows%20and%20locked%20exit%20doors (accessed 2 February 2026)

ILO (1998b) 'Report V (2B) Addendum: Committee on contract labour', Geneva. https://webapps.ilo.org/public/english/standards/relm/ilc/ilc86/rep-vadd.htm (accessed 2 February 2026)

ILO (30 January 2019b) '30th anniversary of the Indigenous and Tribal Peoples Convention, 1989 (No. 169)' https://www.ilo.org/resource/30th-anniversary-indigenous-and-tribal-peoples-convention-1989-no-169#:~:text=169%20has%20been%20ratified%20by,indigenous%20and-%20tribal%20peoples%20worldwide (accessed 2 February 2026)

ILO (April 2023) The Rana Plaza disaster ten years on: What has changed? https://webapps.ilo.org/infostories/en-GB/Stories/Country-Focus/rana-plaza#intro> (accessed 2 February 2026)

Jovanovic M (2021) The business sector and the rights to work and just and favourable conditions of work. In: Bantekas I, Stein MA (eds) The Cambridge companion to business and human rights law. Cambridge University Press, pp 330–358

Kelly A (16 December 2019) Apple and Google named in US lawsuit over Congolese child cobalt mining deaths. Guardian https://www.theguardian.com/global-development/2019/dec/16/apple-and-google-named-in-us-lawsuit-over-congolese-child-cobalt-mining-deaths. Accessed 2 Feb 2026

Kemp D, Owen JR (2017) Corporate readiness and the human rights risks of applying FPIC in the global mining industry. Bus Human Rights J 2(note 1):163–169

Księżak P, Fischbach B (2017) Triple bottom line. J Corporate Responsibility Leadership 14(3):96–110

Lafarre A, Rombouts B (2020) Towards mandatory human rights due diligence: assessing its impact on fundamental labour standards in global value chains. Eur J Risk Regulation 13(4):1–17

Landau I, Howe J (2022) State extraterritorial regulation and decent work in the Asia Pacific. In: Bellace JR, ter Haar B (eds) Research handbook on labour, business and human rights law. Edward Elgar, pp 466–491

Lewis C (2012) Corporate responsibility to respect the rights of minorities and indigenous peoples. Briefing, Minority Rights Group International. https://minorityrights.org/app/uploads/2024/01/download-1157-corporate-responsibility-to-respect-the-rights-of-minorities-and-indigenous-peoples.pdf#page=14.61 (accessed 2 February 2026)

Macchi C (2021) The climate change dimension of business and human rights: the gradual consolidation of a concept of 'climate due diligence. Bus Human Rights J 6(1):93–119

Macchi C, Bernaz N (2021) Business, human rights and climate due diligence: understanding the responsibility of banks. Sustainability 15(13):1–21. https://www.mdpi.com/2071-1050/13/15/8391 (accessed 2 Feb 2026

Martin-Ortega O, Dehbi F (2022) Valerie Nelson and Renginee Pillay 'towards a business, human rights and the environment framework'. MDPI Sustainability 14(11):1–26. https://www.mdpi.com/2071-1050/14/11/6596 (accessed 2 February 2026)

McCorquodale R (2024) Business and human rights: elements of international law. Oxford University Publishing

Meyer N, Patz C (01 June 2024) *Dividing the Indivisible: Human Rights under the EU Corporate Sustainability Due Diligence Directive, Vergassungsblog,* https://verfassungsblog.de/dividing--the-indivisible-human-rights-under-the-eu-corporate-sustainability-due-diligence-directive/ (accessed 2 Feb 2026)

Migration Data Portal (12 June 2024) 'Crossing National Borders to Work Is One of the Key Motivations Behind International Migration, Whether Driven by Economic Inequalities, Seeking Employment, or Both. The Additional Impact of Economic, Political and Environmental Crises and Shifting Demographics, with Ageing Populations in Some Parts of the World and a 'Youth Bulge' in Others, Contribute to Rising Labour Migration.' https://www.migrationdataportal.org/themes/labour-migration#:~:text=According%20to%20the%20latest%20available,force%20(ILO%2C%202021) (accessed 2 Feb 2026)

Mohamadieh K, Davaanyam O (20 March 2025), Stephanie Regalia and Markus Krajewski 'Complementarity of the Legally Binding Instrument on Business and Human Rights and the EU Corporate Sustainability Due Diligence Directive' A study paper CIDSE,

Nagaivska D, Uvarova O (2024) Companies operating in conflict-affected environments without impacting the conflict: between regular and heightened human rights due diligence. Bus Human Rights J 9(2):315–320

New Climate Institute (23 February 2023) 'Report on Corporate Climate Responsibility Monitor 2023'. https://newclimate.org/resources/publications/corporate-climate-responsibility-monitor-2023 (accessed 2 Feb 2026)

Nicolas B (2022) Multinational enterprises and labour rights: concepts and implementation. In: Bellace JR, ter Haar B (eds) Research handbook on labour, business and human rights law. Edward Elgar, pp 421–438

Nissen A (2020) Business and Human Rights: Remediation through agender lens. In The Long Run University of Cambridge https://aleydisnissen.com/gallery/publicationsp-Inthelongrun_Cambridge_Nissen_2.pdf (accessed 2 Feb 2026)

Nolan J, Taylor L (2009) Corporate responsibility for economic, social and cultural rights: rights in search of a remedy? J Bus Ethics 87:443–451. https://link.springer.com/article/10.1007/s10551-009-0295-6 (accessed 2 Feb 2026)

Nollkaemper A (12 Nov 2024) *Lessons of a Landmark Lost: The Judgment of the Hague Court of Appeal in Shell v Milieudefensie, Verfassungsblog,* https://verfassungsblog.de/shell--milieudefensie-climate-litigation/, https://doi.org/10.59704/dd77504c9eae2abd (accessed 2 Feb 2026)

Novitz T (2022) Freedom of association: its emergence and the case for prevention of its decline. In: Bellace JR, ter Haar B (eds) Research handbook on labour, business and human rights law. Edward Elgar, pp 231–252

OECD Watch 'The OECD Guidelines and Indigenous Peoples'. https://www.oecdwatch.org/oecd--ncps/the-oecd-guidelines-for-mnes/what-is-in-the-oecd-guidelines/the-oecd-guidelines-and-indigenous-peoples/#:~:text=You%20can%20use%20the%20OECD,and%20informed%20consent%20(FPIC) (accessed 2 Feb 2026)

Quiroz SO, Seitz K (2021) Corporate accountability: what's gender got to do with it? European Coalition for Corporate Justice. https://corporatejustice.org/news/corporate-accountability-whats-gender-got-to-do-with-it/ (accessed 2 Feb 2026)

Rouas V, Otten J, Daniel (10 June 2024) 'From Paper to Practice: Moving to a Coherent Implementation of the EU Corporate Sustainability Due Diligence Directive's Environmental and Climate Obligations' *Verfassungsblog*, https://verfassungsblog.de/from-paper-to-practice-csddd-implementation (accessed 2 Feb 2026)

Salcito K (2023a) Automotive supply chain links to the Uyghur genocide: reversing a growing crisis. Bus Human Rights J 8(2):265–270

Salcito K (2023b) Rights of indigenous peoples. In: Ewing A (ed) Teaching business and human rights. Edward Elgar, pp 295–313

Seck S, Simons P (2019) Resource extraction and the human rights of women and girls. Can J Women Law 31(1):1–7

Seck S, Simons P (13 April 2020) 'Impact Assessment and Responsible Business Guidance Tools in the Extractive Sector: Implications for Human Rights, Gender and Stakeholder Engagement' (Draft Final Report for the SSHRC Knowledge Synthesis Grant: Informing Best Practices in Environmental and Impact Assessments) https://digitalcommons.schulichlaw.dal.ca/ialaw-rbc/1/ (accessed 2 Feb 2026)

Segall D (2022) Human rights and the global construction sector: deconstructing the challenges faced by. Low-wage workers. In: Marx A, Van Galster G, Wouters J (eds) Research handbook on global governance, business and human rights. Edward Elgar, pp 358–379

Shift (November 2016) Business, Human Rights and the Sustainable Development Goals: Forging a coherent vision and strategy. A paper from Shift commissioned by the Business and Sustainable Development Commission

Simons P, Handl M (2019) Relations of ruling: a feminist critique of the United Nations guiding principles on business and human rights and violence against women in the context of resource extraction. Can J Women Law 31(1):113–150

Tapias Torrado NR (2020) Overcoming silencing practices: indigenous women defending human rights from abuses committed in connection to mega-projects: a case in Colombia. Bus Human Rights J 7(1):29–44

The Korea Bizwire (7 Sept 2018) Outsourced Risk: 80% of Shipyard Deaths Involve Subcontractors, , http://koreabizwire.com/outsourced-risk-80-of-shipyard-deaths-involve-subcontractors/123980 (accessed 2 Feb 2026)

Torkington S (4 June 2024) 'What is the informal economy and how many people work in it?' *World Economic Forum*. https://www.weforum.org/stories/2024/06/what-is-the-informal-economy/ (accessed 2 Feb 2026)

Turner SJ (2021) Business, human rights and the environment—using macro legal analysis to develop a legal framework that coherently addresses the root causes of corporate human rights violations and environmental degradation. Sustainability 13(22):1–31

University of Oxford (8 October 2024) *New report spotlights urgent issues faced by mobile indigenous populations*. https://www.ox.ac.uk/news/2024-10-08-new-report-spotlights-urgent-issues-faced-mobile-indigenous-populations (accessed 2 Feb 2026)

Van Ho T (2020) Business and human rights in transitional justice: challenges for complex environments. In: Deva S, Birchall D (eds) Research handbook on business and human rights. Edward Elgar Publishing, pp 379–401

Vijeyarasa R (2020) Women, work and global supply chains: the gender-blind nature of Australia's modern slavery regulatory regime. Aust J Hum Rights 26(1):74–92

Wegher Osci FS (2023) In: Choudhury B (ed) Guiding principle 22: remediation in *the UN guiding principles on business and human rights: a commentary*. Edward Elgar, pp 171–177

Wettstein F (2012) Corporate responsibility in the collective age: toward a conception of collaborative responsibility. Bus Soc Rev 117(2):155–184

Wettstein F (2015) Normativity, ethics, and the UN guiding principles on business and human rights: critical assessment. J Human Rights 14(2):162–182

Wettstein F (2023) Business and human rights, ethical, legal and managerial perspectives. Cambridge University Press

Workers Support Team and KTNC Watch (20 March 2019) *Complaint to National Contact Point for the OECD Guidelines for Multinational Enterprises*

World Benchmarking Alliance. Financial System Benchmark 2022 report, key findings, https://www.worldbenchmarkingalliance.org/publication/financial-system/ (accessed 2 Feb 2026)

World Economic Forum 'Shared Responsibility: A New Paradigm for Supply Chains' Global Agenda Council 2015. https://www3.weforum.org/docs/WEF_GAC_Supply_Chains_%20A_New_Paradigm_2015.pdf#page=21.05 (accessed 2 Feb 2026)

Young MI (2009) Responsibility for justice. Oxford University Press

Chapter 4
Clarifying Corporate Human Rights Responsibilities Considering Different Corporate Actors Through OECD Case Law

4.1 Introduction

This chapter of this book builds on the foundations laid in the previous chapters and provides a detailed examination of the human rights and environmental responsibilities of companies in different contexts, with a particular focus on the HRDD responsibilities of different corporate actors. This chapter moves from the broader examination of corporate responsibility in Chaps. 2 and 3 to a more focused discussion of the tailored responsibilities of specific actors illuminated by the OECD case law. This chapter examines the critical role of various (corporate) actors, including MNEs with extensive global operations, financial institutions (FIs), state-owned enterprises (SOEs), and even non-profit organisations (NPOs), whose actions and decisions can have a significant impact on rights holders in economic activities (see Fig. 4.1). It is important to note that, although suppliers, technological companies, and audit and consultancy firms were coded in the CSA of the OECD case law under the different corporate actors' responsibilities, their low numbers and lack of substantial analysis meant they were not examined in detail in this book.

Building on the analysis in previous chapters, which has shown that human rights and environmental risks vary significantly depending on the issues and groups affected, the sector and the operating environment, this chapter highlights how different corporate and other actors contribute to these risks through different actions and business relationships. As analysed earlier in this book, corporate responsibility extends beyond mere respect for human rights to include active contribution to the SDGs and collaboration with other companies and other stakeholders. This section examines how the responsibility of different corporate actors is conceptualised and critically assesses whether these conceptualisations are adequate and appropriate to effectively address the specific risks and impacts associated with their actions and relationships. It also explores how tailored approaches to HRDD responsibilities

O. Davaanyam, *Conceptualising the Corporate Human Rights and Environmental Responsibilities*, Interdisciplinary Studies in Human Rights 17,
https://doi.org/10.1007/978-3-032-21430-0_4

Fig. 4.1 Sub-codes of parent code: responsibilities of different corporate actors

can help mitigate these risks by addressing the particular vulnerabilities and needs of specific rights holders and contexts.

Each section of Chapter IV addresses the different responsibilities of different actors, including parent companies, FIs, NPOs and SOEs, as well as the state's duty to protect human rights under the UNGPs and the OECD Guidelines. By combining theoretical insights from international human rights frameworks with practical lessons from the OECD case law, this chapter provides a comprehensive roadmap for actors to understand and fulfil their obligations effectively. For example, it examines the responsibilities of parent companies, highlighting their oversight and group-wide due diligence responsibilities towards subsidiaries, supported by practical case studies from OECD NCP-specific cases.

This chapter also highlights the particular responsibility and accountability of FIs and investors for human rights and environmental risks associated with their investments and emphasises the importance of embedding HRDD in financial and investment decision-making processes. In addition, the analysis is extended to NPOs and SOEs, highlighting their particular role and contributions to the promotion and protection of human rights. The chapter concludes with an examination of the state's multi-layered duty to protect human rights. It examines its role as a regulator (in both home and host states), as an economic actor potentially complicit in corporate abuses, and as the main actor responsible for ensuring access to effective remedies, including participation in NCP procedures. Ultimately, this chapter enriches the book by providing actionable insights and practical guidance tailored to the complex and dynamic contexts in which human rights responsibilities are operationalised, offering stakeholders a nuanced understanding of their role in mitigating risks and promoting corporate accountability.

4.2 Managerial Responsibilities of Parent Companies Towards Subsidiaries

4.2.1 Understanding Parent Company Responsibility Under International BHR Frameworks

Parent companies often benefit from the principle of separate corporate personality, a fundamental concept in corporate law that treats parent and subsidiary companies as distinct legal entities.[1] This framework facilitates business expansion and reduces risks for companies by allowing them to operate globally without being directly responsible for the actions or liabilities of their subsidiaries.[2] While this principle encourages foreign direct investment and the free movement of capital, it raises significant concerns about access to remedy for rights holders who have been harmed by corporate activities. Victims of corporate human rights abuses often face obstacles in obtaining justice, particularly when subsidiaries are uncooperative or when state protection mechanisms fail.[3] In such cases, plaintiffs often target the parent companies, arguing that they are either directly or indirectly responsible for the damage caused by their subsidiaries or that they benefit from it because they own or partially control these companies.[4]

Radu Mares has analysed how parent companies exert control over subsidiaries through mechanisms such as board appointments, voting rights, and managerial oversight, often achieved via operational integration, overlapping leadership roles, and contractual agreements.[5] Furthermore, in terms of different types of corporate group forms, historically, corporate structures relied on centralised models like the pyramidal 'unitary form,' where parent companies exercised strict control over subsidiary layers.[6] Over time, companies transitioned to decentralised 'multi-divisional form' structures, characterised by semi-autonomous divisions that improved profitability and adaptability.[7] Mares further stated that, more recently global value chains have emerged, enabling companies to outsource production and distribution to independent firms through contracts rather than ownership.[8] This shift underlined a

[1] Wilson (2020), p. 161.

[2] Mares (2020), p. 446.

[3] For example, in the case of the Mariana dam collapse, victims sought justice in a London court rather than relying on Brazilian courts, which are known for lengthy proceedings and the risk of inadequate compensation, see Al Jazeera 'Why are victims of a Brazil dam disaster suing miner BHP in a London court?' 23 October 2024 Al Jazeera https://www.aljazeera.com/news/2024/10/23/why-are-victims-of-a-brazil-dam-disaster-suing-miner-bhp-in-a-london-court (accessed 2 February 2026).

[4] Mares (2020), p. 447.

[5] Ibid, 450–451.

[6] Ibid.

[7] Ibid.

[8] Ibid.

trend toward flexibility and efficiency, with limited liability facilitating decentralised operations while allowing parent companies to maintain alignment with broader corporate goals. However, this operational evolution complicates corporate accountability, further highlighting the accountability gap between legal separateness and justice for affected communities.

To close this gap, legal doctrines such as the doctrine of piercing the corporate veil and duty of care under tort law offer ways to hold parent companies accountable. The doctrine of piercing the corporate veil allows courts to suspend the principle of limited liability and hold parent companies accountable when subsidiaries act as their 'alter ego' or when strict adherence to the separation principle would result in fraud or injustice.[9] However, this remedy requires high evidentiary thresholds, including proof of complete control and wrongful intent or fraud, making it a rare and difficult remedy for claimants.[10] In contrast, tort law focuses on the direct acts of parent companies rather than their control over subsidiaries.[11] Under this approach, parent companies can be held liable if their own conduct contributes to harm, regardless of the operational independence of the subsidiary.[12] This framework establishes direct liability, which differs from the piercing the corporate veil doctrine in that it focuses on the parent company's active role in causing the harm.[13]

Recent landmark decisions, such as *Vedanta Resources PLC v Lungowe* in the United Kingdom and *Kiobel v Shell* in the Netherlands, reinforced the growing recognition of parent company liability under tort law for human rights and environmental harms caused by their subsidiaries.[14] The case against Vedanta in the UK Supreme Court established a significant precedent by recognising that a parent company can have a duty of care to individuals harmed by the actions of its subsidiary, regardless of the subsidiary's location.[15] The court emphasised that this duty arises when a parent company actively enforces group-wide policies or publicly holds itself out as supervising and controlling its subsidiaries.[16] Even omissions, such as failing to implement proclaimed responsibilities, can result in liability. This case demonstrated that courts may use public statements, like those in annual reports, to assess a parent company's duty of care.[17] Ultimately, the case was settled with a substantial payment to the claimants, highlighting the potential accountability of parent companies for both their actions and omissions in managing their subsidiaries.

---

[9] The doctrine of separate legal personality states that each company has its own legal personality that is independent of other companies, even if there are ownership or control relationships between them. This distinction is upheld by the concept of the corporate veil in Chambers (2021), p. 529.

[10] Ibid, 528.

[11] Sanger (2019), p. 486.

[12] Ibid, 489.

[13] McCorquodale (2024), p. 208; Chandler v. Cape plc [2012] 1 WLR 3111.

[14] Croser et al. (2020), pp. 130–136.

[15] Vedanta Resources plc v. Lungowe [2019] UKSC 20 [Vedanta].

[16] Ibid., para 53.

[17] McCorquodale (2024), p. 209.

In the Shell cases, which were heard in Dutch courts, plaintiffs from Nigerian villages in the Niger Delta alleged that oil spills caused by subsidiary Shell Nigeria had severely damaged their farmland and fishing grounds. The Court of Appeal in the Hague, found that Shell, as the parent company, had a duty of care to the third parties concerned due to its supervision of the subsidiary's activities.[18] The court held Shell Nigeria responsible for the pipeline leaks and found that the company had been negligent in failing to implement adequate safety measures and leak detection systems.[19] Both companies were ordered to compensate the victims, clean up the leaks and install leak detection systems and impose penalties for non-compliance. This landmark judgment which a parent company was held liable for the actions of its subsidiary in another jurisdiction and sets a significant precedent for victims seeking compensation for human rights and environmental damages.[20] The decisions in the Vedanta and Shell cases reflected a shift in the law that is leading to parent companies being held liable in courts in their own country for damages abroad, particularly in human rights and environmental cases. Scholars see these judgments as a turning point, paving the way for better access to justice and greater accountability for multinational corporations under international legal principles.

In addition to these liability-based approaches, there are also non-liability-based frameworks, such as accounting laws, which impose certain responsibilities on parent companies without requiring remedial action.[21] For example, parent companies may be required to publish consolidated reports on the operations of their subsidiaries to ensure transparency, but without being liable for the loss.[22] While corporate law remains a significant barrier to parent company liability, evolving legal standards in other areas, such as human rights and environmental law, signal a growing recognition of the need for parent companies to take responsibility for managing risk and ensuring justice for affected parties.

Soft law instruments like the UNGPs and the OECD Guidelines suggest, though do not explicitly mandate, parent company accountability for the actions of their subsidiaries. The UNGPs acknowledge that MNEs often function as integrated economic entities while maintaining separate legal structures connected by ownership or contractual relationships. Although the UNGPs uphold the principle of separate legal personality, they emphasise that the responsibility to respect human rights applies universally to all businesses, regardless of size, structure, or operational context.[23] This necessitates tailored approaches to ensure human rights are respected, utilising governance frameworks, management systems, and contractual

[18] Four Nigerian Farmers v Shell, the Hague Court of Appeal, 29 January 2021, ECLI:NL: GHDHA:2021 (Four Nigerian Farmers).

[19] Ibid, para 3.31; McCorquodale (2024), p. 193.

[20] Ibid, 194.

[21] Mares (2020), p. 457.

[22] Ibid, 458.

[23] UN Guiding Principles on Business and Human Rights, Commentaries to Principles 13 and 14.

arrangements.[24] Furthermore, Rachel Chambers highlighted that while the UNGPs acknowledge the role of tort law in providing remedies for victims of corporate human rights abuses and urge states to address barriers like the corporate veil, access to remedy remains the most neglected pillar, leaving victims in extraterritorial cases without effective recourse.[25]

Similarly, the OECD Guidelines, under Chapter 2: General Policies, commentary para 8, emphasise the role of a parent company's board in providing strategic guidance, monitoring management, and ensuring accountability to shareholders and stakeholders.[26] This includes maintaining robust financial reporting systems, independent audits, risk management, operational controls, and compliance with laws and standards, underscoring the broader responsibility of parent companies to uphold integrity and accountability within their corporate groups.[27] Furthermore, in alignment with the UNGPs, the OECD Guidelines uphold the principle that corporations must conduct HRDD across all activities to which they are directly linked through business relationships.[28] These guidelines have provided a critical mechanism for NGOs and affected rights-holders to address corporate accountability by utilising OECD NCPs as forums for mediation. Through this process, allegations of human rights abuses and environmental degradation caused by subsidiaries have been brought directly against parent companies, challenging their HRDD responsibilities for the actions of their subsidiaries. To date, over 100 cases have been concluded, targeting parent companies, with more than 50 of these cases offering detailed analyses on how parent companies discharge their responsibilities over its subsidiary activities.[29] These cases highlight the potential for NCPs to influence corporate behaviour and provide an avenue for victims to seek redress. This research will be explored further in the subsequent section.

Building on the normative framework laid out by the UNGPs and the OECD Guidelines, significant strides have been made in clarifying and enforcing the accountability of parent companies under tort law, particularly through the concept of a duty of care. The recent adoption of the CSDDD has further solidified these responsibilities, introducing legally binding obligations for parent companies. Under Article 6 of the CSDDD, parent companies must actively oversee their subsidiaries, conduct HRDD, and submit consolidated reports that encompass subsidiary activities.[30] Recitals 21 and 22 of the CSDDD highlighted that these obligations extend beyond passive oversight, requiring proactive management to ensure compliance with sustainability and human rights standards.[31] By establishing these clear

[24] Ibid, Commentary to Principle 16.

[25] Chambers (2021), p. 534.

[26] OECD Guidelines for Multinational Enterprises, Chapter 2: General Policies, Commentary para 8.

[27] Ibid.

[28] OECD Guidelines for Multinational Enterprises, Chapter 2: General Policies, sections 11–13.

[29] See Sect. 4.2.2 of this chapter.

[30] Corporate Sustainability Due Diligence Directive, Article 6.

[31] Ibid, Recitals 21 and 22.

and enforceable responsibilities, the CSDDD represents a critical step toward embedding parent companies' accountability into EU law. Parent companies under the scope of the directive are now compelled to implement robust HRDD frameworks and assume responsibility for their subsidiaries' impacts. Collectively, these developments demonstrate a global shift toward enhanced corporate accountability, with parent companies increasingly recognised as central actors in mitigating human rights abuses and environmental harm.

4.2.2 Parent Company Due Diligence Responsibilities: Insights from the OECD Case Law

As noted earlier, the OECD NCP case handling system serves as a crucial platform for CSOs, communities and affected rights-holders to bring parent companies to the table to address alleged harms caused by their subsidiaries. While many cases involve parent companies being challenged, the OECD case law research has identified over 50 cases in which NCPs specifically examined the responsibilities of parent companies, either in detail or in a more general manner. This section will first examine how NCPs generally recognise the parent company and then analyse how they define the specific actions that fall under the parent company's responsibilities.

4.2.2.1 General Concept of Parent Company Responsibility in the OECD Case Law

NCPs began recognising the responsibilities of parent companies well before landmark court cases such as those involving Vedanta and Shell. In many cases, NCPs have observed that parent companies were found to breach the OECD Guidelines when their subsidiaries failed to respect human rights. For instance, in the case against POSCO brought before the Norwegian NCP, POSCO, as a corporate group, was deemed to have violated the OECD Guidelines due to the actions of its wholly owned subsidiary, POSCO India Private Limited. The subsidiary was involved in setting up a steel plant in the Jagatsinghpur District of Odisha, India.[32]

The allegations highlighted POSCO's failure to prevent or mitigate adverse human rights impacts, conduct comprehensive HRDD, and perform adequate environmental due diligence.[33] These shortcomings were identified as substantial violations of the OECD Guidelines, underlining the critical responsibility of parent

[32] NCP Norway, Lok Shakti Abhiyan, Korean Transnational Corporations Watch, Fair Green And Global Alliance and Forum for Environment and Development v. Posco (South Korea), ABP/APG (Netherlands) And NBIM, Final Statement, 27 May 2013.

[33] Ibid, 5–6.

companies to ensure that their subsidiaries adhere to the relevant international standards. This case highlights the necessity for corporate groups to implement comprehensive HRDD processes and actively oversee their subsidiaries' operations to prevent harm and align with BHR principles.

Furthermore, other cases confirm that NCPs recognise the existing responsibility of parent companies for the actions and compliance of their subsidiaries. For example, in the case against Royal Dutch Shell (RDS) concerning oil spills in Nigeria, the issue was first addressed through NCP mediation.[34] Although the voluntary nature of the NCP process meant the compensation awarded fell short of the claimants' expectations, the Dutch NCP's final statement made a significant observation.[35] It emphasised that while parent and subsidiary companies are distinct legal entities, the parent company plays a crucial role in raising standards of responsible business conduct beyond national legal requirements to align with international standards. The NCP asserted that RDS should not disregard its 'ultimate responsibility and accountability' for the actions of its subsidiary in local operations.[36] Furthermore, the NCP recommended that RDS actively use its influence to ensure its subsidiary complies with the OECD Guidelines, including proactive observation and monitoring of its operations on the ground. Although the NCP did not explicitly clarify the meaning of 'ultimate responsibility and accountability of parent company,' it can be inferred that it generally conceptualised the existence of a parent company's responsibility, regardless of the separate legal entity status or independent management and control of its subsidiaries.

In addition, in cases like those involving Unilever, Inter Ikea, and Just Eat, the Dutch NCP clarified and elaborated on the responsibilities of parent companies under the OECD Guidelines. In both cases involved Just Eat and Ikea, the Dutch NCP elaborated on corporate responsibility under the OECD Guidelines, emphasising the shared accountability of all entities within a corporate group to align their actions with the Guidelines. NCP stated that, first, the Guidelines established that every entity within a corporate group carries a collaborative responsibility to ensure compliance, as outlined in the Chapter I: Concepts and Principles, paragraph 4.

Second, the parent company is expected to conduct risk-based due diligence across its corporate group and supply chain to identify, prevent, and mitigate adverse impacts, while taking appropriate actions to align both group entities and business partners with the Guidelines. NCP referred the OECD Guidelines, Chapter 2: General Policies, paragraphs 10 to 13, highlighting due diligence as a key expectation. Lastly, the Guidelines stress the importance of disclosure, urging corporate entities, including the parent, to provide transparent information about their activities, group structure, supply chain, and the origins of their products and resources.

---

[34] NCP Netherlands, Amnesty International, Friends of Earth International and Frriends of Earth Netherlands v. Royal Dutch Shell about the cause of oil spills in the Niger Delta, Final Statement, 21 March 2013.

[35] Ibid, 5.

[36] NCP Netherlands, BWI against IKEA Holding B.V, Final Statement, 25 April 2023; NCP Netherlands, FNV v. Just Eat Takeway.com, Final Statement, 22 March 2023.

Dutch NCP analysis on these cases shows increasing stakeholder demand for corporate accountability and transparency, reinforcing the responsibility that parent companies must actively oversee and disclose their broader operations.

In the recent case against Unilever, the Dutch NCP also addressed key issues regarding the company's obligations as a parent entity in its relationship with subsidiary, Unilever-Marsavco, highlighting it as an example of irresponsible disengagement.[37] It noted that Unilever was obligated to cooperate with its subsidiary during dismissal processes to comply with the Guidelines, which require mitigating adverse effects on employees through reasonable notice and collaboration. Furthermore, post-sale, the NCP emphasised that Unilever retained a supply-chain responsibility to encourage Marsavco to adhere to RBC. Crucially, the NCP pointed out that even prior to the 2011 update, the Guidelines already mandated parent company responsibility for influencing business partners, reinforcing that parent companies cannot evade responsibility through disengagement. In this case, the Dutch NCP conceptualised that parent and subsidiary companies share collective responsibility, requiring them to distribute and allocate their obligations effectively.

The NCP's analysis of the parent company responsibility existed even prior to 2011 was reinforced by the case involving Kongsberg Automotive, brought before the Norwegian NCP. This case addressed the parent company's responsibility for the actions of its subsidiary, which was accused of labour rights violations in Ohio, USA. An ILO representative assisting the Norwegian NCP highlighted the importance of clarifying the scope of Norwegian parent companies' responsibilities under the OECD Guidelines. The representative argued that the Guidelines should cover matters within a parent company's sphere of influence, particularly where it exercises decisive control. It was emphasised that excluding parent companies from accountability for managing their subsidiaries would severely narrow the Guidelines' application and undermine Norway's leadership in promoting responsible business practices. Ultimately, the Norwegian NCP concluded that Kongsberg's parent company had breached the OECD Guidelines by accepting a lockout of approximately 300 employees during wage negotiations and hiring alternative labour.

Adding to this, in the case against Moeller, the Danish NCP set out in detail the responsibilities of parent companies under the OECD Guidelines.[38] It stated that if a subsidiary, especially one that is majority owned by a parent company, is associated with an adverse impact, the parent company is jointly responsible for remedying the harm. The Danish NCP also pointed out in its final statement that this principle of shared responsibility has been reaffirmed in various NCP cases, with reference to Australian and Dutch NCP cases, and stated that both parent companies and their subsidiaries must take measures to ensure compliance with the OECD Guidelines.[39] The Danish NCP further emphasised that these expectations apply to

[37] NCP Netherlands, ATUMA v. Unilever, Final Statement, 7 May 2024.

[38] NCP Denmark. Former employees of the Joint Venture Douala In-ternational Terminal S.A. in Cameroun v. A.P. Moeller - Maersk AS, Final Statement, 6 May 2024.

[39] Ibid, 5.

all organisational structures and that companies cannot avoid responsibility by structuring themselves to avoid responsibility. In this particular case, Moeller was expected to conduct thorough risk-based due diligence within its group of companies and address any potential or actual negative impacts throughout its operations and supply chain.[40] In this case, it is the parent company's responsibility to document its efforts to monitor subsidiaries' compliance with due diligence, where these tasks have been delegated, and leverage its influence to promote RBC within its activities. This decision underlines the obligation of parent companies to proactively manage and monitor their subsidiaries' compliance with international standards.

Overall, the cases demonstrate that parent companies have a clear responsibility to establish BHR standards at the group level and to cooperate with their subsidiaries to ensure these standards are effectively observed at the local level. Some cases further highlight that parent companies are expected to go beyond compliance with national laws, elevating the actions of their subsidiaries to align with international standards.

4.2.2.2 Detailed Specific Actions Constituting Parent Company Responsibility

NCPs have consistently highlighted the pivotal role of parent companies in advancing responsible business practices and ethical standards across their corporate groups. Several NCP cases provide detailed explanations of how parent companies discharge their responsibilities, such as establishing policies, implementing HRDD systems, and engaging with local communities.

Firstly, a recurring expectation is for parent companies to establish and enforce group-wide policies to uphold and elevate standards across their subsidiaries, particularly in industries with significant external engagement. These policies serve as a framework for ensuring that subsidiaries align with international BHR standards and effectively address potential risks. For example, in the cases against Tensa, Flemish Investment Limited and Nidera Holding, in the Chilean, Canadian and Dutch NCPs, all three NCPs have stated that all companies within the group must establish a policy commitment to respect internationally recognised human rights at the highest level of the group's management and conduct a participatory due diligence process to identify and remedy human rights violations throughout their value chain.[41] This includes ensuring remedial actions are taken for suppliers affected by the behaviour of the group's companies in Chile. Furthermore, the NCPs called for the development and implementation of standards and guidelines for the group's companies and suppliers to prevent the recurrence of such issues. Additionally, the

[40] Ibid.

[41] NCP Canada, Former Employees v. Flemish Investment Burundi SA subsidiary of Flemish Investment Limited, Final Statement, 13 June 2019.

Chilean NCP in case against Tensa underlined the importance of adopting strong governance measures at group level.[42] It recommended that enterprises, including their parent companies, implement and periodically review principles of good corporate governance. These principles, promoted by senior management, should translate into effective management systems and self-regulatory practices that are well-communicated throughout the organisation and regularly updated. Together, these measures highlight the dual responsibility of parent companies: not only to ensure compliance with international standards through due diligence and remediation but also to foster a culture of accountability and ethical conduct throughout its governance frameworks.

Secondly, after establishing group-wide policies, NCPs have emphasised the responsibility of parent companies to conduct HRDD at a group-wide level. This was highlighted in cases such as PvM at the Dutch NCP, Nissan in the US NCP and cases involving SOMDIAA, Perenco, DIAM International and Teleperformance at the French NCP.[43] In these cases, NCPs stressed that parent companies must actively support their subsidiaries' due diligence efforts by proactively monitoring how these processes are implemented at the local level and participating in related activities. Specifically, in the cases involving PvM and Nissan at the Dutch and US NCPs, it was noted that parent companies must conduct corporate-wide HRDD, including addressing labour-related risks, and actively engage with local stakeholders to understand how their subsidiaries manage adverse impacts on the ground.[44] This approach emphasises the critical role of parent companies in not only overseeing but also actively participating in their subsidiaries' due diligence efforts, ensuring alignment with international standards.

The implementation of a group-wide consolidated due diligence system is essential, as consistently emphasised by various NCPs. This was notably highlighted in the case involving Perenco and Teleperformance, where the French NCP recommended the establishment of governance mechanisms to ensure the effective implementation of the company's due diligence and sustainability policies at group level.[45] These mechanisms would not only support subsidiaries in aligning with the group's guidelines but also ensure compliance across operations. In case against Perenco, the NCP specifically suggested exploring the feasibility of creating a 'CSR Committee' both at the group and country levels, which would include relevant

[42] NCP Chile, Liquidator v. Tensa, Final Statement, 18 May 2021.

[43] NCP Netherlands 'Final Statement: Notification IUF v. Perfetti Van Melle' 15 June 2020; NCP France UNI v. Teleperformance, Final Statement, 5 July 2021; NCP France, 14 Local Watch Committees and Centre of Actions for Life and Earth v. COPAGEF, SOMDIAA and SOSUCAM in Cameroon' Final Statement, 17 May 2022; NCP France, Birlesik Metal v. DIAM International, Final Statement, 14 May 2019; NCP United States, UAW and IndustriALL Global Union v. Nissan Motor Co Ltd and Nissan Motors America Inc.

[44] For example, NCP United States, UAW and IndustriALL Global Union v. Nissan Motor Co Ltd and Nissan Motors America Inc.

[45] France UNI v. Teleperformance, Final Statement, 5 July 2021.

stakeholders.[46] Furthermore, the NCP urged Perenco to raise awareness and provide training for its subsidiaries on the OECD Due Diligence Guidance on MSE in the extractive sector. In the case against Teleperformance, the French NCP highlighted the importance of a group-wide HRDD system, particularly in managing global crises such as the COVID-19 pandemic, which posed significant health risks to the company's extensive workforce.[47] The NCP noted that, after an initial phase focused on managing the emergency, Teleperformance implemented and continues to deploy a prevention, management, and monitoring policy across all its subsidiaries to address pandemic-related health risks. This policy aligns broadly with the corporate HRDD expectations outlined in the OECD Guidelines. However, the NCP emphasised that such a policy should involve active engagement with stakeholders representing workers, particularly in subsidiaries located in countries lacking collective agreements.[48] The NCP recommended that this engagement should be incorporated into the monitoring of the company's vigilance plan at both subsidiary and group levels, further demonstrating the critical role of integrated HRDD systems in mitigating risks and ensuring accountability during worldwide crises.

However, the group-wide HRDD policy and integrated system is not enough. This was particularly evident in the case against DHL at the German NCP, which addressed allegations of labour rights violations, including rights of collective bargaining.[49] The complainants argued that the current mechanisms for raising and discussing industrial relations issues with the respondent were inadequate. While they acknowledged that DHL regularly met with them to discuss general industrial relations topics until May 2012, they criticised these talks for failing to produce concrete results. Furthermore, they deemed DHL's Code of Conduct insufficient as a tool to address these concerns and highlighted a lack of communication between the company's subsidiaries and its headquarters regarding specific local-level issues.[50] To address these gaps, the complainants proposed the establishment of a grievance mechanism. This case illustrates that parent companies must go beyond adopting group-wide policies and systems by engaging actively with local stakeholders and participating in grievance mechanisms. Such involvement is critical to effectively managing risks and addressing adverse impacts at the local level.

In order to effectively engage in their subsidiaries' HRDD processes, parent companies must exercise their influence and leverage to provide increased support and implement stronger controls. This approach was exemplified in the case against Diam International, where the French NCP highlighted significant actions taken by the parent company to address issues within its Turkish subsidiary, Diam Vitrin.[51]

---

[46] Ibid, 9.

[47] Ibid.

[48] Ibid, 10.

[49] NCP Germany, UNI Global Union (UNI) and International Transport Workers' Federation (ITF) and Deutsche Post DHL (DP-DHL) v. DP-DHL/Bonn, Final Statement, 21 January 2014.

[50] Ibid, 9.

[51] NCP France, Birlesik Metal v. DIAM International, Final Statement, 14 May 2019.

Diam International's due diligence efforts resulted in a range of corrective measures. Legal actions were pursued to address union certification challenges, illegal strikes, and anti-union dismissal disputes. Operationally, the company strengthened its local team by creating a human resources department, disciplining a production manager involved in the 2017 crisis, and hiring a new production manager. Additionally, Diam developed and implemented an action plan focusing on human resources, which included improving employee benefits such as upgrading canteen services, increasing transportation reimbursements, and offering pay raises and bonuses to reach living wage. The plan also prioritised skill development through training and career advancement opportunities, enhanced internal communication through regular updates and meetings, and clarified job roles within departments. The French NCP acknowledged that these efforts, along with external audits and steps toward SA8000 certification, demonstrated Diam International's commitment to addressing adverse impacts in its subsidiary.[52] Although DIAM International demonstrated some willingness to address the issues raised in the NCP proceedings, the NCP criticised and expressed disappointment that the company nevertheless chose to continue its legal action against the workers.

Some cases emphasised the importance of parent companies involving stakeholders in the activities of their subsidiaries at the local level. For example, in the case against Copagef and Somdiaa at the French NCP, the NCP recommended that the parent company Somdiaa support its subsidiary in the development and implementation of a new action plan.[53] This plan should include the reintroduction of a consultation platform or channel as a regular stakeholder engagement through an inclusive and constructive approach. The aim is to promote two-way dialogue and information sharing on measures to identify social and environmental risks and on measures to prevent, mitigate and remedy potential or actual negative impacts on the communities surrounding its plantations. This shows the role of the parent company in exercising its influence over the subsidiary to achieve meaningful stakeholder engagement in improving accountability and managing impacts at the local level.

Adding to this, in the case against Socapalm, the French NCP emphasised that a parent company that exercises HRDD to address adverse impacts and promotes ethical practices in the actions of its subsidiary, such as respect for labour rights at the local level, actively contributes to the achievement of the SDGs.[54] The NCP particularly welcomed the Bolloré Group's commitment to ensure that Socapalm renewed the dialogue structures, as it sees this as a crucial step towards restoring trust between the company and the stakeholders involved.[55] The NCP expressed the hope that the Bolloré Group's commitments will enable Socapalm to make a

---

[52] Ibid, 9.

[53] 14 Local Watch Committees and Centre of Actions for Life and Earth v. Copagef, Somdiaa and Sosucam in Cameroon' Final Statement, 17 May 2022.

[54] Ibid, 3.

[55] Ibid.

meaningful contribution to the sustainable development of the local communities in which it operates. This case illustrated the comprehensive role of parent companies in promoting sustainable practices at local level and building trust through proactive engagement and ethical oversight with the local communities.

The role of parent companies in addressing harm caused, contributed to, or linked to their subsidiaries is a key principle of the OECD Guidelines, as demonstrated by cases reviewed by the Spanish NCP. In the case against Prosegur, the Spanish NCP emphasised the responsibility of the group company to engage actively in HRDD processes and, where necessary, take remedial action for adverse impacts caused by its subsidiaries in Latin America.[56] Similarly, in a case involving a Spanish MNE operating in Guatemala, the NCP highlighted the parent company's responsibility to respect Indigenous Peoples' rights.[57] The NCP recommended that the company revise its human rights policies to align with international standards, such as ensuring FPIC consultation with Indigenous communities before implementing projects.[58]

The NCP further advised that the company integrate active risk monitoring of local partners as part of its structural policy, following the OECD Due Diligence Guidance for Responsible Business Conduct. In light of the Guatemalan Supreme Court's ruling in the case, the NCP urged the Spanish company to encourage its local partner, RENACE, to participate constructively in mandated meetings and work toward improving the quality of life in affected communities. It also recommended that the company demonstrate its commitment to community wellbeing by cooperating with the Supreme Court, submitting relevant environmental and social impact studies, and, if necessary, commissioning new studies through independent experts.[59] These recommendations underlined the role of parent companies in proactively engaging in remediation to respect the rights and livelihoods of impacted stakeholders.

The responsibility of parent companies to remediate harms and adverse impacts caused by their subsidiaries is highlighted in several cases. The UK NCP reviewed a case involving ENRC and its subsidiary's mining activities in the DRC, focusing on the parent company's accountability for addressing community impacts.[60] The complaint, brought by RAID, alleged that ENRC failed to ensure continued community access to a vital water supply established in 2007–2008 and lacked proactive engagement in community development. The NCP emphasised that ENRC, as the parent company, must leverage its influence over its subsidiary, to remediate these harms. Specifically, ENRC was urged to guarantee uninterrupted water access and

[56] NCP Spain, UNI Global Union v. Porsegur subsidiaries in Brazil, Colombia, Paraguay, Peru and Chile, Final Statement, 31 July 2017.

[57] NCP Spain, Alliance for Solidarity v. Spanish MNE in Guatemala, 19 December 2019.

[58] Ibid, 10.

[59] Ibid.

[60] NCP United Kingdom, Rights and Accountability in Development (RAID) v. ENRC, Final Statement, February 2016.

collaborate with affected communities to prioritize early-stage development of essential facilities.[61]

Similarly, the Dutch NCP assessed a case involving SPDC in Nigeria, emphasising the responsibility of RDS, the parent company, to ensure effective remediation processes. The complainant claimed that company failed to adequately address local community grievances.[62] Despite the NCP's recommendation to resolve the issues through SPDC's grievance mechanism, six months of discussions yielded no resolution. When the NCP offered its good offices to mediate, SPDC declined the proposal. In its final statement, the NCP criticised this rejection and emphasised RDS's responsibility to use its leverage to ensure an effective remediation process.[63] The NCP further highlighted that RDS should actively support SPDC in handling complaints in line with the OECD Guidelines and the UNGPs. This case illuminated the role of parent companies in exercising oversight and taking responsibility for preventing and addressing adverse impacts stemming from their subsidiaries' operations.

The analysis of OECD case law explored the critical accountability of parent companies in remediating harms and adverse impacts associated to their subsidiaries. NCP cases here revealed that parent companies should play an important role in upholding international standards of RBC, particularly through group-wide HRDD processes, proactive engagement, and remediation efforts. Key cases, such as those involving ENRC, Shell, and Prosegur, illustrated that parent companies must leverage their influence over subsidiaries to ensure compliance with the OECD Guidelines and the UNGPs. These cases show parent companies' obligations to address community complaints related to their subsidiaries, guarantee access to resources, and proactively participate in remedy mechanisms. Moreover, the cases emphasised that parent companies must actively monitor and enforce compliance at the subsidiary level, ensuring that operations align with both local and international standards.

Overall, OECD case law affirms that, under the international BHR framework, parent companies hold responsibility for their subsidiaries. In particular, they are expected to establish corporate governance structures across their entire organisation that uphold human rights and environmental standards. This includes implementing group-wide policies, conducting group-wide HRDD, and ensuring effective remediation to prevent and mitigate adverse impacts. Although the actual outcomes of these cases were insufficient to hold parent companies fully accountable, the NCPs consistently affirmed parent companies' role in ensuring responsible business conduct within its business structure. These responsibilities reflect evolving global expectations of corporate accountability, requiring parent companies to take a holistic approach that prioritises human rights and sustainable development across their operations.

---

[61] Ibid, 14.

[62] NCP Netherlands, Aminigboko Community v. the Shell Petroleum Development Company of Nigeria Limited and Shell Headquarters, Final Statement, 10 February 2023.

[63] Ibid, 2.

4.3 Responsibilities of Investors and Financial Institutions for Linked Negative Human Rights and Environmental Impacts

4.3.1 Investor and Financial Institutions Obligations Under International Human Rights Regulations

Within international community, the financial sector's funding of major projects with far-reaching impacts on communities has come under increasing scrutiny.[64] Banks are now globally recognised as key actors, not only for their role in enabling problematic business practices but also for their potential to drive comprehensive, systemic solutions.[65] This section critically examines the responsibilities of FIs under global human rights and environmental standards, addressing significant challenges within the current international framework. Drawing on soft law instruments such as the UNGPs, the OECD Guidelines, and the UN Environment Programme Principles for Responsible Banking Guidance Document (UNEP Guidance), as well as binding regulations like the recently adopted CSDDD, it explores the obligations of FIs to prevent, mitigate, and remedy adverse impacts on human rights and the environment.[66]

Additional frameworks from the financial and investment sectors, including the International Finance Corporation's (IFC) Performance Standards on Environmental and Social Sustainability, the Thun Group Discussion Paper, and the Equator Principles, are analysed to highlight their role in shaping FI responsibilities.[67] Despite their collective focus on corporate responsibility, these frameworks expose significant shortcomings in defining, implementing, and enforcing FI responsibilities, particularly in distinguishing between varying degrees of involvement in harm.[68] Clarifying whether FIs contribute to or are merely linked to human rights abuses is crucial for accurately conceptualising their responsibilities and designing

---

[64] For example, the UN Principles for Responsible Investment (PRI) 'The Principles for Responsible Investment Reporting Framework' (23 January 2023) https://www.unpri.org/about-us/what-are-the-principles-for-responsible-investment accessed 26 October 2024; Investor Alliance for Human Rights 'Investor Toolkit for Human Rights' (May 2020); Task force on Climate-related Financial Disclosure (TCFD) 'Recommendations of Task Force on Climate-related Disclosure, Final Report (June 2017); Glasgow Financial Alliance for Net Zero (GFANZ) Towards a Global Baseline for Net-zero Transition Planning (November 2022).

[65] Wettstein (2022), p. 323.

[66] UNEP 'Principles for Responsible Banking' Guidance Document (2021); Corporate Sustainability Due Diligence Directive.

[67] IFC, Performance standard on Social and Environmental Sustainability (2012); Equator Principles 'Equator Principles: A financial industry benchmark for determining, assessing and managing environmental and social risk in projects' 2020.

[68] Macchi and Bernaz (2021); BHRRC 'Switched off: Tech company opacity & Israel's war on Gaza' Briefing 18 April 2024.

effective mitigation and remediation strategies.[69] However, this research revealed that the guidance provided by the UNGPs, the OECD Guidelines, and more recent documents from the OECD and the Office of the High Commissioner for Human Rights (OHCHR) remains inadequate, offering limited clarity in distinguishing between direct and indirect involvement.[70]

The UNGPs and OECD Guidelines are foundational in outlining the responsibilities of businesses, including FIs, to address adverse human rights and environmental impacts. These frameworks emphasise that FIs, when directly linked to harm, are primarily obligated to exert leverage over their clients or investees to ensure mitigation and remediation.[71] However, they provide insufficient guidance on when direct linkage escalates to contribution, particularly in scenarios where FIs facilitate or incentivise harmful practices through inaction or indirect support.[72] The Thun Group's discussion paper initially asserted that FIs are generally 'linked' rather than contributors to harm, a claim that the OHCHR contested.[73] The OHCHR clarified that FIs can indeed contribute to harm by failing to prevent risks or by encouraging harmful practices.[74] For instance, if an FI knowingly overlooks human rights risks and does not take adequate steps to influence client behaviour, it may be seen as incentivising abuse.[75] Despite this, the concepts of 'facilitation' and 'incentivisation' remain underdefined, leaving significant room for interpretative ambiguity.

As Van Ho critiqued, such definitions remain ambiguous and fail to provide a practical distinction between 'contribution' and 'linkage'.[76] This ambiguity is consequential because, as Ruggie noted, the identification of an FI as a contributor obligates it to remediate harms, whereas those merely linked to abuses are not held to the same standard.[77] Van Ho proposed that a company's responsibility for

---

[69] Bordignon (2022), p. 381.

[70] UN Working Group on Business and Human Rights (UN WGBHR) 'Taking stock of investor implementation of the UN Guiding Principles on Business and Human Rights' (2021) Addendum report of the Working Group on the issue of human rights and transnational corporations and other business enterprises corporations A/HRC/47/39/Add.2, 2; OECD 'Responsible business conduct for institutional investors: Key considerations for due diligence under the OECD Guidelines for Multinational Enterprises' (2017); OECD 'Due Diligence for Responsible Corporate Lending and Securities Underwriting: Key considerations for banks implementing the OECD Guidelines for Multinational Enterprises' OECD Publishing, Paris (2019).

[71] UN Guiding Principles on Business and Human Rights, Commentary to Principle 19.

[72] Van Ho (2021), p. 625.

[73] Thun Group of Banks 'Paper on the Implications of UN Guiding Principles 13b & 17 In a Corporate and Investment Banking Context' Paper – Thun Group of Banks, December 2017 https://media.business-humanrights.org/media/documents/files/documents/2017_12_Thun_Group_of_Banks_Paper_UNGPs_13b_and_17.pdf#page=5.08 (accessed 2 February 2026).

[74] OHCHR, Response to Request from BankTrack for Advice Regarding the Application of the UN Guiding Principles on Business and Human Rights in the context of the Banking Sector 5 (2017).

[75] Ibid.

[76] Van Ho (2021), p. 647.

[77] Ruggie (2017).

providing remedies should be determined by its power and independence to facilitate or prevent harm.[78] Building on this idea, the current understanding of FIs in the context of human rights and accountability could be redefined. This redefinition would consider their power and their actual or potential capacity to influence companies (leverage) to prevent, mitigate, and address human rights violations effectively.[79]

Scholars have consistently highlighted that FIs, particularly banks, are frequently identified as being directly linked to human rights and environmental harms, primarily through their investment and financial relationships with corporations.[80] In these scenarios, the primary obligation placed on FIs under frameworks such as the UNGPs and the OECD Guidelines is to exert leverage over their clients or investees. Leverage, in this context, is intended as a means to influence these entities to address and mitigate harms.[81] However, as Bordignon argued, leverage is not formally conceptualised as a legal responsibility.[82] Instead, it is regarded as a capacity or ability that one entity possesses, enabling it to influence another entity due to the nature of their business relationship. This distinction shows a significant gap: leverage is framed as an operational tool rather than an enforceable obligation.

Despite this legal ambiguity, leverage is widely acknowledged as an essential mechanism for FIs to address adverse impacts effectively. By using leverage, FIs can encourage or pressure the direct causer or contributor of harm to take corrective action. The UNGPs and OECD Guidance documents encourage FIs to utilise their influence to promote responsible practices within their client or investee relationships.[83] However, the lack of a clear legal framework around leverage limits its consistent and effective implementation.

Moreover, while the importance of leverage is recognised in principle, its practical application often falls short. Frameworks such as the Equator Principles and the IFC Performance Standards provide valuable guidance for identifying and managing risks within financial relationships.[84] However, they lack provisions for more concrete and decisive measures, such as divestment or termination of business relationships, when leveraging influence fails to achieve the desired outcomes.[85] This absence of clear escalation mechanisms weakens the practical effectiveness of leverage as a tool for addressing human rights violations and environmental harm. The failure to operationalise leverage as a legally binding responsibility creates further challenges. For instance, in cases where FIs are directly linked to harm but not

[78] Van Ho (2021), p. 648.

[79] Davaanyam (2025), pp. 56–57.

[80] Macchi and Bernaz (2021), pp. 647–648; Bordignon (2022), p. 381.

[81] Wettstein (2022), p. 324.

[82] Bordignon (2022), p. 393.

[83] UN WGBHR, Taking stock of investor implementation of the UN Guiding Principles on Business and Human Rights; OECD Due Diligence for Responsible Corporate Lending and Securities Underwriting.

[84] IFC performance Standard, Equator Principles.

[85] Davaanyam (2025), pp. 59–60.

considered contributors, their obligations are limited to exerting influence rather than implementing corrective or remedial actions. This delineation allows some FIs to adopt a minimalist approach, fulfilling nominal responsibilities without driving meaningful change. The lack of explicit provisions for situations where leverage fails—such as guidance on divestment or stricter accountability measures—reinforces the perception that FIs prioritise financial performance over substantive commitments to human rights and environmental sustainability.

Respond to this, international organisations have made considerable efforts to conceptualise the responsibilities of FIs, particularly focusing on the application and operationalisation of leverage. The WGBHR, in its report, mentioned the concept of 'rights-respecting investing', which advocates for FIs to leverage their influence through active stakeholder collaboration and sustained engagement with investee companies.[86] This approach emphasises the importance of fostering responsible practices and mitigating harm through continuous dialogue and partnership.[87] Building on this, the OECD's recent policy paper on Responsible Business Conduct Due Diligence for FIs offer a more detailed framework. This document emphasises proactive measures such as scoping, risk screening, and early stakeholder engagement. These steps are designed to pre-emptively identify and address risks, while also clarifying the often-ambiguous boundaries between 'linkage' and 'contribution' within the context of FIs' responsibilities. By providing guidance on early intervention and risk management, these frameworks aim to enhance the effectiveness of leverage as a tool for preventing harm and fostering accountability.[88]

However, despite these comprehensive recommendations, the practical implementation by FIs often falls short. Many FIs continue to prioritise financial returns over the adoption of meaningful remedial actions.[89] The inconsistency in applying leverage and the reluctance to employ divestment as a corrective measure affirms this challenge.[90] As highlighted in a recent BankTrack report, numerous FIs demonstrate a lack of commitment to human rights and environment, failing to leveraging their influence effectively, often opting for superficial compliance rather than substantive engagement with human rights and environmental concerns.[91] This gap between policy recommendations and practical application reveals a critical barrier

[86] UN WGBHR, Taking stock of investor implementation of the UN Guiding Principles on Business and Human Rights, 3.

[87] OECD, OECD Due Diligence for Responsible Corporate Lending and Securities Underwriting, Chapter 2.

[88] Ibid, 35, 47–48.

[89] BankTrack 'Coal Havens: The Policy Loopholes keeping coal finance alive in Asia' January 2024 https://www.banktrack.org/download/coal_havens/240122_coal_havens_opt.pdf (accessed 2 February 2026).

[90] Davaanyam (2025), pp. 58–60.

[91] No bank yet fully meets its human rights responsibilities under the UN Guiding Principles. Of the 50 banks assessed, 36 scored below 7.5 points out of 15, indicating that they are less than half-way to implementing the requirements of the UN Guiding Principles, and are therefore ranked as 'laggards' or 'followers'. The BankTrack 'Global Human Rights Benchmark 2024' November 2024 https://www.banktrack.org/download/the_banktrack_global_human_rights_benchmark_2024/banktrack_human_rights_benchmark_2024_1.pdf#page=6.25 (accessed 2 February 2026).

to progress. While frameworks like the WGBHR report, and OECD policy paper provide detailed guidance, their impact is undermined by the failure of FIs to integrate these principles into their core operational strategies. Without a stronger commitment to prioritising human rights and environmental sustainability over financial gains, the potential of these international efforts remains unrealised.[92] Binding clear regulatory frameworks and stricter enforcement mechanisms may be essential to align FI practices with the expectations set forth in these initiatives. The inclusion of FIs in the recently adopted CSDDD represents progress but remains insufficient, as it excluded the FIs in downstream supply chain and also it lacks clarity in defining their specific human rights and environmental responsibilities tailored to the financial sector.[93]

The recent article on many banks' involvement in arm trade industry shows the importance of FIs in downstream supply chain.[94] Nevertheless, starting in 2027, 'regulated financial undertakings' operating or generating income within the EU and meeting the thresholds of €450 million in turnover and relevant employee numbers will be required to conduct due diligence.[95] This involves assessing, addressing, and reporting on the actual and potential adverse impacts of their operations, subsidiaries, and supply chains on human rights and the environment. The scope of this regulation encompasses investment firms, alternative investment fund managers, insurance providers, credit institutions, central securities depositories, financial holding companies, and crypto companies.[96] BSR noted that the CSDDD marks a shift in focus from traditional financial risks to the risks businesses pose to individuals and the environment.[97] It necessitates a cultural transformation, where

[92] WBA's recent report states that 'The 2,000 most influential companies are leaving hundreds of millions of people behind 90% of companies are not even halfway to meeting fundamental societal expectations on human rights, decent work and ethical conduct. Efforts to respect human rights are evident among the top 10% of companies that surpass the halfway mark' WBA 2024 Social Benchmark https://www.worldbenchmarkingalliance.org/publication/social/ (accessed 2 February 2026).

[93] Corporate Sustainability Due Diligence Directive. FAQ: While the personal scope of application of the Directive also covers financial undertakings, financial services provided in the context of relationships with clients are excluded from its material scope. The possible inclusion of the client relationships will be considered under a specific review clause within two years after entry into force of the Directive. Financial undertakings are nevertheless required to adopt and put into effect a climate transition plan, including absolute emission reduction targets for scope 3 greenhouse gas emissions, where appropriate https://commission.europa.eu/document/download/7a3e9980-5fda-4760-8f25-bc5571806033_en?filename=240719_CSDD_FAQ_final.pdf#page=3.35 (accessed 2 February 2026).

[94] Alwishewa (2024), pp. 1–7.

[95] SCDDD (Article 3.1. a(3)).

[96] Ibid.

[97] Quick et al. 'The CSDDD: Implications for the Finance Industry' BSR Blog 4 September 2024 https://www.bsr.org/en/blog/the-csddd-implications-for-the-finance-industry (accessed 2 February 2026).

organisations allocate time and resources to integrate human rights and environmental concerns into their operations and foster transparency.[98] However, it will become evident over time how these general due diligence obligations will impact the operations of FIs and what measures are needed to effectively address their accountability for associated harms.

There is a pressing need for clearer procedural and substantive rules. Substantive obligations, such as conducting effective HRDD and meaningfully engaging with stakeholders, must be complemented by procedural measures, including transparent impact assessments, leveraging influence, and ensuring accountability in divestment decisions.[99] Also, it must be supported by more detailed guidance to ensure consistent application. Morgera highlighted the importance of a process-oriented approach to implementing these obligations effectively.[100] Recent regulatory advancements, such as the EU's adoption of 'double materiality' in sustainability-related disclosure regulations, reinforce the dual responsibility of FIs to address both investor risks and broader societal impacts.[101] Binding international instruments are necessary to standardise these responsibilities across jurisdictions.

Furthermore, in addition to beyond respect, there is a growing expectation for FIs to actively contribute to the SDGs. Unlike the UNGPs, which primarily focus on harm mitigation, the OECD Guidelines explicitly encourage MNEs to align their operations with the SDGs.[102] The UN Working Group on Business and Human Rights (WGBHR) further emphasises that institutional investors should integrate SDG principles into their policies and investment strategies, promoting sustainable economic development.[103] However, this alignment remains challenging. As previous academic literature has argued, FIs hold significant power to influence corporations but often fail to leverage this power effectively to achieve SDG-as well as human rights related commitments.[104] However, for instance, while the OECD encourages MNEs to contribute to the SDGs, there are no binding rules requiring FIs to align their investments with sustainability objectives, leaving a gap in accountability.

To conclude, while existing frameworks provide a foundational structure for the responsibilities of FIs in human rights and environmental protection, significant gaps remain in the conceptualisation, implementation, and enforcement of these obligations. By addressing these shortcomings through binding regulations, enhanced procedural requirements, and clearer distinctions between 'contribution' and 'linkage,' FIs can assume a more proactive role in mitigating harm. A clear and

---

[98] Ibid.

[99] Davaanyam (2025), p. 60.

[100] Morgera (2020), p. 230.

[101] Regulation (EU) 2019/2088 on sustainability-related disclosures in the financial services sector [2019] OJ L317/1; Mohr et al. (2022).

[102] OECD Guidelines for Multinational Enterprises, Chapter 2: General Policies. Section 1.

[103] UN WGBHR, Taking stock of investor implementation of the UN Guiding Principles on Business and Human Rights, 5.

[104] Van Dijk et al. (2018), pp. 105–11.

concrete international framework, supported by robust due diligence and accountability mechanisms, is critical for ensuring that FIs contribute to sustainable development and the protection of human rights.

4.3.2 *Human Rights and Environmental Impacts: OECD Case Law Perspectives on Investor Responsibility*

This section explores different NCP cases, focusing on how international standards, particularly the OECD Guidelines, are applied to FIs in specific contexts. The cases involve NCPs from various countries, including Australia, Denmark, France, Japan, Korea, the Netherlands, Norway, Poland, Switzerland, the United Kingdom, and the United States. These cases primarily involve FIs accused of being complicit in human rights abuses and environmental harm through their financial services. They cover a variety of FIs, such as asset owners (e.g., pension funds, sovereign wealth funds, development finance institutions), asset managers (including investment advisors), banks, and insurance companies. While these FIs are mainly headquartered in the global North (Europe and the United States), the cases focus on their financial activities worldwide, particularly in relation to environmental degradation, climate change, and violations impacting indigenous and local communities.

Several OECD cases involving diverse FIs—including banks, institutional investors, state-backed export credit agencies, and minority shareholders—have significantly contributed to the understanding and conceptualisation of FIs' responsibilities concerning human rights. These cases have also guided OECD and other institutions, as well as scholars, in refining the framework for FI accountability.

A crucial example is the case against the Government Pension Fund Global, managed by Norway's Norges Bank Investment Management (NBIM), which demonstrated how the OECD Guidelines apply to minority shareholders.[105] NBIM, holding only 0.9% of shares in POSCO, was found to be directly linked to alleged human rights violations by the company through its investment relationship.[106] The Norwegian NCP ruled that the small shareholding size did not exempt NBIM from responsibility, as it had the capacity to influence POSCO's actions.[107] The NCP recommended that NBIM leverage its influence to urge POSCO to address the human rights issues associated with its operations. This case set a critical precedent, establishing that even minority shareholders bear obligations under the OECD Guidelines if their financial involvement links them to human rights abuses.

---

105 NCP Norway, Lok Shakti Abhiyan, Korean Transnational Corporations Watch, Fair Green And Global Alliance and Forum for Environment and Development v. Posco (South Korea), ABP/ABP (Netherlands) and NBIM (Norway), Final Statement, 27 May 2013.

106 Ibid, 6.

107 Ibid.

The Dutch NCP also assessed the role of the ABP/APG pension fund, which held a relatively small stake in POSCO. Despite the modest shareholding, the NCP emphasised the fund's heightened responsibility due to its significant influence in the investment market. It underlined the importance of leverage, noting that a major investor's ability to influence corporate behaviour often surpasses the size of its stake. Furthermore, the NCP highlighted that the degree of leverage an FI can exert depends on its capacity and potential within the economic market, given its prominent role and profile. This aligns with the analysis from the previous section, suggesting that the responsibilities of FIs may extend further when considering the power and autonomy they wield in the market. This reinforces the principle that large investors, by virtue of their market influence, carry broader obligations to address human rights issues.

Other cases, such as those involving Rabobank and Atradius Dutch State Business (ADSB), further clarified the role of FIs in managing human rights and environmental risks linked to their financial activities.[108] In Rabobank's case, the Dutch NCP emphasised that the bank should not rely solely on multi-stakeholder initiatives to fulfil its responsibilities but must also take direct action to prevent and mitigate negative impacts by leveraging its influence.[109] Similarly, in the ADSB case, the NCP draw attention to the importance of monitoring and engaging with stakeholders, recommending that ADSB adopt a more proactive approach to ensure its clients comply with social and environmental standards.

There are also cases that have shaped the understanding of FIs influence on climate change, particularly their investments in fossil fuels and the resulting environmental impacts, as well as how international regulations define their responsibilities. CSOs have criticised several FIs for financing fossil fuel projects while failing to demonstrate a clear commitment to the Paris Agreement. Cases brought before NCPs in Australia, the Netherlands, and Poland—against ANZ, ING, and the PZU Group, respectively—highlight the role of FIs in reducing greenhouse gas emissions through their investment strategies. These cases explore specific climate change approaches, including emissions measurement, target-setting, and alignment with sustainable goals.

In the case of ING, the Dutch NCP acknowledged the challenges posed by financed emissions, as these are indirect and difficult to measure and control.[110] Nevertheless, the NCP recommended that ING enhance its efforts to balance immediate climate goals with long-term sustainable objectives and to regularly review

[108] NCP Netherlands, Both ENDS, Associação Fórum Suape Espaço Socioambiental, Conectas Direitos Humanos and Colônia de Pescadores do Município do Cabo de Santo Agostinho v. Atradius Dutch State Business, Final Statement, 30 November 2016; NCP Netherlands, Friends of the Earth Europe and Friends of the Earth Netherlands/Milieudefensie v. Rabobank, Final Statement, 15 January 2016.

[109] NCP Netherlands, Friends of the Earth Europe and Friends of the Earth Netherlands/Milieudefensie v. Rabobank, Final Statement, 15 January 2016.

[110] NCP Netherlands, Oxfam Novib, Greenpeace Netherlands, BankTrack and Friends of the Earth Netherlands (Milieudefensie) v. ING, Final Statement, 19 April 2019.

and refine its emissions measurements and targets in alignment with the Paris Agreement. It also emphasised that the absence of an established methodology or globally recognised standard should not deter companies from taking proactive steps to measure and disclose their environmental impacts. This aligns with the corporate responsibility for environmental sustainability outlined in the OECD Guidelines, which encourage continuous improvement despite gaps in guidance.[111]

The case also underlined the broader expectations under frameworks such as the UNGPs, OECD Guidelines, and other international standards, which call on companies, including FIs, to strengthen their efforts to meet climate goals and align decision-making with the SDGs. While these standards may lack explicit instructions for reducing greenhouse gas emissions, they broadly advocate for heightened climate action.

In the ANZ case, the bank was accused of financing fossil fuel projects that allegedly contributed to climate crises, including the devastating Australian bushfires of 2020. The complainants demanded full transparency from ANZ regarding its greenhouse gas emissions, encompassing all financial activities.[112] However, the Australian NCP concluded that the existing OECD Guidelines and UNGPs were too broad and lacked specific requirements for climate-related disclosures or assessments. Consequently, the NCP found that ANZ had fulfilled its obligations under the current framework. This case highlighted the need to update the OECD Guidelines (2011) to set higher expectations for corporate climate action and risk management.[113] Following this and similar cases, the updated 2023 OECD Guidelines introduced more robust recommendations for companies to align with international climate and biodiversity agreements. These updates addressed the urgency of transparent, progressive climate risk disclosure, requiring FIs to provide detailed information about their environmental impacts. This evolution in standards reflects the pressing need for FIs to proactively manage climate risks and demonstrate accountability in addressing the climate emergency.

These cases collectively highlighted the evolving expectations for FIs to address human rights and environmental concerns, not only through indirect mechanisms but also through direct involvement. They demonstrate the increasing responsibility of FIs to use their market power and influence to mitigate and prevent harm associated with the projects and entities they finance.

Adding to this, some of these cases provide valuable examples of how FIs can effectively fulfil their HREDD responsibilities by engaging proactively with stakeholders and using their leverage. These best-practice examples demonstrate how FIs can exceed the basic expectations outlined in the OECD Guidelines by taking additional steps to address human rights and environmental concerns. In these instances, FIs not only meet the basic requirements but also engage more robustly with the

[111] Ibid, 5–6.

[112] NCP Australia, Friends of the Earth, Egan, Dodds and Simons v. ANZ Group, Final Statement, 15 December 2021.

[113] Ibid, 4.

entities in which they invest, seek out innovative solutions, and take corrective actions to mitigate harm. These cases also serve as lessons for improving how existing laws and regulations can be developed to ensure that FIs take a more active role in addressing the adverse human rights and environmental impacts linked to their activities.

A case, involving a Danish FI financing a mining project in Armenia, exemplified how extensive due diligence can help FIs manage human rights and environmental risks.[114] This case demonstrated the importance of stakeholder engagement and proactive monitoring. Specifically, the case revolved around the institution providing a financial guarantee for a loan issued by a Danish pension fund to a Russian bank, which in turn financed a loan to Company A, an operator of a mine in Armenia.[115] The Danish institution entered into a direct bilateral agreement with Company A, stipulating compliance with specific requirements under the IFC Performance Standards. As part of this agreement, Company A was obligated to conduct third-party social and environmental impact assessments and report the monitoring results to the Danish institution in a timely manner. Moreover, before the project commenced, the Danish institution engaged in extensive stakeholder consultations. These consultations included local officials, NGOs, and representatives from communities near the mine, allowing the institution to gather valuable input on the implementation of the project's plans.

The Danish institution also conducted on-site visits to the mines, received and addressed complaints from stakeholders, and engaged directly with them to follow up on their concerns. Additionally, representatives from the institution travelled to Armenia to meet with the company's management after Company A failed to comply with its contractual obligations related to social and environmental impacts. When the company's response proved inadequate, the Danish institution chose to terminate the agreement. This case serves as an exemplary model of how financial institutions can actively engage with both companies and stakeholders to fulfil their human rights and environmental responsibilities. It demonstrates the effective use of influence and highlights the importance of proactive measures, such as the OECD's recommended practices of 'early warning systems' and MSE.

Another example is in Australia, the ANZ Bank faced accusations of financing a sugar plantation project in Cambodia that resulted in forced evictions of local communities.[116] In this case, ANZ initially refused to acknowledge responsibility for the alleged human rights violations associated with its financing of a sugar plantation project in Cambodia, however, the Australian NCP highlighted that ANZ approved the loan despite being aware of widespread protests and allegations of abuse surrounding the project, emphasizing the bank's failure to conduct adequate human rights due diligence. Furthermore, as public pressure mounted, ANZ reconsidered

[114] NCP Denmark, Two NGOs v. Danish Financial Institution, Final Statement, 19 June 2018.

[115] Ibid, 6–7.

[116] NCP Australia, Equitable Cambodia (EC) and Inclusive Development International (IDI) v. Australian and New Zealand Banking Group Limited (ANZ Group) and its group entity ANZ Royal Bank (Cambodia) Limited (ANZ Royal), Final Statement, 27 June 2018.

its position and agreed to take responsibility for its involvement. The bank pledged to address the harm caused and compensate the displaced communities. In a public statement, ANZ committed to aligning its practices with its human rights policies and promised to donate the profits earned from the controversial sugar plantation loan in Phnom Penh. ANZ's response marked a rare instance of an FI publicly accepting responsibility for its investments' link to human rights violations and taking remedial action.[117] This case illustrates the power of public accountability and the importance of FIs' willingness to engage in remedying the harm caused by their investments, especially when human rights violations are involved.

Also, in a case reviewed by the French NCP, French bank Natixis and its asset management arm, Natixis Global Asset Management (NGAM), faced allegations of failing to adequately leverage their influence over their U.S. subsidiary, AEW Capital Management (AEW). AEW, a real estate management company, oversaw assets including the Westin Long Beach Hotel, which was accused of violating workers' rights by engaging in anti-union practices and denying employees the right to collective bargaining. Following an in-depth examination of the relationships between the entities, the French NCP determined that Natixis and NGAM had not conducted sufficient due diligence regarding AEW's activities. It recommended that they use their influence to ensure AEW implemented proper due diligence measures, both in this case and across its operations more broadly.[118] After the French NCP initiated proceedings, Natixis and NGAM reached out to their U.S. subsidiary to address the alleged violations at the hotel. This engagement led to the sale of the hotel's management to a new company, which promptly recognized the labour unions of the hotel employees. The case demonstrates the importance of parent companies taking proactive steps to oversee their subsidiaries and highlights how the effective use of influence can lead to the remedial outcome of the BHR related harms.

However, despite these positive examples, significant challenges remain in ensuring FIs meet their responsibilities. In many cases, mediation processes have focused more on future improvements than on determining whether FIs' past actions were compliant with the Guidelines. For example, the Swiss NCP's handling of the Credit Suisse case, involving the North Dakota Access Pipeline (NDAP), revealed that while Credit Suisse promised to incorporate Free, Prior, and Informed Consent (FPIC) into its internal policies, no substantial progress occurred.[119] A year later, another NGO filed a similar complaint to the US NCP, showing that Credit Suisse had not implemented the changes it had committed to. Regrettably, the U.S. NCP

---

[117] Inclusive Development International 'ANZ payment to displaces Cambodian families brings landmark human rights case to a close' 3 November 2021 https://www.inclusivedevelopment.net/equator-banks/anz-payment-to-displaced-cambodian-families-brings-landmark-human-rights-case-to-a-close/ (accessed 2 February 2026).

[118] NCP France, Unite here v. Natixis and NGAM in the United States of America, Detailed Report, 5 December 2017.

[119] NCP United States, Divest Invest Protect, Indigenous Peoples Law and Policy Program, Women's Earth and Climate Action Network v. Credit Suisse, Final Statement, 31 August 2021.

dismissed the case, reasoning that mediation would not be productive as a similar dialogue had already taken place under the Swiss NCP.

Similarly, cases involving ING and UBS also demonstrated a reliance on dialogue-based approaches, with little focus on holding the FIs accountable for past harm. This pattern raises concerns about the effectiveness of mediation if it does not result in tangible change or clear accountability. To elaborate, a recent case involving ING, reviewed by the Dutch NCP in 2022, illustrates the challenges in holding FIs accountable in climate change impact. ING acknowledged its connection to the alleged negative impacts but denied causing or contributing to them, asserting that it was not obligated to participate in or facilitate remediation efforts. In its final statement, the Dutch NCP noted that the parties failed to agree on whether ING had contributed to or was merely directly linked to the impacts through its business relationships. Importantly, the NCP highlighted that a direct link could escalate to a contribution if a financial institution is aware of the harm but neglects to address it or take adequate measures to mitigate its effects. However, the NCP refrained from making a definitive determination in this case.

A similar approach was seen in the UBS case handled by the Swiss NCP.[120] Here, the Swiss NCP used dialogue-based methods to address the financial institution's role in the alleged harm. UBS avoided reflecting on its own activities linked to the harm, maintaining that such issues could only be resolved through a multi-stakeholder approach. Despite the complainant's argument that UBS could take specific actions to address the harm and improve its policies, the company insisted on the multi-stakeholder route, and the case was closed without clearly determining the company's responsibility.[121] These cases reveal the limitations of mediation-based approaches employed by NCPs, particularly when they aim to create a platform for effective redress. They suggest that such strategies may not be well-suited to addressing the complexities of corporate accountability in human rights violations. Moving forward, it may be necessary to critically evaluate whether these mediation frameworks are adequate for handling cases involving financial institutions and their links to adverse impacts on human rights.

One of the most significant challenges revealed by these cases is the lack of clear guidance on how FIs should exercise leverage, assess human rights impacts, and address complaints. While NCPs encourage FIs to engage with stakeholders and increase leverage, the term 'leverage' remains undefined, and there are no clear criteria for determining what constitutes effective action. This lack of clarity makes it difficult for FIs to understand the full scope of their responsibilities, leaving them room to avoid meaningful action. In several cases, such as those involving ANZ and ING, the NCPs emphasised the importance of transparency in disclosing greenhouse gas emissions, but the current OECD Guidelines provide limited guidance on how to measure and report these emissions. The absence of clear expectations

[120] NCP Switzerland, Society for Threatened Peoples v. UBS Group AG, Final Statement, 20 December 2021.

[121] Ibid, 5–6.

regarding climate-related disclosures and human rights impact assessments shows the need for more detailed guidance for FIs.

The cases involving government export credit agencies (ECAs), such as the United Kingdom's Export Finance (UKEF), New Zealand's Permanent Trustees Ltd, and Korea's Export-Import Bank (KEXIM), also highlight the gaps in the application of the OECD Guidelines.[122] Specifically, in the case against UKEF, Global Witness alleged that UKEF, as a public FI, plays a significant role in facilitating fossil fuel projects by providing substantial financial support for such initiatives.[123] They also referenced other NCP cases, such as the Dutch NCP's review of ADSB, which examined the actions of export credit agencies. However, UKEF argued that its role differs from other export credit agencies because it operates as a ministerial government department without its own resources.[124] It issues guidelines on behalf of the Minister for International Trade and serves a statutory purpose. The UK NCP did not delve further into UKEF's claim that the OECD Guidelines do not apply to it and ultimately dismissed the case.

In response, OECD Watch expressed disagreement with this decision, asserting that state export credit agencies actively engage in and facilitate commercial activities covered by the OECD Guidelines. OECD Watch argued that dismissing complaints against ECAs undermines the state's ability to demonstrate leadership in promoting RBC through its own state-affiliated entities.[125] The dismissal of such cases undermines the role of state-affiliated entities in promoting responsible business conduct. Furthermore, the UNGPs affirm that all investment entities, including public pension funds, sovereign wealth funds, and development finance institutions, must respect human rights, a standard that should apply equally to public ECAs. The ongoing debate around the applicability of the OECD Guidelines to public FIs highlights a key area that needs further clarification in future cases.

In conclusion, while the OECD case law provides important insights into the responsibilities of FIs in addressing human rights and environmental and climate change impacts, there are still significant gaps in how these responsibilities are conceptualised, enforced, and clarified. Strengthening NCP procedures, providing clearer definitions of key terms like 'leverage', and ensuring that FIs are held accountable for both past and future actions are essential steps to improve the effectiveness of the OECD Guidelines and foster greater accountability among FIs. These improvements are critical to ensuring that FIs contribute to sustainable development and respect human rights and the environment in all their operations.

---

[122] NCP UK, Global Witness v. UK Export Finance, Initial assessment, 9 September 2020; NCP New Zealand, Mr and Mrs C/Southern Response v. NZ Permanent Trustees Ltd, Final Statement, 9 March 2016; OECD Watch, KTNC Watch et al., v. KEXIM Violations of FPIC, consultation at Philippine Jalaur dam, 18 January 2019.

[123] NCP UK, Global Witness v. UK Export Finance, Initial assessment, 9 September 2020.

[124] Ibid.

[125] OECD Watch (2020), Global Witness vs. UK Export Finance 'UK Export Finance Fails Climate Commitments, Disclosures' September 2020, https://www.oecdwatch.org/complaint/global-witness-vs-uk-export-finance/ (accessed 2 February 2026).

4.4 Responsibilities of Non-Profit/ Non-Governmental Organisations

4.4.1 Non-Profit Organisations Roles in Upholding Human Rights Under International BHR Guidelines

Non-profit organisations (NPOs) encompass a wide range of entities, including non-governmental organisations (NGOs) and other organisations whose primary objective is not profit generation but rather the pursuit of social, cultural, educational, or humanitarian goals. NPOs including NGOs vary significantly in terms of geographical scope, organisational type, and area of operation.[126] Geographically, they function at international, national, and local levels.[127] As Domenico Carolei emphasised, a legal distinction exists between these terms.[128] From a legal perspective, NPOs are defined and established under domestic legislation, while the term NGO is widely used in international legal discourse.[129] Notably, as he mentioned in his other article, the first official mention of NGO in international law appears in the 1945 United Nations Charter.[130] The term NPO broadly refers to organisations outside the government and business sectors, including NGOs, charitable organizations, faith-based groups, professional associations, and foundations.[131]

According to Carolei, what sets NPOs apart from business and governmental entities are their distinct characteristics: they are (a) voluntarily and formally organised, (b) private, (c) self-governing, (d) non-profit-distributing, and (e) significantly voluntary in their operations.[132] This differentiation highlights the unique role NPOs play in addressing societal needs while maintaining independence from both state control and market-driven motives.

Building on Carolei's observations, other scholars have highlighted that the accountability and responsibility of NPOs under international law and regulations remain insufficiently developed.[133] However, Rosana Garciandia emphasised the growing significance of NPOs across various domains, particularly their direct influence in the BHR field.[134] For example, high-profile cases such as FIFA's involvement in the abuse of migrant workers in Qatar during preparations for the 2022 World Cup indicated the urgent need to assess whether BHR legal frameworks

---

[126] Martens (2003), pp. 3–4.

[127] Ibid.

[128] Carolei (2022a), p. 34.

[129] Ibid.

[130] Carolei (2022b), p. 868.

[131] Carolei (2022a), p. 34.

[132] Ibid.

[133] Garciandia (2023), pp. 524–545; Woods and Stokes (2019), pp. 49–85; Lin et al. (2024), pp. 1–12; Byrne and Ludvigsen (2023), pp. 217–234.

[134] Ibid, Garciandia (2023), pp. 531–533.

can be applied to NPOs.[135] This includes examining how BHR frameworks might enhance their accountability, especially regarding their due diligence obligations to mitigate associated human rights and environmental harms.

Garciandia argued that while the fundamental differences between companies and NPOs must be acknowledged, there are notable commonalities and potential synergies.[136] These, coupled with the broad interpretation of 'companies' within BHR frameworks, justify exploring the application of these legal principles to NPOs.[137] Accordingly, this section of the book will analyse whether integrating BHR perspectives could strengthen due diligence practices within the self-regulation of the NPO sector. This evaluation will draw on insights from various scholars and precedents established in OECD case law, where similar approaches have demonstrated potential to enhance institutional accountability and operational standards.

NPOs, especially one with the multiple global locations are governed by domestic laws in both their home and host countries, with regulatory approaches differing significantly across jurisdictions. Home governments typically focus on areas such as registration, political activities, and economic operations.[138] State regulation of NPOs often risks imposing restrictive policies that undermine their operational effectiveness and limit their capacity for self-regulation, as argued by Garciandia.[139] Referring the International Centre for Not-for-Profit Law, Carolei noted that, since 2012, 161 restrictive laws worldwide have targeted critical aspects of NPO operations, including funding, service delivery, and oversight, further complicating their ability to function effectively.[140] He further highlighted additional challenges, such as chronic underfunding, limited jurisdiction over overseas activities, and the absence of mechanisms to address misconduct or provide remedies to victims.[141] These systemic weaknesses exacerbate the difficulties in achieving sector-wide accountability, leaving substantial gaps in oversight and enforcement.

At the international level, regulating and ensuring the accountability of NPOs is equally fraught. While their roles and statuses are acknowledged in key treaties like the UN Charter and the Geneva Conventions, international law does not impose direct obligations on NPOs due to their lack of legal personality within the state-centric global system.[142] As Kerstin Martens observed, NGOs remain a legal 'terra incognita' in international affairs, with no clear legal standards governing their

[135] BHRRC 'Saudi Arabia: BWI files ILO forced labour complaint ahead of 2034 FIFA World Cup bid amid 'epidemic' of migrant worker abuse' 22 October 2024 https://www.bhrrc.org/en/latest-news/saudi-arabia-bwi-files-ilo-forced-labour-complaint-ahead-of-2034-fifa-world-cup-bid-amid-epidemic-of-migrant-worker-abuse/ (accessed 2 February 2026).

[136] Garciandia (2023), p. 537.

[137] Ibid.

[138] Carolei (2022b), p. 871.

[139] Garciandia (2023), p. 537.

[140] Carolei (2022b), pp. 871–872.

[141] Ibid.

[142] Ibid.

transnational operations despite their growing role in global governance.[143] While states recognise NGOs' contributions to international negotiations and grant some recognition at the national level, there is no uniform framework to govern their responsibilities or accountability in the international sphere.

Unlike states, NPOs are not bound by international human rights regimes, and as Carolei argued, their accountability was notably excluded from the International Law Commission's 2011 study on the responsibilities of international organisations.[144] Instead, their obligations typically arise from cooperative arrangements, such as ECOSOC Resolution 1996/31, which outlines consultative status requirements with the UN.[145] Carolei also pointed out the stereotypical portrayal of NGOs as morally impeccable champions of human rights, which has shielded them from accountability, even as multinational corporations have been subjected to frameworks like the OECD Guidelines and the UNGPs since the 1970s.[146] This regulatory gap leaves NPOs without an equivalent framework to address their responsibilities, despite growing concerns over their legitimacy, transparency, and impact on communities.

As Garciandia observed, NGOs as part of the NPOs are primarily self-regulated under international law, with domestic regulations often unsuitable due to the risks of restrictive actions that undermine their efficiency.[147] In response, the sector has increasingly relied on voluntary, institutionalised self-regulation frameworks, such as the INGO Accountability Charter ('Accountable Now') or HAP International.[148] The Global Accountability Communities (GACs), established through frameworks often facilitated by NGO networks or international institutions, aim to enhance accountability by engaging key stakeholders in external oversight processes.[149] These frameworks provide structured and consistent mechanisms for governance and engagement, addressing the risks of fragmented or inconsistent implementation of accountability standards.

However, a key challenge with these widely recognised self-regulation initiatives is their sector-specific nature, limiting their applicability across all NGOs.[150] Moreover, these regulations typically address only certain types of nonprofit organizations, focusing primarily on NGOs, while excluding other forms of nonprofits. For instance, the Conservation and Human Rights Framework, launched in 2009 by the Conservation Initiative on Human Rights, is tailored to integrate human rights into conservation practices, emphasizing the perspectives and needs of local

---

[143] Martens (2003), p. 23.

[144] Carolei (2022b), p. 871.

[145] Carolei and Bernaz (2021), p. 508.

[146] Carolei (2022b), p. 872.

[147] Ibid.

[148] Garciandia (2023), pp. 527–528.

[149] Ibid.

[150] Ibid, 529–531.

communities.[151] While such frameworks are valuable within their specific sectors, the existing regulations for NPOs remain inadequate compared to those for corporations, particularly in addressing broader accountability needs across the NGO sector.[152]

Against this backdrop, scholars Bernaz, Carolei and Garciandia proposed that the accountability of NPOs can be more effectively conceptualised using international BHR frameworks, such as the UNGPs and the OECD Guidelines.[153] They argue that there is a compelling case for including NGOs within the scope of the UNGPs, which outline due diligence as a process for identifying, assessing, and addressing actual or potential adverse human rights and environmental impacts. General Principle 14 of the UNGPs explicitly states that the framework applies to 'all enterprises regardless of their size, sector, operational context, ownership, and structure'.[154] Since NGOs frequently engage in business-like activities to sustain their operations beyond relying solely on donations—such as employing staff, leasing office spaces, procuring goods, and managing investments—they clearly fit within the broad definition of business enterprises.[155] Furthermore, Carolei and Bernaz further asserted that these standards provide a complementary approach to traditional mechanisms for NGO accountability.[156]

The OECD Guidelines present a compelling case for their applicability to NGOs, as their flexible and inclusive framework extends to organisations engaging in commercial activities, regardless of their legal form or purpose. This perspective has been further validated by cases reviewed by the Swiss NCP, including those involving FIFA, WWF, the International Olympic Committee, and the International Hockey Federation, as well as a case involving Norwegian Church Aid addressed by the Norwegian NCP. These cases focused on the organisations' commercial activities rather than their non-profit status. The updated OECD Guidelines enhance this applicability by expanding HRDD requirements to cover conflict contexts and vulnerable groups—key areas of NGO operations—and by addressing issues such as the embezzlement or misuse of charitable donations.[157] This evolving framework highlights the potential for NPOs including NGOs to align with the due diligence expectations already reshaping corporate accountability narratives under business and human rights frameworks like the UNGPs.

By integrating established frameworks like the UNGPs and the OECD Guidelines, NPOs have the opportunity to enhance their accountability practices through well-defined, cohesive standards that build upon existing self-regulation mechanisms. These frameworks could provide clear guidance for embedding human rights due

[151] Ibid.

[152] Ibid.

[153] Carolei and Bernaz (2021), pp. 513–520; Garciandia (2023), pp. 531–537.

[154] Ibid; UN Guiding Principles on Business and Human Rights, Principle 14.

[155] Ibid.

[156] Ibid.

[157] Garciandia (2023), p. 537.

diligence into organisational models and emphasise the importance of stakeholder engagement as a fundamental element of effective accountability. For example, the UNGPs advocate for harmonised standards, encouraging organisations to identify, address, and mitigate adverse impacts on human rights while fostering transparency and accountability in their operations. This alignment could push NGOs to refine their consultation processes with stakeholders, improve their mechanisms for tracking and communicating progress, and ensure that human rights considerations are systematically integrated into their decision-making and operational strategies. However, while these frameworks hold substantial promise for strengthening NPO accountability, considerable effort and adaptation will be required to implement them effectively in the diverse and complex context of NPOs.

4.4.2 OECD Case Analysis: Non-Profit Organisations' Accountability in Human Rights Contexts

Out of the 394 cases in OECD case law research, 9 cases specifically address organisations that are neither MNEs nor state-based commercial entities like export credit agencies. Instead, these organisations operate with objectives beyond profit-making, focusing on advancing the public good or serving the interests of their members. These cases include prominent sports organisations such as FIFA, the International Olympic Committee (IOC), and the International Ice Hockey Federation (IIHF); global trade unions like the International Trade Union Confederation (ITUC); international humanitarian organisations such as the World Wide Fund for Nature (WWF) and Norwegian Church Aid; and multi-stakeholder initiatives like Bonsucro and the Roundtable on Sustainable Palm Oil (RSPO), which function to support and represent their members.

The very first case filed against a NPO under the OECD Guidelines was the complaint against Norwegian Church Aid (NCA) by 129 Roma individuals in Kosovo in June 2011.[158] The complainants alleged that NCA violated the Guidelines on general policies, human rights, and the environment by failing to prevent severe health risks, including lead poisoning, in a camp it managed. NCA assumed responsibility for the camp on behalf local government, although the camp had been established prior to its involvement. NCA argued that it used health risk data in its advocacy efforts with the UN and EU to push for the relocation of Roma families and the camp's closure.[159] However, these efforts were unsuccessful, and the detrimental conditions persisted, prompting the Roma families to file the complaint.

The Norwegian NCP concluded that the complaint was inadmissible under the OECD Guidelines, as NCA did not meet the Guidelines' 'business nexus'

[158] NCP Norway, 129 Roma in Kosovo v. Norwegian Church Aid, Initial Assessment and Final Report, 30 August 2011.

[159] Ibid, 3.

requirement.[160] Registered in Norway as a non-profit organisation under the Register for Voluntary Organizations, NCA was not classified as a business enterprise, which is a prerequisite for the Guidelines' applicability. This strict interpretation was upheld by the OECD Investment Committee, which supported the NCP's determination that the case fell outside the Guidelines' scope. Consequently, the NCP did not assess whether NCA had breached the Guidelines. This case represents the first attempt to address the accountability of NPOs under the OECD Guidelines, raising broader questions about the capacity of NCPs to assess such accountability. It shows the limitations and inadequacies of existing frameworks in regulating the actions of non-profit organisations engaged in quasi-commercial activities.

Later, cases were brought against various NPOs, including FIFA, the IOC, and WWF, between 2016 and 2017 before the Swiss NCP. The first case, filed in 2016 by Americans for Democracy and Human Rights in Bahrain (ADHRB) against FIFA, also serves as an example of a case that was ultimately deemed inadmissible.[161] The complaint alleged that FIFA failed to incorporate human rights due diligence into its governance processes, specifically in its presidential election procedures, and raised concerns about human rights abuses by Sheikh Salman, a presidential candidate and former chairman of the Bahrain Football Association, during pro-democracy protests in 2011.[162] The Swiss NCP accepted the case, even though FIFA's classification as a multinational enterprise under the OECD Guidelines was debatable.

The Swiss NCP examined the applicability of the OECD Guidelines to FIFA, an association registered under Swiss law and operating in both commercial and non-commercial activities. FIFA's dual objectives—promoting football globally and organising international competitions such as the FIFA World Cup—include significant commercial activities, such as revenue generation and investment in football development projects.[163] However, the Swiss NCP determined that FIFA's governance processes, including its presidential election procedures, are internal organisational matters not directly linked to its commercial activities. Additionally, the alleged human rights violations involving Sheikh Salman were found to be unrelated to any commercial relationship between FIFA and the Bahrain Football Association. Based on these considerations, the Swiss NCP concluded that the OECD Guidelines did not apply to the issues raised in the submission, as the case lacked a clear nexus to FIFA's commercial operations.

Contrary to this, the second case filed against FIFA by the Building and Wood Workers' International (BWI) was a successful example of the application of the OECD Guidelines to the NPO.[164] On May 28, 2015, BWI submitted a request to the

---

[160] Ibid, 6.

[161] NCP Switzerland, Americans for Democracy and Human Rights in Bahrain (ADHRB) v. FIFA, Final Statement, 17 August 2016.

[162] Ibid, 4.

[163] NCP Switzerland, BWI v. FIFA, Final Statement, 2 May 2017.

[164] Ibid, 2.

Swiss NCP to address a specific instance involving FIFA regarding alleged human rights violations of migrant workers involved in the construction of facilities for the 2022 FIFA World Cup in Qatar. Unlike previous cases, the Swiss NCP determined that FIFA fell within the scope of the OECD Guidelines due to its commercial activities and multinational operations.[165]

In its initial statement, the Swiss NCP noted that while the OECD Guidelines do not provide a precise definition of MNE, they apply to entities operating across multiple countries and engaging in coordinated global activities. FIFA, registered as an association in Switzerland, operates through various subsidiaries, such as FIFA Development Zürich Ltd and FIFA Ticketing Ltd, and oversees international activities involving contractual agreements with commercial elements.[166] The NCP highlighted that FIFA's bidding agreement with Qatar's Bid Committee included provisions of a commercial nature, such as media marketing rights and financial arrangements, thereby establishing FIFA's involvement in business activities.[167] The Swiss NCP concluded that FIFA's international operations and commercial agreements linked to the World Cup constituted activities of a commercial nature, making the OECD Guidelines applicable. This case demonstrated a successful application of the Guidelines to an NPO and emphasised the importance of case-specific analysis in determining whether an entity's activities meet the criteria for responsible business conduct under the Guidelines.

In the case, filed by BWI, centred on human rights violations involving migrant workers during the construction of facilities for the 2022 FIFA World Cup in Qatar. By this time, global awareness and criticism of labour in Qatar had reached a critical level, putting FIFA under intense international rights abuses scrutiny. This public pressure likely contributed to the Swiss NCP approaching the case differently, as it faced increased pressure to ensure accountability. The Swiss NCP ultimately determined that FIFA's involvement in organising the World Cup and its contractual relationships with entities in Qatar constituted commercial activities. After the successful resolution of the case between FIFA and BWI, additional cases targeting major sports organisations which are classified as NPOs were brought before the Swiss NCP. Notable cases were involving the IOC and the IIHF, resolved in 2019 and 2021, respectively.

The case against IIHF, however, was dismissed as the Swiss NCP determined that the alleged breaches of the OECD Guidelines were not sufficiently materialised or substantiated.[168] The underlying issue, concerning alleged violations of players' rights by the Polish Ice Hockey Federation (PIHF), was deemed outside the scope of the Swiss NCP's mandate, as the matter was a contractual issue of national interest between PIHF and the players. Despite dismissing the case, the Swiss NCP

---

[165] Ibid, 3.

[166] Ibid.

[167] Ibid, 4.

[168] NCP Switzerland, Stowarzyszenie Zawodników Hokeja na Lodzie v. International Ice Hockey Federation, Final Statement, 24 July 2019.

noted IIHF's offer to mediate between the PIHF and the affected players, though it required the consent of both parties.[169] In its analysis, the Swiss NCP evaluated the IIHF's eligibility under the OECD Guidelines. While IIHF, as the global governing body for ice hockey, operates as a NPO, it was found to have multinational operations through its 76 Member National Associations (MNAs) and its subsidiary, Parkring AG. Despite its international scope, the NCP concluded that IIHF's activities are largely non-commercial, focused on fostering ice hockey globally rather than pursuing business or profit-based activities.[170] While the relationship between IIHF and its MNAs involves financial transactions, these are aimed at promoting the sport rather than governed by business interests. The NCP emphasised that the applicability of the OECD Guidelines to NPOs like IIHF must be assessed on a case-by-case basis, with particular attention to the commercial nature of their activities.[171] This case shows the complexities in determining the accountability of NPOs under the OECD Guidelines, particularly for organisations whose operations straddle both non-commercial and commercial activities.

The case against the IOC, filed by the Tibetan community in Switzerland, alleged that the IOC failed to conduct adequate risk-based due diligence under the OECD Guidelines, thereby contributing to potential violations of internationally recognised human rights and abusive employment practices in China.[172] The complaint focused on the IOC's decision to award the 2022 Winter Olympics to Beijing, highlighting concerns over its responsibility to prevent human rights violations associated with its activities.[173] Similar to other cases involving NPOs, the Swiss NCP conducted an analysis of the IOC's eligibility under the OECD Guidelines, assessing its multinational operations and the commercial nature of its activities. While the mediation process was ultimately unsuccessful, the NCP recognised the IOC's obligations under the Guidelines and issued specific recommendations for improving its practices. In its final statement, the Swiss NCP recommended that the IOC maintain an ongoing dialogue with all stakeholders, including the Tibetan community and other interested parties, to address concerns raised during the proceedings.[174] It further advised the IOC to disclose its policies and practices regarding HRDD, particularly in relation to awarding and hosting the Olympic Games. This included emphasising the IOC's responsibility to set clear expectations for business partners, such as sponsors and suppliers directly linked to its operations, to uphold human rights standards.

Beyond the high-profile cases involving sports giants like FIFA, IOC, and IIHF, the Swiss NCP has also successfully resolved cases involving other global NPOs,

[169] Ibid, 2–3.

[170] Ibid, 7.

[171] Ibid.

[172] NCP Switzerland, Swiss-Tibetan Friendship Association, Tibetan Youth Association in Europe, Tibetan Community in Switzerland and Liechtenstein as well as the Tibetan Women's Association Switzerland v. International Olympic Committee IOC, Final Statement, 21 December 2021.

[173] Ibid, 1.

[174] Ibid, 3.

such as the RSPO and WWF International.[175] In the RSPO case, the complaint was filed by the Indonesian NGO TuK Indonesia on behalf of the Dayak Hibun communities of West Kalimantan, Indonesia. The case concerned an unresolved land conflict related to palm oil production involving the Malaysian enterprise Sime Darby and its subsidiary PT Mitra Austral Sejahtera. The submission sought Swiss NCP's support to create an action plan between RSPO and TuK to resolve the ongoing complaint, including clear deadlines for action steps.[176] The Swiss NCP facilitated a constructive dialogue between the parties, resulting in an agreement on a transparent and fair legal review process by the RSPO Complaint Panel, a clear action plan with deadlines, and a commitment to regular exchanges until the complaint is fully resolved.

In the case against WWF International, Survival International filed a complaint with the Swiss NCP on behalf of the Baka people of southeast Cameroon.[177] The submission alleged that WWF failed to conduct adequate HRDD and violated the OECD Guidelines by supporting the demarcation of environmentally protected areas in Cameroon without ensuring the FPIC of the Baka people.[178] The complaint also raised concerns about WWF's role in supporting Ecoguard patrols, which allegedly focused on subsistence hunting by the Baka rather than commercial poaching and, in some cases, involved abuse and violence against the Baka people. The mediation process facilitated by the Swiss NCP focused on four key areas: the management of environmentally protected areas, the implementation of WWF's Indigenous Peoples and Conservation Principles, securing FPIC from the Baka people, and preventing human rights adverse impacts.[179] The dialogue led to agreements on future interactions with stakeholders and commitments to improve WWF's due diligence processes and accountability mechanisms.

Both cases underlined the Swiss NCP's capacity to address intricate issues concerning the responsibilities of NPOs, particularly in mitigating risks to local and indigenous communities' rights arising from their activities. The WWF case highlighted a significant failure in due diligence, as the organisation did not adequately ensure the FPIC of the Baka people, nor did it effectively safeguard them against abuses tied to its conservation initiatives. Meanwhile, the RSPO case focused on shortcomings in resolving conflicts between member companies and affected communities, reflecting a failure from an access-to-remedy perspective. However, the Swiss NCP's final statements could have provided a more substantive analysis to conceptualise the responsibility of the NPO in implementing the OECD Guidelines. Moreover, the long-term impact of these cases remains uncertain, as the Swiss NCP

[175] NCP Switzerland, TUK Indonesia v. Roundtable Sustainable Palm Oil, Final Statement, 5 June 2019.

[176] Ibid, 1.

[177] NCP Switzerland, Survival International v. Wolrd Wide Fund, Final Statement, 21 November 2017.

[178] Ibid, 1.

[179] Ibid, 4.

has not issued any follow-up reports to assess the implementation of the agreements or subsequent progress.

The last case to be analysed is the complaint against Bonsucro, brought to the UK NCP by Inclusive Development International (IDI), Equitable Cambodia (EC), and the Cambodian League for the Promotion and Defence of Human Rights (LICADHO).[180] The case highlights significant due diligence failures by Bonsucro, a multi-stakeholder NPO promoting sustainable sugarcane projects. The complainants alleged that Bonsucro failed to assess human rights risks adequately and did not use its leverage over its member, Mitr Phol Group (MPG-T), regarding documented human rights abuses in Cambodia. Despite reports and complaints dating back to 2011, Bonsucro admitted MPG-T as a member in 2010 and readmitted it in 2015 without evidence of meaningful corrective actions. Moreover, Bonsucro awarded MPG-T a Sustainability Award and promoted it as a 'leading member' shortly after a Thai National Human Rights Commission report confirmed severe human rights violations.

While Bonsucro argued that its approach aligns with its goal of continuous improvement, it failed to demonstrate due diligence process or verify its members' compliance with its Code of Conduct. This lack of transparency undermined its credibility and raised questions about its commitment to human rights and RBC. The UK NCP recommended that Bonsucro strengthen its due diligence processes and apply adequate leverage over its members to address risks associated with their operations.[181] Elena Corcoine observed that cases like Bonsucro, a NPO providing voluntary sustainability standards (VSS), reflect a growing awareness of the critical role such actors can play in deterring human rights violations.[182] However, Corcoine further argued that their responsibilities remain insufficiently defined within NCP practices.[183] The UK NCP case underline the failure of sustainability label providers in shaping corporate responsible behaviour and calls for a potential framework for holding other VSS actors accountable under the OECD Guidelines when they occupy similarly powerful and influential positions.

The analysed cases demonstrate the evolving role of NCPs in addressing accountability for NPOs under the OECD Guidelines. These cases highlight the growing recognition of the responsibilities of NPOs, particularly those engaged in quasi-commercial activities or wielding significant influence, such as multi-stakeholder initiatives and sustainability standard-setters. While some cases, like those against FIFA and Bonsucro highlighted successful applications of the Guidelines through constructive dialogue and actionable recommendations, others reveal limitations, such as the dismissal of cases against IIHF and the lack of clear follow-up mechanisms. The Swiss and UK NCPs set important precedents by emphasising the need

---

[180] NCP United Kingdom, IDI, EC and LICADHO v. Bonsucro Ltd, Final Statement, 11 January 2022.

[181] Ibid.

[182] Corcoine (2023), p. 276.

[183] Ibid.

for NPOs to strengthen their HRDD, enhance stakeholder engagement, and exercise leverage over business partners to prevent and mitigate human rights risks. However, these cases also revealed gaps in the consistency and clarity of NCP practices, particularly regarding the accountability of NPOs and voluntary sustainability actors. Going forward, these insights show the need for stronger enforcement mechanisms and a more coherent conceptualisation towards the NPO accountability within BHR frameworks.

4.5 Responsibilities of State-Owned Enterprises

4.5.1 State-Owned Enterprises Human Rights Obligations Within International Frameworks

According to the OECD, in 2023, the public sector held over 25% ownership in 2037 listed companies globally, accounting for 11.6% of total market capitalisation.[184] However, the significance of SOEs varies widely between markets. In the OECD countries, such entities represent only 2% of market capitalisation, compared to 16% in Latin America and Asia, and 50% or more in certain other markets.[185] Furthermore, SOEs as entities that are commonly found in utilities and infrastructure sectors, such as energy, transport, and telecommunications, where their performance significantly impacts large portions of the population and other areas of the business sector.[186] Larry Catá Backer stated that, SOEs occupy a distinct and complex role within the framework of globalisation, balancing the intersecting dynamics of markets, states, and corporations.[187] Unlike private enterprises, SOEs merge commercial activities with state influence, challenging traditional classifications of economic actors.[188] The UNGPs, particularly Principles 4 to 6, under the concept of the state-business nexus, emphasise the unique obligations of states to integrate HRDD into the operations of SOEs and incentivise human rights and environmental sustainability commitments among businesses engaging in commercial transactions with the state.[189] Additionally, Principles 8 to 10 call for policy coherence between governmental departments that shape business practices and the

[184] OECD 'Corporate governance of state-owned enterprises' https://www.oecd.org/en/topics/sub-issues/corporate-governance-of-state-owned-enterprises.html (accessed 2 February 2026).

[185] Ibid.

[186] OECD Guidelines on Corporate Governance of State-Owned Enterprises 'Annotations to Chapter 3: State-owned enterprises in the marketplace' 2024, OECD Publishing. Paris.

[187] Catá Backer (2020), p. 223.

[188] Ibid.

[189] UN Guiding Principles on Business and Human Rights, Principles 4–6.

state's broader international human rights obligations.[190] These principles highlight the critical role of SOEs as both economic agents and instruments of state policy.

Catá Backer further argued that SOEs have a dual responsibility: advancing the political and strategic interests of their home states while adhering to international human rights standards and market-based frameworks.[191] Key reasons include the state's legal obligation to prevent human rights abuses, the need for policy coherence across government departments, and the imperative for states to maintain legitimacy and credibility by holding SOEs to the same or higher standards than private enterprises.[192] International frameworks like the OECD Guidelines on Corporate Governance of SOEs (OECD Guidelines for SOEs) advocate for 'active ownership', encouraging states to adopt transparent, accountable, and efficient management practices to align SOEs with international human rights and governance standards.[193]

However, Catá Backer noted that the duality of SOEs—as state instruments and commercial entities—creates inherent tensions.[194] Operating across diverse sectors such as energy, telecommunications, and infrastructure, SOEs are regulated by domestic legal frameworks while also being subject to international regulatory regimes that may conflict with their national obligations.[195] This tension indicated the challenges of ensuring that SOEs effectively uphold human rights while navigating complex legal and market environments. Moreover, their close association with the state means that any human rights violations committed by SOEs could also implicate the state in breaching its international legal obligations.[196] These dynamics make SOEs critical yet challenging actors in advancing human rights and meeting global economic and legal standards, demanding a balanced approach that integrates active ownership, coherent policy frameworks, and strong accountability mechanisms.

Specifically, as argued by Judith Schönsteiner, in practice, numerous well-documented case studies reveal that SOEs, particularly in sectors such as energy, extractives, services, banking, transportation, and telecommunications, have been implicated in significant human rights violations.[197] These violations frequently impact Indigenous Peoples, minorities, and local communities. Examples include forced evictions and resettlements conducted without FPIC; breaches of the right to health, water, and a healthy environment due to emissions, spills, ruptures of tailing

---

190 Ibid, Principles 8–10.

191 Catá Backer (2020), pp. 224–225.

192 Ibid, paras 1–9; UN WGBHR 'The State as an economic actor and human rights' https://www.ohchr.org/en/special-procedures/wg-business/state-economic-actor-and-human-rights (accessed 2 February 2026).

193 OECD Guidelines on Corporate Governance of State-Owned Enterprises, I. Rationales for state ownership.

194 Catá Backer (2020), p. 229.

195 Barnes (2021), pp. 1–49.

196 Ibid.

197 Schönsteiner (2019), p. 896.

dams, and other forms of severe environmental contamination; violations of both individual and collective labour rights; and the suppression of civic freedoms, including the rights to life, personal integrity, freedom of assembly, and freedom of expression, often in response to social protests against business projects.[198] Furthermore, Schönsteiner also mentioned that potential violations may arise regarding the right to information or the right to participation during various phases of a project, including planning, design, exploration, operation, and closure.[199] In the context of community and client relations within the service sector, additional violations could result from discrimination based on race, ethnicity, gender, sexual orientation, national origin, religion, trade union involvement, or socio-economic status, among other factors.[200]

Although there are numerous causes of human rights violations attributed to SOEs, holding them accountable is significantly more challenging compared to MNEs. This difficulty arises from the unique characteristics of SOEs, including their close connection to and control by the state.[201] Mihaela Maria Barnes highlighted the distinctiveness of SOEs, emphasising their intrinsic connection to the public domain and the state and Backer pointed out that since SOEs are owned and operated by governments, ultimate accountability must inherently lie with the state.[202] As highlighted by the WGBHR, SOEs, like other private businesses, are required to conduct HRDD in their operations. They must be held accountable for damages they cause, contribute to, or are directly linked to, and fulfil their responsibility to provide and participate in remediation.[203] However, state involvement adds complexity to these obligations. Camilla Wee argued that unlike private shareholders, the state as a controlling owner holds unique powers, such as nominating and electing SOE boards without the consent of other shareholders, as highlighted by the OECD Guidelines for SOEs.[204] The guidelines also note that SOE boards often face encroachment from both state ownership entities and management, with senior management typically appointed by and reporting to state entities.[205] Additionally, ownership entities are often accountable to political bodies, such as parliaments, representing public interests.[206] These layers of state influence—over board composition, senior management, and accountability structures—distinguish

198 Ibid, 896–897.

199 Ibid.

200 Ibid.

201 Uvarova (2022), pp. 301–303.

202 Ibid, Catá Backer (2020), pp. 225–227.

203 WGBHR 'Report of the Working Group on the issue of human rights and transnational corporations and other business enterprises' 4 May 2016 UN Doc A/HRC/32/45, para 77.

204 Wee (2008), pp. 18–19.

205 The OECD, OECD Guidelines on Corporate Governance of State-owned Enterprises, 2005, 192. https://www.oecd-ilibrary.org/docserver/9789264009431-10-en.pdf?expires=1733743228&id=id&accname=ocid54016941&checksum=8D03696EF7ED5EC2D41FEDB0A5A38364 (accessed 2 February 2026).

206 Ibid, 196.

SOEs from private corporations.[207] This unique position supports the argument that SOEs cannot be held accountable for their actions in the same manner as private enterprises. Given the significant influence of state decisions on their operations, the focus must primarily be on state responsibility.

Furthermore, as Schönsteiner argued that, a central issue lies in determining when SOE actions or omissions can be attributed to the state, as this attribution is pivotal for ensuring accountability and access to justice for victims.[208] The complexity of attribution is further exacerbated by inconsistent legal frameworks and the frequent invocation of state immunity by SOEs, which can effectively block mechanisms for accountability.[209] This issue calls for the urgent need to address the legal and structural gaps that allow SOEs to evade responsibility for human rights violations.

Thus, scholars such as Catá Backer, Schönsteiner, and Wee have explored a range of international instruments to examine the responsibilities of SOEs and their potential accountability for human rights violations.[210] These include the Draft Articles on Responsibility of States for Internationally Wrongful Acts (Draft Articles 2001), case law from human rights courts like the European Court of Human Rights (ECHR) and the Inter-American Court for Human Rights (IACtHR), the UNGPs, the WGBHR report on SOEs, and the OECD Guidelines for SOEs.[211]

The Draft Articles 2001 provide limited guidance on the attribution of SOE actions to the state, particularly through Articles 4, 5, and 8.[212] Wee argued that Article 4 offers a narrow scope for considering SOEs as state organs. Unless national legislation explicitly designates a SOE as such, the enterprise must perform traditional state functions to be considered part of the state.[213] However, given the commercial nature of most SOEs, this designation is typically unlikely, though exceptions may exist depending on the state's traditions.[214] Article 5 addresses SOEs' actions when they exercise functions of a public character typically associated with state organs.[215] Their conduct must relate to 'governmental authority' to be attributable to the state. However, the absence of clear definitions for terms like 'governmental authority' and 'governmental functions' introduces interpretative ambiguities.[216] This lack of clarity often allows SOEs to exploit their hybrid nature,

[207] Wee (2008), p. 19.

[208] Schönsteiner (2019), pp. 898–899.

[209] Ibid.

[210] Catá Backer (2020), Schönsteiner (2019), and Wee (2008).

[211] Ibid; International Law Commission 'Draft articles on Responsibility of States for Internationally Wrongful Acts, with commentaries 2001' 2008 https://legal.un.org/ilc/texts/instruments/english/commentaries/9_6_2001.pdf (accessed 2 February 2026).

[212] Ibid, Article 4. Conduct of organs of a State; Article 5. Conduct of persons or entities exercising elements of governmental authority; Article 8. Conduct directed or controlled by a State.

[213] Wee (2008), pp. 22–23.

[214] Ibid.

[215] Ibid, 23–27.

[216] Ibid.

invoking state immunity to avoid liability. Lastly, Article 8 broadens the scope of state responsibility by attributing actions to the state when an entity operates under its instructions, direction, or control, even if the entity is not a state organ or engaged in governmental functions.[217] For SOEs, this is especially significant, as their actions—commercial or otherwise—can be linked to the state when substantial influence is evident. By emphasising the state's involvement, Article 8 reinforces the obligation to ensure accountability for wrongful acts, including human rights abuses, committed by entities under its substantial control.[218]

Schönsteiner argued that SOEs, citing the UNGPs, they are required to respect human rights like any other business entity (Pillar 2).[219] Additionally, as state-owned entities, SOEs bear an elevated responsibility to align their operations with the state's duty to protect human rights. States must also take additional measures, as outlined in the WGBHR report, to ensure that SOEs comply with the UNGPs (Pillar 1).[220] These dual obligations position SOEs as critical actors in upholding human rights standards, yet their accountability mechanisms remain underdeveloped. She further added that the historical legacy of SOEs further complicates their role in human rights abuses. In industries such as mining, energy, and oil, SOEs have often been implicated in widespread environmental degradation and human rights violations.[221] These legacies persist even when such enterprises are privatised or dissolved, as the state remains responsible for failing to regulate or oversee their operations adequately. For example, abandoned contaminated sites resulting from SOE activities continue to harm communities, infringing on rights such as health, water, and a safe environment.[222] International human rights jurisprudence has consistently held states responsible for such ongoing violations, asserting that the dissolution or privatisation of an SOE does not absolve the state of its obligations to remedy past harms.

Schönsteiner, after analysing a variety of court cases, emphasised the crucial role of international and regional human rights mechanisms in ensuring the accountability of SOEs. She further asserted that ECtHR has established criteria for attributing SOE actions to the state, focusing on whether the enterprise performs governmental functions or operates under significant state control.[223] In contrast, the IACtHR adopts a more streamlined approach, often treating SOEs as state organs without requiring detailed attribution criteria.[224] This stance is justified by the inherently close relationship between SOEs and the state, particularly when these entities

---

[217] Ibid, 27–28.

[218] Ibid, 30–31.

[219] Schönsteiner (2019), p. 921.

[220] Ibid.

[221] Ibid, 907–908.

[222] Ibid, 905.

[223] Schönsteiner (2019), Section 3.1 912; Fadeyeva v Russia, Judgment, 45 Eur.Ct.H.R. 10, para. 92 (2005).

[224] Ibid, Section 3.2; Pueblo Ind.gena Kichwa de Sarayaku v Ecuador, Preliminary Exceptions, Merits, Reparations and Costs, Judgment, Inter-Am. Ct. H.R., (ser. C) 245 (Jun. 27, 2012).

perform regulatory or governmental functions.[225] However, the absence of uniform attribution standards across different jurisdictions demonstrates the urgent need for greater coherence in addressing SOE-related human rights violations within the framework of international law.

Analysing these various cases, she further argued that state responsibility for human rights abuses extends beyond the direct attribution of SOE actions.[226] States are also accountable for failing to regulate or oversee SOEs effectively and for providing inadequate remedies for victims. For example, underfunded SOEs often lack the resources to compensate victims, yet the state remains responsible for ensuring access to justice and remediation.[227] This obligation includes assigning additional funds to fulfil human rights obligations and addressing systemic issues such as the excessive reintegration of SOE revenues into the state budget. States cannot escape their human rights obligations by creating SOEs; they remain responsible for ensuring that these entities comply with international standards and provide effective remedies for harm caused.

International law also recognises the need for states to address historical injustices linked to SOEs. For example, contaminated sites abandoned by SOEs continue to harm communities, and states are obligated to provide remediation and compensation.[228] This responsibility cannot be avoided by invoking the corporate veil or claiming that the SOE operates as a private business. Attribution rules in international human rights law focus on the control exerted by the state over the SOE and the public service functions performed by the entity.[229] These rules reinforce the importance of addressing ongoing violations and providing effective remedies for victims.

A thorough analysis of the challenges within the relationship between SOEs and the state stresses the critical need for greater clarity in defining SOEs' responsibilities. These challenges, including the tension between state duties and corporate accountability, the ambiguities in attribution rules under international law, and the fragmentation of accountability frameworks, reveal significant gaps in governance and enforcement. As Catá Backer argued, the state-business nexus, articulated in Principles 4 and 8 of the UNGPs, raises critical questions of policy coherence, especially concerning the disparity between a state's legal obligations and an enterprise's broader responsibility to respect human rights.[230] He further argued that the ambiguity is intensified by the 'take additional steps' principle, as reflected in the WGBHR report on SOE responsibilities.[231] This principle risks conflating the roles of SOEs

[225] Ibid.

[226] Ibid, 920.

[227] Ibid, 920–921.

[228] Ibid, Sect. 4.2, 923–924.

[229] Ibid.

[230] Catá Backer (2020), p. 242.

[231] Ibid, 243.

and states, potentially limiting the scope of SOEs' Pillar 2 obligations to align with the state's narrower legal duties under Pillar 1.

Moreover, the fragmentation of accountability frameworks and the inconsistent application of human rights obligations to SOEs across jurisdictions further illustrate the pressing need for reform.[232] This is exacerbated by the ambiguity of the "public function" of state-based economic activities and the tension between the public and commercial roles of SOEs contribute to governance gaps that undermine accountability.[233] Addressing these gaps requires states to prioritise the regulation of SOEs, adopt customised HRDD frameworks, and ensure effective remedies for victims. Strengthening oversight and transparency mechanisms is essential to mitigate policy incoherence and to extend human rights obligations to SOEs, regardless of whether their functions are economic or governmental in nature. Further research and legal development are crucial to clarifying the scope of SOEs' responsibilities and strengthening the mechanisms for their accountability under international law.

4.5.2 OECD Case Law on State-Owned Enterprises' Accountability for Human Rights Impacts

The analysis of OECD cases involving SOEs reveals significant variation in how NCPs interpret and address the unique challenges and responsibilities of these entities under the OECD Guidelines. While export credit agencies (ECAs) were examined in detail in this chapter as it included as FIs, this section expands the focus to include other types of SOEs. It assesses whether NCPs effectively adapt their recommendations to the specific characteristics and operations of SOEs. Among the 16 cases reviewed, several involved SOEs, including ECAs, highlighting inconsistencies in the recommendations and actions taken by different NCPs. This addresses the need for clear and consistent guidance to ensure these entities meet their obligations under the OECD Guidelines.

In many cases, SOEs were mentioned only in passing without any substantive examination of their specific responsibilities. For example, in the case against Nykomb at the Swedish NCP and the case against KBC and KBL at the Belgium NCP, the companies were identified as SOEs, yet no further analysis or tailored recommendations were provided.[234] Such missed opportunities fail to capture the complexities of SOEs' operations and the heightened expectations placed upon them.

Furthermore, some cases explicitly identified SOEs as the respondent companies but failed to issue specific recommendations addressing their unique characteristics.

[232] Ibid, 243–244.

[233] Ibid.

[234] NCP Sweden, Takkom Jerry and Lumiere Synergie Developpement v. Nykomb Synergetics Development AB, Final Statement. 15 December 2015; NCP Belgium, Open Secrets v. KBC – KBL, Initial Assessment, 24 June 2019.

For instance, the case against Van Oord at the Brazilian NCP involved allegations that the Port of Suape as well as ADSB, both are SOEs neglected to demand high standards of transparency and conduct during dredging activities, resulting in socio-environmental harm.[235] The complaint also highlighted the port's failure to implement participatory measures to mitigate the socio-environmental impact of the dredging, a responsibility compounded by its state ownership. Despite these serious allegations, the Brazilian NCP did not provide specific recommendations tailored to the state-owned nature of the port and investor, reflecting a missed opportunity to address governance and accountability challenges unique to SOEs.

Conversely, certain NCPs demonstrated an understanding of the need for SOE-specific guidance. In the case against Kone Oyj at the Finnish NCP, the recommendations included conducting due diligence specific to bribery risks in transactions with SOEs and maintaining transparency regarding agents involved in such dealings.[236] Similarly, in the case against Accenture at the Irish NCP, detailed recommendations were provided on prohibiting facilitation payments, enhancing transparency in anti-bribery measures, and fostering public cooperation in the fight against corruption.[237]

Several cases brought human rights concerns related to SOEs into sharper focus, highlighting inconsistencies between national commitments to international human rights standards and the conduct of SOEs. The Norwegian NCP's case against Statkraft drew significant attention to Norway's ratification of key international conventions on Indigenous Peoples' rights, including ILO Convention 169, CERD, ICCPR, ECHR, and UDHR.[238] These conventions obligate states to protect Indigenous Peoples' rights to land and to participate in decisions affecting their natural resources. Despite these commitments, Statkraft, a Norwegian state-owned company, was found to have failed to meet these expectations, exposing a gap between Norway's international obligations and the actions of its SOE.[239] The case demonstrates the heightened expectations for SOEs to align their operations with human rights standards upheld by their owning states, particularly in contexts involving vulnerable populations.

Another important case involved NBIM, also reviewed by the Norwegian NCP.[240] The complaint centred on NBIM's failure to provide a meaningful response to the

[235] NCP Brazil, Association Forum Suape Environmental Space, Conectas Human Rights, Fishermen's Colony Z8 – Gaibu Both ENDS v. Van Oord, Atradius Dutch State Business and Industrial Port Complex Eraldo Gueiros – Suape Enterprise, Pernambuco, Final Statement, 5 June 2020.

[236] NCP Finland, Haidir Hussen v. Mone Oyj, Kone middle East, Initial Statement, 24 September 2020.

[237] NCP Ireland, Daphne Caruana Galizia Foundation v. Accenture PLC, Statement, 7 October 2022.

[238] NCP Sweden, Jijnjevaerie Saami village v. Statkraft SCA Vind AB (SSVAB) 10 February 2016.

[239] Ibid, 1.

[240] NCP Norway, Cotton Campaign, Anti-Slavery International and KTNC Watch v. Norges Bank Investment Management, Initial and Final Statement, 2 July 2015; Lok Shakti Abhiyan, Korean Transnational Corporations Watch, Fair Green and Global Alliance And Forum for Environment

NCP's specific inquiries regarding its adherence to the OECD Guidelines.[241] NBIM chose a general written response over engaging in dialogue or addressing the detailed questions posed by the NCP. This lack of engagement was particularly concerning given NBIM's status as a SOE, which, under the OECD Guidelines, is subject to heightened public scrutiny and accountability. The Norwegian NCP concluded that NBIM's actions breached the Guidelines, reinforcing the principle that SOEs are not exempt from responsibility and must proactively engage to address human rights concerns.[242]

The interplay between state responsibilities and corporate conduct was also shown in the UK NCP's case against six telecommunication companies.[243] The complaint focused on allegations of human rights violations under Article 8 of the ECHR, which guarantees the right to privacy.[244] UK domestic law places responsibility on UK government entities to ensure that any infringement on human rights is proportionate and pursues legitimate aims, such as crime prevention or safeguarding economic well-being. Although the complaint rejected by the UK NCP, this case highlights business enterprises, including SOEs, in ensuring compliance with human rights obligations while maintaining transparency and proportionality in their actions.

However, certain cases revealed disappointing gaps where NCPs rejected complaints involving SOEs, citing their state-owned nature as outside the scope of the OECD Guidelines. For instance, in the case against KEXIM at the Korean NCP, the NCP concluded that the Guidelines may not apply to KEXIM due to its role as a loan provider, despite its commercial nature as an export credit agency.[245] Similarly, the UK NCP rejected the case against UKEF, stating that it was not a multinational enterprise under the OECD Guidelines.[246] Another example is the case against Southern Response at the New Zealand NCP, where the NCP dismissed the complaint, citing the company's domestic focus and lack of a transnational character.[247] These rejections reflect inconsistencies in how NCPs apply the Guidelines to SOEs, often excluding them from scrutiny despite their significant impact on human rights and environmental issues.

In other cases, the difficulties in influencing SOEs as business partners were evident. The German NCP's case against Otto Stadtlander highlighted the

---

and Development v. Posco (South Korea), ABP/APG (Netherlands) and NBIM (Norway), Final Statement, 2 May 2013.

[241] Ibid, 5.

[242] Ibid, 8.

[243] NCP United Kingdom, An NGO v. 6 UK-based Telecommunication Companies, Initial Statement, July 2014.

[244] Ibid, 3.

[245] OECD Watch, KTNC Watch et al v. KEXIM Violations of FPIC, consultation at Philippine Jalaur dam, 18 January 2019.

[246] NCP UK, Global Witness v. UK Export Finance, Initial assessment, 9 September 2020.

[247] NCP New Zealand, Mr and Mrs C/Southern Response against NZ Permanent Trustees Ltd, Final Statement, 9 March 2016.

challenges private companies face in addressing the practices of SOEs.[248] The complaint alleged that the company's purchase of Uzbek cotton from state-owned suppliers indirectly supported child labour. While the complainants argued that Otto Stadtlander could have used its business links to exert influence on the Uzbek SOEs or government, the case highlighted the limits of private entities' ability to drive change within state-controlled systems.

Overall, these cases reveal significant inconsistencies and failures in how NCPs interpret and address the responsibilities of SOEs. While some NCPs issue tailored recommendations that consider the unique risks and challenges posed by SOEs, others fail to go beyond acknowledging their involvement, leaving critical governance gaps unaddressed. Strengthening oversight mechanisms, aligning SOE practices with international human rights commitments, and fostering greater engagement within the NCP framework are critical steps to ensuring that SOEs contribute positively to the protection of human rights and the promotion of sustainable development.

4.6 Understanding State Duty to Protect Human Rights from Corporate Actors Through OECD Case Law

4.6.1 Introduction

The traditional human rights approach upholds that states have a fundamental obligation to respect, fulfil and protect the human rights of individuals.[249] The UNGPs embody the fundamental role of the state in protecting human rights from abuse by non-state actors.[250] Pillar 1 and 3 of the UNGPs require states to ensure that businesses do not violate human rights by enacting enforceable or voluntary laws and providing remedies for violations.[251] However, the complexity of global supply chains, economic markets, and the entrenched power imbalance between the Global North and Global South make the state's duty to protect human rights from corporate exploitation a highly challenging endeavour.[252] Under the UNGPs, the state's responsibility to protect human rights from corporate abuse is built upon a 'smart mix' of regulatory measures, encompassing both binding and non-binding approaches, as well as extraterritorial obligations and policy coherence. One of the most common, yet challenging, obligations is the home state's extraterritorial duty to regulate the overseas activities of MNEs headquartered within its jurisdiction.[253]

---

[248] NCP Germany, ECCHR v. Otto Stadtlander GmbH/Bremen, Final Statement, 7 November 2011.

[249] De Schutter (2020), p. 291.

[250] UN Guiding Principles on Business and Human Rights. Pillar 1: Principles 1–10, Commentary.

[251] Ibid.

[252] Krajewski (2018), p. 20.

[253] Ibid, 33–38; Augenstein (2022), pp. 284–298.

The EU, which is home to many MNEs that cause and contribute human rights abuses and environmental damage internationally, has recently developed a mandatory regulation requiring all applicable multinational corporations to conduct responsible business.[254]

The state's duty to protect under international law incorporates principles such as the 'smart mix' of regulatory measures, policy coherence, and extraterritorial obligations, forming a framework for safeguarding human rights. This duty includes an obligation of result, requiring states to achieve specific outcomes, and an obligation of conduct, requiring states to take concrete steps or adopt measures to fulfil their responsibilities.[255] Under the UNGPs, progress has been made through domestic legislation, including laws with extraterritorial effects.[256] However, the exact scope and definition of these obligations—whether of result or conduct—remain ambiguous and insufficiently explored. As De Schutter notes, 'international human rights instruments generally prescribe only the result to be achieved, leaving the state to choose the means by which it will provide that protection.'[257] This highlights the need to interpret the state's duty as both a procedural obligation and a substantive requirement tied to achieving meaningful outcomes, particularly in addressing corporate abuses.

In particular, the obligation of conduct (referred to in De Schutter as the obligation of means), which demands the state to take certain measures to achieve the result of the duty to protect, has not been adequately discussed in terms of the meaning of the UNGPs. One of the approaches to exercising the duty to protect as an obligation of result is to establish judicial and non-judicial mechanisms to prevent and punish human rights violations by corporations.[258] According to Maria Monnheimer, the obligation of conduct, which complements the duty to protect, would consist of a number of measures, including effective and diligent investigation, redress and punishment of offenders.[259] Member countries of the OECD are required to establish a NCP to act as a state-based non-judicial mechanism to advise companies on responsible business conduct in accordance with the OECD Guidelines and to resolve complaints from individuals about corporate misconduct by offering its good offices between the parties.[260] Despite the fact that NCPs are mandated to promote the implementation of the OECD Guidelines, which focus exclusively on the conduct of MNEs and not on the state's duty to protect human rights from corporate misconduct, some specific cases that have been referred to NCPs (OECD case law) reflect the existing duty of the home and host state and shed

[254] Corporate Sustainability Due Diligence Directive.

[255] De Schutter (2020), p. 436.

[256] UN Guiding Principles on Business and Human Rights, Commentary to the Principle 2.

[257] De Schutter (2020), p. 436.

[258] UN Guiding Principles on Business and Human Rights, Principle 3(c).

[259] Monnheimer (2021), p. 69.

[260] Černic (2008), p. 71.

light on how the state fulfils its obligations to protect as a means of the obligation of result as well as the obligation of conduct.

Some cases show how NCPs fulfil their extraterritorial duties as home state by addressing specific human rights violations that are not subject to their territorial jurisdiction but to their legal jurisdiction. In addition, a number of cases illustrated how states fulfil their duty to protect as a means of fulfilling their obligation of conduct. Based on these analyses, this section of the book argues that the NCP case handling system can be seen as a tool that complements the state duty to protect, in particular the home state's duty to comply with extraterritorial human rights obligations, and that the analysis of the state duty to protect as a means of a obligation of conduct can be derived from the study of OECD cases. This topic should be further discussed to address the critical question of what appropriate conducts entail the state's duty to protect under the meaning of the UNGPs. This section is divided into two sub parts. The first part analyses the state's duty to protect by examining the two forms of obligations under international human rights law: obligations of result and obligations of conduct. It also explores the specific interpretations of the duty to protect under the UNGPs, including both territorial and extraterritorial obligations of host and home states. The second part examines the OECD case law to analyse how states fulfil their duty to protect human rights by dealing with the various cases under the NCP system.

4.6.2 The State's Duty to Protect Individuals from Corporate Abuse: A Perspective on Obligations of Conduct and Result

The UNGPs recall that all States have a positive obligation to protect the human rights of individuals within their territory or jurisdiction from interference by third parties.[261] The duty to protect requires that 'all appropriate measures' be taken to prevent such interference and that, in the event of violations, all necessary legal, regulatory and judicial measures be taken to remedy the harm.[262] De Schutter took a close look at the state's positive duty to protect, arguing that it is not an obligation of result but an obligation of means (in other words, an obligation of conduct), as the obligation to protect requires that all reasonable measures be taken to prevent the breaches and remedy the harm.[263] In order to establish whether the state has breached its duty to protect, it must demonstrate that state could have taken certain measures that could have prevented the event, but yet failed to take such measures.[264] Monnheimer, who has written extensively on the obligation of conduct, argues that

[261] UN Guiding Principles on Business and Human Rights, Commentary to Principle 1.

[262] Ibid, Principle 3.

[263] De Schutter (2020), p. 480.

[264] Ibid.

international human rights law merely requires states to take some kind of action to fulfil their duty to protect.[265] Additionally, she argued that the current international framework does not offer any additional guidance, either on the exact form of positive action that must be taken or on how and when it must be carried out.[266] She also noted that, while there are few recommended positive actions, such as the enactment and implementation of appropriate legal frameworks, the establishment of adequate reparation mechanisms, and the existence and maintenance of effective administrative and judicial institutions, these are more illustrated as an obligation of result.[267]

Although, due to its non-binding nature, the UNGPs are neither comprehensive nor authoritative, it encourage states to take some appropriate measures to protect individuals from corporate human rights abuses.[268] The UNGPs have explicitly emphasised that the state's duty to protect is a norm of conduct, reminding states of their duty to prevent, investigate, punish and remedy violations by third parties.[269] The first 10 principles of Pillar 1 of the UNGPs direct states to fulfil their duty to protect through various actions.[270] Examples include setting explicit expectations and rules for all businesses regarding their responsibility to protect human rights, emphasising responsible business conduct by state-owned or state-affiliated enterprises, and privatisation and doing business in conflict zones. However, according to the standards of an obligation of conduct as set out in Monnheimer's argument, which states that every obligatory action must include all the necessary specific activities to be done step by step and in a timely manner, these recommendations could be considered vague and indeterminate.[271]

However, on some specific issues, such as the enactment of relevant legislation under Principle 3, the UNGPs recommend rather specific measures as a means to fulfil its duty to protect. For example, the state is recommended to focus on specific laws, such as the Securities Act and the Companies Act, in order to influence corporate conduct in relation to human rights.[272]

Additionally, in establishing rules governing corporate obligations to respect human rights, states are encouraged to give particular attention to groups that are especially vulnerable to business-related harm, including Indigenous Peoples, women, national or ethnic minorities, religious and linguistic minorities, children, persons with disabilities, and migrant workers and their families.[273] According to Monnheimer, however, these specific measures could be understood as an obligation of result, because the obligation of conduct that complements this obligation to

[265] Monnheimer (2021), p. 53.

[266] Ibid.

[267] Ibid, 54.

[268] UN Guiding Principles on Business and Human Rights, Principle 1and its Commentary.

[269] Ibid.

[270] Ibid, Principles 1–10.

[271] Monnheimer (2021), p. 53.

[272] UN Guiding Principles on Business and Human Rights, Principle 1 and its Commentary.

[273] Ibid.

enact relevant laws under the third principle of the UNGPs goes beyond the context of the laws and focuses on how the state effectively and diligently implements these laws, taking into account its administrative, budgetary and human resource capacities.[274] Of course, the application of the obligation of conduct could be seen as an unnecessary, comprehensive and unpalatable detail, although the application of this concept is useful for determining the effectiveness of certain actions undertaken by states to fulfil their duty to protect.

Apart from the typology of the state's duty to protect, the limitation of the duty to protect raises some questions. As De Schutter analysed, there may be certain factors that limit the state in fulfilling its duty to protect.[275] In the Osman case, the European Court of Human Rights (ECHR) found that the unpredictability of risks, the capacity of the state, including budgetary constraints due to limited resources, and the conflict between different human rights and obligations can be considered as limiting the fulfilment of the duty to protect.[276] International law expert have expressed similar concern about the limits of the state's duty to protect.[277] Some states, particularly developing countries in the Global South with limited financial resources and structurally weak legal and administrative systems, are more vulnerable to exploitation and corruption and, due to their economic situation, are often unable or unwilling to effectively enforce the duty to protect against powerful transnational corporations.[278]

4.6.2.1 Home States' Extraterritorial Duty to Regulate Corporate Human Rights Impacts

Scholars argued that home state governments should proactively monitor multinational corporations headquartered in their territory and subject to their jurisdiction for human rights violations.[279] When it comes to the home state's duty to protect human rights, there are two aspects to consider: first, the home state's international extraterritorial obligation; and second, the home state's approach to adopting domestic laws with extraterritorial effect to regulate corporations operating in overseas.[280]

Scholars argued that the home state has a duty under international law to control MNEs operating abroad, and some UN treaty bodies have already called on states

---

[274] Monnheimer (2021), p. 69.

[275] De Schutter (2020), p. 481.

[276] European Court of Human Rights Osman v. United Kingdom (Appl. No. 23452/94) judgment of 28 October 1998, paras 115–22.

[277] Krajewski (2018), p. 20.

[278] Ibid.

[279] Augenstein (2022); O'Brien (2018), pp. 47–73; Seck (2011), pp. 25–51.

[280] Augenstein (2022), p. 285.

to apply such a duty when upholding certain human rights.[281] However, the UNGPs have explicitly stated that home states do not have a general duty to regulate the extraterritorial activities of companies domiciled in their territory, raising the argument that the UNGPs are a weak formulation of home states' duty to protect, encouraging them to hesitate in recognising such obligations.[282] O'Brien takes issue with the inability of UNGPs to recognise extraterritorial jurisdiction under international human rights law, arguing that states may have a duty not only to regulate MNEs within their territorial jurisdiction, but also those subject to their legal jurisdiction.[283] She also argued that although under international law the general jurisdiction of each state is primarily territorial, states may seek to control the conduct of their nationals or protect them outside their territory.[284] However, O'Brien doubted the existence of a concrete obligation on the home state to control MNEs abroad, referring case law and the provisions of UN in the context of international human rights. She argued that the home state's extraterritorial human rights obligations lack legal basis in international human rights law, after examining the scope and limits of the state's extraterritorial human rights obligations in both the spatial and personal models.[285]

Adding to this, Markus Krajewski argued that the duty of the home state to regulate MNEs outside its territory should not be examined solely on the basis of territorial or jurisdictional requirements, but should be discussed on the basis of the scope of the duty to protect under international human rights law.[286] Referring to the comments of the UN Committee on the Rights of Child, he argued that this duty to protect should be reasonably linked to human rights risks and whether the fulfilment of this duty can prevent or mitigate human rights risks.[287] Furthermore, he argued that the duty of the home state does not depend on the host state's inability and weakness in protecting human rights, but is an independent obligation based on its own human rights responsibilities.[288] Looking at the recent practises of states in adopting certain laws and requirements to control the activities of MNEs outside their territory, he argued that there is a strong argument that states have a duty to regulate the transnational business activities of corporations beyond their territory.[289]

---

281 UN Committee on the Rights of the Child (CRC), General Comment No. 16 (2013) on State Obligations regarding the Impact of the Business Sector on Children's Rights, UN Doc CRC/C/GC/16 (17 April 2013); UN Committee on Economic, Social and Cultural Rights, General Comment No. 24 (2017) on State obligations under the International Covenant on Economic, Social and Cultural Rights in the context of business activities, UN Doc E/C.12/GC/24 (10 August 2017).

282 UN Guiding Principles on Business and Human Rights, Principle 2 and its Commentary.

283 O'Brien (2018), p. 51.

284 Ibid.

285 Ibid, 61.

286 Krajewski (2018), p. 23.

287 Ibid, 27.

288 Ibid, 23.

289 Ibid, 30.

Daniel Augenstein also refers to the comments of the UN Committee on the Rights of the Child and other UN treaty bodies, as well as the Maastricht Principles on the extraterritorial obligations of states in the area of economic, social and cultural rights (the Maastricht Principles), and argues that extraterritorial obligations can be recognised in international human rights law.[290] The Maastricht Principles, which specifies in its Principle 24 that 'states must take the necessary measures to ensure that non-state actors they can regulate… do not undermine or interfere with economic, social and cultural rights'.[291] Following Krajewski, Augenstein also examined recent state practise in the development of domestic regulations and found that the increasing development of domestic regulations with extraterritorial effect also influences the recognition of the state's extraterritorial duty to regulate the activities of multinational corporations abroad.[292]

These analysis show that while there are persistent arguments denying an extraterritorial duty of the state to protect human rights from corporate abuse outside its territory, the increasing development of domestic legislation focusing on transparency, corporate or supply chain due diligence strengthens the argument in favour of the duty of the home state to protect cross-border human rights risks from corporate abuse. Moreover, Seck argued that if international law recognises the home state's extraterritorial duty to protect, compliance with that duty requires further scrutiny of the state's conduct, including facilitating corporate compliance with its responsibility to respect rights and facilitating access to remedies for victims of human rights violations.[293] Therefore, the future discourse on business and human rights should be further developed to explore the strengthening of such a duty to protect, rather than continuing the debate on the existence of such a responsibility in the international human rights framework. Thus, further analysis on the state's duty to protect against extraterritorial human rights violations could focus on the question of what appropriate conduct the state's extraterritorial duty to protect entails from the perspective of the concept of the obligation of conduct and its connection to the requirements under the Pillar I of the UNGPs.

4.6.2.2 State Duty to Employ Regulative Measures: Advancing a Smart Mix Approach

Alongside the state's extraterritorial duty to regulate MNEs, domestic regulatory approaches and policy measures have become central to ensuring corporate compliance with international human rights and environmental standards. These measures reflect a combination of binding and non-binding regulatory frameworks aimed at

[290] The Maastricht Principles on the Extraterritorial Obligations of States in the Area of Economic, Social and Cultural Rights https://www.fidh.org/IMG/pdf/maastricht-eto-principles-uk_web.pdf (accessed 2 February 2026).

[291] Ibid, Principle 24.

[292] Augenstein (2022), p. 285.

[293] Seck (2011), p. 31.

addressing corporate conduct, as highlighted by Wettstein, who categorised binding measures into three key groups: transparency and disclosure legislation, HRDD legislation, and HRDD laws incorporating corporate liability provisions.[294] The first category of transparency and disclosure legislation require companies to report on their processes and practices in relation to specific BHR issues. Such laws primarily focus on enhancing corporate accountability by making business operations more transparent.[295] Examples of these laws include the UK Modern Slavery Act, the Australian Modern Slavery Act, and the California Transparency in Supply Chains Act.[296] These legislative measures compel companies to publicly disclose information about their efforts to combat modern slavery and human trafficking within their supply chains.[297] As Wettstein argued, while such laws represent significant progress in promoting corporate transparency, they often fail to impose substantive obligations on companies to mitigate human rights risks or ensure actual compliance.[298] For example, the UK Modern Slavery Act mandates companies to publish annual statements detailing measures taken to combat slavery and human trafficking, but it lacks enforcement mechanisms to penalise non-compliance or ensure meaningful action. Similarly, the California Transparency in Supply Chains Act requires companies to disclose their policies and supply chain practices but does not compel them to actively prevent or address abuses.

The second category includes HRDD legislation that requires companies to identify, prevent, and mitigate human rights risks in their operations and supply chains. Examples include LkSG, the Dutch Child Labour Due Diligence Law, and the Dodd-Frank Act.[299] These laws extend beyond transparency requirements, imposing proactive obligations on companies to conduct due diligence, assess risks, establish grievance mechanisms, and report their measures. The Dodd-Frank Act specifically addresses BHR issues such as the use of conflict minerals, requiring companies to disclose sourcing practices to avoid contributing to conflicts or human rights abuses.[300] This legislation illustrates how HRDD measures can adapt to address sector-specific risks effectively. However, the Dodd-Frank Act has faced legal and practical challenges.[301] For instance, under the Trump administration, the Securities and Exchange Commission (SEC) suspended enforcement of the rule. Also, opinions on

---

294 Wettstein (2022), pp. 240–241.

295 Ibid, 242–244.

296 UK Modern Slavery Act and Australian Modern Slavery Act; The California Transparency in Supply Chains Act.

297 Wettstein (2022), pp. 244–245.

298 Ibid, 246–247.

299 The Act on Corporate Due Diligence Obligations in Supply Chains (Lieferkettensorgfaltspflichtengesetz, LkSG) 22 July 2021; Child Labour Due Diligence Act; The United States Securities and Exchange Commission (SEC), Section 1502 of the 2010 Dodd-Frank Wall Street Reform and Consumer Protection Act (Dodd-Frank Act) https://www.sec.gov/files/rules/final/2012/34-67716.pdf (accessed 2 February 2026).

300 Wettstein (2022), pp. 248–251.

301 Ibid.

its impact also vary significantly.[302] Some scholars argue that the Act helped reduce the black market for conflict minerals, which fuels violence and human rights violations.[303] Conversely, others contend that such Western interventions can harm local communities, increasing smuggling and other illicit activities among artisanal miners.[304]

Under the LkSG, companies within its scope must fulfil HRDD obligations and notify the Federal Office for Economic Affairs and Export Control (BAFA) of any identified adverse impacts.[305] Non-compliance can result in fines (up to 50,000 euros and up to 2 percent of their annual turnover) and reputational damage, while affected rights-holders can file complaints with BAFA, initiating investigations.[306] However, Germany appears hesitant to enforce the law rigorously. According to BAFA's 2023 Accountability Report, 30 complaints were filed in the first year, involving 40 companies, with six leading to investigations.[307] Rather than imposing significant sanctions, BAFA has prioritised cooperation and auditing to support companies in developing their HRDD processes effectively.[308]

The most advanced HRDD legislation includes corporate liability provisions, enabling victims to seek remedies when companies fail to meet their due diligence obligations. France's Duty of Vigilance Law is a key example, requiring large companies to establish and implement vigilance plans to identify and mitigate human rights and environmental risks.[309] What distinguishes this legislation is its corporate liability framework, allowing affected individuals to hold companies accountable for harm caused by inadequate vigilance plans.[310] By linking due diligence with legal liability, the Duty of Vigilance Law significantly advances corporate accountability and access to remedies, providing a strong incentive for companies to address risks effectively. However, practical challenges persist, particularly in proving causation between corporate actions and harm suffered, which can limit the effectiveness of liability provisions.[311] This was evident in the first case under the Duty of

302 Sadaf Naushad 'Why Section 1502 of The Dodd-Frank Act Cannot Solve the Humanitarian Crisis in the Democratic Republic of Congo' University of Denver https://djilp.org/why-section-1502-of-the-dodd-frank-act-cannot-solve-the-humanitarian-crisis-in-the-democratic-republic-of-congo/#_ftn1 (accessed 2 February 2026).

303 Wettstein (2022), p. 250; Whitney (2015), pp. 182–200.

304 Ibid; Taylor (2015), p. 205.

305 The Act on Corporate Due Diligence Obligations in Supply Chains (Lieferkettensorgfaltspflichtengesetz, LkSG) 22 July 2021, Section 19.

306 The Act on Corporate Due Diligence Obligations in Supply Chains (Lieferkettensorgfaltspflichtengesetz, LkSG) 22 July 2021, Sections 23 and 24(3).

307 BAFA 'Rechenschaftsbericht 2023' https://www.bafa.de/SharedDocs/Downloads/DE/Lieferketten/rechenschaftsbericht_2023.html (accessed 2 February 2026).

308 Linklaters 'German watchdog reports on the first year of the Supply Chain Act' 15 October 2024 https://sustainablefutures.linklaters.com/post/102jlse/german-watchdog-reports-on-the-first-year-of-the-supply-chain-act (accessed 2 February 2026).

309 Duty of Vigilance Law; Savourey and Brabant (2021), pp. 141–152.

310 Ibid, 144–145.

311 Soilihi and Haranger (2024).

Vigilance Law, where six CSOs sued Total for allegedly omitting its Ugandan oil project from its vigilance plan, claiming violations of the law.[312] Total denied the allegations, asserting its plan adequately addressed risks. Despite jurisdictional disputes, France's Supreme Court ruled in December 2021 that the civil court had authority to hear the case.[313] However, in February 2023, the court dismissed the case on procedural grounds, citing inconsistencies in the plaintiffs' submissions.[314] The decision affirms the persistent challenges in using liability provisions to enforce corporate accountability.

The adoption of these legislative measures reflects the state's obligation of result, aiming to protect individuals from corporate abuses. However, their effective implementation and enforcement represent an obligation of conduct, requiring ongoing action to fulfil this commitment. Transparency and disclosure laws have laid the groundwork for accountability, while HRDD legislation takes a more proactive approach by directly addressing risk mitigation. The inclusion of corporate liability provisions strengthens these frameworks by providing mechanisms for remedy and deterrence. Nevertheless, further attention is needed to examine how enforcement, implementation, and specific actions fulfil the state's obligation of conduct in realising this state duty to protect.

In addition to legislative measures, states are encouraged to implement complementary policy initiatives that enhance corporate accountability and strengthen human rights protections. These include the adoption of NAPs on BHR, public procurement reforms, and leveraging the influence of export credit agencies and investment guarantees.[315] NAPs serve as critical policy tools, providing governments with strategic orientation and a roadmap to address key BHR challenges within their territories.[316] These plans help states align their policies with the UNGPs by outlining priorities, proposing legislative and policy measures to regulate companies, and setting mechanisms for monitoring and enforcement.[317] Importantly, NAPs also create a platform for stakeholder engagement, allowing diverse groups, including civil society, businesses, and affected communities, to voice their concerns and contribute to solutions.[318] By integrating input from multiple actors, NAPs offer a comprehensive framework for advancing corporate accountability and human rights protection.

Public procurement, a powerful policy tool for promoting sustainable and ethical practices, represents another significant area for enhancing human rights

---

[312] BHRRC, Total Lawsuit (Re Failure To Respect French Duty Of Vigilance Law In Operations In Uganda) 23 October 2019 Https://Www.Business-Humanrights.Org/En/Latest-News/Total-Lawsuit-Re-Failure-To-Respect-French-Duty-Of-Vigilance-Law-In-Operations-In-Uganda/ (accessed 2 February 2026).

[313] Ibid.

[314] Ibid.

[315] Wettstein (2022), pp. 233–240.

[316] Ibid, 234–235.

[317] O'Brien et al. (2022), p. 72.

[318] Ibid, 79.

compliance.[319] Procurement procedures, however, are primarily regulated by the WTO's Plurilateral Agreement on Government Procurement, which, as Wettstein highlights, has traditionally prioritised competition and non-discrimination over sustainability and human rights.[320] Recent efforts, such as new EU public procurement directives, aim to incorporate human rights considerations into procurement policies. Despite these advancements, gaps remain, as these directives often fail to fully address human rights concerns.[321] In contrast, the UK Modern Slavery Act explicitly mandates public buyers to consider human rights in their procurement processes, representing a progressive step towards embedding human rights into state purchasing practices.[322] As for the ECAs and investment guarantees, they are also essential tools for promoting cross-border trade and investment, as they provide financing and risk mitigation for exporting companies.[323] These agencies hold significant leverage over MNEs, given their role in facilitating global business activities.[324] By linking state-backed financial support to compliance with human rights due diligence and ethical standards, ECAs can influence corporate practices, ensuring that businesses benefiting from these guarantees align with international human rights norms.[325] Such conditionality enhances the accountability of companies operating in complex global markets and supports the broader goal of integrating human rights into international trade and investment.

These policy measures—NAPs, public procurement reforms, and export credit conditions—work alongside legislative frameworks to create a more cohesive and effective system for clarifying the state's duty to protect. By addressing critical gaps and leveraging state influence across various sectors, these initiatives strengthen the state's obligation of conduct. They also complement the state's duty to regulate MNEs, ensuring respect for human rights and environmental rights within economic activities conducted in the state's territory.

From the perspective of the state's duty to protect, these measures embody a combination of obligations of result and obligations of conduct. On the one hand, they pursue concrete outcomes—such as reducing human rights abuses and strengthening corporate accountability—thereby reflecting obligations of result. For instance, NAPs establish explicit objectives to address BHR issues, public procurement policies integrate human rights criteria, and export credit conditions enforce compliance through financial leverage. On the other hand, these measures also entail obligations of conduct, emphasising procedural dimensions such as stakeholder engagement, institutional reform, and monitoring frameworks. While such

---

[319] Martin-Ortega (2018), pp. 75–95.

[320] World Trade Organisation 'Agreement on Government Procurement' (GPA) 2012 https://www.wto.org/english/docs_e/legal_e/rev-gpr-94_01_e.pdf (accessed 2 February 2026).

[321] Wettstein (2022), p. 237.

[322] Ibid.

[323] Ibid, 238–239.

[324] Ibid.

[325] Ibid.

procedural efforts may not guarantee immediate or quantifiable results, they underline the state's duty to act in good faith and to take proactive, continuous steps towards fulfilment. Effectively promoting corporate accountability therefore requires states to balance these two dimensions—ensuring that robust procedural mechanisms (obligations of conduct) are accompanied by tangible and measurable outcomes (obligations of result).

4.6.2.3 Critical Analysis and Conclusion: Scrutinising the State's Duty to Protect the BHR Related Potential and Actual Harms

This section shifts the focus to critically analysing how the legislative and policy measures discussed—legislative and policy frameworks such as NAPs, public procurement reforms, and export credit conditions—align with the dual concepts of obligations of result and conduct. These two obligations provide a lens to evaluate the effectiveness of state actions in fulfilling their duty to protect under the UNGPs. Monnheimer's suggested obligation of conduct goes beyond the obligation of result by looking not only at the implementation of the obligation, but at the effectiveness and diligence to analyse how this implementation achieves the effective outcomes.[326] For example, if the obligation of result is the enactment of specific laws and regulations to fulfil the duty to prevent the potential harms and protect human rights, the obligation of conduct will consider the course of action that establishes an adequate budget, human resources, and administrative capacity to oversee and ensure the implementation of such obligation.[327] If the obligation arising from the duty to protect is to establish a judicial or non-judicial mechanism to punish companies that have violated human rights, the corresponding obligation to conduct means that States should ensure that this redress mechanism diligently carries out the relevant concrete measures, including effective investigation and the imposition of an appropriate penalty.[328]

Applying this concept to the state's duty to protect, including the extraterritorial duty to protect, examines what measures the state takes to effectively implement this duty to protect. Although there are many ways to examine how States implement their duty to protect and what concrete measures they take by examining their State initiatives on corporate social responsibility, their adopted domestic HRDD legislation and the NAPs,[329] one effective way is to examine how they deal with the specific alleged extraterritorial human rights violations caused by companies domiciled in their territory.[330] Therefore, examining the OECD cases, which are one of the most

[326] Monnheimer (2021), p. 69.

[327] Ibid, 71.

[328] Ibid, 71–72.

[329] Catá Backer (2014).

[330] United Nations. Human Rights Council 'Report of the United Nations High Commissioner for Human Rights: Improving accountability and access to remedy for victims of business-related human rights abuses' 10 May 2016 Un Doc A/HRC/32/19.

effective non-judicial state mechanisms for dealing with the various human rights violations committed by MNEs allows us to see how the duty of conduct can be developed by strengthening the specific measures that give rise to the duty to protect.

The purpose of the research of this section was to analyse the state's duty to protect human rights under the UNGPs and how it reflected on the OECD case law when the NCPs handled human rights violations by MNEs. First, it examined the state's duty to protect using the concept of 'obligation of conduct' that De Schutter and Monnheimer had previously examined. According to De Schutter and Monnheimer, state responsibility for the protection of human rights should be assessed on the basis of the concept of the obligation of conduct rather than the obligation of result, since international law obliges states to take all necessary reasonable means to fulfil their duty to protect. Further, it examined the specific legislative and policy measures that states implement to fulfil their duty to protect individuals and victims from potential and actual corporate abuses, analysing arguments surrounding their effectiveness. This raises the question of whether a state has adequately fulfilled its duty to protect, considering the full scope of measures it has to undertake. According to Monnheimer's extensive research, the obligation of conduct should therefore complement the state duty to protect as the obligation of result, by looking at the concrete actions states have taken in fulfilling their duty. For this reason, this section highlights the importance of concrete actions and policy measures taken by states in fulfilling their duties. However, further attention must be given to other critical issues, such as establishing adequate state agencies equipped with sufficient human and financial resources to effectively implement and monitor compliance with state policies and regulations. These aspects need to be thoroughly examined and evaluated in the context of the UNGPs.

In addition, next subsection will examine various OECD cases handled by different states, such as the UK, the Netherlands, France and Norway, to analyse how states fulfil their duty to protect as a means of the duty to conduct by bringing their own state commitment to international human rights standards to bear on the cases they handle. In addition, states fulfil their duty to protect by addressing the extraterritorial human rights violations of multinational corporations seated at their territory and recommending that they comply with international human rights laws endorsed by their own state in their overseas activities. Following some of these good examples set under the NCP system, states, especially the home states of MNEs, can fulfil their duty to protect by taking a number of concrete measures that could actually give effect to their duty.

4.6.3 OECD Case Law Insights: The Role of the State in Ensuring Corporate Human Rights Compliance

NCPs are one of the most important tools for holding companies accountable for their human rights violations and enabling them to take meaningful corrective action. They also contribute to the current development of corporate responsibility in the field of human rights, which affects various industries and economic actors. NCPs are also distinct in enabling affected rights holders to directly approach company management or the parent company to bring the misconduct of their foreign subsidiaries to their attention. However, as mentioned above, NCPs are exclusively focused on the human rights and environmental activities of companies and not on examining the responsibility of the State to respect, fulfil and protect human rights on its territory. This was confirmed by the OECD Investment Committee when it responded to OECD Watch's letter regarding the Australian NCPs handling the complaint submitted by the Human Rights Law Centre (HRLC) and Rights and Accountability in Development (RAID) against G4S Australia Pty Ltd.[331] OECD Watch reported to the Investment Committee that the Australian NCP did not handle the case against G4S in an accessible and impartial manner, given the company's service contract with the state, and thus incorrectly mixed the state obligation to protect human rights and corporate responsibility to respect human rights.[332] In its response, the OECD Investment Committee explicitly pointed out that the NCP deals with the responsibility of companies to respect human rights and the related due diligence obligations, but not with the duty of the state to protect human rights.[333]

Nevertheless, the Investment Committee pointed out that the OECD Guidelines briefly mention the responsibility of the state in its Chapter IV: Human Rights, and recommended that NCPs should clearly distinguish between these different obligations when handling cases.[334] However, since in most countries NCPs are located within the government and the state is mandated to operate NCPs as part of its commitment to sustainable development and the protection of human rights, as stated in the foreword to the OECD Guidelines, it is not possible for NCPs to distinguish between the responsibility of the state and that of the company when handling cases. In resolving various matters, NCPs often consider cases on the basis of their own state's human rights obligations, commitments, practises and perspectives. States' responsibility to protect human rights, including their extraterritorial obligations, may thus be reflected in how they resolve human rights violations committed abroad. In this subsection, various OECD cases will be analysed to examine different forms of state involvement and assess how OECD case law contributes to understanding the state's duty to protect.

---

[331] OECD Investment Committee 'Response by the Investment Committee to the Substantiated Submission by OECD Watch regarding the Australian National Contact Point' 30 November 2018 DAF/INV (2018)34/FINAL.

[332] Ibid, para 13a.

[333] Ibid, para 42.

[334] Ibid, para 41.

4.6.3.1 State Complicity in Human Rights Violations by Multinational Enterprises

Research into the OECD case law reveals instances where states have been complicit in human rights violations alleged against MNEs. These cases are crucial to include in this book to understand how NCPs approach and address situations where state involvement is evident. In some cases, states are not only complicit but also act as primary perpetrators of human rights violations, often in facilitation or collaboration with companies. This cooperation raises significant challenges for NCPs, as they must navigate the complexity of addressing corporate complicity while also holding states accountable for their own human rights violations. These cases highlight the difficulty of ensuring accountability when both state and corporate actors are implicated.

Adding to the above-mentioned case against G4S Australia Pty Ltd filed with the Australian NCP by HRLC and RAID, there are several other cases, including the case against Serco Group Pty Ltd filed with the Australian NCP by Professor Ben Saul, the case against British Telecommunications PLC filed by Reprieve at UK NCP and the case against G4S filed by LPHR at UK NCP, all of which show how the NCP ignores the human rights violations of the state and the complicity of the company.[335] Similar to G4S Australia Pty Ltd, Serco Group Pty Ltd had a service contract with the Australian Department of Immigration to provide refugee detention services in Australia.[336] The complainant Ben Saul referred to the report of the UN Human Rights Committee to highlight the human rights violations in these detention centres and called on Serco to review its contract with the Australian government to comply with its obligation under the OECD Guidelines.[337] However, the Australian NCP rejected the case on the grounds that the NCP could not resolve this case due to a number of complex political and national security considerations and that the matter in this case was not covered by the OECD Guidelines.[338]

UK NCP also handled the case against BT in the similar way. In this particular case, Reprieve stated that BT had allowed UK and US intelligence agencies to intercept customers' communications in order to obtain information for US military operations in Yemen.[339] UK NCP also pointed out that this matter was not covered by the obligations of the OECD Guidelines and that the allegation had already been resolved by the Investigatory Powers Tribunal, a UK judicial body that hears

[335] NCP Australia 'Statement by the Australian National Contact Point: Specific Instance – G4S Australia Pty Ltd' 10 June 2015; NCP Australia, Ben Saul on behalf of refugees detained in Australia, v. SERCO Group Pty Ltd' Final Statement, 10 August 2017; NCP United Kingdom, Lawyers for Palestinian Human Rights (LPHR) v. G4S, Final Statement, 7 July 2016; NCP United Kingdom, Reprieve v. BT, Initial Statement, 10 February 2015.

[336] Ibid, NCP Australia, Ben Saul v. Serco, paras 1–2.

[337] Ibid, paras 15–16.

[338] Ibid, paras 24–25.

[339] UK NCP, Reprieve v. BT, Initial Statement.

complaints about surveillance by public bodies, and was considered a lawful action.[340] Also, in case against Corriente Resources in Canadian NCP, the complainant also stated in the complaint that the government of Ecuador is complicit in forced evictions and violence against communities by Corriente Resources.[341] In its initial decision, the Canadian NCP specifically pointed out that the state's conduct was beyond the powers of the Canadian NCP and dismissed the complaint because there was insufficient evidence of a link between the alleged abuse and the company.[342]

On contrary to the NCPs of the United Kingdom and Australia, some NCPs set a good but rare example by successfully and impartially resolving cases related to their own and other state's misconduct. For example, in the case against Atradius Dutch State Business (ADSB), the Dutch NCP engaged with the Ministry of Finance in addition to the ADSB and recommended that both develop a more specific policy to comply with the OECD Guidelines.[343] Above analysed cases show that NCPs are often not able to impartially resolve cases where the state itself has committed the human rights violations and where the companies are involved. The current discourse on BHR and recent legal developments often ignore the interrelationship between the state and business when it comes to addressing human rights violations.[344]

4.6.3.2 Examples of Home States' Duty to Regulate MNEs Abroad in OECD Cases

Due to sovereignty and non-interference in the affairs of the other state, NCPs are of course not obliged to solve the cases of human rights violations of the other state, but since the home state is obliged to protect human rights, it still has control over the companies located in its territory. The UNGPs, Principle 7 require States to ensure that companies operating in high-risk areas are not implicated in human rights abuses by adopting regulatory measures and providing assistance in conducting risk assessments.[345] While this principle does not explicitly refer to the interrelationship between the state and corporations, it states that corporations should not take advantage of the weak situation of the state and should not be complicit in the violation of human rights. According to this Principle 7, states, particularly home states, should ensure that they have a policy that requires their companies not to

[340] Ibid, paras 20, 25.

[341] NCP Canada, CEDHU and Mining Watch against Corriente Resources in Mirador Mine in Ecuador, Initial Statement, 24 July 2014.

[342] Ibid.

[343] Dutch NCP 'NCP Evaluation Final Statement Both Ends v. ADSB' 3 May 2018 https://www.oecdguidelines.nl/latest/news/2018/05/03/ncp-evaluation-final-statement-both-ends-vs-adsb (accessed 2 February 2026).

[344] Davies (2022).

[345] UN Guiding Principles on Business and Human Rights, Commentary to Principle 7.

cooperate with foreign states in human rights violations.[346] This state duty to protect needs to be further explored under the concept of the obligation to conduct. This means that states must not only adopt policies and regulations but also take effective measures to monitor and control compliance with these policies. From this point of view, some cases could have been strategically handled differently.

For example, the case against Serco should have been filed with the UK NCP rather than the Australian NCP. Because Serco is a UK-based company, the UK NCP has the option of resolving the case through Serco's detention services in Australia and simply recommending that Serco review its contract with the Australian government to comply with the OECD Guidelines. It can also further recommend Serco to terminate its contract with the Australian government if Serco believes that it cannot leverage Australian government to mitigate the negative human rights impacts associated with the detention services contract. According to this analysis of OECD cases, states, especially home states, must take and effectively implement measures to ensure that companies based in their country cannot collude with the government of the other state to commit human rights violations.

Several states, including the UK, pursue this type of policy. For example, in the case against G4S in the UK NCP, G4S was accused of supplying security products to the Israeli government that were used for Israeli operations in the OPT.[347] In the context of the case against G4S, UK NCP pointed out that the UK's Overseas Commercial Risk Guidance clearly states that the UK government does not promote commercial links with settlements in the occupied Palestinian territories, as these are illegal under international law and have corresponding negative consequences.[348] Therefore, UK NCP recommended G4S to review its business activities with Israeli partners in order to address the negative impacts mentioned in the complaint.[349]

In addition, In the NCP complaint mechanism, it is common for complainants to file cases concerning human rights violations committed by foreign subsidiaries with the NCP of the parent company's home state. Such complaints have frequently been accepted, reflecting a growing recognition that parent companies bear responsibility for overseeing the conduct of their subsidiaries abroad. This practice also illustrates how home states may fulfil their extraterritorial obligation to protect human rights by addressing transnational corporate structures. NCPs play a pivotal role in linking harms caused by subsidiaries to the responsibility of parent companies, thereby operationalising the notion of shared accountability across corporate groups. However, an examination of concrete cases reveals that the scope and effectiveness of this extraterritorial obligation vary significantly, depending on the political will, interpretative approach, and human rights commitments of the respective home state.

---

346 Ibid.

347 NPC United Kingdom, LPHR against G4S, Final Statement, 10 June 2015.

348 Ibid, para 49.

349 Ibid, para 80.

4.6.3.3 State Policy and Regulatory Measures Reflected in OECD Case Law

The leading NCPs, including those of the Netherlands and Norway, often take into account their own country's practise and commitment to human rights when investigating human rights violations by companies based in their territory. For example, in the cases against ING and Mylan, in which these companies are accused of violating human rights obligations related to the death penalty and climate change, the Dutch NCP took into account both the Netherlands' commitment to the Paris Agreement and the Netherlands' views on the death penalty.[350] In the case of the pharmaceutical company Mylan, which is accused of supplying lethal injections to US prisons for capital punishment, members of the Dutch Parliament and the Ministry of Foreign Trade and Development Cooperation took the allegation seriously and informed Mylan to adhere to the Dutch CSR policy to avoid involvement in human rights violations anywhere in the world.[351] They also claimed that the Netherlands considers the death penalty to be a significant violation of human rights and therefore advised Mylan to make contractual arrangements with its US partners to reduce the risk of its drugs being used in executions.[352]

In the case against Statkraft SCA Vind AB (SSVAB), the Norwegian NCP pointed out that Norway has ratified the ILO Convention 169—the Indigenous and Tribal Peoples Convention—and claimed that the Norwegian authorities expect state-owned enterprises like SSVAB to respect human rights in their activities.[353] This practise by NCPs of handling certain cases in light of their own human rights commitments demonstrate that the duty of the home state to protect human rights can be strengthened if it embeds its own strong human rights obligations in its governance structure. Furthermore, some NCPs, such as the French NCP, appear to attempt to link the NCP case handling system to their own binding human rights due diligence legislation by assessing compliance and implementation of the Duty of Vigilance Act when evaluating the company's RBC following a complaint received by their NCP. In the cases concerning the COPAGEF Group and Teleperformance, the French NCP assessed the vigilance plan of both companies in the context of human rights due diligence.[354] In the case of Teleperformance, the French NCP paid particular attention to Teleperformance's vigilance plan to assess whether it contained a sufficient policy and plan to protect workers' health and safety related rights during the Covid-19 pandemic and provided specific guidance on how to

---

[350] OECD Watch 'Final Statement: Bart Stapert attorneys v. Mylan:' 3 March 2015 https://www.oecdwatch.org/complaint/bart-stapert-vs-mylan/ (accessed 2 February 2026).

[351] Ibid, 3.

[352] Ibid.

[353] NCP Sweden, Jijnjevaerie Saami village v. Statkraft SCA Vind AB (SSVAB), Final Statement, 8 February 2016.

[354] NCP France UNI v. Teleperformance, Final Statement, 5 July 2021; NCP France, 14 Local Watch Committees and Centre of Actions for Life and Earth against COPAGEF, SOMDIAA and SOSUCAM in Cameroon, Final Statement, 17 May 2022.

improve the plan.[355] These examples show that the NCP system can complement the duty of home state to protect human rights by imposing a human rights due diligence obligation on multinational corporations established in its territory and monitoring their compliance.

In addition, there are some notable cases that have actually provided actual remedy to the affected rightsholders under the NCP system. One of them is the case between the former Bralima employees and Bralima and Heineken, which has already been extensively analysed by human rights scholars.[356] As Bhatt and Türkelli noted, the political will of the Dutch government, which paid for the participants in this case to work on the ground and for several face-to-face meetings to successfully mediate between the parties, was crucial to this successful case.[357] Bhatt and Türkelli, in their analysis of the background to this case, highlighted that 'the success or failure of accountability sought through NCPs depends on an NCP's own networks, funding and priorities, such as the individual quality of a particular NCP, budgetary resources, flexibility of the process and the people sitting at the mediation table. This means that extremely fragmented, unpredictable and opaque institutional variables determine whether a case is successful or not'.[358] This analysis reaffirms earlier research suggesting that international law should offer more precise guidance to states in fulfilling their duty to protect human rights. In particular, the OECD NCP case examples provide valuable insights into the concrete measures that states can adopt to give practical effect to this obligation.

In order to strengthen the State's duty to protect human rights, in particular the home state's duty to protect human rights extraterritorially, further guidance and analysis is needed to discuss specific concrete measures as a means to fulfil 'the obligation of conduct' mentioned in the previous chapter, including the appropriate human and resource capacities to implement some of the measures, including specific measures for the operation of the NCP and the monitoring of mandatory HRDD. Thus, when it comes to operating non-judicial mechanisms such as NCPs within their government agencies, states should, in line with the obligation of conduct, consider an approach that provides for adequate budget, staff and administrative capacity to monitor and ensure implementation so that NCPs can achieve more effective and successful outcomes in the cases they handle. Moreover, the OECD case law mentioned above are examples of how states can link their duty to enforce mandatory HRDD legislations with the help of NCPs in assessing corporate responsible business conduct under the NCP system to their own international human rights obligations, and how they can also link the case handling process to their own international human rights commitments.

---

[355] Ibid, Teleperformance case.

[356] Bhatt and Türkelli (2021), pp. 423–448.

[357] Ibid, 438–439.

[358] Ibid, 432.

4.6.3.4 Preliminary Conclusion

The analysis of OECD case law provided valuable insights into how states address their duty to protect human rights, particularly in the context of business-related harms. NCPs serve as a crucial mechanism for holding companies accountable, facilitating meaningful dialogue, and recommending corrective action. However, the findings indicate that NCPs primarily focus on corporate responsibilities rather than directly addressing the state's obligations to respect, protect, and fulfil human rights. This limitation is evident in cases where state complicity in human rights violations complicates the accountability process, as seen in examples involving G4S, Serco, and other MNEs.

While some NCPs, such as those in the Netherlands, Norway, and France, have demonstrated innovative approaches by linking their case handling to domestic human rights obligations and mandatory HRDD legislation, others have struggled to impartially resolve cases involving state actors. For instance, the UK and Australian NCPs dismissed cases involving state complicity, citing jurisdictional or political limitations. This inconsistency highlights the need for stronger guidance and institutional capacity to address both corporate and state responsibilities effectively.

The concept of the state's 'obligation of conduct,' as discussed in earlier chapters, is particularly relevant here. To fulfil this obligation, states must not only enact policies and regulations but also ensure their implementation through adequate resources, monitoring mechanisms, and institutional support. Successful cases, such as the Bralima-Heineken case, demonstrated that the effectiveness of NCPs depends heavily on the political will, funding, and operational capacity of the home state.[359] This reflects the importance of embedding human rights commitments within state governance structures and ensuring that NCPs are equipped to handle complex cases involving both corporate and state actors. Ultimately, the analysis highlighted that NCPs could play a pivotal role in bridging the gap between corporate accountability and state responsibility. However, for this potential to be fully realised, states must strengthen the institutional capacity of NCPs, align their domestic policies with international human rights standards, and integrate mandatory due diligence requirements into their case-handling processes.

Cases

Chandler v. Cape plc [2012] 1 WLR 3111.
Fadeyeva v. Russia, Judgment, 45 Eur.Ct.H.R. 10, para. 92 (2005).
Four Nigerian Farmers v. Shell, the Hague Court of Appeal, 29 January 2021, ECLI:NL:GHDHA:2021.
Vedanta Resources plc v. Lungowe [2019] UKSC 20 [Vedanta].

[359] NCP Netherlands, Former employees vs. Bralima, Heineken, Final Statement, 18 August 2017.

Legislations

Australia. *Modern Slavery Act 2018 (Cth)*. No. 153. Canberra: Federal Register of Legislation, 2018.

European Union. Regulation 2019/2088 on sustainability-related disclosures in the financial services sector. [2019] OJ L317/1.

European Court of Human Rights Osman v. United Kingdom (Appl. No. 23452/94) judgment of 28 October 1998.

Germany. *Act on Corporate Due Diligence Obligations in Supply Chains (Lieferkettensorgfaltspflichtengesetz, LkSG)*. 22 July 2021.

The United States Securities and Exchange Commission (SEC). *Section 1502 of the 2010 Dodd-Frank Wall Street Reform and Consumer Protection Act (Dodd-Frank Act)* 2012 https://www.sec.gov/files/rules/final/2012/34-67716.pdf (accessed 2 February 2026).

United Kingdom. *Modern Slavery Act 2015*. c. 30.

Documents

BankTrack 'Global Human Rights Benchmark 2024' November 2024 https://www.banktrack.org/download/the_banktrack_global_human_rights_benchmark_2024/banktrack_human_rights_benchmark_2024_1.pdf#page=6.25 (accessed 2 February 2026).

Equator Principles 'Equator Principles: A financial industry benchmark for determining, assessing and managing environmental and social risk in projects' 2020 https://equator-principles.com/about-the-equator-principles/ (accessed 2 February 2026).

Glasgow Financial Alliance for Net Zero (GFANZ). *Towards a Global Baseline for Net-zero Transition Planning*. November 2022. https://www.gfanzero.com (accessed 2 February 2026).

Investor Alliance for Human Rights. *Investor Toolkit for Human Rights*. (May 2020) https://investorsforhumanrights.org/sites/default/files/attachments/2020-05/Full%20Report-%20Investor%20Toolkit%20on%20Human%20Rights%20May%202020c.pdf (accessed 2 February 2026).

International Law Commission. *Draft articles on Responsibility of States for Internationally Wrongful Acts with commentaries 2001*. 2008 https://legal.un.org/ilc/texts/instruments/english/commentaries/9_6_2001.pdf (accessed 2 February 2026).

OECD. *OECD Guidelines on Corporate governance of state-owned enterprises*' 2024. https://www.oecd.org/en/topics/sub-issues/corporate-governance-of-state-owned-enterprises.html (accessed 2 February 2026).

OECD. *OECD Due Diligence for Responsible Corporate Lending and Securities Underwriting: Key considerations for banks implementing the OECD Guidelines for Multinational Enterprises* OECD Publishing, Paris (2019).

Organisation for Economic Cooperation and Development (OECD) 'OECD Guidelines for Multinational Enterprises on Responsible Business Conduct' OECD Publication 2023.

OECD Investment Committee. *Response by the Investment Committee to the Substantiated Submission by OECD Watch regarding the Australian National Contact Point* 30 November 2018 DAF/INV (2018)34/Final.

OECD 'Responsible business conduct for institutional investors: Key considerations for due diligence under the OECD Guidelines for Multinational Enterprises' 2017.

Office of the United Nations High Commissioner for Human Rights (OHCHR). *Response to Request from BankTrack for Advice Regarding the Application of the UN Guiding Principles on Business and Human Rights in the Context of the Banking Sector.* 2017.

Task Force on Climate-related Financial Disclosures (TCFD). *Recommendations of the Task Force on Climate-related Financial Disclosures: Final Report.* June 2017. https://www.fsb-tcfd.org.

ETO Consortium '*The Maastricht Principles on the Extraterritorial Obligations of States in the Area of Economic, Social and Cultural Rights'* 2013 https://www.fidh.org/IMG/pdf/maastricht-eto-principles-uk_web.pdf (accessed 2 February 2026).

Thun Group of Banks 'Paper on the Implications of UN Guiding Principles 13b & 17 In a Corporate and Investment Banking Context' Paper – Thun Group of Banks, December 2017 https://media.business-humanrights.org/media/documents/files/documents/2017_12_Thun_Group_of_Banks_Paper_UNGPs_13b_and_17.pdf#page=5.08 (accessed 2 February 2026).

United Nations. Committee on the Rights of the Child (CRC), General Comment No. 16 (2013) on State Obligations regarding the Impact of the Business Sector on Children's Rights, UN Doc CRC/C/GC/16 (17 April 2013).

United Nations. Committee on Economic, Social and Cultural Rights, General Comment No. 24 (2017) on State obligations under the International Covenant on Economic, Social and Cultural Rights in the context of business activities, UN Doc E/C.12/GC/24 (10 August 2017).

United Nations. *Guiding Principles on Business and Human Rights: Implementing the United Nations "Protect, Respect and Remedy" Framework.* New York and Geneva: United Nations, 2011.

United Nations. Working Group on Business and Human Rights 'Report of the Working Group on the issue of human rights and transnational corporations and other business enterprises' 4 May 2016. A/HRC/32/45.

United Nations. Principles for Responsible Investment (PRI) 'The Principles for Responsible Investment Reporting Framework' (23 January 2023) https://www.unpri.org/about-us/what-are-the-principles-for-responsible-investment (accessed 2 February 2026).

United Nations. Working Group on Business and Human Rights 'Taking stock of investor implementation of the UN Guiding Principles on Business and Human Rights' (2021) Addendum report of the Working Group on the issue of human rights and transnational corporations and other business enterprises corporations. A/HRC/47/39/Add.2, 2.

United Nations. Working Group on Business and Human Rights 'The State as an economic actor and human rights' https://www.ohchr.org/en/special-procedures/wg-business/state-economic-actor-and-human-rights (accessed 2 February 2026).

United Nations. Human Rights Council 'Report of the United Nations High Commissioner for Human Rights: Improving accountability and access to remedy for victims of business-related human rights abuses' 10 May 2016 Un Doc A/HRC/32/19.

World Benchmark Alliance 2024 Social Benchmark https://www.worldbenchmarkingalliance.org/publication/social/ (accessed 2 February 2026).

World Trade Organisation 'Agreement on Government Procurement' (GPA) 2012 https://www.wto.org/english/docs_e/legal_e/rev-gpr-94_01_e.pdf (accessed 2 February 2026).

References

Al Jazeera Why are victims of a Brazil dam disaster suing miner BHP in a London court? 23 October 2024. Al Jazeera https://www.aljazeera.com/news/2024/10/23/why-are-victims-of-a-brazil-dam-disaster-suing-miner-bhp-in-a-london-court. Accessed 2 Feb 2026

Alwishewa H (2024) Addressing the human rights risks of financing the arms industry: insights from banks' corporate policies. Bus Hum Rights J:1–7

Augenstein D (2022) Home-state regulations of corporations. In: Gibney M, Türkelli GE, Krajewski M, Vandenhole W (eds) The Routledge handbook on extraterritorial human rights obligations. Routledge, pp 284–298

BankTrack 'Coal Havens: The Policy Loopholes keeping coal finance alive in Asia' January 2024. https://www.banktrack.org/download/coal_havens/240122_coal_havens_opt.pdf. Accessed 2 Feb 2026

Barnes MM (2021) State-owned entities and human rights: the role of international law. Cambridge University Press

Bhatt K, Türkelli GE (2021) OECD national contact points as sites of effective remedy: new expressions of the role and rule of law within market globalization? Bus Hum Rights J 6(3):423–448

Bordignon M (2022) Ensuring financial sector compliance with human rights: from the UNGPs to complicity. In: Marx A, Van CG, Wouters J (eds) Research handbook on global governance, business and human rights. Edward Elgar Publishing, pp 81–90

Bundesamt für Wirtschaft und Ausfuhrkontrolle (BAFA). Rechenschaftsbericht 2023. https://www.bafa.de/SharedDocs/Downloads/DE/Lieferketten/rechenschaftsbericht_2023.html. Accessed 2 Feb 2026

Business and Human Rights Resource Centre. Total Lawsuit (Re Failure To Respect French Duty Of Vigilance Law In Operations In Uganda) 23 October 2019 Https://Www.Business-Humanrights.Org/En/Latest-News/Total-Lawsuit-Re-Failure-To-Respect-French-Duty-Of-Vigilance-Law-In-Operations-In-Uganda/. Accessed 2 Feb 2026

Business and Human Rights Resource Centre. Saudi Arabia: BWI files ILO forced labour complaint ahead of 2034 FIFA World Cup bid amid 'epidemic' of migrant worker abuse. 22

October 2024. https://www.bhrrc.org/en/latest-news/saudi-arabia-bwi-files-ilo-forced-labour-complaint-ahead-of-2034-fifa-world-cup-bid-amid-epidemic-of-migrant-worker-abuse/. Accessed 2 Feb 2026

Business and Human Rights Resource Centre. Switched off: Tech company opacity & Israel's war on Gaza. Briefing 18 April 2024. https://www.business-humanrights.org/de/from-us/briefings/tech-sector-opt-analysis-2024/. Accessed 2 Feb 2026

Byrne S, Ludvigsen JAL (2023) An Olympic Embrace? A critical evaluation of the IOC's Commitment to Human Rights. Int J Sport Policy Polit 16(2):217–234

Carolei D (2022a) Accountability beyond corporations: the applicability of the OECD guidelines for multinational enterprises to non-profit organisations. Nonprofit Policy Forum 13(1):31–47

Carolei D (2022b) An International Ombudsman to make non-governmental organizations more accountable? Too good to be true .... Leiden J Int Law 35(4):867–886

Carolei D, Bernaz N (2021) Accountability for human rights: applying business and human rights instruments to non-governmental organizations. Oxford J Hum Rights Pract 13(3):507–528

Catá Backer L (2014) On the problem of the state in the state duty to protect human rights - fostering national action plans as a means of refocusing the state duty on the business of the state itself. 10 May 2014 LC Backer Blog https://lcbackerblog.blogspot.com/2014/05/on-problem-of-state-in-state-duty-to.html. Accessed 2 Feb 2026

Catá Backer L (2020) Human rights responsibilities of state-owned enterprises. In: Deva S, Birchall D (eds) Research handbook on human rights and business. Edward Elgar Publishing, pp 223–244

Černic JL (2008) Corporate responsibility human rights: a critical analysis of the OECD guidelines for multinational enterprises. Hanse Law Rev 4(1):71–101

Chambers R (2021) Parent company direct liability for overseas human rights violations: lessons from the U.K. Supreme Court. Univ Pa J Int Law 42:519–579

Corcoine E (2023) In the wake of Bonsucro: multi-stakeholder initiatives and third-party certifiers at the test bench of OECD national contact points. Bus Hum Rights J 8:271–276

Croser M, Day M, Van Huijstee M, Samkalden C (2020) Vedanta v Lungowe and Kiobel v Shell: the implications for parent company accountability. Bus Hum Rights J 5:130–136

Davaanyam O (2025) Articulating responsibility for human rights and the environment in the financial sector: outlook on the concrete cases of the OECD national contact points. In: Davaanyam O, Krajewski M (eds) Exploring corporate human rights responsibilities in OECD case law. Springer Nature, pp 51–84

Davies P Qc (2022) Ending human rights abuses in which companies and states are complicit. Oxford Business Law Blog 5 April 2022 Https://Blogs.Law.Ox.Ac.Uk/Business-Law-Blog/Blog/2022/04/Ending-Human-Rights-Abuses-Which-Companies-And-States-Are-Complicit. Accessed 2 Feb 2026

De Schutter O (2020) International human rights law: cases, materials, commentary, 3rd edn. Cambridge University Press

Garciandia R (2023) Accountability of NGOs: the potential of business and human rights frameworks for NGO due diligence. King's Law J 34(3):524–545

Krajewski M (2018) The state duty to protect against human rights violations through transnational business activities. Deakin Law Rev 23:20

Lin S, Khan A, Song Y (2024) Upholding human rights in mega sports: a study of governance practices within the IOC and FIFA through the lens of the Ruggie Principle. Elsevier 10(16):1–12

Linklaters (2024) German watchdog reports on the first year of the Supply Chain Act. 15 October 2024 https://sustainablefutures.linklaters.com/post/102jlse/german-watchdog-reports-on-the-first-year-of-the-supply-chain-act. Accessed 2 Feb 2026

Macchi C, Bernaz N (2021) Business, human rights and climate due diligence: understanding the responsibility of banks. Sustainability 15(13):1–21. https://www.mdpi.com/2071-1050/13/15/8391. Accessed 2 Feb 2026

Mares R (2020) Liability within corporate groups: parent companies' accountability for subsidiary human rights abuses. In: Deva S, Birchall D (eds) Research handbook on human rights and business. Edward Elgar Publishing, pp 446–470

Martens K (2003) Examining the (non-)status of NGOs in international law. Indiana J Global Leg Stud 10:1–25

Martin-Ortega O (2018) Public procurement as a tool for the protection and promotion of human rights: a study of collaboration, due diligence and leverage in the electronics industry. Bus Hum Rights J 3(1):75–95

McCorquodale R (2024) Business and human rights: element of international law. Oxford University Press

Mohr K, Riquelme M, Quick PM (2022) Double materiality for financial institutions survey findings and recommendations. BSR 2022 https://www.bsr.org/reports/BSR_Issue_Brief_Materiality_Survey_December_2022_final.pdf. Accessed 2 Feb 2026

Monnheimer M (2021) Due diligence obligations in international human rights law. Cambridge University Press, p 69

Morgera E (2020) Corporate environmental accountability in international law, 2nd edn. Oxford University Press

Naushad S. Why Section 1502 of The Dodd-Frank Act Cannot Solve the Humanitarian Crisis in the Democratic Republic of Congo. University of Denver https://djilp.org/why-section-1502-of-the-dodd-frank-act-cannot-solve-the-humanitarian-crisis-in-the-democratic-republic-of-congo/#_ftn1. Accessed 2 Feb 2026

O'Brien CM (2018) The home state duty to regulate the human rights impacts of TNCs abroad: rebuttal. Bus Hum Rights J 3:47–73

O'Brien CM, Ferguson J, McVey M (2022) National action plans on business and human rights: an experimentalist governance analysis. Hum Rights Rev 23:71–99

OECD Watch, KTNC Watch et al against KEXIM Violations of FPIC, consultation at Philippine Jalaur dam, 18 January 2019

OECD Watch, Global Witness vs. UK Export Finance 'UK Export Finance Fails Climate Commitments, Disclosures' September 2020., https://www.oecdwatch.org/complaint/global-witness-vs-uk-export-finance/. Accessed 2 Feb 2026

Quick PM, Mohr K, Fisher B. The CSDDD: implications for the finance industry. BSR Blog 4 September 2024. https://www.bsr.org/en/blog/the-csddd-implications-for-the-finance-industry. Accessed 2 Feb 2026

Ruggie J (2017) Comments on Thun Group of Banks Discussion Paper on the Implications of UN Guiding Principles 13 & 17 In a Corporate and Investment Banking Context. Harvard Kennedy School, 21 February 2017

Sanger A (2019) Parent company duty of care to third parties harmed by overseas subsidiaries. Camb Law J 78:486–490

Savourey E, Brabant S (2021) The French Law on the duty of vigilance: theoretical and practical challenges since its adoption. Bus Hum Rights J 6(1):141–152

Schönsteiner J (2019) Attribution of state responsibility for actions or omissions of State-owned enterprises in human rights matters. Univ Pa J Int Law 40:895–936

Seck SL (2011) Conceptualising the home state duty to protect human rights. In: Buhmann K, Morsing M, Roseberry L (eds) Corporate social and human rights responsibilities: global legal and management perspectives. Palgrave Macmillan, pp 25–51

Soilihi A, Haranger X (2024) The First French Court Rulings on the Duty of Vigilance. Morgan Lewis Law Flash 5 March 2024 https://www.morganlewis.com/pubs/2024/03/the-first-french-court-rulings-on-the-duty-of-vigilance. Accessed 2 Feb 2026

Taylor CR (2015) Using securities disclosures to advance human rights: a consideration of Dodd-Frank Section 1502 and the Securities and Exchange Commission Conflict Minerals Rule. J Hum Rights 14(2):201–217

Uvarova O (2022) Mihaela Maria Barnes, state-owned entities and human rights. The role of international law. Bus Hum Rights J 8(2):301–303

Van Dijk MA, De Haas M, Zandvliet R (2018) Banks and human trafficking: rethinking human rights due diligence. Bus Hum Rights J 3(1):105–111

Van Ho T (2021) Defining the relationships: "Cause, Contribute, and Directly Linked to" in the UN Guiding Principles on Business and Human Rights. Hum Rights Q 43(4):625–658. https://muse.jhu.edu/article/837782. Accessed 2 Feb 2026

Wee C (2008) Regulating the human rights impact of state-owned enterprises: tendencies of corporate accountability and state responsibility. International Commission of Jurists, Danish Section, October 2008

Wettstein F (2022) Business and human rights: ethical, legal, and managerial perspectives. Cambridge University Press

Whitney T (2015) Conflict minerals, black markets and transparency: the legislative background of Dodd-Frank Section 1502 and its historical lessons. J Hum Rights 14:182–200

Wilson N (2020) When is a subsidiary's negligence the parent company's problem? Canterbury Law Rev 26:161–195

Woods CL, Stokes AQ (2019) 'For the game, for the world': an analysis of FIFA's CSR initiatives. Public Relat Inq 8, 1: 49-85

Chapter 5
Conclusion—From Soft Law to Influence: The Normative Authority of OECD NCP Statements in Shaping Corporate Responsibility

5.1 Introduction

This book sought to explore corporate human rights and environmental responsibilities through an in-depth analysis of OECD case law, focusing on specific responsibilities articulated in the OECD Guidelines and the UNGPs. By systematically analysing 394 specific instances handled by NCPs from 2000s to 2024, the research illuminated the expectations placed upon corporations to fulfil their responsibilities and to navigate complex challenges related to adverse human rights, environmental as well as climate impacts. The findings provide a critical perspective on the substantive dimensions of corporate responsibility for human rights and environment.

This book delved into the substantive dimensions of corporate human rights and environmental responsibility, providing a detailed analysis of HRDD responsibilities as outlined in the OECD Guidelines. It examined the six steps of the risk-based due diligence concept, including the responsibility to conduct MSE and the imperative to ensure the effectiveness of HRDD processes. Beyond these procedural considerations, the second part explored substantive responsibilities in diverse contexts, such as corporate responsibility for group rights, particularly for marginalised populations including women, workers, Indigenous Peoples, and minorities. Furthermore, it addressed corporations' responsibilities regarding environmental protection, climate change mitigation, and their operational conduct in conflict affected areas. The analysis extended beyond the corporate responsibility to respect human rights, emphasising the role of MNEs in contributing to the SDGs at the local level. It also explored collective and shared responsibilities, particularly in scenarios involving groups of companies or collaborations with other organisations and stakeholders. In the third part, the research scrutinised the varied responsibilities of corporate actors, such as parent companies, FIs, and SOEs, while also addressing the interplay between corporate and state responsibilities in ensuring accountability in business activities.

O. Davaanyam, *Conceptualising the Corporate Human Rights and Environmental Responsibilities*, Interdisciplinary Studies in Human Rights 17,
https://doi.org/10.1007/978-3-032-21430-0_5

This concluding chapter critically synthesises the analytical gaps and conceptual tensions identified throughout the preceding chapters, offering an integrated assessment of the study's principal findings and implications. It aims not merely to summarise but to interrogate how OECD NCP practice contributes to shaping the concepts of corporate human rights and environmental responsibility. While serving as a concise reference for policymakers, NCP practitioners, and other stakeholders, the chapter situates OECD case law within broader debates on corporate accountability and transnational governance. The first section distils the substantive findings and overarching recommendations concerning corporate responsibility for human rights and environmental protection. The final section advances a critical reflection on the authoritative and normative role of NCP statements—examining how their determinations, reasoning, and recommendations influence the evolving jurisprudence and normative development of business and human rights standards.

This research provides a deeper and more nuanced understanding of corporate human rights and environmental responsibilities, revealing the dual function of the OECD NCP system—both as a facilitator of corporate accountability through non-judicial grievance mechanisms and as a contributor to the evolving legal and ethical conceptualisation of corporate responsibility. The findings draw attention to the considerable potential of NCPs to clarify corporate duties in complex transnational contexts, adopt a more proactive stance in strengthening effective HRDD, and monitor the implementation of remedial actions. NCPs can act as crucial intermediaries between companies and complainants, fostering constructive dialogue and enabling more cooperative and sustainable forms of dispute resolution.

Although many cases fall short of producing transformative outcomes, several have yielded tangible results: negotiated agreements, the creation of grievance mechanisms, collaborative initiatives, and cases in which parent companies exercised leverage to uphold labour rights and collective bargaining. These examples demonstrate the practical impact that OECD NCP proceedings can generate. However, such successes remain exceptional due to systemic constraints—limited follow-up procedures, uneven analytical depth in NCP reasoning, and the voluntary, non-binding nature of the OECD Guidelines. The heterogeneity of NCP approaches and interpretive practices ultimately impedes the emergence of a coherent and authoritative body of case law capable of consistently delineating the scope of corporate human rights and environmental responsibility.

5.2 Key Findings: Re-Conceptualising Corporate Human Rights and Environmental Responsibility Through OECD Case Law

This research demonstrates that the OECD NCP mechanism functions as a distinct quasi-juridical site of normative practice through which the operationalisation of HRDD responsibilities can be critically examined. Drawing on 394 cases, the analysis reveals both the normative diffusion of the UNGPs and OECD Guidelines and the persistent implementation deficit that continues to characterise corporate conduct under the rubric of RBC. While HRDD has attained global recognition as the procedural backbone of corporate accountability, its translation from normative aspiration into operational reality remains partial, fragmented, and frequently performative.

A central finding concerns the disjunction between policy commitment and institutional internalisation. Corporate human rights policies, often couched in aspirational language, tend to remain declaratory instruments rather than transformative governance tools. They frequently fail to permeate managerial hierarchies, incentive structures, and decision-making processes in a manner that substantively reorients corporate behaviour. OECD case law evidences that HRDD is too often operationalised as an externalised compliance or reporting function—an add-on to business operations rather than an organising principle of corporate governance. NCPs have consistently pointed out that HRDD must be institutionalised within corporate governance architecture, with clear lines of responsibility, accountability, and monitoring. The persistence of this gap underlines the structural limitations of voluntarism within soft-law regimes and reinforces the need for a paradigmatic shift from procedural compliance towards embedded, and enforceable accountability.

Secondly, the case law demonstrates that corporate approaches to risk identification and assessment remain largely cosmetic forms of compliance, characterised by fragmented methodologies, superficial impact assessments, and the systematic exclusion of affected rights-holders. NCP findings consistently reveal that companies tend to treat risk assessment as a procedural formality rather than a substantive exercise in rights-based governance. In response, NCPs have repeatedly urged corporations to adopt context-sensitive and participatory methodologies that incorporate rights-holders' perspectives and reflect the differentiated risks faced by different vulnerable groups. This is particularly imperative in sectors where structural inequalities—such as gender-based violence, violations of Indigenous Peoples' rights, and labour exploitation—are entrenched within production and value chains. The uneven quality of corporate risk assessments marked the absence of a shared interpretative framework defining what constitutes 'adequate' or 'effective' human rights due diligence under international soft-law standards.

Thirdly, the dimensions of prevention, mitigation, and leverage are conceptualised inconsistently across OECD NCP statements. While the UNGPs articulate leverage as a continuum of responsibility for enterprises 'directly linked' to adverse impacts, NCPs have seldom clarified its operational parameters or the extent to which it must traverse complex contractual, financial, and supply-chain relationships. The analysis reveals that leverage remains an underestimated yet pivotal responsibility—particularly given that most corporate actors are not direct perpetrators but facilitators of harm through their business relationships. Too often, leverage is invoked rhetorically to signal awareness rather than deployed strategically to prevent or mitigate harm. This evidences a deeper conceptual tension within HRDD practice: rather than functioning as a narrow risk-management tool, HRDD must be reconceived as a responsibility-sharing framework that distributes differentiated yet interdependent duties among parent companies, financial institutions, state-owned enterprises, and non-profit entities.

A further insight concerns the weak institutionalisation of monitoring, transparency, and remediation mechanisms within corporate HRDD practice. The OECD case law reveals that only a limited number of companies have developed systematic approaches to tracking the effectiveness of HRDD measures or disclosing results to stakeholders. While NCPs routinely recommend independent verification, multi-stakeholder monitoring, and periodic review, the non-binding character of their determinations significantly constrains the effectiveness of follow-up. The combination of uneven NCP reasoning and states' discretionary political will has produced a fragmented enforcement landscape, where accountability and learning depend largely on voluntary corporate initiative rather than structural obligation. Moreover, transparency remains equally underdeveloped. Many NCP cases demonstrate that companies frequently invoke business confidentiality to justify withholding essential information—such as environmental impact assessments or risk analyses—from affected rights-holders. This lack of disclosure undermines participatory governance and erodes trust between corporations and communities. Although NCPs consistently urge companies to establish communication channels with affected rights-holders and engage in open dialogue to build trust and prevent conflict escalation, compliance remains largely exceptional. Where implemented, transparent engagement has proven instrumental in rebuilding relationships and enhancing the social legitimacy of corporate operations, underscoring its function as a substantive component of HRDD rather than a discretionary act of goodwill.

Critically, remediation persists as the least operationalised pillar of corporate responsibility. Even when companies acknowledge adverse impacts, NCPs rarely delineate concrete remedial measures or ensure post-mediation monitoring. In several instances, NCPs have expressly discouraged complainants from pursuing remedial outcomes, reiterating the mechanism's non-binding mandate—thereby diluting the remedial dimension of corporate accountability under the OECD framework. This institutional restraint stands in tension with the UNGPs and the OECD Guidelines, both of which explicitly embed remediation within the HRDD continuum. Nonetheless, a limited number of cases indicate emerging best practices, where NCP-facilitated mediation has led to the creation of grievance mechanisms, compensation schemes, or structural reforms. These incremental developments signify the gradual emergence of a rights-based remedial culture within the NCP system, though still constrained by voluntarism and the absence of formal enforcement powers.

The book further emphasises the cross-cutting dimensions of corporate responsibility, revealing persistent gaps between the rhetorical expansion of HRDD and its substantive implementation. Despite the growing integration of gender, environmental, and climate-related concerns into the HRDD discourse, OECD case law demonstrates that these dimensions remain largely peripheral and selectively operationalised. Corporate neglect of women's rights, inadequate attention to Indigenous Peoples' right to FPIC, and weak climate-related due diligence all illustrate how the universality of the 'do no harm' principle is frequently diluted in practice. Such omissions reflect a broader pattern of performative alignment with the Sustainable Development Goals (SDGs), where companies invoke sustainability language without embedding it into decision-making or impact assessment processes. The 2023 revision of the OECD Guidelines represents a normative advancement by explicitly linking environmental and climate due diligence to human rights responsibilities; however, its effectiveness depends on consistent interpretation and political commitment by both states and NCPs.

Moreover, OECD case law reveals the under-theorised potential to conceptualise corporate responsibility not merely as avoidance of harm but as a positive duty to contribute to sustainable development and to address structural and systemic harms that transcend the capacity of individual actors. The NCP mechanism provides a valuable interpretive space to articulate such positive responsibilities among corporations, financial institutions, and state actors—particularly in addressing transnational environmental degradation, labour exploitation, and climate impacts. Some NCPs have already begun assessing MNEs actions in developing countries through the lens of the SDGs, emphasising that failure to contribute to local social and environmental well-being constitutes a breach of responsible business conduct obligations under the OECD Guidelines.

From a structural perspective, the findings reaffirm that corporate accountability under the OECD framework is relational and networked, dispersed across parent companies, subsidiaries, investors, and state entities. NCP case law increasingly recognises parent companies as duty-bearers for group-wide conduct, establishing a normative expectation that they exercise oversight and ensure HRDD implementation throughout corporate groups. While enforcement remains voluntary, numerous NCPs have begun explicitly connecting parent company responsibility to harms caused by subsidiaries, advancing stronger governance, monitoring, and remedial engagement at the local level. Similarly, financial institutions—despite their systemic leverage—continue to rely on dialogue-based mediation with limited binding outcomes. Yet, NCPs have progressively advanced the conceptualisation of financial-sector accountability, clarifying the due diligence obligations of investors and lenders and their responsibility to leverage influence over investee companies. These developments mark a gradual but significant expansion of the HRDD paradigm toward encompassing the financial ecosystem. By contrast, the accountability of (NPOs) and state-owned enterprises (SOEs) remains conceptually underdeveloped in the OECD NCP mechanism. However, OECD case law has increasingly scrutinised the quasi-commercial activities of NPOs, applying the OECD Guidelines to their operations and thereby affirming that entities exercising economic power or normative influence, irrespective of their formal legal status, fall within the regulatory and normative ambit of RBC.

Finally, the analysis underlines that the state duty to protect—the foundational first pillar of the UNGPs—remains largely implicit and under-theorised within NCP practice. Although certain NCPs, notably in France and the Netherlands, have sought to align case handling with domestic human rights and environmental frameworks, the majority refrain from interrogating *state complicity* or addressing underlying regulatory deficiencies. Cases such as those in Belgium and Finland illustrate instances where states have acted as constructive participants in NCP mediation, using their influence to steer corporate practice towards more responsible business conduct. In contrast, other jurisdictions—particularly the United Kingdom, Australia, and Canada—demonstrate how governmental prioritisation of trade and investment interests can undermine the quasi-regulatory mandate of NCPs and dilute their accountability function. Moreover, several cases reveal that states themselves often constitute primary enablers or direct perpetrators of harm, particularly in developing-country contexts where weak governance facilitates corporate misconduct. Yet, despite these dynamics, NCPs—mandated to address only MNEs—rarely acknowledge or reflect on the state's contributory role in their statements. This analytical omission highlights a broader institutional reluctance to engage with the structural interplay between corporate abuse and state failure. To strengthen NCPs as effective quasi-regulatory instruments, there is a pressing need to enhance state capacity, standardise follow-up procedures, and ensure systematic integration with emerging mandatory due diligence regimes at both national and regional levels. Only through such alignment can the NCP mechanism evolve beyond voluntary facilitation and contribute meaningfully to the enforcement of the state's duty to protect within the global BHR framework.

To conclude, the OECD NCP mechanism functions as a quasi-juridical and interpretive system that contributes to the progressive norm-formation of corporate human rights and environmental responsibilities. When examined cumulatively, NCP statements reveal an emerging yet fragmented body of interpretive practice that provides concrete illustrations of how corporate actors operationalise—or fail to operationalise—the OECD Guidelines and the UNGPs. While the case law has not yet produced a coherent or generalised body of jurisprudence capable of refining standards and obligations in the abstract, it nevertheless offers valuable context-specific precedents that delineate the contours of corporate due diligence in practice. These cases—through their reasoning, recommendations, and negotiated outcomes—constitute a growing repository of applied normative guidance for companies, policymakers, and regulators seeking to translate the 'responsibility to respect' into operational and measurable standards.

However, the system's authoritative potential remains constrained by its voluntary design, the absence of binding force, and the uneven quality of NCP reasoning across jurisdictions. The lack of interpretive coherence prevents the emergence of a fully-fledged transnational jurisprudence and limits the persuasive authority of NCP determinations. To strengthen their normative weight, NCPs must adopt principled consistency and interpretive discipline, articulating reasoned findings that move beyond procedural facilitation toward substantive clarification of corporate obligations. This requires transparent justification of outcomes, doctrinal cross-referencing between NCPs, and systematic follow-up mechanisms capable of reinforcing compliance and learning.

Ultimately, the legal significance of OECD NCP practice lies in its contribution to the juridification of corporate due diligence obligations. By transforming the aspirational vocabulary of responsible business conduct into concrete expectations of compliance and accountability, NCPs bridge the gap between soft-law governance and emergent hard-law regimes such as the EU CSDDD and France's Duty of Vigilance. Properly institutionalised, the cumulative body of NCP statements could evolve into a form of transnational law, in which iterative reasoning, peer review, and cross-jurisdictional convergence gradually crystallise an authoritative corpus of norms governing corporate accountability beyond the state.

Table of OECD NCP Cases

(sorted first by NCP country name in descending by year, then alphabetical order)

NCP country	Completed year	Complaint	Status	Source link:
NCP Australia	2023	GLAN v. BHP Group Ltd and other enterprises	Completed without agreement	https://ausncp.gov.au/sites/default/files/2023-07/final-statement-complaint-21.pdf
NCP Australia	2023	Project Sepik and Jubilee Australia Research Centre on behalf of Sepik River communities v. PanAust Limited	Completed without agreement	https://ausncp.gov.au/complaints/complaint-29
NCP Australia	2023	Publish What You Pay Australia v. Mallee Resources Limited	Closed (withdrawal of participation)	https://ausncp.gov.au/complaints/complaint-27
NCP Australia	2021	Andrew Starkey and Robert Starkey v. ElectraNet Pty Lt	Completed without agreement	https://ausncp.gov.au/complaints/complaint-22
NCP Australia	2021	Friends of Earth v. ANZ Group	Completed without agreement	
NCP Australia	2019	Australian Women Without Borders v. Mercer PR for its conduct in relation to activity in Nauru.	Closed (withdrawal of participation)	https://ausncp.gov.au/complaints/complaint-15

NCP Australia	2019	Mr Yacouba Traoré on behalf of the Former Employees Collective of the Australian Laboratory Services Mali SARL Laboratory Group against Australian Laboratory Services (ALS)	Completed without agreement	https://ausncp.gov.au/complaints/complaint-13
NCP Australia	2018	Equitable Cambodia and Inclusive Development International v. ANZ Group	Completed without agreement	https://ausncp.gov.au/complaints/complaint-11
NCP Australia	2017	Ben Saul on behalf of refugees detained in Australia, v. SERCO Group Pty Ltd	Rejected	https://mneguidelines.oecd.org/database/instances/au0010.htm
NCP Australia	2015	Statement by the Australian National Contact Point: Specific Instance – G4S Australia Pty Ltd	Rejected	https://ausncp.gov.au/sites/default/files/2023-01/G4S_aus.pdf
NCP Belgium	2019	Open Secrets v. KBC – KBL	Rejected	https://www.oecdwatch.org/complaint/open-secrets-cals-vs-kbc-group/
NCP Belgium	2018	Adimed-Kilu Group v. ES-KO International	Rejected	https://mneguidelines.oecd.org/database/instances/be0019.htm
NCP Belgium	2017	Building and Wood Workers' International (BWI) v. Etex Group	Completed without agreement	https://mneguidelines.oecd.org/database/instances/be0016.htm
NCP Belgium	2014	Greenpeace v. Jan De Nul NV.	Completed without agreement	https://mneguidelines.oecd.org/database/instances/be0015.htm

(continued)

NCP country	Completed year	Complaint	Status	Source link:
NCP Belgium	2011	Greenpeace India v. Dredging International.	Completed without agreement	https://mneguidelines.oecd.org/database/instances/be0012.htm
NCP Belgium	2011	Mr. Vincent Van Quickenborne, Minister for Enterprises v. Brink	Completed without agreement	https://mneguidelines.oecd.org/database/instances/be0013.htm
NCP Brazil	2021	A Group of Individuals v. VALE S.A	Closed (withdrawal of participation)	https://mneguidelines.oecd.org/database/instances/br0029.htm
NCP Brazil	2021	Carlos Cleber Guimarães Júnior and Carla de Laci França v. VALE S.A	Closed (withdrawal of participation)	https://mneguidelines.oecd.org/database/instances/br0030.htm
NCP Brazil	2021	Izabel Lopes Soares da Silva, represented by José Reinaldo Soares da Silva v. Bracell Bahia Specialty Cellulose S.A	Completed without agreement	https://www.gov.br/mdic/pt-br/assuntos/camex/pcn/produtos/alegacoes-de-inobservancia/banco-de-dados-de-alegacoes-de-inobservancia/BSCDeclaracao_Final_IE_06_2020_EN.pdf#page=3.55
NCP Brazil	2021	Vila Solaris Hospedagens e Eventos, represented by Rogério Mário Ziviani Gomes v. VALE S.A	Closed (withdrawal of participation)	https://mneguidelines.oecd.org/database/instances/br0031.htm

NCP Brazil	2020	Association Forum Suape Environmental Space, Conectas Human Rights, Fishermen's Colony Z8 – Gaibu Both ENDS v. Van Oord, Atradius Dutch State Business and Industrial Port Complex Eraldo Gueiros – Suape Enterprise, Pernambuco	Completed without agreement	https://www.oecdwatch.org/complaint/forum-suape-et-al-vs-atradius-dutch-state-business/
NCP Brazil	2016	Association of Neighborhoods v. Kinross Gold	Agreement	https://www.oecdwatch.org/complaint/paracuta-vs-kinross-gold-corporation-1/
NCP Brazil	2013	The Trade Union Bank Workers Union of São Paulo, v. Itau-Unibanco Bank	Closed (withdrawal of participation)	https://mneguidelines.oecd.org/database/instances/br0017.htm
NCP Canada	2024	Individuals v. Barrick Gold	Completed without agreement	https://www.international.gc.ca/trade-commerce/ncp-pcn/2024-05-17-barrick-gold.aspx?lang=eng
NCP Canada	2024	United Tegaru Canada v. Sun Peak Metals Corp	Rejected	https://www.international.gc.ca/trade-commerce/ncp-pcn/statement-sun-peak-metals-communique.aspx?lang=eng
NCP Canada	2020	SEACC v. Imperial Metals Corporation	Completed without agreement	https://www.international.gc.ca/trade-agreements-accords-commerciaux/ncp-pcn/2020-05-07-ncp-pcn.aspx?lang=eng
NCP Canada	2019	Former Employees v. Flemish Investment Burundi SA subsidiary of Flemish Investment Limited	Completed without agreement	https://www.international.gc.ca/trade-agreements-accords-commerciaux/ncp-pcn/2019-06-13-ncp-pcn.aspx?lang=eng

(continued)

NCP country	Completed year	Complaint	Status	Source link:
NCP Canada	2017	The Secretary General of the Labour Union Federation nationale des Mines et de l'Energie (FENAME) v. Endeavour Mining.	Agreement	https://www.international.gc.ca/trade-agreements-accords-commerciaux/ncp-pcn/2017-10-24-final_stat-comm_finale.aspx?lang=eng
NCP Canada	2015	NCP Canada, The Canada Tibet Committee v. China Gold International	Closed (withdrawal of participation)	https://www.international.gc.ca/trade-agreements-accords-commerciaux/ncp-pcn/statement-gyama-valley.aspx?lang=eng
NCP Canada	2014	CEDHU and Mining Watch v. Corriente Resources in Mirador Mine in Ecuador	Closed (withdrawal of participation)	https://www.international.gc.ca/trade-agreements-accords-commerciaux/ncp-pcn/initial-assessment-evaluation-initiale.aspx?lang=eng
NCP Canada	2014	The Porgera Landowners Association (PLOA), a Papua New Guinean association, and the Akali Tange Association (ATA), a Papua New Guinean NGO, assisted by Mining Watch Canada (MWC), a Canadian NGO v. Porgera Gold Mine in Papua New Guinea, Barrick Gold	Completed without agreement	https://www.international.gc.ca/trade-agreements-accords-commerciaux/ncp-pcn/statement-declaration.aspx?lang=eng
NCP Chile	2022	A Group of 26 neighbours v. Minera Candelaria	Closed (withdrawal of participation)	https://mneguidelines.oecd.org/database/instances/cl0028.htm
NCP Chile	2021	Arpal SpA v. Walmart	Completed without agreement	https://mneguidelines.oecd.org/database/instances/cl0015.htm

NCP Chile	2021	Liquidator v. Tensa		
NCP Chile	2020	Quebrada Blanca Trade Union v. Teck	Agreement	https://mneguidelines.oecd.org/database/instances/cl0013.htm
NCP Chile	2015	The Starbucks Coffee Chile S.A. Workers' Union, the Central Unitaria de Trabajadores (CUT) v. Starbucks Coffee Chile S.A	Agreement	https://mneguidelines.oecd.org/database/instances/cl0008.htm
NCP Colombia	2018	Sindicato de Trabajadores Enfermos y Discapacitados del Sector Minero (SINTRADEM) And the Federación General el Trabajo CGT Seccional Cesar (CGT) v. Drummond Ltd.	Closed (withdrawal of participation)	https://mneguidelines.oecd.org/database/instances/co0002.htm
NCP Czech Republic	2022	A Czech Interest Group v. A Czech Company in Textile Industry	Agreement	https://mpo.gov.cz/assets/cz/zahranicni-obchod/narodni-kontaktni-misto-pro-smernici-oecd/projednavani-stiznosti/2023/1/Zaverecna-zprava_EN.pdf
NCP Denmark	2024	Former Employees of the Joint Venture Douala International Terminal S.A. in Cameroun v. A.P. Moeller – Maersk A/S.	Completed without agreement	https://ncp-danmark.dk/sites/default/files/2024-05/Final%20Statement%20-%20A%20P%20Moeller%20-%20Maersk_WA.pdf
NCP Denmark	2022	Christian Juhl v. Bestseller AS	Rejected	https://mneguidelines.oecd.org/database/instances/dk0020.htm

(continued)

NCP country	Completed year	Complaint	Status	Source link:
NCP Denmark	2021	West Virginians for Sustainable Development (WVSD) v. Rockwool International AS.	Completed without agreement	https://www.oecdwatch.org/complaint/west-virginians-for-sustainable-development-v-rockwool/#:~:text=The%20complaint%20alleges%20Rockwool%20has,to%20air%20and%20water%20pollution.
NCP Denmark	2018	Two NGOs v. a Danish Financial Institutions.	Rejected	https://mneguidelines.oecd.org/database/instances/dk0016.htm
NCP Denmark	2016	Clean Clothes Campaign and Active Consumers v. PWT Group	Completed without agreement	https://mneguidelines.oecd.org/database/instances/dk0015.htm
NCP Finland	2020	Haidir Hussen v. Mone Oyj, Kone middle East	Rejected	https://mneguidelines.oecd.org/database/instances/fi0005.htm
NCP Finland	2013	The Siemenpuu Foundation, Friends of the Earth Finland, and 13 other NGOs v. Pöyry Plc and the Xayaburi hydropower project.	Completed without agreement	https://mneguidelines.oecd.org/database/instances/fi0003.htm
NCP France	2022	14 Local Watch Committees ("Comités Riverains de Veille") and Centre of Actions for Life and Earth ("Centre d'Action pour la Vie et la Terre") v. COPAGEF, SOMDIAA and SOSUCAM in Cameroon	Closed (withdrawal of participation)	https://www.tresor.economie.gouv.fr/tresor-international/pcn-france/circonstance-specifique-copagef-somdiaa-et-sosucam-au-cameroun
NCP France	2022	ASF v. Perenco	Closed (withdrawal of participation)	https://www.tresor.economie.gouv.fr/tresor-international/pcn-france/circonstance-specifique-du-pcn-francais-perenco-en-tunisie
NCP France	2022	A foreign national v. a French MNE in Poland	Completed without agreement	https://www.tresor.economie.gouv.fr/tresor-international/pcn-france/circonstance-specifique-du-pcn-francais-un-ressortissant-etranger-et-une-entreprise-multinationale-francaise-en-pologne

NCP France	2022	Intersyndicate Atos v. Atos Group	Agreement	https://mneguidelines.oecd.org/database/instances/fr0036.htm
NCP France	2021	ASF and IWATCH v. Perenco	Closed (withdrawal of participation)	https://mneguidelines.oecd.org/database/instances/fr0029.htm
NCP France	2021	UNI v. Teleperformance	Completed without agreement	https://www.tresor.economie.gouv.fr/tresor-international/pcn-france/circonstance-specifique-teleperformance-en-france-et-dans-le-monde
NCP France	2020	ProDESC v. EDF Group and EDF Renewables	Completed without agreement	https://www.tresor.economie.gouv.fr/tresor-international/pcn-france/circonstance-specifique-edf-et-edf-en-au-mexique
NCP France	2019	Avocats Sans Frontières (ASF) and I WATCH v. Perenco (initial statement)	Initial statement	https://www.tresor.economie.gouv.fr/tresor-international/pcn-france/circonstance-specifique-du-pcn-francais-perenco-en-tunisie
NCP France	2019	Birlesik Metal v. DIAM International	Completed without agreement	https://www.tresor.economie.gouv.fr/tresor-international/pcn-france/circonstance-specifique-diam-international-en-turquie
NCP France	2018	The International Trade Union Confederation (ITUC) and the Cambodian Labour Confederation v. VINCI Airports in Cambodia	Completed without agreement	https://www.tresor.economie.gouv.fr/tresor-international/pcn-france/circonstance-specifique-vinci-vinci-airports-au-cambodge
NCP France	2017	Unite Here v. Natixis/NGAM	Agreement	https://www.tresor.economie.gouv.fr/tresor-international/pcn-france/circonstance-specifique-natixis-et-ngam-aux-etats-unis
NCP France	2013	Group of four non-governmental organisations (NGOs) and associations from Cameroon, France and Germany v. SOCAPALM, Bollore Group.	Agreement	https://www.tresor.economie.gouv.fr/tresor-international/pcn-france/circonstance-specifique-groupes-bollore-et-socfin-socapalm-au-cameroun

(continued)

NCP country	Completed year	Complaint	Status	Source link:
NCP France	2013	Sherpa et al. v. Michelin Group	Completed without agreement	https://www.tresor.economie.gouv.fr/tresor-international/pcn-france/circonstance-specifique-groupe-michelin-en-inde
NCP France	2012	IUF v. Accor Group	Agreement	https://www.tresor.economie.gouv.fr/Institutionnel/Niveau3/Pages/328fe721-9fbe-4431-959d-ea720fa1e511/files/45610f54-3e68-4d2c-b554-696dc0ca2908
NCP Germany	2018	European Center for Constitutional and Human rights et al v. TUV Rheinland, Final Statement	Completed without agreement	https://www.oecdwatch.org/complaint/ecchr-et-al-vs-tuv-rheinland-ag/
NCP Germany	2018	SÜDWIND Institut, Sedane Labour Resource Centre (Lembaga Informasi Perburuhan Sedane, (LIPS"), Bogor (West Java, Indonesia), Clean Clothes Campaign v. Adidas.	Completed without agreement	https://www.bmwk.de/Redaktion/EN/Beschwerdefaelle-NKS/Follow-Up/follow-up-report-on-the-complaint-by-sudwind-aa-against-adidas-ag.pdf?__blob=publicationFile&v=1
NCP Germany	2016	Mr. Dominic Whiting v. Nordex SE	Completed without agreement	https://www.bmwk.de/Redaktion/EN/Downloads/abschlusserklaerung-nks-dominic-whiting-gegen-nordex-se.pdf?__blob=publicationFile&v=1
NCP Germany	2014	UNI Global Union (UNI) and International Transport Workers' Federation (ITF) and Deutsche Post DHL (DP-DHL) v. DP-DHL/Bonn	Agreement	https://uniglobalunion.org/news/dhl-adopts-new-oecd-protocol-2022/

NCP Germany	2014	Uwe Kekeritz, Member of the German Bundestag, v. KiK Textilien and Non-Food GmbH, C&A Mode GmbH & Co., and Karl Rieker GmbH & Co.KG.	Completed without agreement	https://www.bmwk.de/Redaktion/EN/Downloads/oecd-ac-final-statement-kik.pdf?__blob=publicationFile&v=1
NCP Germany	2011	ECCHR v. Otto Stadtlander GmbH/ Bremen	Agreement	https://www.ecchr.eu/fileadmin/Juristische_Dokumente/final_statement_NCP_-_Stadtlander__Uzbekistan_dt_.pdf
NCP Germany	2010	Greenpeace v. Vattenfall, Summary	Rejected	https://www.oecdwatch.org/complaint/greenpeace-germany-vs-vattenfall/
NCP Ireland	2022	Daphne Caruana Galizia Foundation v. Accenture PLC	Rejected	https://www.oecdwatch.org/complaint/daphne-caruana-galizia-foundation-vs-accenture/
NCP Italy	2022	The Legalità per il clima on behalf of 45 individuals and Italian CSOs v. Cremonini S.p.A	Pending	https://www.oecdwatch.org/complaint/legalita-per-il-clima-on-behalf-of-45-individuals-and-italian-csos-vs-cremonini-s-p-a/
NCP Italy	2022	Rete Legalità Per Il Clima (Legality For Climate Network) and others v. Eni	Pending	https://www.oecdwatch.org/complaint/legalita-per-il-clima-on-behalf-of-10-csos-vs-eni-s-p-a/
NCP Italy	2017	Survival International Italia v. Salini Impregilo S.p.A	Completed without agreement	https://www.oecdwatch.org/complaint/survival-international-vs-salini-impregilo/
NCP Japan	2021	Market Forces v. SMBC, MUFG and Mizuho	Completed without agreement	https://www.oecdwatch.org/complaint/market-forces-v-smbc-mufg-and-mizuho/

(continued)

NCP country	Completed year	Complaint	Status	Source link:
NCP Korea	2023	Chanel Korea Branch of the Department Store Sales and Service Workers' Union v. Chanel Korea YH	Agreement	https://mneguidelines.oecd.org/database/instances/kr0024.htm
NCP Korea	2018	KTNC Watch et al v. KEXIM	Rejected	https://www.oecdwatch.org/complaint/ktnc-watch-et-al-vs-kexim/
NCP Luxembourg	2024	Friends of Earth Europre and Sustainable Development Institute of Liberia v. ArcelorMittal Liberia	Agreement	https://www.oecdwatch.org/complaint/friends-of-the-earth-vs-arcelor-mittal/
NCP Netherlands	2024	ATUMA v. Unilever	Completed without agreement	https://www.oecdguidelines.nl/latest/news/2024/5/7/final-statement-notification-atuma-vs-unilever
NCP Netherlands	2023	Aminigboko Community v. the Shell Petroleum Development Company of Nigeria Limited and Shell Headquarters	Completed without agreement	https://www.oecdguidelines.nl/latest/news/2023/02/10/final-statement-aminigboko-community-vs.-the-shell-petroleum-development-company-nigeria-of-nigeria-limited-and-shell-headquarters
NCP Netherlands	2023	Building and Wood Workers International (BWI) et al. v. IKEA Holding B.V.	Agreement	https://mneguidelines.oecd.org/database/instances/nl0044.htm
NCP Netherlands	2023	FNV v. Just Eat Takeway.com	Closed without participation	https://www.oecdguidelines.nl/latest/news/2023/03/22/final-statement-fnv-vs-just-eat-takeaway.com
NCP Netherlands	2023	Italian CSOs v. Stellantis NV and Stellantis Italy, Initial Statement	Pending	https://www.oecdwatch.org/complaint/italian-csos-vs-stellantis-italy-and-stellantis-nv/

NCP Netherlands	2023	4 Trade Unions (IUF, EFFAT-IUF, SEIU, UGT) v. APG Asset Management	Agreement	https://www.oecdguidelines.nl/latest/news/2022/02/03/fs-4-trade-unions-vs-apg
NCP Netherlands	2022	FNV, ITF, PSI, IndustriALL Global Union v. Chevron Netherlands BV et al	Completed without agreement	https://www.oecdguidelines.nl/latest/news/2022/03/24/fs-fnv-vs-chevron
NCP Netherlands	2022	Milieudefensie/Friends of the Earth Netherlands, WALHI/Friends of the Earth Indonesia and SDI/Friends of the Earth Liberia v. ING.	Closed (withdrawal of participation)	https://www.oecdguidelines.nl/latest/news/2022/04/07/foe-ing-final-statement
NCP Netherlands	2022	4 Trade Unions International Union of Food, Agriculture, Hotel, Restaurant, Catering, Tobacco, and Allied Workers Associations (IUF), European Federation of Food, Agriculture and Tourism (EFFAT), Service Employees International Union (SEIU), Unión General de Trabalhadores (UGT) (IUF, EFFAT-IUF, SEIU, UGT) v. APG Asset Management	Agreement	https://mneguidelines.oecd.org/database/instances/nl0042.htm

(continued)

NCP country	Completed year	Complaint	Status	Source link:
NCP Netherlands	2020	IUF v. Perfetti Van Melle	Agreement	https://www.oecdguidelines.nl/latest/news/2020/06/15/final-statement-iuf-vs.-perfetti-van-melle
NCP Netherlands	2019	Oxfam Novib, Greenpeace Netherlands, BankTrack and Friends of the Earth Netherlands (Milieudefensie) v. ING	Agreement	https://www.oecdwatch.org/complaint/dutch-ngos-vs-ing-bank/
NCP Netherlands	2017	Former employees v. Bralima, Heineken	Agreement	https://www.oecdwatch.org/complaint/former-employees-vs-heineken/
NCP Netherlands	2016	Bart Stapert attorney v. Mylan	Agreement	https://www.oecdwatch.org/complaint/bart-stapert-vs-mylan/#:~:text=Attorney%20Bart%20Stapert%20filed%20a,from%20being%20used%20in%20executions.
NCP Netherlands	2016	Both ENDS, Associação Fórum Suape Espaço Socioambiental, Conectas Direitos Humanos and Colônia de Pescadores do Município do Cabo de Santo Agostinho v. Atradius Dutch State Business.	Agreement	https://mneguidelines.oecd.org/database/instances/nl0026.htm
NCP Netherlands	2016	Friends of the Earth Europe and Friends of the Earth Netherlands/Milieudefensie v. Rabobank	Agreement	https://www.oecdwatch.org/complaint/friends-of-the-earth-vs-rabobank/

NCP Netherlands	2013	Amnesty International, Friends of Earth International and Frriends of Earth Netherlands v. Royal Dutch Shell about the cause of oil spills in the Niger Delta	Completed without agreement	https://www.oecdwatch.org/complaint/amnesty-international-and-friends-of-the-earth-vs-shell/
NCP Netherlands	2013	Lok Shakti Abhiyan, KTNC Watch, Fair Green and Global Alliance, Forum for Environment and Development v. ABP/APG	Agreement	https://mneguidelines.oecd.org/database/instances/nl0023.htm
NCP Netherlands	2010	Final Statement of the Irish and Netherlands National Contact Points (NCPs) on the notification dated 21st August, 2008 concerning the Corrib Gas project, 30 July 2010.	Completed without agreement	https://enterprise.gov.ie/en/publications/publication-files/final-statement-irish-and-netherlands-ncps-10-july-2010.pdf
NCP Netherlands	2008	Clean Clothes Campaign and Landelijke India Werkgroep (India Committee of the Netherlands, LIW) v. G-Star International BV.	Closed (withdrawal of participation)	https://www.oecdwatch.org/complaint/ccc-icn-vs-g-star/

(continued)

NCP country	Completed year	Complaint	Status	Source link:
NCP New Zealand	2015	Mr and Mrs C/Southern Response v. NZ Permanent Trustees Ltd	Rejected	https://www.oecdwatch.org/complaint/wecan-vs-southern-response-nz-permanent-trustees-ltd/
NCP Norway	2023	Eight civil society organisations from South Sudan, Norway, Sweden, and the Netherlands v. Aker BP ASA and Aker ASA	Pending	https://www.oecdwatch.org/complaint/eight-civil-society-organisations-from-south-sudan-norway-sweden-and-the-netherlands-vs-aker-bp-asa-and-aker-asa/
NCP Norway	2023	Samsung Heavy Industries Martin Linge Project Crane Accident Workers Support Team and Korean Transnational Corporations Watch v. Totalenergies E&P Norge As, Equinor Asa, Technip Energies N.V.	Closed (withdrawal of participation)	https://www.oecdwatch.org/complaint/ktnc-watch-and-samsung-heavy-industries-martin-linge-project-crane-accident-workers-support-team-vs-total-et-al/
NCP Norway	2022	Agreement between IUF, EFFAT-IUF, SEIU and UGT against NBIM.	Agreement	https://www.responsiblebusiness.no/news/agreement-between-trade-unions-and-nbim-in-specific-instance/
NCP Norway	2022	Committee Seeking Justice for Alethankyaw v. Telenor ASA	Completed without agreement	https://www.oecdwatch.org/complaint/committee-seeking-justice-for-alethankyaw-vs-telenor/
NCP Norway	2018	Industri Energi v. DNO ASA	Closed (withdrawal of participation)	https://files.nettsteder.regjeringen.no/wpuploads01/blogs.dir/263/files/2018/04/Final-statement-DNO-Industri-Energi_EN.pdf

NCP Norway	2015	Association for International Water Studies (FIVAS) v. Norconsult AS	Agreement	https://www.responsiblebusiness.no/dialogue-and-mediation/specific-instances/fivas-vs-norconsult-asnorpower-sdn-bhd/
NCP Norway	2015	Cotton Campaign, Anti-Slavery International and KTNC Watch v. Norges Bank Investment Management	Rejected	https://www.responsiblebusiness.no/dialogue-and-mediation/specific-instances/cotton-campaign-anti-slavery-international-and-ktnc-watch-vs-nbim/
NCP Norway	2013	Lok Shakti Abhiyan, Korean Transnational Corporations Watch, Fair Green And Global Alliance And Forum for Environment and Development v. Posco (South Korea), ABP/APG (Netherlands) And NBIM (Norway)	Rejected	https://www.oecdwatch.org/complaint/lok-shakti-abhiyan-et-al-vs-posco/
NCP Norway	2013	Norwegian Support Committee for Western Sahara v. Sjøvik AS	Agreement	https://www.oecdwatch.org/complaint/norwegian-support-committee-for-western-sahara-vs-sjovik/
NCP Norway	2011	The Future In Our Hands (FIOH) v. Intex Resources ASA and The Mindoro Nickel Project	Closed (withdrawal of participation)	https://www.oecdwatch.org/complaint/framtiden-i-vare-hender-vs-intex-resources/
NCP Norway	2011	Norwegian Climate Network v. Statoil	Rejected	https://www.oecdwatch.org/complaint/norwegian-climate-network-et-al-vs-statoil/

(continued)

NCP country	Completed year	Complaint	Status	Source link:
NCP Norway	2011	129 Roma in Kosovo v. Norwegian Church Aid, Initial Assessment and Final Report	Rejected	https://www.oecdwatch.org/complaint/roma-people-vs-norwegian-church-aid/
NCP Poland	2019	Development Yes v. PZU Group	Agreement	https://www.oecdwatch.org/complaint/development-yes-open-pit-mines-no-vs-group-pzu-s-a/
NCP Spain	2022	Committee for Solidarity with the Arab Cause v. Spanish MNE	Completed without agreement	https://mneguidelines.oecd.org/database/instances/es0012.htm
NCP Spain	2019	Alliance for Solidarity v. Spanish MNE in Guatemala	Completed without agreement	https://mneguidelines.oecd.org/database/instances/es0008.htm
NCP Spain	2017	UNI Global Union v. Porsegur subsidiaries in Brazil, Colombia, Paraguay, Peru and Chile	Completed without agreement	https://www.oecdwatch.org/complaint/alianza-por-la-solidaridad-v-grupo-acs-cobra/
NCP Sweden	2016	Jijnjevaerie Saami village v. Statkraft SCA Vind AB.	Closed (withdrawal of participation)	https://www.oecdwatch.org/complaint/jijnjevaerie-saami-village-vs-statkraft/
NCP Sweden	2015	Takkom Jerry and Lumiere Synergie Developpement v. Nykomb Synergetics Development AB	Completed without agreement	https://www.oecdwatch.org/complaint/takkom-jerry-lsd-vs-nykomb-synergetics-development-ab/

NCP Switzerland	2022	Maharashtra Association of Pesticide Poisoned Persons, Pesticide Action Network India, Public Eye, European Centre for Constitutional and Human Rights, Pesticides Action Network Asia Pacific v. Syngenta AG.	Closed (withdrawal of participation)	https://www.oecdwatch.org/complaint/public-eye-et-al-vs-syngenta/
NCP Switzerland	2021	Society for Threatened Peoples v. BKW Group.	Agreement	https://www.oecdwatch.org/complaint/society-for-threatened-peoples-vs-bkw-energie-ag/
NCP Switzerland	2021	Society for Threatened People v. USB Group AG	Completed without agreement	https://www.oecdwatch.org/complaint/society-for-threatened-peoples-switzerland-vs-ubs-group/
NCP Switzerland	2021	Swiss-Tibetan Friendship Association, Tibetan Youth Association in Europe, Tibetan Community in Switzerland and Liechtenstein as well as the Tibetan Women's Association Switzerland v. International Olympic Committee IOC	Completed without agreement	https://www.oecdwatch.org/complaint/swiss-tibetan-friendship-association-and-others-vs-international-olympic-committee/
NCP Switzerland	2019	Society for Threatened People v. Credit Suisse	Agreement	https://www.oecdwatch.org/complaint/society-for-threatened-peoples-vs-credit-suisse/#:~:text=Mainly%2C%20it%20alleges%20that%20Credit,of%20the%20pipeline%2C%20the%20bank

(continued)

NCP country	Completed year	Complaint	Status	Source link:
NCP Switzerland	2019	Stowarzyszenie Zawodników Hokeja na Lodzie v. International Ice Hockey Federation	Rejected	https://mneguidelines.oecd.org/database/instances/ch0018.htm
NCP Switzerland	2019	TUK Indonesia v. Roundtable Sustainable Palm Oil	Agreement	https://www.oecdwatch.org/complaint/tuk-indonesia-vs-roundtable-on-sustainable-palm-oil-rspo/
NCP Switzerland	2017	BWI against FIFA	Agreement	https://mneguidelines.oecd.org/database/instances/ch0013.htm
NCP Switzerland	2017	Survival international v. WWF	Withdrawn	https://www.oecdwatch.org/complaint/survival-international-vs-wwf/
NCP Switzerland	2016	Americans for Democracy and Human Rights in Bahrain (ADHRB) v. FIFA	Rejected	https://www.oecdwatch.org/complaint/adhrb-vs-fifa/
NCP Switzerland	2014	Pragatisheel Cement Shramik Sangh (PCSS) v. Holcim India and Holcim Group	Agreement	https://mneguidelines.oecd.org/database/instances/ch0011.htm
NCP Turkey	2021	Lumiere Synergie pour le Developpement" and "l'Association des femmes transformatrices de poissons de Bargny Guèdj (Khelcom)" v. Tosyalı Iron And Steel Senegal S.A	Completed without agreement	https://www.sanayi.gov.tr/assets/pdf/anlasmalar/OECDInitialAssesmentLSDvsTosyaliENG.pdf

NCP United Kingdom	2023	Association des Habitants de Ndogpassi 1, 2 et 3 [Ndogpassi 1, 2 and 3 Residents Association] (AHN) and Cercle de Bon Voisinage de Logmayangui [Logmayangui Good Neighbours Circle] (CBVL) v. Victoria Oil and Gas PLC	Completed without agreement	https://www.gov.uk/government/publications/ahn-and-cbvl-complaint-to-uk-ncp-about-victoria-oil-gas-plc-vog/final-statement-ahn-and-cbvl-complaint-to-the-uk-ncp-about-victoria-oil-gas-plc-vog
NCP United Kingdom	2022	Global Legal Action Network (GLAN) v. Anglo American	Completed without agreement	https://www.oecdwatch.org/complaint/glan-vs-anglo-american-plc/
NCP United Kingdom	2022	IDI, EC and LICADHO v. Bonsucro Ltd.	Completed without agreement	https://www.oecdwatch.org/complaint/idi-ec-and-licadho-v-bonsucro/
NCP United Kingdom	2022	IUF and FLOC v. BAT	Completed without agreement	https://www.gov.uk/government/publications/iuf-and-floc-complaint-to-uk-ncp-about-bat/final-statement-iuf-and-floc-complaint-to-uk-ncp-about-bat
NCP United Kingdom	2021	Lawyers for Palestinian Human Rights v. JCB	Completed without agreement	https://www.oecdwatch.org/complaint/lawyers-for-palestinian-human-rights-vs-j-c-bamford-ltd/
NCP United Kingdom	2021	AJTZP, RAID and PILC v. Glencore UK Ltd	Completed without agreement	https://www.gov.uk/government/publications/ajtzp-raid-pilc-complaint-to-the-uk-ncp-about-glencore-uk-ltd/final-statement-ajtzp-raid-pilc-complaint-to-the-uk-ncp-about-glencore-uk-ltd
NCP United Kingdom	2020	ClientEarth v. BP, Initial Statement	Withdrawn	https://www.gov.uk/government/publications/client-earth-complaint-to-the-uk-ncp-about-bp/initial-assessment-clientearth-complaint-to-the-uk-ncp-about-bp

(continued)

NCP country	Completed year	Complaint	Status	Source link:
NCP United Kingdom	2020	Global Witness v. UK Export Finance	Rejected	https://www.gov.uk/government/publications/global-witness-complaint-to-the-uk-ncp-about-uk-export-finance/initial-assessment-global-witness-complaint-to-the-uk-ncp-about-uk-export-finance
NCP United Kingdom	2019	Crude Accountability v. KPO Consortium	Completed without agreement	https://www.gov.uk/government/publications/crude-accountability-complaint-to-uk-ncp-about-kpo-consortium
NCP United Kingdom	2016	An individual in Cameroon v. UK-based MNE	Rejected	https://assets.publishing.service.gov.uk/media/5dd3d308ed915d08a146d5e4/uk-ncp-initial-assessment-Cameroon-individual.pdf
NCP United Kingdom	2016	LPHR v. G4S.	Completed without agreement	https://www.oecdwatch.org/complaint/lawyers-for-palestinian-human-rights-vs-g4s/
NCP United Kingdom	2016	Rights and Accountability in Development (RAID) v. ENRC	Completed without agreement	https://assets.publishing.service.gov.uk/media/5dd2a0a140f0b606ee65ea84/BIS-16-156-raid-and-enrc-final-statement-after-complaint.pdf
NCP United Kingdom	2015	Reprieve v. BT	Rejected	https://www.oecdwatch.org/complaint/reprieve-vs-british-telecommunications-plc/
NCP United Kingdom	2014	An NGO v. 6 UK-based Telecommunication Companies	Rejected	https://www.gov.uk/government/publications/ngo-complaint-to-uk-ncp-about-6-uk-based-telecommunication-companies

NCP United Kingdom	2014	International Accountability Project and World Development Movement v. GCM Resources PLC	Completed without agreement	https://www.oecdwatch.org/complaint/iac-wdm-vs-gcm-resources-plc/
NCP United Kingdom	2011	Corner house et al., v. BTC Pipeline.	Completed without agreement	https://www.oecdwatch.org/complaint/corner-house-et-al-vs-bp/
NCP United Kingdom	2009	Survival International v. Vedanta Resources PLC	Completed without agreement	https://www.oecdwatch.org/complaint/survival-international-vs-vedanta-resources-plc/
NCP United Kingdom	2008	RAID v. DAS Air	Completed without agreement	https://www.oecdwatch.org/complaint/raid-vs-das-air/#:~:text=In%20July%202008%2C%20a%20strongly,of%20international%20civil%20aviation%20regulations. https://www.oecdwatch.org/complaint/raid-vs-das-air/#:~:text=In%20July%202008%2C%20a%20strongly,of%20international%20civil%20aviation%20regulations.
NCP United States	2022	André Amisi Rushingwa, Delvaux Bwisibo Mukunda, and Raymond Minani Muganira, v. Gramercy Funds Management LLC	Rejected	https://www.state.gov/specific-instance-between-andre-amisi-rushingwa-delvaux-bwisibo-mukunda-raymond-minani-muganira-and-gramercy-funds-management-llc-regarding-events-in-the-democratic-republic-of-the-congo/
NCP United States	2022	Formed employees v. Coca Cola	Rejected	https://www.state.gov/specific-instance-between-leonce-safari-kajangu-anicet-tambwe-byadunia-and-francois-zabene-zagabe-and-the-coca-cola-company-regarding-events-in-the-democratic-republic-of-the-congo/

(continued)

NCP United States	2022	International Union of Food, Agriculture, Hotel, Restaurant, Catering, Tobacco, and Allied Workers Associations (IUF), European Federation of Food, Agriculture and Tourism (EFFAT), Service Employees International Union (SEIU), Unión General de Trabalhadores (UGT) v. McDonald' s Corporation.	Agreement	https://www.state.gov/specific-instance-between-international-union-of-food-agriculture-hotel-restaurant-catering-tobacco-and-allied-workers-associations-iuf-european-federation-of-food-agriculture-and-tourism-e/
NCP United States	2021	Divest Invest Protect, Indigenous Peoples Law and Policy Program, Women's Earth and Climate Action Network v. Credit Suisse	Rejected	https://www.state.gov/specific-instance-between-divest-invest-protect-indigenous-peoples-law-and-policy-program-womens-earth-and-climate-action-network-and-credit-suisse/
NCP United States	2018	The International Union of Food, Agriculture, Hotel, Restaurant, Catering, Tobacco, and Allied Workers Associations v. Coca Cola Amatil	Closed (withdrawal of participation)	https://www.state.gov/u-s-national-contact-point-for-the-oecd-guidelines-for-multinational-enterprises/specific-instance-final-statements/specific-instance-between-the-international-union-of-food-agriculture-hotel-restaurant-catering-tobacco-and-allied-workers-associations-and-the-coca-cola-company-related-to-alleged-conduct-in/

NCP United States	2016	European Centre for Democracy and Human Rights et al v. the Boeing Company and Lockheed Martin Corporation	Rejected	https://www.oecdwatch.org/complaint/ecdhr-et-al-vs-boeing-lockheed-martin/
NCP United States	2015	UAW and IndustriALL Global Union v. Nissan Motor Co Ltd and Nissan Motors America Inc	Completed without agreement	https://2009-2017.state.gov/e/eb/oecd/usncp/links/rls/236972.htm

MIX
Papier aus verantwortungsvollen Quellen
Paper from responsible sources
FSC® C105338

FSC
www.fsc.org

If you have any concerns about our products,
you can contact us on
ProductSafety@springernature.com

In case Publisher is established outside the EU,
the EU authorized representative is:
Springer Nature Customer Service Center GmbH
Europaplatz 3, 69115 Heidelberg, Germany

Printed by Libri Plureos GmbH
in Hamburg, Germany